Teaching English to Young Learners

Teaching English to Young Learners: Critical Issues in Language Teaching with 3–12 Year Olds

EDITED BY JANICE BLAND

Bloomsbury Academic
An imprint of Bloomsbury Publishing Plc

B L O O M S B U R Y
LONDON · OXFORD · NEW YORK · NEW DELHI · SYDNEY

Bloomsbury Academic

An imprint of Bloomsbury Publishing Plc

50 Bedford Square	1385 Broadway
London	New York
WC1B 3DP	NY 10018
UK	USA

www.bloomsbury.com

BLOOMSBURY and the Diana logo are trademarks of Bloomsbury Publishing Plc

First published 2015
Reprinted by Bloomsbury Academic 2016 (three times)

© Janice Bland and Contributors, 2015

Janice Bland and Contributors have asserted their right under the Copyright, Designs and Patents Act, 1988, to be identified as Author of this work.

British Library Cataloguing-in-Publication Data
A catalogue record for this book is available from the British Library.

ISBN: HB: 978-1-4725-8857-9
PB: 978-1-4725-8856-2
ePDF: 978-1-4725-8859-3
ePub: 978-1-4725-8858-6

Library of Congress Cataloging-in-Publication Data
A catalog record for this book is available from the Library of Congress.

Typeset by Integra Software Services Pvt. Ltd.
Printed and bound in Great Britain

Contents

List of Contributors   vii

Foreword *Carol Read*   xi

Acknowledgement   xiv

Introduction *Janice Bland*   1

1   The Advantages and Disadvantages of English as a Foreign
    Language with Young Learners *Janet Enever*   13

2   Primary English and Critical Issues: A Worldwide
    Perspective *Shelagh Rixon*   31

3   English in Pre-primary: The Challenges of Getting It
    Right *Sandie Mourão*   51

4   Immersion Teaching in English with Young Learners
    Kristin Kersten and Andreas Rohde   71

5   CLIL Scenarios with Young Learners *Kay Bentley*   91

6   Task-Based Learning with Children *Annamaria Pinter*   113

7   Language Development in Young Learners: The Role of
    Formulaic Language *Saskia Kersten*   129

8   Grammar Templates for the Future with Poetry for
    Children *Janice Bland*   147

9   Developing Intercultural Understanding in Primary
    Schools *Patricia Driscoll and Helen Simpson*   167

10 Oral Storytelling in the Primary English Classroom
Janice Bland 183

11 The Potential of Picturebooks with Young
Learners *Sandie Mourão* 199

12 Drama with Young Learners *Janice Bland* 219

13 Teaching Young Learners with Technology
Euline Cutrim Schmid and Shona Whyte 239

14 Assessment and Portfolios *Carmen Becker* 261

15 Developing Principled Materials for Young Learners of English
as a Foreign Language *Brian Tomlinson* 279

Index 294

List of Contributors

Carmen Becker is Visiting Professor of English Language Teaching at TU Braunschweig and holds a doctoral degree from the University of Hannover. She is co-editor of the journal *Grundschule Englisch*, has been an English and science teacher and a member of several commissions for the development of the English curriculum guidelines at the Ministry of Education of Lower Saxony, Germany. Carmen has a number of publications on portfolio assessment and interaction including *Portfolio als Baustein einer neuen Lernkultur. Eine empirische Studie zur Implementierung des Europäischen Portfolios der Sprachen* and the co-edited book *Content and Language Integrated Learning by Interaction* (2014).

Kay Bentley has wide experience of teaching, training and writing materials for Content and Language Integrated Learning (CLIL). She authored *Primary Curriculum Box* (2009), a young learner CLIL resource book and *The Teaching Knowledge Test Course, CLIL Module* (2010), both for Cambridge University Press. Kay wrote primary maths and science materials for Egyptian bilingual schools and primary cross-curricular materials for Kazakh trilingual schools. She authored an online CLIL course for Cambridge English Teacher and wrote *Let's Draw* (2014), a CLIL book for New Penguin Young Readers. Kay is Chair of the TKT: CLIL Module for Cambridge English Language Assessment.

Janice Bland is Deputy Chair of TEFL at the University of Münster. She holds a doctoral degree from Jena University, Germany, and has worked in the English Departments of Duisburg-Essen, Hildesheim and Paderborn Universities and as Visiting Professor of English Language and Literature Teaching at Vechta University, Germany. Her research interests are language and literacy development in the second language, visual and critical literacy, intercultural learning and global issues, drama methodology and creative writing. She is the author of *Children's Literature and Learner Empowerment. Children and Teenagers in English Language Education* (Bloomsbury, 2013). Janice is co-editor of CLELEjournal: *Children's Literature in English Language Education*.

Euline Cutrim Schmid is Professor of TEFL and Applied Linguistics at the University of Education Schwaebisch Gmuend, Germany. She teaches at undergraduate and postgraduate levels on a variety of topics including Computer Assisted Language Learning (CALL), applied linguistics and qualitative research methodologies. Her recent academic publications have focused mainly on the use of interactive technologies in the English language-teaching context. She is the author of *Interactive Whiteboard Technology in the Language Classroom: Exploring New Pedagogical Opportunities* (2009) and co-editor of *Interactive Whiteboards for Education: Theory, Research and Practice* (2010) and *Teaching Languages with Technology: Communicative Approaches to Interactive Whiteboard Use* (2014).

Patricia Driscoll is Reader in Education and the Director of Research Development at Canterbury Christ Church University, UK. She has worked in the field of languages for over twenty-five years. Patricia teaches on a range of initial teacher, masters- and doctoral-level programmes and conducts both small- and large-scale studies in early language learning. Patricia's publications include: 'The sustainable impact of a short comparative teaching placement abroad on primary teachers' professional, linguistic and cultural skills', *The Language Learning Journal* (special edition, 2014) and *A New Era for Languages in Debates in Modern Languages Education* (edited with Ernesto Macaro and Ann Swarbrick, 2014).

Janet Enever is Professor of Language Teaching and Learning at Umeå University, Sweden, teaching courses in research methods, primary ELT and issues related to language and globalization. She holds a doctoral degree from Bristol University, UK, in Primary Foreign Languages Policy and has worked at universities in London, Krakow, Budapest and now Umeå. She has advised on language policy, early language learning and teacher education for ministries in a number of Asian, Latin American and European countries. Currently she is working on a critical examination of supranational patterns of policymaking in relation to early English language learning in schools.

Kristin Kersten is Professor of EFL and Language Acquisition at the University of Hildesheim, Germany. She coordinated the multilateral EU COMENIUS project ELIAS, an international study of bilingual preschools. She has published books and articles on second language acquisition and young learners, language learning, intercultural competence and bilingual environmental education in bilingual preschools, and language input in bilingual classrooms. Her current research in psycholinguistics and foreign-language teaching focuses on variables of language acquisition, with a special emphasis on bilingual education (CLIL/immersion). She is involved in teacher training at the university level and for practitioners in preschools and schools.

Saskia Kersten is Lecturer in English Language and Communication in the School of Humanities at the University of Hertfordshire, UK. She obtained her PhD from Hildesheim University, Germany, in 2009. Her research interests are computer-mediated communication, with a focus on the different varieties of English and communicative strategies used in English language tweets, second language development in young learners and the role of formulaic language in both these areas. Her monograph, *The Mental Lexicon and Vocabulary Learning: Implications for the foreign language classroom* (a study of L2 vocabulary acquisition in primary school), was published in 2010.

Sandie Mourão is an independent scholar, teacher educator, author and educational consultant specializing in early years language education with a PhD in didactics and teacher education from the University of Aveiro, Portugal, and over twenty-five years of experience in the field of English language education. She is co-editor of *Early Years Second Language Education: International Perspectives on Theories and Practice* (2015) and the open access journal *Children's Literature in English Language Education* (CLELEjournal), as well as author of a number of language-learning courses and resource books. Her main research interests focus on early years language learning, picturebooks in language learning and classroom-based research.

Annamaria Pinter is Associate Professor in the Centre for Applied Linguistics at the University of Warwick, UK. She has published widely in the area of teaching English to young learners. She is the author of *Teaching Young Language Learners Oxford Handbooks for Language Teachers* (2006) and *Children Learning Second Languages* (2011). She is also an editor of an e-book series entitled *Teaching English to Young Learners* (http://www.candlinandmynard.com/series.html). Her research interests include all aspects of second language learning in childhood and teacher development.

Shelagh Rixon worked for The British Council, including five years as English Language Officer in Italy, where in the 1980s she first encountered teachers needing to retrain in order to teach English to primary-school children. Between 1991 and 2010, she lectured at the University of Warwick, UK, coordinating the Young Learners strand of the masters programme in English Language Teaching. She is the author of textbooks and research works including *Young Learners of English: Some Research Perspectives* (1999) and the 2013 British Council Survey of Policy and Practice in Primary English Language Teaching Worldwide.

Andreas Rohde is Professor of Linguistics and Second Language Teaching and Learning at the University of Cologne, Germany. He has been a participant in several projects to assess bilingual preschool and school programmes

(Comenius Project ENEMU – Enhancing Early Multilingualism, 2005–2008, Comenius Project ELIAS – Early Language and Intercultural Acquisition Studies, 2008–2010). He is currently involved in the Grundtvig Project 'EU Speak II' on low literate adults and in the PKE Project on the development of foreign-language teachers' professional knowledge.

Helen Simpson has wide experience of teaching modern languages in both primary and secondary schools. More recently, she has been involved in primary languages research, consultancy and Initial Teacher Education. As Director of the Development Education charity, World Education Development Group (WEDG), she developed her interest in the value of language awareness and intercultural understanding through related project work. The projects included trialling and developing methodologies to audit attitudes towards aspects of global citizenship and, building on an earlier study, testing ways of developing language awareness through use of stories in different languages with young children.

Brian Tomlinson has worked as a teacher, teacher trainer, curriculum developer, football coach and university academic in Indonesia, Japan, Nigeria, Oman, Singapore, UK, Vanuatu and Zambia, as Visiting Professor at Leeds Metropolitan University and TESOL Professor at Anaheim University, USA. He is Founder and President of MATSDA (the international Materials Development Association), and is currently Honorary Visiting Professor at the University of Liverpool. He has over 100 publications on materials development, language through literature, the teaching of reading, language awareness and teacher development, including *Discover English* (with Rod Bolitho, 2005), *Openings* (1989), *Materials Development in Language Teaching* (2011), *Developing Materials for Language Teaching* (2003), *Research for Materials Development in Language Learning* (with Hitomi Masuhara, 2010) and *Applied Linguistics and Materials Development* (2012).

Shona Whyte is Associate Professor in English at Nice University, France, teaching EFL and Second Language Acquisition (SLA), and training pre- and in-service primary and secondary teachers (http://efl.unice.fr). Her research focuses on young learners and teacher education, with a particular interest in technology. She is the author of *Implementing and Researching Technological Innovation in Language Teaching: The Case of Interactive Whiteboards for EFL in French Schools* (2015) and co-editor of *Teaching Languages with Technology: Communicative Approaches to Interactive whiteboard Use* (Bloomsbury, 2014).

Foreword

Carol Read

This book is timely and significant for a number of key reasons.

First, the book adds substance to the growing body of theoretical and research-based literature on teaching young learners which has been much needed in recent years. Despite the fact that, globally, there are many more young learners than adults learning English as a foreign language, English language teaching to adults has nevertheless continued to be the 'default' in areas such as teacher education, SLA studies, syllabus design and classroom methodology, as well as the principal focus of research. Unfortunately, this has also at times been accompanied by negative attitudes towards foreign-language teachers of children who have been characterized as doing little more than playing games, singing songs and telling stories in their classrooms in a way that does not recognize the competences and skills needed by a professional foreign-language educator of children. This book not only contributes to setting a new 'default' for teaching young learners but also serves to unpack the range of knowledge, skills, attitudes and professional qualities that are needed to teach children successfully.

Second, in the context of an educational climate which increasingly seeks to standardize, measure and test language performance, this book explores those factors in early foreign-language learning which are hard to pin down and provide empirical evidence for, but which nevertheless are likely to be at the heart of teaching and learning success. As well as a focus on the key role of holistic learning with young learners, there is a welcome emphasis on the importance of rich exposure to language, including repeated patterns, formulaic sequences and 'chunks' which can be remembered and transferred to other contexts. Opportunities for natural interaction and meaningful repetition in engaging contexts, leading to creative outcomes, whether through the use of drama, play, oral storytelling, picturebooks or poetry, are also seen as crucial to learning. The advantages of such an approach are not seen narrowly in terms of measurable linguistic outcomes but rather in terms of the whole learner and the more elusive social, psychological, cognitive, metacognitive, affective and emotional benefits that underpin children's motivation and learning success. Early foreign-language learning is also integrally linked to the development of intercultural understanding, empathy, self-awareness and respect for others, and to broadening children's view of the world.

Third, the book reveals the gap between the competences and qualities that are needed by teachers of young learners in order to be effective and actual practice in many classrooms, which highlights the need for more specialized teacher education.

It is clear that teaching children in the ways suggested in this book requires a high level of skill and language competence. It is also not surprising that many teachers reportedly shy away from using more risk-taking activities such as drama and storytelling in their classes and prefer to stay on safer, more formal instructional ground with activities such as sentence repetition or gap-fill texts. This understandable reluctance highlights a pressing need for more in-depth, specialized teacher education for young-learner teachers. As well as knowledge and understanding about children's development and when, why and how to best scaffold and support their learning, teachers need to develop a range of multiple practitioner skills and sub-skills such as designing and sequencing age-appropriate activities and tasks, developing children's critical and creative thinking skills, providing feedback which supports learning and assessing learning.

Finally, through the book's discussion of ways to most appropriately support children's foreign-language learning, certain limitations of some existing published English language teaching materials for young learners are revealed. Aspects of these include limited opportunities for language exposure, teaching vocabulary in isolation, 'stories' labelled as such but which are in fact situational sequences rather than well-constructed stories and 'CLIL' content, also labelled as such, but which lacks the academic vocabulary and language needed to adequately explore concepts from other areas of the curriculum. While the depth of theoretical understanding and insight which informs primary English language teaching materials vary hugely in different contexts and countries, it is also important to remember that publishers do their main market research by asking primary-language teachers what they want to see in their materials, as well as of course keeping a close eye on the syllabuses and formats of external EYL tests and examinations. Increased knowledge, understanding and awareness of the processes of children's foreign-language learning by teachers through more specialized young-learner teacher education courses would not only increase the effectiveness of classroom practice but also raise awareness of principled criteria for quality materials that are most suitable to use. This would potentially lead to changes in some of the currently available published language teaching materials for children and possibly in EYL tests and examinations too.

In conclusion, by reading this book, as an academic, a student or a researcher, you will gain a thought-provoking, up-to-date overview and understanding of current theoretical issues in teaching English to young learners and how they relate to the classroom. As a young-learner teacher, you will deepen your knowledge of how children learn a foreign language and be able to use many of the suggestions and recommendations to enrich and enhance your classroom practice. As a young-learner teacher educator, you will discover a wealth of ideas, which will enable you to make links between theory and practice to your trainees in a meaningful and digestible way. For everyone involved in, and passionate about, teaching English to young learners, this is an important book.

Carol Read
Primary ELT specialist
IATEFL President & Vice President, 2012–2016

Acknowledgement

I am deeply grateful to all the contributors of the chapters in this volume, for their support in the endeavour to accomplish a thoroughly multifaceted picture of teaching English to young learners. My sincere thanks go to Carol Read for honouring our work with her generous Foreword. I would also like to thank Svenja Brinkmann and Chris Pesch for most helpfully and thoughtfully reading through the final manuscript of *Teaching English to Young Learners* for clarity and readability.

Introduction

Janice Bland

This book is about the teaching of English to young learners in school settings. While several of the chapters cover issues that are relevant for all foreign language teaching to a young age group, others relate specifically to *English* for young learners (EYL). In this book the term *primary* refers to children from circa five years of age to circa eleven. The number of years of primary schooling varies considerably from country to country, but so do many other conditions of English teaching to young learners, so that approximations cannot, unfortunately, always be avoided. The expression *young learner* is, for this publication, applied to children from the age of three to twelve. This is in order to reflect the steadily lowering age of English learning to include pre-primary in many contexts. Additionally, there is no sudden cut-off at age ten or eleven with regard to a need for a child-centred pedagogy, rich in oral input and meaning-centred learning. The transitional years at the beginning of secondary schooling should arguably be studied at least as much from the perspective of primary pedagogy as from the perspective of a more strictly cognitive and analytic secondary pedagogy, which tends to place less weight on the affective, sociological and physiological dimensions of education. Many of the chapters are the result of research conducted foremostly in Europe and focusing on children and their learning in mainstream schooling. The authors are aware that not all the situations described are necessarily typical of the innumerable different contexts worldwide, but we do hope that many of the insights and findings presented here will be useful to all those involved in English for young learners.

In education generally, a shift towards learning outcomes and competences can be observed. This shift is intended to be student centred, in order to structure children's learning around their (future) needs, and support their involvement in their own learning. It is, however, crucial that the holistic approach to learning is not lost, as will be seen with reference to language learning in the following chapters. According to the Common European Framework of References for Languages (CEFR): 'All human competences contribute in one way or another to the language user's ability to communicate and may be regarded as aspects of communicative competence' (Council of Europe 2001: 101). Several contributions in this volume point to the short-sightedness of a too instrumental approach to EYL (e.g. Rixon 2015: 42–43). Considering young children's drive to construct meaning and interact on meaning (their oracy), innate ability to learn playfully (holistic learning), interest in reading (literacy), interest in the world around them and respect for self and others (intercultural understanding), language learning is understood in this volume as a major opportunity for the widening of children's horizons. According to Johnstone (2002: 12), early foreign language learning can have an important educational outcome: 'there can be a positive influence on children's general educational development (e.g. cognitive, emotional, cultural) and on the formation of a multilingual and intercultural identity.'

Such a catalogue of competences and multiple outcomes will not be given due value by a classroom assessment method with a narrow understanding of standardization and accountability. Similarly, the educational goals and outcomes outlined above are easily neglected by empirical research projects investigating foreign language learning (FLL) with young learners, as Enever writes in this volume: 'The measurement of affective skills, broader educational skills and the development of intercultural learning that occurs during the process of early FLL has a qualitative resonance that does not lend itself to large-scale statistical analysis. As a result, what cannot be easily measured tends to be overlooked and undervalued' (2015: 25–26). It is important to remember that competence is a wider category than skills:

> Competence is a 'can-do' category; it is something a student is able to perform. Students are competent when they have knowledge and skills at their disposal, know how to employ them, and are also able to reflect independently on their knowledge and skills. [...] Creativity and innovative skills – as well as critical thinking and problem solving skills – are essential qualities in modern societies. [...] Creativity, problem-solving and innovation often go hand in hand, which means that knowledge and skills as well as competences are seen as important prerequisites for creativity and innovation – not as tight limitations. (Rasmussen 2013: 7)

The language development of young learners, although not the only aim of plurilingual education, is of course a central aim. The usage-based approach to language acquisition, which is one of the theoretical underpinnings of several of the chapters in this volume, provides a valuable understanding of the role of context, formulaic language and usage (both receptive and productive) in children's language acquisition.[1] This approach highlights the exemplar-based nature of language acquisition and how lexical and grammatical knowledge can emerge through engaging with input, 'with language, as with other cognitive realms, our experiences conspire to give us competence' (Ellis, O'Donnell and Römer 2013: 45), that is, we learn through experience. However, in an EYL setting with extremely limited input, frequency and salience (which includes prominence of meaning and whether the feature – from a morpheme to a formulaic sequence – is easy to notice) are crucial. While focus on form is one useful way of making language features salient, an explicit focus on form is not the most efficient means for most children of primary-school age: 'Children are argued to use largely implicit mechanisms, whereas older, adult learners, have been argued to use more explicit learning mechanisms' (Murphy 2014: 5). Other methods of helping children notice language are suggested in the contributions to this volume. Usage frequency is the ideal condition: 'Psycholinguistic research provides the evidence of usage-based acquisition in its demonstrations that language processing is exquisitely sensitive to usage frequency at all levels of language representation' (Ellis et al. 2013: 30). This is usually difficult to achieve in EYL classroom settings (other than through Content and Language Integrated Learning (CLIL) and immersion teaching). Fortunately there are methods that support discourse skills, while making language pleasurable and salient for young learners: 'The ability to understand, recall, and produce songs, rhymes, chants, and stories [...] are all examples of discourse skills' (Cameron 2003: 109).

This volume includes research from various disciplines in order to more fully understand children's language learning: 'The field of Applied Linguistics speaks with multiple voices, depending on whether one's original training was in linguistics, anthropology, psychology, sociology, education, or literature' (Kramsch 2000: 317). A number of the chapters in this book include children's literature scholarship as well as pedagogy and a more purely linguistic understanding of language education. This is highly significant in the area of EYL, for children must learn English over many years and need to be motivated in ways that make sense to them as seekers of meaningful patterns. Boyd argues that humans have evolved 'pattern-matching neural processing' (2009: 134), and explains art and stories as patterned cognitive play, which tones neural wiring. In the children's literature chapters, the patterned nature of poems, storytelling and picturebooks is shown to connect to concerns such as literacy (reading and writing skills) as well as oracy (listening and speaking skills), which are essential aspects of EYL.

Young learners are highly dependent on the teacher; therefore teacher education is of paramount importance. Children do not yet have many general learning strategies, and need to learn strategies while they are learning language. Thus innate abilities are particularly important for this age group: their pleasure in rhythm, their curiosity and interest in technology, as novice readers their excitement over picturebooks, their interest in others and intercultural mediation, children's interest in collecting and portfolios, the connection of drama to play and also task-based learning, Content and Language Integrated Learning and immersion approaches that meet children's need to learn implicitly. All this is highly challenging for teachers, who must often extend their craft repertoire and their language competence, and even additionally develop or search for suitable materials. But as the following chapters hopefully show, the interdisciplinary nature of EYL can be deeply rewarding, for practitioners as well as for researchers and teacher educators: 'Because of its position at the confluence of several disciplines and at the intersection of theory and practice, Applied Linguistics is the site of unusual intellectual ferment' (Kramsch 2000: 317).

This volume offers a study of EYL based on empirical research, theoretical research, action research and teaching observation over many years. Some of the chapters include reports on the authors' recent research studies; others are reviews of the research literature, leading to concept development and theory building often with a 'sense of educational mission' (Kramsch 2000: 320). I consider this many-faceted combination, including dialogue with teachers, head teachers and structured observations of lessons with young learners, crucial for theoretical legitimacy in a still emerging yet fast expanding field. As an editor, I have selected the issues I consider to be critical for EYL, and most in need of attention, and this has influenced the choice of topics covered in this volume. One area that steadily increases in importance is intercultural learning. According to many researchers, intercultural understanding is a central component of foreign language education (Byram and Doyé 1999, Beacco and Byram 2007, Legutke, Müller-Hartmann and Schocker von Ditfurth 2009: 84–93, Bland 2013: 207–291). These issues are critical in the sense that it is important that well-recognized approaches actually reach the children in their language classrooms, for, as Garton, Copland and Burns have observed, there is a too frequent 'gap between pedagogic policy and classroom practice' (2011: 6). It is my hope that this volume is a useful contribution towards closing that gap.

Enever contributes the first chapter, beginning with a historical perspective on EYL. She follows with a call for far more heed to be paid to which are the most auspicious conditions for teaching foreign languages to young learners in order to 'ensure appropriate learning outcomes across a range of contexts' (Enever 2015: 13). The author considers the factor of age, and whether an early start is indeed such an advantage. The two main strands of teacher expertise are considered, an 'advanced level of language fluency and the ability to implement age-appropriate methodological skills' (2015: 22). The continuity of teaching from primary to secondary school is seen to be a problem that in many contexts is as yet unresolved, for the project of EYL is, according to Enever, a demanding and long-term process. Following this, Rixon looks at the reasons why English has taken hold as a global language, and the consequences and tensions, as reported in her recent large-scale survey into EYL, are discussed. Sho takes the historical status of English in the various contexts into account, and refers to the negative social consequences when there is no equity with regard to provision. Rixon points to the weakness of the often uncritical discussion of 'the Younger the Better' position by politicians and administrators, who neglect the 'more tenable arguments about the general educational, affective and cognitive benefits that can be associated with early language learning [but which] tend not to be in the forefront of much public debate' (Rixon 2015: 35). This is against the advice of researchers who have 'supported the introduction of English for reasons beyond the instrumental, as an enrichment of the curriculum and as leading to an opening out of cultural, imaginative and cognitive horizons along with language development' (2015: 42). The British Council survey conducted by Rixon reveals the diversity of conditions across the world and identifies a number of critical issues.

Mourão reports on a pressing yet makeshift worldwide development, English for pre-primary, which it seems has so far largely been ignored by policymakers. This is likely to change very soon: 'On a European level, the most recent Eurydice report (2012) shows that by September 2015, just over a third of the European community will officially implement second or foreign-language teaching to children of six years and under' (Mourão 2015a: 52). The author describes the extremely ad hoc nature of pre-primary provision to date, along with a pedagogical concept she has developed and trialled, the *English learning area*, where 'children can engage in child-initiated play with and through English' (Mourão 2015a: 58).

The next focus of the volume is on contexts in which the foreign language is, to different extents, the medium of instruction in school. Immersion programmes and CLIL are covered in separate chapters, as the approaches are usually distinguished by intensity (in immersion programmes the foreign language is used as the vehicle of teaching at least 50 per cent of the time) and by the fact that while the children in CLIL programmes learn certain subjects through the medium of English (e.g. music or PE lessons, or both), they have English lessons in addition. Recently researchers have, however, tended to highlight the core aspect shared by CLIL and immersion – the teaching of non-language subjects in the foreign language – more than the differences. This view is taken by K. Kersten and Rohde, who begin by defining CLIL as the umbrella term. Their chapter then reviews the impressive results of the systematic evaluation of immersion programmes worldwide, which demonstrate its high effectiveness as a means of second language (L2) acquisition in school settings. Counter-intuitively, immersion programmes do not limit progress in the mother tongue: 'three years of instruction entirely in French from kindergarten through Grade 2 produces no long-term negative effects on either English oral or literacy skills' (K. Kersten and Rohde 2015: 74). The authors conclude that children in immersion programmes may enjoy the same benefits as children who grow up bilingually, including mental flexibility and other cognitive advantages due to the 'effortful attention and training effect' (2015: 78). Bentley provides a rich description of current CLIL scenarios with young learners throughout Europe, and introduces a number of key concepts, including the 4Cs Framework: content, communication, cognition and culture, as a means to map out effective CLIL practice. The author refers to planning for competency-based education and the development of higher-order thinking processes such as predicting, observing and evaluation. Subsequently she provides an insight into assessment in CLIL scenarios, and how to evaluate ELT publications that purport to offer CLIL, but which 'lack the range of subject-specific and academic vocabulary to explore and communicate ideas about [for example] science and history to match what young learners would do in subject lessons learned through CLIL' (Bentley 2015: 99).

   The focus now switches to the currently more typical situation of extremely limited exposure to the foreign language in the primary school, and how the teacher in these conditions can best exploit the characteristics of young learner L2 acquisition. Pinter explores the benefits of task-based language teaching (TBLT) with young learners. TBLT shares the underlying principle of communicative language teaching that 'authentic learner interaction, motivated engagement and purposefulness are important in making progress in language learning' (Pinter 2015: 114). The author first seeks to define tasks and reviews the academic research that uses task-based interactions as a means to study the nature of collaborative dialogue, following which different types of classroom tasks are identified. For the older age group of young learners TBLT can include a delayed focus on form, which is considered 'more beneficial than focusing on form upfront, since the learners can see how the need arose for the use of those forms and the language is both contextualized and personalized' (2015: 117). Pinter writes of tasks that there can be multiple demands, linguistic, social, cognitive or metacognitive, and TBLT should challenge the children, promoting playful and confident participation and the willingness to take risks.

   Following this, S. Kersten provides an insight into the lexically driven nature of language and the ubiquity of formulaic language (often known as chunks). S. Kersten reviews the characteristics of formulaicity and explains its importance for EYL and language development, as communication is speeded up from the outset. Beyond this, the author illustrates that even in the input-limited

EYL context children are able to work productively with multiword units they have acquired. It is therefore counterproductive that L2 coursebooks 'tend to view vocabulary to consist of single words only, rather than prefabricated expressions, in some cases even to the extent of providing vocabulary lists in which L2 words are presented as being translation equivalents of L1 words' (S. Korsten 2015: 136). Instead, the author suggests more effective ways of 'familiarizing learners with authentic language which is also rich in formulaic language, fairly restricted and repetitive' (2015: 138), and provides evidence that formulaic language not only is highly useful input but also allows new language competence to develop. In the following chapter, Bland illustrates how children's poetry as pattern-rich language can stimulate the emergence of grammar sensitivity: 'Through salience, repetition and exaggerated prosodic features in performance, the latent structures, lexical patterns and grammatical units within playful language' can help children notice features (2015a: 149). A *leitmotif* of this chapter is the need for repetition and perceptual salience in the classroom discourse as highly supportive of L2 acquisition, and Bland cites many authentic poems of childhood that can offer delight, satisfy children's cognitive need for pattern and even stimulate cultural awareness.

For the focus on intercultural understanding, a different perspective is taken. In the UK English is not, of course, taught as a foreign language, although there is a growing need of English as an Additional Language (EAL) support in schools for recent arrivals to the UK. In Scotland, Wales and Northern Ireland plurilingualism is valued – for the heritage languages Scottish Gaelic, Welsh and Irish are soundly supported. It is, perhaps, particularly significant to investigate foreign languages in the primary school and intercultural learning in England, a multicultural country with a monolingual ethnic majority. Driscoll and Simpson refer to a British Council report (2014) on the foreign languages most needed in the UK, which takes account of cultural, intellectual, individual and societal factors. Driscoll and Simpson (2015: 168) set out the arguments for intercultural understanding: 'Fostering an open mindset, developing tolerance, cultural sensitivity and an acceptance and understanding of diversity in increasingly multilingual and multicultural societies are essential features in preparing young people for a future which is not confined by local, regional or national borders.' The authors found 'a clear commitment to promote a global mindset and recognition of the importance of intercultural skills' (2015: 174) in their study of forty primary schools in England; however intercultural practice was evidenced in less than 25 per cent of lessons. After introducing the complexity of intercultural learning as set out in Byram and Doyé (1999), Driscoll and Simpson suggest possible whole-school solutions, noting the necessity for long-term planning: 'Creative solutions are needed if children are to develop the intercultural knowledge, skills, attributes and mindset for the global world of the twenty-first century' (Driscoll and Simpson 2015: 176).

The next two chapters refer to the use of narrative in the EYL classroom, first oral storytelling (Bland) followed by picturebooks (Mourão). The two approaches are similar with regard to the centrality of *story*, but otherwise quite different. Bland begins her chapter by distinguishing the approaches: on the one hand the flexibility of oral storytelling and shaping the story to the audience, and on the other hand the sharing of a picturebook, whereby not only the words and the book itself but particularly the pictures 'can arrest and focus the children's attention through their continuous and repeated presence' (Bland 2015b: 186). Bland then introduces the characteristics of oral tales, referring to *orality*, and the relevance for language teaching of their template-like structure. The educational value of stories for empathy and intercultural understanding is discussed, and the critical role of the teacher-storyteller and creative teacher talk is detailed. Mourão takes up the children's literature focus beginning with a definition of the picturebook, emphasizing its compound nature and total design. She explains how multilayered picturebooks 'that provide multiple opportunities for interpretation' (Mourão 2015b: 200) promote more active learners. Mourão proffers an insight into the wealth of topics picturebooks can provide and details a rationale for considering the whole picturebook design in EYL. The author then illustrates the potential of picturebooks with young learners with reference to four picturebooks; the children's response to them as literary texts, including the use of L1 that is then rephrased into English by the teacher, is exemplified.

Drama is the next focus, and Bland begins by discussing the cognitive, sociological, affective and physiological dimensions of holistic language learning, and refers to the centrality of sociocultural context, as 'children are extremely involved in learning through imitation and playful experimentation' (Bland 2015c: 222). She continues with the uses of drama for literacy as well as oracy, referring to motivated reading and creative writing. Warming-up activities, scripted and unscripted drama are illustrated, as well as a range of drama strategies useful for exercising higher-order thinking processes. With Cutrim Schmid and Whyte on technology in teaching language to young learners, the focus remains on interaction in the young-learner classroom. The authors discuss the affordances of technology-enhanced tasks, and emphasize that the focus must be placed on the pedagogy not the tools. They describe and evaluate a tandem project that studied interaction via videoconferencing sessions between French and German young learners, aiming to 'allow learners to negotiate meaning and repair communication breakdowns on their own' (Cutrim Schmid and Whyte 2015: 249). The authors report on motivated children and considerable opportunities, as well as the challenges of computer-mediated communication.

Becker provides an introduction to the complexities of assessment within EYL. The author discusses the development of portfolio work in education, referring to constructivism, self-efficacy, self-determination and learner autonomy. The European Language Portfolio is introduced as a common European instrument that can help learners maintain a record of their language-learning achievements. Becker points to the documentation and pedagogic functions of portfolios, and how they can increase children's enthusiasm for learning. This chapter also reports on a study that showed that 'large-scale implementation is not a sure-fire success' (Becker 2015: 272). The author outlines the far-reaching changes that need to be made in order for portfolio work to develop to its full potential.

In the final chapter, Tomlinson argues for the consideration of both local and universal principled criteria in materials development. He discusses the importance of input: 'If the input is minimal, as it often is for learners of a foreign language whose coursebooks restrict their input to tiny texts and who have little or no access to the language outside the classroom, then the intake will be miniscule' (Tomlinson 2015: 282). The author then considers how children need to make hypotheses about a linguistic feature in order for acquisition to result 'from repeated and meaningful exposure to the feature in use' (2015: 283). Tomlinson shares his rich experience of meaningful and less-meaningful language-learning contexts around the world, always referring to the priority of providing 'an engaging and enjoyable experience of English' (2015: 290). And this, in the end, is the most efficient use of young learners' time, and certainly, as I believe this volume shows, the most effective.

Notes

1 All language-learning terminology is explained in the chapters. Please check the index to find where specific terms occur in the volume.

References

Beacco, Jean-Claude and Byram, Michael (2007), *From Linguistic Diversity to Plurilingual Education: Guide for the Development of Language Education Policies in Europe*, Strasbourg: Council of Europe.

Becker, Carmen (2015), 'Assessment and portfolios', in Janice Bland (ed.), *Teaching English to Young Learners. Critical Issues in Language Teaching with 3–12 Year Olds*, London: Bloomsbury Academic, pp. 262–278.

Bentley, Kay (2015), 'CLIL scenarios with young learners', in Janice Bland (ed.), *Teaching English to Young Learners. Critical Issues in Language Teaching with 3–12 Year Olds*, London: Bloomsbury Academic, pp. 91–111.

Bland, Janice (2013), *Children's Literature and Learner Empowerment. Children and Teenagers in English Language Education*, London: Bloomsbury.

Bland, Janice (2015a), 'Grammar Templates for the Future with Poetry for Children', in Janice Bland (ed.), *Teaching English to Young Learners. Critical Issues in Language Teaching with 3–12 Year Olds*, London: Bloomsbury Academic, pp. 147–166.

Bland, Janice (2015b), 'Oral storytelling in the primary English classroom', in Janice Bland (ed.), *Teaching English to Young Learners. Critical Issues in Language Teaching with 3–12 Year Olds*, London: Bloomsbury Academic, pp. 183–198.

Bland, Janice (2015c), 'Drama with young learners', in Janice Bland (ed.), *Teaching English to Young Learners. Critical Issues in Language Teaching with 3–12 Year Olds*, London: Bloomsbury Academic, pp. 219–238.

Boyd, Brian (2009), *On the Origin of Stories: Evolution, Cognition, and Fiction*, Harvard: Harvard University Press.

British Council (2014) *Languages for the Future. Which Languages the UK Needs Most and Why.* UK: British Council. Available at <http://www.britishcouncil. org/sites/britishcouncil.uk2/files/languages-for-the-future.pdf> [accessed 3 December 2014]

Byram, Michael and Doyé, Peter (1999), 'Intercultural competence and foreign language learning in the primary school', in Patricia Driscoll and David Frost (eds), *The Teaching of Modern Foreign Languages in the Primary School.* London: Routledge, pp. 138–151.

Cameron, Lynne (2003), 'Challenges for ELT from the expansion in teaching children', *ELT Journal*, 57/2: 105–112.

Council of Europe (eds) (2001), *Common European Framework of Reference for Languages: Learning, Teaching, Assessment*, Cambridge: Cambridge University Press.

Cutrim Schmid, Euline and Whyte, Shona (2015), 'Teaching Young Learners with Technology', in Janice Bland (ed.), *Teaching English to Young Learners. Critical Issues in Language Teaching with 3–12 Year Olds*, London: Bloomsbury Academic, pp. 239–259.

Driscoll, Patricia and Simpson, Helen (2015), 'Developing intercultural understanding in primary schools', in Janice Bland (ed.), *Teaching English to Young Learners. Critical Issues in Language Teaching with 3–12 Year Olds*, London: Bloomsbury Academic, pp. 167–182.

Ellis, Nick, O'Donnell, Matthew and Römer, Ute (2013), 'Usage-Based Language: Investigating the Latent Structures that Underpin Acquisition', *Language Learning*, 63/Supp. 1: 25–51.

Enever, Janet (2015), 'The advantages and disadvantages of English as a foreign language with young learners', in Janice Bland (ed.), *Teaching English to Young Learners. Critical Issues in Language Teaching with 3–12 Year Olds*, London: Bloomsbury Academic, pp. 13–29.

Garton, Susan; Copland, Fiona, and Burns, Ann (2011), *Investigating Global Practices in Teaching English to Young Learners.* <http://www.teachingenglish. org.uk/publications/global-practices-teachingenglish-young-learners> [accessed 4 October 2014].

Johnstone, Richard (2002), *Addressing 'The Age Factor': Some Implications for Languages Policy*, Strasbourg: Council of Europe. <http://www.coe.int/t/dg4/ linguistic/Source/JohnstoneEN.pdf> [accessed 27 November 2014].

Kersten, Kristin and Rohde, Andreas (2015), 'Immersion Teaching in English with Young Learners', in Janice Bland (ed.), *Teaching English to Young Learners.*

Critical Issues in Language Teaching with 3–12 Year Olds, London: Bloomsbury Academic, pp. 71–89.

Kersten, Saskia (2015), 'Language development in young learners: the role of formulaic language', in Janice Bland (ed.), *Teaching English to Young Learners. Critical Issues in Language Teaching with 3–12 Year Olds*, London: Bloomsbury Academic, pp. 129–145.

Kramsch, Claire (2000), 'Second language acquisition, applied linguistics, and the teaching of foreign languages', *The Modern Language Journal*, 84/3: 311–126.

Mourão, Sandie (2015a), 'English in pre-primary: The challenges of getting it right', in Janice Bland (ed.), *Teaching English to Young Learners. Critical Issues in Language Teaching with 3–12 Year Olds*, London: Bloomsbury Academic, pp. 51–69.

Mourão, Sandie (2015b), 'The potential of picturebooks with young learners', in Janice Bland (ed.), *Teaching English to Young Learners. Critical Issues in Language Teaching with 3–12 Year Olds*, London: Bloomsbury Academic, pp. 199–217.

Murphy, Victoria (2014), *Second Language Learning in the Early School Years: Trends and Contexts*, Oxford: Oxford University Press.

Legutke, Michael; Müller-Hartmann, Andreas and Schocker-von Ditfurth, Marita (2009), *Teaching English in the Primary School*, Stuttgart: Klett.

Pinter, Annamaria (2015), 'Task-based learning with children', in Janice Bland (ed.), *Teaching English to Young Learners. Critical Issues in Language Teaching with 3–12 Year Olds*, London: Bloomsbury Academic, pp. 113–127.

Rasmussen, Jens (2013), 'Competence goal-driven education in school and teacher education', Keynote lecture, *Transforming Learning and Teaching to Meet the Challenges of 21st Century Education*, Ministry of Education, Kuala Lumpur. <http://pure.au.dk/portal/files/68371248/Competence_goal_driven_education_KL030713.pdf> [accessed 25 October 2014].

Rixon, Shelagh (2015), 'Primary English and critical issues: A worldwide perspective', in Janice Bland (ed.), *Teaching English to Young Learners. Critical Issues in Language Teaching with 3–12 Year Olds*, London: Bloomsbury Academic, pp. 31–50.

Tomlinson, Brian (2015), 'Developing Principled Materials for Young Learners of English as a Foreign Language', in Janice Bland (ed.), *Teaching English to Young Learners. Critical Issues in Language Teaching with 3–12 Year Olds*, London: Bloomsbury Academic, pp. 279–293.

1

The Advantages and Disadvantages of English as a Foreign Language with Young Learners

Janet Enever

Introduction

For more than fifty years now there has been a general trend worldwide towards introducing the teaching of additional languages from the very earliest phases of compulsory schooling. More recently, a trend towards introduction during the preschool years can be identified in particular contexts. The term 'additional languages' is used here to include foreign languages, minority languages and home/heritage languages across a range of contexts. However, overwhelmingly the trend has been towards English becoming the priority language introduced to young children the world over. This chapter seeks to identify the advantages and disadvantages of an early start to English language learning, examining a range of interconnected themes to shed further light on the question. The chapter begins by clarifying the influences that have led to this current circumstance, focusing first on why age has been considered a key factor in this trend. From this analysis, I move on to argue that we need to pay far more attention to understanding the conditions for effective foreign language learning (FLL) today if we are to ensure appropriate learning outcomes across a range of contexts. This section also discusses the importance of understanding how to plan for realistic outcomes, given the limitations of some contexts. Here, I review recent evidence which indicates that we should also develop greater understanding of the potential impact of out-of-school environments and children's exposure to languages via digital media, acknowledging the likelihood of its having an increasing influence on their engagement and achievements in the future.

A historical perspective

Published research reporting on the early years of introducing additional languages to young children is limited, but some key studies should be mentioned here to contextualize the more recent patterns. Increasingly widespread introduction of FLL developed across Europe during the post-war period and particularly in the 1960s, mainly taking the form of smaller-scale projects or individual school initiatives. Notably, a report on a large-scale pilot study conducted in the UK was influential in bringing to a halt much of this expansion following publication of the report (Burstall, Jamieson, Cohen and Hargreaves 1974). In essence, the report concluded that there was no advantage in introducing languages to the primary curriculum since the evidence indicated that children had made little progress. The conclusions were later challenged from a number of perspectives, particularly citing the evidence that languages had been taught by secondary-school-trained teachers with little or no knowledge of age-appropriate methodological skills (Buckby 1976: 340). This issue continues to be a significant factor in many primary-school contexts worldwide today where teachers have been trained as specialist language teachers (trained to teach across the whole age range) with only limited attention given to the specific challenges of maintaining a strong focus on the general development of oral skills with young children. Under such conditions it is possible that any potential advantage may be lost, even resulting in young children developing a negative attitude towards the learning of foreign languages.

Subsequent initiatives for the introduction of early FLs began to expand again in various parts of the world during the 1980s/1990s, with much more rapid expansion becoming visible as one outcome of the changing political climate post-1990 in Europe. In an effort to capture these developments, Blondin, Candelier, Edelenbos, Johnstone, Kubanek-German and Taeschner (1998) conducted a review of published research, aiming to identify the extent to which specific factors contributed to effective learning. Their synthesis of available European research included themes related to society, schools, teachers, learners, start age and diversity. This provided something of a baseline study establishing principles for later research to be conducted.

Some eight years later the European Commission published a more extensive review of current research (Edelenbos, Johnstone and Kubanek

2006). The timing of this review is significant in that it encompassed the period of large-scale expansion of English provision in primary schools, both across Europe and through many regions of Asia. Importantly, the review moved away from a central focus on age as the determining factor, providing a broader understanding of the advantages and disadvantages of an early start and highlighting the very varied conditions and contexts for learning that existed. With this stress on the importance of gaining a detailed understanding of how conditions might impact on learning, the review sheds light on potential new directions for research which may, in time, contribute to developing teacherly skills able to maximize the potential advantages of an early start.

The shift to English during the second half of the twentieth century is clearly revealed in a review by Cha and Ham (2008), reporting that during the period between 1945 and 1969 English as a foreign language was evident in approximately 32.8 per cent of all primary-school curriculum programmes worldwide, rising to nearly 70 per cent by 2005 (Cha and Ham 2008: 317). While the accuracy of these figures may be difficult to verify, given the complexity of access for such multiple sources, nonetheless, they reveal the broad pattern of unprecedented growth in English language provision that has occurred at primary level globally. This trend is reflected in Europe also where the rise in popularity of English at primary level has been charted by three publications: Eurydice (2005: 44) reported that in ten member countries of the European Union (EU) English as a Foreign Language had been introduced in over 50 per cent of all primary schools in each country; by 2008 this figure had risen to seventeen countries (Eurydice 2008: 64) while Eurydice (2012: 60) records English taught in 72 per cent of all primary schools across the EU. From the summary of studies presented here it can be concluded that an earlier start has become a key factor in changing perceptions that this offers an advantage for the learner in terms of final achievement levels. The following section discusses evidence that has helped shape this viewpoint.

Age – is it the key factor?

Much debate related to early language learning has focused on age as a central factor in deciding when to introduce FLL in schools (e.g. Muñoz 2006, Nikolov 2009). In a review of various studies Nikolov (2009: 4) concludes that there are mixed views on how to interpret the evidence from research. Summarizing, she cites Singleton's view that there may be no definitive answer, where he argues finally that the question of age is 'impossible to deal with' (Singleton 2005: 280).

Before moving on to the main focus of this chapter, I will briefly present here the three main themes that may account for the strong focus given to age as the most important determining 'condition' for curriculum decision-makers to take into account during the planning process. These include language acquisition, neuroscience and socio-political perspectives.

Language acquisition perspective

Opinions have been much influenced in the past by evidence from two main areas: bilingual home environments and immersion schooling. With regard to bilingualism, a substantial number of research studies have illustrated how successfully children can learn two or more languages simply by exposure in the home environment (Genesee 1989). In the one-to-one atmosphere of child and parent/caretaker, the child often seems to effortlessly acquire both languages, although sometimes one will be more dominant than the other (Genesee 2006). Similarly impressive results have been charted from contexts where immersion schooling has been developed. Here, particularly noteworthy is the evidence from Canada, where many primary schools were established to provide full immersion in French throughout the school day. Results clearly demonstrated how successfully children from English-speaking home backgrounds quickly became able French speakers (Genesee 1987). Many similar initiatives have been taken following the Canadian model, or some adaptation of this, around the world (Johnson and Swain 1997; Dobson, Murillo and Johnstone 2010; for a detailed discussion see K. Kersten and Rohde 2015, this volume).

From evidence of impressive language acquisition results in both the home environment and immersion schooling contexts, parents, policymakers and many researchers have generalized such successes to an assumption that similar results can be achieved in the ordinary school classroom, often ignoring factors such as the larger number of pupils involved and the limited curriculum time available for foreign-language lessons.

Neuroscience

This field is rapidly becoming an exciting area of relevant research. With the development of neuroimaging techniques, opportunities to actually see brain activity have become increasingly possible, offering the prospect of perhaps gaining insights into cognition. It now seems evident from research that the child's brain functions differently from the adult brain. From these findings some extrapolate that children may learn languages differently from adults (Sabourin and Stowe 2008: 425). Much of the brain research on children to date has centred on children in bilingual contexts, also increasingly in multilingual contexts (Wattendorf and Festman 2008: 4). So far, it is difficult to be sure of how these findings might relate to contexts where children begin learning a second/foreign language some years after they acquired their first language. Functional magnetic resonance imaging (fMRI) has identified changes in the structural plasticity of the brain that occurs during learning, but how this might relate to the age factor is not yet fully determined. Studies on early bilinguals using voxel-based morphometry (VBM) have shown increased neural activity during the early stages of language processing, together with evidence of the expanded size of the neural pathways (Mechelli, Crinion, Noppeney, O'Doherty, Ashburner, Frackowiak and Price 2004: 757). From this, it is hypothesized that the learning of more than one language at a young age increases the capacity for cognitive processing.

One recent study employing fMRI to compare two groups of adult multilinguals, one of which was bilingual by the age of three years and the other after the age of nine years, moves our knowledge further forward in this field. The study provided evidence that 'the early learning of two languages has a pervasive effect on a neuronal network that is presumed to regulate language control in bilinguals at different processing levels' (Wattendorf et al. 2014: 61). Nonetheless, despite these highly informative studies, much further interdisciplinary research in this area is needed before we can reach conclusions that indicate clear relevance to the more formal instructional context of the primary foreign-language classroom.

Socio-political context

The next theme that can be identified as having a significant impact on views related to the benefits of an early start to FLL is best described as the socio-political context. Globally, both parents and politicians have been influential in promoting the perceived benefits of an early start over the last thirty years or so. With a heightened sense of global interconnectivity that has emerged as a result of economic globalization and digital technology advances, politicians have argued for the importance of a plurilingual citizenry equipped to operate in the global marketplace. From this, the argument follows that it is valuable to start learning languages early, to become fluent by adulthood. Parents have been much influenced by this rhetoric, linking it with the evidence from bilingual families and immersion schooling to conclude that an early start is automatically an advantage. Deeply embedded in this rhetoric, English is positioned centrally as the global language – hence, the first language to learn.

The above factors have combined to stimulate rapid growth in the provision of primary English language teaching worldwide, with the socio-political viewpoint drawing on the first two influences to provide a rationale for an early start during a period of intense globalization.

Advantages and disadvantages

The developments summarized above have stimulated a growing body of research, contributing valuable new clarifications in relation to the age question. However, research from varied global contexts consistently fails to offer a definitive voice on this question, a situation in which Johnstone (2009: 34) helpfully provided a measured response to the debate, proposing that:

> Overall, an advantage of an early start is that in principle at least it allows young beginners to exploit such advantages as they possess, but in addition, as they become older, to make use of the advantages that older learners possess. So, over time, both sets of advantages are available to those making the early start, whereas only the second set of advantages is available to those beginning later.

Here, Johnstone tends to come out in favour of an earlier start to language learning, but in later sections of his paper he makes clear his view that the advantages of an early start may be lost if what he describes as conditions for *generalized success* are not available. By generalized success, Johnstone indicates that the conditions should be such that not only highly skilled teachers but also 'ordinary' teachers should be able to succeed. This key point will be returned to later in this chapter.

Returning firstly, however, to evidence presented above from the field of neuroscience, Johansen-Berg (2013) – a leading researcher in brain plasticity – suggests that current literature from neuroimaging studies can generally be summarized as indicating that language learning 'does seem to get harder as you get older' (Johansen-Berg, 26/12/2013). With increasingly clear evidence from neuroscience of the potential for young language learning, it is perhaps surprising that classrooms worldwide are not always managing to fully capitalize on this potential to produce the outcomes that research indicates should be achievable. Accounting for this is a complex undertaking; however, it is important to acknowledge that the scale of this kind of reform is huge and expertise takes time to establish. At present, we are still in the early stages of building this expertise – a process that may well take more than one generation to establish and consolidate. Understanding more clearly the advantages for language learning that the young child brings to the classroom and ensuring that teachers are equipped with the skills to capitalize on these in the ordinary school classroom must be viewed as a priority aspect of contemporary research in pedagogy if children are to benefit sufficiently from the weekly dose of just one to two hours focusing on English language. Here, I will briefly discuss overviews put forward by Halliwell (1992) and Johnstone

(2009), reflecting the considered opinions at particular points in the developing phases of research in this field. Following this, I will discuss the extent to which the advantages of an early start may be fully exploited or lost completely, as a result of contextual conditions.

Insights into advantages: 1992–2009

Halliwell (1992) was writing during the period before the most major expansion of primary and pre-primary English had occurred across the Asian region. As such, the approach adopted in the teachers' handbook referred to here is likely to have drawn mainly on her knowledge and experience of classrooms and teacher education in Europe. Nonetheless, Halliwell's six main categories of young children's abilities have much resonance in today's vastly expanded global context for learning English early. She begins by highlighting children's ability to grasp meaning, relating this to their recently learnt ability to 'read the general message' (Halliwell 1992: 3) in their first language (mother tongue). Here, she suggests that children are drawing on the paralinguistic features of communication such as 'intonation, gesture, facial expression, actions' (1992: 3) and on the wider context in which the communication occurs. This ability is linked closely with Halliwell's second point, which she describes as 'children's creative use of language', referring to young children's willingness to focus on communication rather than accuracy in their first steps towards getting across their meaning in a foreign language. For example, children may form negatives incorrectly, invent new words or include words from their first language (L1) spoken with a foreign accent (1992: 4). She emphasizes the benefits of making mistakes during this process, arguing that much learning is thereby facilitated. Third, Halliwell suggests that the ability to be creative with language can also be linked closely to children's capacity for what she describes as 'indirect learning' (1992: 5). Essentially, the term suggests an ability to guess at language and a tolerance of ambiguity in the process of meaning making. She explains this capacity by drawing on evidence of how children acquire their first language, which she proposes is 'acquired through continuous exposure and use' (1992: 5). Here, she is careful to indicate that conscious direct learning also plays a part in the learning of a new language, arguing that classroom tasks need to provide opportunities for both and suggesting that different children may respond more or less to each of these processes in their early stages of learning (1992: 5). The fourth item on Halliwell's list of capacities that young children bring to the English language classroom relates to 'children's instinct for play and fun' (1992: 6), proposing that this instinct can be turned to great advantage in the early phases of learning by creating engaging activities which children will enjoy and 'play' with. By way of clarification, I include one of Halliwell's examples here. She reports on a class of 9–10-year-olds asked to follow directions to navigate their way around a map and reach a particular shop. During the activity one pair chose to 'navigate' their way using a paper clip to trace the route, making cornering noises as they turned corners and screeching brake noises in drawing to a halt. Wisely, the teacher recognized the value of these children 'translating' verbal instructions into physical actions in the process of powerfully making their own meanings. For these children, she reports, 'the children are living the language for real' (1992: 7). This evidence is again closely linked to the role of imagination in young children's lives. Fifth, she suggests that fantasy plays a very big part in how young children test out and make sense of the world around them. Indeed, some children appear to often exist almost completely in a world of fantasy. This willingness to suspend disbelief for periods of the day offers great potential for the early FL classroom, where children may be encouraged to create a new identity within the classroom in order to participate in a make-believe game *in the foreign language*. Halliwell (1992: 7) offers the example of how children's picturebooks can replicate and support this experience, for example, *The Tiger Who Came to Tea* (Kerr 1968). As a final and all-encompassing point Halliwell concludes by citing possibly the most important one for the language classroom, 'children's instinct for interaction and talk' (1992: 8). She argues that 'without talking they cannot become good at talking' and that 'the only way to learn to *use* it *is* to use it' (italics in the original). Creating opportunities for this to occur through a variety of more and less structured activities is the most important priority for teachers of this age group.

Johnstone, writing some seventeen years later, provides a summary with a slightly different focus to that of Halliwell's. In addressing an audience of researchers rather than practitioners (the focus of Halliwell's publication) he nonetheless raises very similar points. His introduction indicates that his summary draws on a research overview presented in an earlier report to the Council of Europe (Johnstone 2002). This perhaps gives some hint that the advantages of younger learners may have something of a timeless quality that has been unshaken by research evidence in the interim.

Johnstone (2009: 34) begins by proposing that young children are likely to have relative ease in acquiring the sound system of a new language, including both the pronunciation of individual sounds and the patterns of intonation (Johnstone 2002: 12). While this point is not emphasized specifically by Halliwell, it could be said to be embedded in a number of her themes. Johnstone's second point proposes that young children are 'less likely to be "language anxious"' (Johnstone 2009: 34), a view very much in line with Halliwell's comments on children's ability to use language creatively, indicating their willingness to take risks and tolerate ambiguity in an effort to convey meaning. Here, Johnstone refers to some of the extensive research conducted by Mihaljević Djigunović (1995) on language anxiety, attitudes and motivation, which finds that children mainly exhibit a distinct advantage in all three during the early phases of language learning. The third advantage that Johnstone identifies is an expansion of Johnstone (2009) quoted above, where he provides an illustration comparing the language achievements for five-year-old beginners after one year of learning with the achievements of ten-year-old beginners after a similar period. He concludes that older beginners are more likely to be ahead as a result of their more analytic approach to learning, which allows them to learn more rapidly. However, he goes on to assert that if both groups are then compared again at the age of fourteen, it is likely that the younger beginners will then be ahead, simply because they have been learning for a longer period and been able to employ the advantages of both younger learners and older learners (Johnstone 2002: 12).

It should be noted that this example relies on all other variables of the comparison being equal. These findings are further supported by a review of research conducted by Singleton (1989), who additionally emphasized the role that particular conditions may play in whether or not good progress is made. In his summary Johnstone (2009) goes on to propose that there are a number of advantages which young children bring to the language classroom related to acquisition over time. He cites evidence of the initial mainly intuitive abilities, together with more analytical processes at a later stage, arguing that the combination of these two processes can enable the language 'to become more deeply embedded in the person' (Johnstone 2002: 12). Johnstone (2009: 34) concludes by suggesting that an early start to language learning may contribute positively to many broader educational aims. These might include: 'cognitive, linguistic, emotional, and social skills' (Johnstone 2009: 34), together with laying the foundations of a 'multilingual and intercultural identity' (Johnstone 2002: 12).

Disadvantages of an early start

Given the wealth of evidence now accumulating in support of the advantages of an early start, it is becoming increasingly difficult today to pinpoint any single factor that can be identified as a disadvantage *under any circumstance.* Johnstone (2009: 34) suggests that young children's less developed knowledge of how language works (e.g. grammatical structures, limited experience of a range of discourses, etc.) may place them at a disadvantage in grasping new concepts. He proposes that older learners are better equipped to draw on a more sophisticated knowledge of the world and more advanced analytical skills in making sense of how the new language functions. Research by both García Mayo (2003: 106) and Cenoz (2003: 89) seems to support this also.

While there are many ways in which a skilled teacher can work around this limitation, evidence of the relatively slow progress of younger children learning languages tends to confirm this viewpoint (Muñoz 2006).

Johnstone (2009: 34) also suggests that older learners have greater experience of engaging in different forms of communication and thus have more familiarity with how to negotiate and clarify meanings. Similarly, they may well have developed a range of learning strategies (e.g. note taking, revising) – skills that are immediately transferable to the task of learning an FL. For younger children, they are likely to be only just beginning to learn these skills in the first few years of compulsory schooling, while preschool children are unlikely to have any such knowledge or experience. Still, the question remains, is it better to begin early, including these learning strategies as part of the broad educational aims for this subject within the primary curriculum, or should we wait until learners have developed these skills before introducing them to FL learning? In the next section I return to Johnstone's notion of *generalized success* in order to review the conditions that will allow this to be achieved, ensuring that any potential advantages of any early start are actually advantageous.

Conditions necessary for *generalized success*

In adopting a global perspective on the question of conditions it is difficult to generalize from research since contexts worldwide are so diverse. Here I limit myself to a focus on five main areas of evidence that seem to be areas of remaining weakness within some learning environments today. Unless policymakers pay attention to overcoming these weaknesses, the significant advantages that young children bring to the classroom may be all but lost. These themes include teacher expertise, the role of motivation, establishing continuity of learning, setting realistic aims and the role of out-of-school learning. Each of these themes is briefly discussed in the following sections.

Teacher expertise

It is now generally accepted that the teacher expertise needed for EYL includes two main strands: an advanced level of language fluency and the ability to implement age-appropriate methodological skills. Decisions on what precise level of fluency is acceptable vary, but recent research indicates that oral fluency in particular needs to be at an advanced level for teachers to be able to respond to the many informal uses of language that are likely to occur in the young-learner classroom (Enever 2011). The more highly skilled the teacher is in using English for some of the many incidental communications that children engage in during daily routines, the more rapidly children are likely to adjust to the new experience of taking their first steps in communicating in an FL. In a number of European contexts this level has now been established at a minimum of B2, based on the Common European Framework of Reference for Languages (CEFR) descriptors (Council of Europe 2001).

Interpretations of the necessary methodological skills for teaching young learners vary considerably, both as a result of widely differing understandings of the nature of learning in educational institutions worldwide and because of the limited attention paid to the specific needs of children in EYL. As a result, some countries continue to prepare language teachers for teaching across the whole age range, from preschool to adulthood, allocating little or no time to the development of the specialist skills needed for teaching EYL, while also failing to include supportive learning modules on child development. The outcome of such an inappropriate preparation for EYL may be a complete failure to build on the young child's potential, particularly in circumstances where little or no continuous professional development opportunities are available. As one illustration of how a language teacher with age-appropriate teacherly skills can overcome difficulties such as poor resource provision, an example from lesson observations conducted in Hungary during the mid-1990s (Enever 2001) is briefly summarized below.

Responsibility for decisions on teaching materials varies in different parts of the world. In some countries materials may be issued to schools free of charge, selected by a central committee, while in others decisions are devolved to regional authorities, individual schools or to teachers – sometimes with the cost being met by parents. Evidence from Hungary reflected devolution of decision making on the choice of course materials to individual schools, with parents covering the cost. This often resulted in decisions to continue the use of somewhat out-of-date materials, saving money by passing the books on from older to younger siblings in relatively low-economy households. However, this did not necessarily result in weak outcomes for these early learners. Where teachers were highly skilled primary specialists, often they chose to adapt the main theme of a coursebook topic to create a lesson that offered a contemporary, engaging and age-appropriate challenge to the children. Where teachers lacked this skill (insufficient pre- and in-service training was available during this period), then many of the advantages of an early start were lost, with significant evidence of a rapid decline in learner motivation (Enever 2001).

Sustaining motivation over time

It has often been claimed that one of the principal advantages of learning languages early is the high level of motivation for engaging in enjoyable new experiences that children have. Halliwell's (1992) key text for teacher education includes a number of references to fun and enjoyment, emphasizing the importance of balancing enjoyment with cognitive engagement in the task, in order to stimulate motivation. This argument relates to the role of play in early childhood as part of the developmental process. However, in many schooling systems the emphasis is placed on formality and concentrated effort, both of which tend not to support environments where children might be making a noise – thus placing much stress on the teacher who attempts to introduce activities where children have fun, in the process of learning the FL.

The question of how motivation can be maintained over time provides a serious challenge for language teachers in contexts where English may be taught for periods of up to fourteen years now (including preschool). Nikolov (1999: 53) indicated that children's motivation may begin high, but later decline as the challenges increase. Only limited research on this topic with young learners is so far available owing to the difficulties of mounting longitudinal studies. One recent study to shed some light has been the ELLiE study (Enever 2011), which followed the experiences of young language learners in seven European countries over a period of four years in total. Lesson observations and interview data revealed frequent fluctuations in motivation, both during lessons and over longer periods of time. Much of this could be attributed to limited teacherly skills of classroom management, poor choice of age-appropriate methodology, tasks/activities, but also to peer and wider societal influences. In an analysis of variations in motivation over time, Mihaljevic Djigunovic and Lopriore (2011: 44) reported that children's responses to questions about their foreign-language lessons continued to indicate a generally positive attitude, but negative responses were more frequent in the later years of the study. These responses were 'most probably, informed by their whole primary learning experience' (Mihaljević Djigunović and Lopriore 2011: 44).

Continuity

Linked to the above discussion of maintaining motivation is the challenge of achieving continuity of the learning process over time. One of the problems that has arisen as a result of the rapid introduction of primary English has been the much slower provision of curricula documents to support the implementation process, in many contexts. In the introduction of large-scale reform to an education system, the failure to support it with appropriate curricula guidelines can result in a tendency for teachers to simply 'do their own thing' with little attention to what has come before, or what will follow. Li (2011) reports on this occurrence during the early phases of the introduction of English in China, prior to the development of curricula to fully support teachers. Similarly in the ELLiE study school principals often reported little or no contact with the schools their children might transfer to at age eleven or twelve (unpublished data from ELLiE study). Continuity was generally more effectively maintained in those countries where children remained in the same school throughout the period of compulsory schooling – albeit sometimes in different buildings for each period of the process. Where information on individual learner achievements was transferred to a new school, it tended to be only in the form of numerical data, offering little detail to fully support continuity. Without the benefits of continuity throughout schooling, it seems unlikely that learners will experience the advantages of an early start and achieve the higher outcomes predicted.

Aims

In a discussion of the conditions necessary for effective language learning we need to be clear about the desired outcomes if we are to provide conditions that will enable learners to be successful. Defining these outcomes has proved to be an imprecise process. This particularly applies to the age group in question given the tendency for progress to be non-linear for language learners of this young age. The entanglement of affective responses with language production in the young child's cognitive functioning at this stage of development may result in spiral, erratic or even recursive outcomes as children become familiar with a new way of communicating, through the medium of a foreign language, during these early years. From a wider perspective, the problem is further compounded by the scale and speed of reform that has been attempted in some countries, inevitably leading to somewhat varied patterns of provision across regions, with a general trend towards increased inequalities between urban and rural environments and thus concerns that not all learners have an equal opportunity to achieve the desired outcomes. Most recently, global interconnectivity has contributed to shaping a measurement culture, nurturing the production of comparative statistics in all fields of education, including the outcomes of language education (see, e.g., Eurydice 2005, 2008 and 2012, ESLC SurveyLang 2012).

In this heady environment of measurement, comparisons and competition, one of the key tenets of the argument for an early start to language learning may be overlooked – that of the potential for establishing early positive attitudes which will sustain children's motivation and engagement through the many years of future language learning. The measurement of affective skills, broader educational skills and the development of intercultural learning that occurs during the process of early FLL has a qualitative resonance that does not lend itself to large-scale statistical analysis. As a result, what cannot be easily measured tends to be overlooked and undervalued. Given this, contemporary approaches to defining outcomes for early language learners mostly refer to aspects of linguistic measurement, using terms such as 'elementary' or 'intermediate' level, or language descriptor scales such as those available in the CEFR (Council of Europe 2001). Alternatively, some countries/individual schools rely on an exit exam at the end of the primary phase of schooling. Where national decisions are made on the form of measurement to be used, these rarely include any differentiation for the varying modes of provision that may be available in the country. These may range from one or two hours per week to full or partial immersion (sometimes known as bilingual provision). Broadly speaking, the model of one to two hours per week is most commonly found worldwide today, with possibly only thirty minutes per week being not uncommon at the preschool level. While each of these models will clearly have different outcomes, it is important to note that it is unrealistic to expect substantial progress from one hour per week.

Out-of-school learning

English is available to young children beyond the classroom increasingly in many contexts worldwide. The growing opportunities for this cannot be understated in terms of their impact on young children's familiarity and general sense of ease with pronunciation and prosodic features even before they begin learning English formally in some contexts. Studies from northern Europe with often high levels of digital interconnectivity may give a hint of future possibilities worldwide. Lefever (2010) reports on how children in Iceland have picked up words and phrases from subtitled films, while Kuppens (2010) reported that Flemish children (Dutch-speaking) who watched subtitled TV in English more frequently outperformed those who watched less, in an oral translation task. Similarly, Lindgren and Muñoz (2013: 119) report findings indicating that watching subtitled films and TV had a positive effect on listening and reading skills. Additionally, listening to music and playing games in the FL had an effect, albeit of lesser statistical significance. Muñoz and Lindgren (2011: 117) reported that children in the ELLiE study made use of the internet generally to find information, to watch programmes online without subtitles and to chat with children in other countries for fun. These studies indicate the potential that digital technology might offer for the future, particularly in creating a stronger home/school partnership where families can be guided to identify appropriately engaging online materials/programmes for children's use in the relaxed environment of the home. This may prove highly relevant in contexts where generally there are few opportunities for access to the FL beyond school, and time spent on FLs in school is limited to one or two hours per week.

Conclusions

While the evidence for the advantages of an early start is far from conclusive, there is much to be said for Johnstone's (2009) view that the longer period of learning offered by an early start pays dividends over time. Johansen-Berg's (2013) weighing of the evidence from neuroscience further supports this as she states that language learning 'does seem to get harder as you get older'. However, while the potential advantage is significant, the implementation process is a demanding long-term project. Unless or until policymakers fully come to terms with this and invest in ensuring that appropriate conditions for implementation are achieved as quickly as possible, the whole initiative may risk the same downfall as occurred in the UK during the 1970s (Burstall et al. 1974).

Two related factors require the urgent attention of researchers: the question of aims and outcomes. Currently, experimentation with a range of intensity of provision is happening worldwide. Insights into the aims and realistically achievable outcomes for each of these models are now needed, providing a mechanism for schools to negotiate their individual school aims within/despite a culture of increasing measurement, accountability and comparison. National and local education authorities also need to establish a realistic, time-bound development plan for embedding quality early provision within the school system. Only then will we be able to accurately evaluate the advantages or disadvantages of an early start.

References

Blondin, Christiane; Candelier, Michel; Edelenbos, Peter; Johnstone, Richard; Kubanek-German, Angelika and Taeschner, Traute (1998), *Foreign Languages in Primary and Pre-school Education: Contexts and Outcomes. A Review of Recent Research within the European Union*, London: CILT.

Buckby, Michael (1976). Is Primary French Really in the Balance? *Modern Language Journal*, 60/7: 340–346

Burstall, Clare; Jamieson, Monika; Cohen, Susan and Hargreaves, Margaret (1974), *Primary French in the Balance*, Slough: NFER Publishing Co.

Cenoz, Jasone (2003), 'The influence of age on the acquisition of English: General proficiency, attitudes and code-mixing', in Maria García Mayo and Maria García Lecumberri (eds), *Age and the Acquisition of English as a Foreign Language*, Clevedon: Multilingual Matters, pp. 77–92.

Cha, Yun-Kyung and Ham, Seung-Hwan (2008), 'The impact of English on the school curriculum', in Bernard Spolsky and Francis Hult (eds), *The Handbook of Educational Linguistics*, London: Blackwell, pp. 313–328.

Dobson, Alan; Murillo, Maria Delores Perez and Johnstone, Richard (2010), *Bilingual Education Project Spain*, Spain: Ministry of Education/British Council.

Council of Europe (2001), *Common European Framework of Reference for Languages: Learning, Teaching, Assessment*, Cambridge: Cambridge University Press.

Edelenbos, Peter; Johnstone, Richard and Kubanek, Angelika (2006), *Languages for the Children of Europe: Published Research, Good Practice and Main Principles. Final Report of the EAC 89/04, Lot 1 Study*, Brussels: European Commission. <http://ec.europa.eu/languages/policy/language-policy/documents/young_en.pdf> [accessed 15 July 2014].

Enever, Janet (ed.) (2011), *ELLiE. Early Language Learning in Europe*, London: British Council.

Enever, Janet (2001), *The Politics of Non-decision Making in Language Policy in Hungary, Unpublished* doctoral thesis, Bristol: University of Bristol.

ESLC SurveyLang (2012), *First European Survey on Language Competences: Final Report*, Brussels: European Commission.

Eurydice (2012), *Eurydice: Key Data on Teaching Languages at Schools in Europe*, Brussels: Commission of the European Communities. <http://eacea.ec.europa.eu/education/eurydice/key_data_en.php> [accessed 15 July 2014].

Eurydice (2008), *Eurydice: Key data on Teaching Languages at Schools in Europe*, Brussels: Commission of the European Communities. <http://eacea.ec.europa.eu/education/eurydice/key_data_en.php> [accessed 15 July 2014].

Eurydice (2005), *Eurydice: Key Data on Teaching Languages at Schools in Europe*, Brussels: Commission of the European Communities. <http://bookshop.europa.eu/en/key-data-on-teaching-languages-at-school-in-europe-pbNCXA04001/> [accessed 15 July 2014].

García Mayo, Maria (2003), 'Age, length of exposure and grammaticality judgements in the acquisition of English as a foreign language', in Maria García Mayo and Maria García Lecumberri (eds), *Age and the Acquisition of English as a Foreign Language*, Clevedon: Multilingual Matters, pp. 94–114.

Genesee, Fred (1987), *Learning through Two Languages. Studies of Immersion and Bilingual Education*, Cambridge, MA: Newbury House.

Genesee, Fred (1989), 'Early bilingual development: One language or two?' *Journal of Child Language*, 16/1: 161–179.

Genesee, Fred (2006), 'Bilingual first language acquisition in perspective', in McCardle, Peggy and Hoff, Erika (eds), *Childhood Bilingualism: Research on Infancy through School Age*, Clevedon: Multilingual Matters.

Halliwell, Susan (1992), *Teaching English in the Primary Classroom*, Harlow: Longman.

Johansen-Berg, Heidi (2013), *You and Yours interview, BBC Radio 4*, 26/12/2013.

Johnstone, Richard (2002), *Addressing 'The Age Factor': Some Implications for Languages Policy. Guide for the Development of Language Education Policies in Europe: From Linguistic Diversity to Plurilingual Education*, Strasbourg: Council of Europe. <http://www.coe.int/t/dg4/linguistic/Source/JohnstoneEN.pdf> [accessed 15 July 2014].

Johnstone, Richard (2009), 'An early start: What are the key conditions for generalized success?' in Janet Enever, Jayne Moon and Uma Raman (eds), *Young Learner English Language Policy and Implementation: International Perspectives*, Reading: Garnet Education, pp. 31–41.

Johnson, Keith and Swain, Merrill (eds) (1997), *Immersion Education: International Perspectives*, Cambridge: Cambridge University Press.

Kerr, Judith (1968), *The Tiger Who Came to Tea*, Glasgow: William Collins & Sons.

Kersten, Kristin and Rohde, Andreas (2015), 'Immersion Teaching in English with Young Learners', in Janice Bland (ed.), *Teaching English to Young Learners. Critical Issues in Language Teaching with 3–12 Year Olds*, London: Bloomsbury Academic, pp. 71–89.

Kuppens, Ari (2010), 'Incidental foreign language acquisition from media exposure', *Learning, Media and Technology*, 35/1: 65–85.

Li, Minglin (2011), 'Shaping socialist ideology through language education policy for primary schools in the PRC', *Current Issues in Language Planning*, 12/2: 185–204.

Lindgren, Eva and Muñoz, Carmen (2013), 'The influence of exposure, parents and linguistic distance on young European learners' foreign language comprehension', *International Journal of Multilingualism*, 10/1: 105–129.

Lefever, Samuel (2010), *English Skills for Young Learners in Iceland*, paper presented at Menntakvika Conference, Reykjavik.

Mechelli, Andrea; Crinion, Jenny; Noppeney, Uta; O'Doherty, John; Ashburner, John; Frackowiak, Richard and Price, Cathy (2004), 'Neurolinguistics: Structural plasticity in the bilingual brain', *Nature*, 14.10.2004, p. 757.

Mihaljević Djigunović, Jelena (1995), 'Attitudes of young foreign language learners: A follow-up study', in Vilke Mirjana and Vrhovac Yvonne (eds), *Children and Foreign Languages*, University of Zagreb: Faculty of Philosophy, pp. 16–33.

Mihaljević Djigunović, Jelena and Lopriore, Lucilla (2011), 'The Learner: Do individual differences matter?' in Janet Enever (ed.), *ELLiE. Early Language Learning in Europe*, London: British Council.

Muñoz, Carmen (ed.) (2006), *Age and the Rate of Foreign Language Learning*, Clevedon: Multilingual Matters.

Muñoz, Carmen and Lindgren, Eva (2011), 'Out-of-school factors: The home', in Janet Enever (ed.), *ELLiE. Early Language Learning in Europe*, London: British Council.

Nikolov, Marianne (1999), '"Why do you learn English?" "Because my teacher is short". A study of Hungarian children's foreign language learning motivation', *Language Teaching Research*, 3/1: 33–56.

Nikolov, Marianne (2009) (ed.), *The Age Factor and Early Language Learning*, Berlin & New York: Mouton de Gruyter.

Sabourin, Laura and Stowe, Laurie (2008), 'Second language processing: When are first and second languages processed the same?' *Second Language Research*, 24/3: 397–430.

Singleton, David (1989), *Language Acquisition: The Age Factor*, Clevedon: Multilingual Matters.

Singleton, David (2005), 'The critical period hypothesis: A coat of many colours.' *International Review of Applied Linguistics*, 43: 269–286.

Wattendorf, Elsie and Festman, Julia (2008), 'Images of the multilingual brain: The effect of age of second language acquisition', *Annual Review of Applied Linguistics*, 28: 3–24.

Wattendorf, Elsie; Festman, Julia; Westermann, Birgit; Keil, Ursula; Zappatore, Daniela; Franceschini, Rita; Luedi, Georges; Radue, Ernst-Wilhelm; Münte, Thomas; Rager, Günter and NitschEarly, Cordula (2014), 'Bilingualism influences early and subsequently later acquired languages in cortical regions representing control functions', *International Journal of Bilingualism*, 18/1: 48–66.

2

Primary English and Critical Issues: A Worldwide Perspective

Shelagh Rixon

Introduction

In this chapter I aim to do two things: *Firstly* it seems useful to provide an update on the state internationally of the teaching of English as a foreign or second language to primary-school-aged children. This is a movement that by the time of writing has had a thirty-five-year or so history since the first stirrings of interest in the subject on the European continent lit the fuse of English as a school subject for young children. This interest then quickly spread to other parts of the world, notably East Asia. See Rixon (1992) and Kubanek-German (1998) for accounts of these early years. The update aspect of this chapter is based on the results of a recent worldwide survey carried out for the British Council in 2011 (Rixon 2013). The teaching and learning contexts in the survey are divided according to Kachru's scheme (1985) of Inner Circle, Outer Circle and Expanding Circle contexts. Inner Circle contexts are those such as the UK, the USA and Australia in which English has been the predominant first language for some considerable time. Outer Circle countries, which were largely previously colonized by one of the Inner Circle countries, have a legacy of widespread English language use in law, government and education and often a recognition of English as one of the official languages. Expanding Circle areas are those in which English has been traditionally classified as a foreign language, where English has no embedded role in administration or governance. There are diversities in the linguistic situations in contexts placed within the same category and these have increased with increasing globalization since Kachru first proposed the scheme. Indeed, the amounts of English use may be higher in some present-day Expanding Circle countries than they are in some regions of Outer Circle countries. However, the labels remain useful for making broad divisions in a discussion such as this one. The focus of the survey, and of this chapter, is the state school system, although some discussion of the private sector is also included because of the important interactions between the two that can be discerned in many countries.

This chapter would quickly go out of date if it were no more than a facts-and-figures exercise. *Secondly*, therefore, through the headings to the different sections of this chapter, I shall try to link the reported data with critical issues and with some anomalies concerning how English language teaching to young learners is being conceptualized and implemented in different parts of the world.

Why has English for young learners taken such a hold?

Increasing the grasp within a nation of a politically and economically important language such as English sounds to many politicians and their public to be an uncontroversially desirable proposition. Many of them then envision the main way to achieve this as teaching the language to young children in school. Graddol (2006: 88–91) claims that, in the view of many governments, English for young learners is 'not just an educational project, but also a political and economic one'. This linkage has been experienced in places all over the world by now. However, as I will suggest below, the aim of ensuring that key people in a nation are linguistically well equipped could potentially be approached by a variety of ways and means, not all of them involving teaching English to young children. Many of these alternatives might give rise to rather less expenditure and upheaval of career paths and school dynamics than current policies concerning teaching English to children have caused. If we are looking for one overarching critical issue, it is the need to consider the rationales for primary-school English language teaching from a number of points of view rather than to focus mainly or exclusively on the age of the learners.

Contextual factors affecting young learners' English

In a global survey of English language learning, very varied conditions will be found and not all influencing factors or emerging consequences will apply everywhere equally or in exactly the same ways. We have seen above that very broad classifications can be made according to the historical and existing status of English in different countries around the world. Beyond that, however, we could also consider the different sorts of access to English in the environment that younger learners in particular might have. It has been suggested that access to English via 'out of school' means such as internet use, video games and watching non-dubbed English language films and TV programmes can these days constitute significant levels of informal learning for children. See, for example, Kuppens (2010), Lefever (2009) and Sayer and Ban (2014), on how this can apply to young learners in places as diverse as Belgium, Iceland and Mexico, respectively. Linguistic landscapes (Landry and Bourhis 1997) such as are contributed to by signage and advertisements and other environmental print in English (see Hudelson 1994) should also be considered, with all the non-standard, creative or eccentric models of English that may well be found on such signs in streets and public places.

English as a life-changer? High-stakes and really high-stakes English learning

In most Expanding Circle countries in which English has been introduced as a subject into the primary curriculum, it is generally perceived as a high-stakes school subject. As we shall see later, many parents are prepared to make considerable sacrifices to ensure that their children do well in English. However, in many Outer Circle countries, the stakes are realistically even higher. In many of these, English is not only a subject on the school curriculum but a medium of education as well (but see Bentley 2015, and K. Kersten and Rohde 2015, both this volume, for developments in this direction in the Expanding Circle). Where English is needed for study purposes in primary or secondary education, as in Kenya or Zambia, very high stakes will be attached. Using the terms coined by Cummins (1991), the ability to make use of the language on the level of Cognitive Academic Language Proficiency (CALP) as well as for Basic Interpersonal Communicative Skills (BICS) is crucial in these contexts for access to the school curriculum itself. On the other hand, in a country such as Japan, where English has no major role in government or in society at large, the stakes as perceived by parents and administrators may indeed be high but failure to learn English well at an early age need not place a totally impassable barrier in the way of future educational or other opportunities. As Rogers (1982) suggested, in a deliberately provocative article, English in many contexts might more rationally and cost-effectively be started or re-tried at a later stage in life when the specific need arose. What stands in the way of this being seriously considered in many contexts, as Rogers claims, are a number of widely accepted beliefs, some concerning the optimum age for language learning, others connected with views of educational opportunities and social justice.

Who benefits from an early start?

As mentioned above, the arguments given for the teaching of English to young children in school often focus on national needs and the enhancement of individual opportunities. However, a fundamental question that must be asked is how evenly spread facilities for successful language learning are in a given society. This comes within the larger question of how evenly spread access to good, or indeed any, education may be in the same society. The urban–rural divide within a country concerning quality of English language education is often mentioned by British Council survey respondents and is often also cited as a reflection of the same divide concerning all educational subjects. This example is from Yemen:

> Some of the English teachers in primary schools are graduates from teachers' institutes who completed a 2-year course in English. In the rural areas there are some teachers who have just completed their secondary schools and worse is that some teach English just because they know some English. This happens because some of the schools in these rural areas can't get qualified teachers. (Yemen)

Another divide is in those countries in which access to secondary schooling is not provided for all, which means that many children leave school after their primary education. One simplistic social justification for an early start in English in those societies is that starting early is the only way to ensure that everyone has at least some chance of contact with English. An exacting critic might, however, ask how much value there is in a little English learned young by a child who later faces the overriding disadvantage of being excluded from the full panoply of what education in his or her country has to offer. We might question whether even developing a substantial grasp of English would be sufficient to change the fortunes of the less privileged in the absence of other enabling conditions and relevant opportunities. The role of assessment in English as either a neutral or a filtering device concerning access to secondary education in some contexts is also relevant. In a few of the contexts surveyed, results in English were taken into consideration in the decision whether to allow a child to attend secondary school or not.

The disconnects in the optimum age for language-learning arguments

Singleton (1989), Enever and Moon (2009), Johnstone (2009) and Murphy (2014), among others, have provided insightful analyses of why making simplistic connections between age and success in language learning is misguided. As has often been pointed out, evidence in support of an early start at school has frequently been taken from children's success with language learning undertaken in very different circumstances: the language acquisition paths of children in bilingual families, children in immersion conditions or of children settling into a new country, for example. In addition, many commentators such as Rixon (1992) have, from the early stages of the present trend, questioned the uncritical application of 'the Younger the Better' slogan to the hurly-burly and different variables that school instructional conditions present.

However, even now, the same understandings do not yet seem to have reached the public arena in all places. Given the many attempts to refine the debate about potential linguistic gains, the *uncritical* use of 'the Younger the Better' mantra by politicians and administrators anxious to get on board with an easy argument for an electorate-pleasing initiative should have been discredited by now. The more tenable arguments about the general educational, affective and cognitive benefits that can be associated with early language learning tend not to be in the forefront of much public debate.

Learning to meet the needs of ever-younger learners

Whatever the educational and psycholinguistic arguments may be, young learners are getting ever younger. One of the most striking findings of the recent British Council survey was a trend for starting to teach children English at ever younger ages, even when this put increased pressure on educational resources. In response to a question on recent policy changes regarding the teaching of English in primary schools, many local experts (twenty out of sixty-four) signalled that the starting age for English within the primary-school system had been lowered in the past few years (Rixon 2013: 9). In just under half of the contexts, year one of schooling was the official or target starting stage for English (Rixon 2013: 15). More striking still was the frequency with which a start with very young learners (VYLs) at pre-primary level was mentioned as a recent change or future plan (Rixon 2013: 9) (see Mourão 2015a, this volume). In countries where pre-primary education was not offered by the state, there seemed to be interest in private nurseries and kindergartens offering English. However, the reports in the survey were often accompanied by comments from respondents that suggested that the quality of provision at pre-primary level, both state and private, was not always high.

Optimizing the situations we have

As Enever puts it in her summary of her contribution to the EYL Debate (English for young learners) at the 2014 Harrogate IATEFL conference: '... we have now reached a point where primary ELT is sufficiently embedded in the national curriculum documents of so many countries that, realistically "the deed is done" – an early start is here to stay' (Copland and Enever 2015: 75). In line with Enever's view, it could be that it is time for commentators to focus not so much on whether lowering the age for starting English is a well-founded project but on making the most of the situations and of the opportunities offered. What follows, therefore, is a series of reflections on how we can optimize what we have.

Optimizing English learning over the primary and secondary levels: Transition effects

Another aspect of 'the Younger the Better' position involves considering the total quantity of exposure to a language over a whole school career that an earlier start may provide. In other words, if learners learn a language at primary and secondary school instead of only at secondary school, there are bound to be better outcomes at the end of secondary school. Evidence on this stance is mixed (see, e.g., Johnstone 2009), but the majority of research suggests that this is not an unproblematic conclusion to draw.

One reason for this, long understood since the report on early French learning in England and Wales of Burstall, Jamieson, Cohen and Hargreaves (1974), but little acted upon, is the tendency for there to be a disconnect between what happens regarding language learning at primary-school level and the content and methods used at secondary school. See Hunt, Barnes, Powell and Martin (2008) and Bolster, Balandier-Brown and Rea-Dickins (2004) for accounts of the lack of change in this situation within the UK with respect to the teaching of Modern Foreign Languages. It was decided in the British Council survey to spotlight this issue and seek for detailed information about how transition was addressed in other countries nearly forty years after Burstall et al. highlighted the problem. Table 2.1, adapted from that in Rixon (2013: 39), shows the answers given. The first six questions concerned practical measures that might be adopted to improve transition while the last addressed the commonly found practice of starting again from zero in the new level of schooling. In some contexts, such as Sweden, care seemed to be applied to ensure a good transition experience, with teachers from both levels of schooling consulting and assessment results being shared. In some cases (e.g. Armenia, Denmark, Egypt, Israel, Italy, Jordan, Montenegro, Pakistan, Russia, Zambia, Zimbabwe) it was claimed that publishers regularly ensure that their course materials for the first year of secondary school contain a brief revision of what was supposed to have been learned at primary school, before new ground with the language is broken. A very interesting strategy in Norway (not part of the survey) concerns

Table 2.1 Responses from worldwide contexts concerning how transition is handled between primary-school English language learning and that at the next stage of schooling.

	Always	Often	Quite often	Sometimes	Rarely	Never	I don't know/ no info
Teachers from the two levels of schooling meet to discuss the transition	2	1	2	8	14	24	13
Children are given special 'bridging' courses to help them make the transition	0	2	1	2	10	36	13
Teachers in the new school are well informed about the type of work that has been done at primary/elementary school	10	6	7	7	14	10	10
Publishers make sure that their course materials for the next level of school contain revision material that covers what children should have learned at primary/elementary school	5	9	5	8	11	9	17
Information on children's levels from externally provided formal testing at the end of primary school is passed to the new school	7	0	3	4	8	25	17
Information on children's levels from school-based assessment is passed to the new school	14	4	3	4	5	21	13
When children start their new school they are treated as absolute beginners in English	4	8	5	10	2	13	16

the timing of the examination used to evaluate the success of primary English learning. This is placed early in the first year of secondary school and thus attracts the attention of both sets of teachers.

These findings suggest that, in spite of what we have long known about the importance of continuity and coherence in transition, in many countries there are still steps to be taken so that achievement in English in the primary school is built upon rather than ignored (see Becker 2015 on assessment culture and transition, this volume). It is not heartening that in some contexts in which *pre*-primary English was an innovation, similar problems of transition between pre-primary and primary English learning were commented upon by respondents.

Realistic returns on number of hours spent

Another aspect of the quantity of learning time concerns the actual hours dedicated to English within the school year. It seems from the British Council survey that at primary-school level, in many contexts, high ambitions rest upon extremely modest amounts of planned exposure to the language. In about 16 per cent of contexts, totals of only thirty to fifty hours per year were given as the target amount, and in a further 28 per cent, fifty to eighty hours was claimed as the range. About 30 per cent of reports gave targets of over 100 hours of English per year for some or all grades in primary school (Rixon 2013: 29–30).

In terms of total hours of English provided over an entire primary-school career, there are difficulties in comparing like with like since the number of years of primary schooling differs from place to place. In most cases, compulsory primary-school attendance starts at the age of five or six. In many cases children leave primary school for the next level of schooling at the age of eleven or twelve, but there are educational systems, particularly in Northern and Eastern Europe, where primary schooling continues until the age of thirteen or fourteen. There are also differences in the school grade at which English starts. Some illustrative examples may be useful, however.

Cameroon, an Outer Circle country, has English as both a school subject and, in Anglophone schools, the medium of primary-school education. In Francophone schools it is a school subject only, with French the medium of education. The figures given for hours of English were very high in both cases. Over the six years of primary education, Anglophone schools had an official target of 1,404 hours and Francophone schools of 972. These were the highest overall figures for hours of learning English found in this survey.

In those Expanding Circle countries with a five- or six-year period spent at primary school, between 400 and 500 hours seemed a common range. In China, for example, the figure given was 432 hours and for Italy it was 468 hours.

As mentioned above, in some educational systems, primary schooling lasts longer. Croatia, in common with many other Eastern European education systems, has eight grades at elementary school with a transition to the next level of school at the age of about fourteen. The total figure given of 367 officially required hours overall for Croatia thus averages out at lower than fifty hours per year. This is interesting in that Croatia has a high reputation for the achievement in English of its primary-school children. Given that the literature also points to the child-friendly and interactive methods that have been employed for a great number of years in that context (Stokic and Mihaljevic Djigunovic 2000, Vilke 1993), this might support the view that, in young-learner teaching, the number of hours well spent is the key rather than the total number of hours in absolute. This theme will be continued in the section on optimizing teaching approaches.

Public and private sector issues

A concern in many contexts is the dynamic that exists between provision of English in state primary schools and private sector provision, in private mainstream schools or private language institutes. This may result in some children having increased quantity of learning time and in some cases (though not all) enhanced quality of learning.

In the very few contexts surveyed in which English had not yet been established as part of the state primary-school curriculum, access to the subject was available to children attending either private mainstream schools or private language institutes. These comments from the British Council survey concerning Colombia reflect the complex range of provisions that can be found:

In Colombia, there are several types of private primary schools [...] according to a study developed by a local university in 2006 [...] Apart from bilingual schools there are other types of private schools that are affordable to parents with average incomes, and that teach less than five hours of English per week.

There are differences between private and state sectors: Parents who pay a private school are commonly more concerned about supporting their children's English Learning, and if they make an effort, they can pay for extra support. Parents of children attending state schools have more economical constraints and are less worried about English learning. (Colombia)

Most contexts seem to support a vigorous sector of private language institutes. It was in only a very few contexts that attendance at private language institutes by primary-school-aged children was reported as low or non-existent. There seems to be a split here between countries in which financial constraints may put private lessons out of the reach of many families (e.g. Azerbaijan,

India, Zambia) and affluent countries (e.g. Denmark, Finland, Sweden) with good-quality school English learning and other facilitating circumstances such as access to non-dubbed English media. This comment from Sweden is very unusual: 'There is no market for private language institutions....'

In most of the other contexts surveyed varying numbers of children studying English at school also attended private lessons in language institutes. Respondents from just over 20 per cent of contexts claimed attendance at such institutes by more than 40 per cent of children. In contexts in which parental or societal confidence in state school provision for English is low, a vigorous private sector seems ready to play its part. For example, the following comment came from Greece, where it was reported that more than 60 per cent of primary-school-aged children attended private language institutes: 'English is considered to be an unimportant subject at school as it is seriously offered at private language institutions.'

The disparities between families who can afford to send their children to private language institutes for extra English and those who cannot were highlighted by some respondents to the survey as creating problems. In some cases these problems were seen in mainly pedagogic terms, with children within the same state-school class having very different levels of English as a result of some taking private lessons and some not. However, in a few other cases deeper issues of social equity were highlighted. We know from the literature, for example Lee (2009: 98), that the government of South Korea has taken action a number of times to try to equalize the chances of all children to have access to the 'extra' English that more prosperous parents could afford to pay for. However, this level of concern for equity was not found in many contexts.

Finding the optimum teachers for primary-school English learners

At the heart of most successful learning in a school situation are teachers professionally trained and experienced to provide, at a minimum, appropriate input, structured learning opportunities and feedback that supports learning. Different contexts may interpret the components of this minimum provision differently or may require more than the minimum, but it seems a reasonable core set of expectations. This is where, historically, many of the more hastily introduced young-learner programmes have fallen short. Rixon (2000) reported a number of years ago on a previous survey which revealed that in many places there were either not enough teachers or not enough teachers with the background and training that were judged in each context to be appropriate. The same situation seemed to obtain in 2011 according to the British Council survey. Only 17 per cent of contexts reported having no teacher-supply problems. In 36 per cent of contexts respondents chose an answer suggesting that teacher supply was patchy: 'There are sufficient English teachers in some parts of the country but not in others' and a further 28 per cent chose 'There are problems with supply of English teachers in all areas of my country'.

The type of teacher expected to be appropriate for young learners of English varies across different contexts. Interestingly, the category of teacher often cited in the literature as possibly the most suitable for the role, that is a generalist class teacher or home-room teacher, who is also equipped to teach English, was mentioned only twenty-five times (39 per cent) and in only six contexts was the generalist class teacher the *only* type of teacher officially approved. In many contexts, some sort of specialist English teacher, moving from class to class or even from school to school, was expected to fill the role.

In most contexts, there was a variety of acceptable qualifications. The seven possibilities below were listed as alternatives in the questionnaire:

1. a native or other very competent speaker of English with no formal teaching qualifications

2. a primary-school teacher who has followed a specialist pre-service training course in teaching primary-school English at college or university

3. a qualified generalist primary teacher who has passed a special local test or examination of proficiency in English

4. a qualified secondary school teacher of English who is willing to work in primary schools

5. a university graduate in English language and/or literature who did not take courses in education or methodology while at university

6. an already qualified generalist primary teacher who has successfully completed a special in-service training course of preparation to teach English to primary-school children

7. a qualified generalist primary teacher who has passed an international test or examination of proficiency in English.

Three places, Palestine, Portugal and Russia, gave all seven options as acceptable and nearly 50 per cent of contexts accepted three or more. However, a rider to the responses about officially accepted qualifications was frequently found in the open comments section. It seems that in many countries where there are teacher-supply problems (and these often occur each time there is a reduction of the age at which English is taught) the 'official' standards may become elastic and individuals who do not strictly fit the criteria are accepted as teachers of English. This situation was noted a number of years previously by Rixon (2000), and it seems that there has been little change since then.

Optimizing teaching approaches

In the many countries where little contact with English outside school is readily available, it is the teacher who is the major source and catalyst for children's development in English. Norms of teacher behaviour in class will vary from teaching culture to teaching culture (see Alexander 2000 for international comparisons) but a crux comes when culturally expected and sanctioned classroom behaviour differs strongly from the best that research can suggest about effective language teaching. For example, it is widely agreed that interaction in and use of the language, rather than mere exposure, are what is required for optimum take-up and development. This appears to be a psycholinguistic fact rather than a matter of cultural choice. As Halliwell (1992: 8) put it, 'without talking they cannot become good at talking' and 'the only way to learn to *use* it *is* to use it' (emphasis in the original). Meeting learners' needs in this way may require major accommodations on the part of some teachers, especially if they have never taught a language before. Firstly, some may need to change the classroom approaches that they have previously used for other subjects to one that favours language uptake. This may require a considerable shift, since in many areas of the world, classroom discourse patterns that involve teacher–pupil or pupil–pupil interaction are not familiar or favoured. Secondly, to be able to achieve this optimal interactive approach, teachers' subject knowledge and skills in English need to be more than basic. They need a confident and fluent command of English if interaction and linguistic accommodation to the learners are to be feasible in class. If learners are in the care of teachers who are able to provide such optimal approaches, they may be able to make the most of their capacities as young learners even with relatively little exposure to the language in school. On the contrary, if their teachers are not convinced about or capable of providing optimal conditions for language learning, the mere fact that the learners are young will not be enough for language-learning success.

Early English learning as an enrichment of the curriculum

Many commentators (e.g. Pinter 2006, Bland 2010) have supported the introduction of English for reasons beyond the instrumental, as an enrichment of the curriculum and as leading to an opening out of cultural, imaginative and cognitive horizons along with language development. There are numerous examples of approaches to EYL that can clearly be seen as at least making language learning meaningful and, when used best, putting it at the service of widening horizons and adding to the quality of children's engagement with learning. These approaches reach beyond being effective methods to teach languages into providing worthwhile experiences in themselves. There is not space to discuss them at length here, but other chapters in this volume discuss some well-known examples. CLIL or Content and Language Integrated Language Learning (Coyle, Hood and Marsh 2010) commands a strong following in some parts of the world (see Bentley 2015, this volume). Literature-based approaches such as those promoted by Bland (2013) are also clear examples as are the uses of storytelling and drama and song-based experiences. It is notable that in Cyprus, after dedicated induction and training of teaching personnel, picturebook use has become a backbone of the new English language-learning curriculum (see also Mourão 2015b, this volume).

However, the prominence of approaches such as these in the literature, and their undoubted success in a number of contexts, may not reflect the degree to which they are actually present in the wider world or the everyday classroom. Difficulties with resources, teacher preparation and language levels may lie behind this, or there may simply be different priorities and interests in different parts of the world. The survey presently under discussion did not look closely at classroom practices, but the survey by Garton, Copland and Burns (2011: 12) gives us a detailed and balanced picture of the most prevalent classroom practices in primary-school English language teaching worldwide. The 'top 5' classroom practices based on responses to their questionnaire may repay reflection:

1. repeating after the teacher
2. listening to tape recorder/CD
3. pupils reading aloud
4. playing games
5. songs.

The role, quality and availability of published teaching materials

In a field where considerable numbers of newly appointed or created teachers enter the young-learner classroom each time a lowering of the start age is put in place, it is prudent to make sure that at least some of the teaching materials available have been designed to support and guide teachers through

Table 2.2 Official position regarding course materials in state primary schools.

	Number of responses
Teachers may use any published materials (local or international) if they are within the school budget	13
Teachers make their own materials in addition to any published materials that they use	14
There is no school budget for books or other materials – teachers must make their own	1
Teachers may only use material that has received official approval and appears on a list of permitted works	16
There is only one approved set of course materials and this is written and published specially for schools in this country or region	14
There is only one approved set of course materials but this was not written and published specially for schools in this country or region	3
Other/no information	5

an appropriate repertoire of activities to promote language learning besides providing an appropriate syllabus and sequencing of language items. A wide range of sources for class materials was found among the sixty-four contexts, as shown in Table 2.2. Some respondents chose more than one answer.

A particular issue with materials in published book form, and books are still the norm, is that they tend to favour 'words on the page'. Teachers (especially if they have previously taught older learners) may assume that words on the page (e.g. in dialogues or vocabulary labels) are facilitators of early language learning, whereas for many beginning young learners, especially those whose mother tongue uses a different script or even a different writing system, the written or printed words in English are a challenge in themselves. Cameron (2003: 108) sees the view of early reading and writing as a prop to other learning, as one of the key problems in the practice of EYL:

[. . .] it takes time for reading and writing to reach a level at which they can support foreign language learning. Before that point is reached, there is what we might call a 'literacy skills lag', in which the written form of English creates such high cognitive and motor skills demands for pupils that the oral component of a task may have to be backgrounded to cope with the written demands. [. . .] Careful analysis of activities by teachers is necessary to ensure that language learning opportunities are not overwhelmed by literacy demands.

If Cameron's view is correct it is of concern that the survey by Garton, Copland and Burns (2011) suggests that decoding words on the page in order to read aloud is a crucial skill for many young learners for them *simply to participate* in lessons. In relation to a question on the most favoured modes of operating in class, an activity called 'children reading out loud' had a more than 70 per cent combined response rate for being used either 'every lesson' or 'often' and, as we have seen, came third in the 'Top 5' classroom practices. Rixon (2012: 79) concurs with Cameron that this hidden dependence on the written word in primary English teaching seems very widespread even when the declared and official priorities are the development of listening and speaking.

Clarity in setting goals and levels

The need for greater clarity about priorities and goals, such as is discussed immediately above, is an area which, judging by the findings of the British Council survey, is being seriously addressed in more and more contexts. A considerable quantity of information on goal setting and assessment was volunteered in the survey as a response to a question about recent policy changes. There were reports from eleven out of the sixty-four contexts that there had been changes within the last decade involving setting target levels for English.

Although some countries, particularly Outer Circle countries, assessed the English of children at the end of primary schooling using their own examination or assessment instruments and setting their own standards, the Common European Framework of Reference for Languages (CEFR) was a particularly widely used instrument, mentioned in connection both with goal setting and with assessment. It was cited by respondents from twenty-one countries (33 per cent), not all of them in Europe itself, as providing a way of expressing the level of English required at the end of primary schooling. On the other hand, it should be noted that an equal number of countries still had no stated level for children to reach by the end of primary school. Table 2.3, adapted from a table in Rixon (2013), sets out the overall picture.

Standards setting as a step on the way to clarity of goals for primary English is potentially highly beneficial. However, it is important to look beneath the surface at a number of problematic issues. Firstly, assessment

Table 2.3 Required levels of English by the end of primary schooling.

	Number of responses	Percentage (rounded)
I have no information on this topic/other	9	14%
There is no stated level for children to reach by the end of primary school	21	33%
The required level is A1	8	13%
The required level is A2	12	19%
The required level is B1	1	2%
The required level is B2	0	0%
There is a locally set examination or test with its own standards that cannot be referred to the Common European Framework	13	20%
Total	64	

seems to be seen predominantly in terms of assessment of linguistic attainment. It is acknowledged that it is very difficult to assess affective areas such as motivation for language learning, attitudes to English and degree of intercultural understanding, which are often to be found among the stated educational goals of teaching English to young children. Indeed, trying to assess them may involve ethical issues of what types of responses by pupils may be most favoured. Might low motivation or a neutral attitude to English, for example, be penalized in a less-than-enlightened assessment regime? However, educational goals may easily be ignored or bypassed in actual classroom practice if there is no officially required verification that they are being attained.

An additional issue is that standards setting and related assessment, seen as aspects of accountability, have become implicated with much of the managerialism and attempts at top-down control that is spreading through modern-day education (McKay 2005). In one or two contexts (Russia, Bahrein) new end of primary-school exam systems which included English were reported, with one, at least, of the purposes being to evaluate and compare schools' performances. On the other hand, many of the contexts in which the required level (often a CEFR level) was cited for the end of primary school did not yet appear to have formal or informal instruments in place to ascertain whether or not it was reached. The CEFR seems in many cases to have provided no more than a convenient label to indicate the language levels aimed at.

A key issue where there is scope for considerable work for the future is the fact that currently the CEFR is not an ideal framework for EYL purposes, particularly in terms of its content and topic areas (Hasselgren 2005; Bland 2013: 6–7). In addition, given that the majority of goals for the end of primary-school English were expressed as one or other of the A bands in the CEFR, which represent very modest attainments, we are left with the problem of how to break the levels down into sub-levels to cater for assessment during the several years of English learning that normally precede the end of primary school.

Conclusion

The British Council survey has served to highlight and illustrate a number of critical issues in present-day EYL, although, of course, it is not equipped to offer solutions. A survey such as this can, however, start to reveal the diversity of conditions across contexts as well as those factors that are more widely shared across the world. There is a growing tendency to focus on local conditions and situations in EYL research, which is good news. As an example of extended research covering the views of different stakeholders in a particular context, Kuchah (2013) has looked in depth at what it means to be considered as a good and effective primary-school teacher of English in the often-challenging circumstances of Cameroon. See also Rich (2014) for a volume in which EYL teaching in a range of different countries is discussed in detail. It is heartening that there is a growing mass of specific research into EYL in particular contexts that takes account of all the factors that make it as it is in any given place.

References

Alexander, Robin (2000), *Culture and Pedagogy: International Comparisons in Primary Education*, Oxford: Blackwell Publishers Inc.

Becker, Carmen (2015), 'Assessment and portfolios', in Janice Bland (ed.), *Teaching English to Young Learners. Critical Issues in Language Teaching with 3–12 Year Olds*, London: Bloomsbury Academic, pp. 262–278.

Bentley, Kay (2015), 'CLIL scenarios with young learners', in Janice Bland (ed.), *Teaching English to Young Learners. Critical Issues in Language Teaching with 3–12 Year Olds*, London: Bloomsbury Academic, pp. 91–111.

Bland, Janice (2010), 'Using pictures and picture books to create readers and thoughtful readings', in Hania Kryszewska (ed.), *Humanising Language Learning*, 12/6. <http://www.hltmag.co.uk/dec10/sart12.htm> [accessed 14 September 2014].

Bland, Janice (2013), *Children's Literature and Learner Empowerment. Children and Teenagers in English Language Education*, London: Bloomsbury.

Bolster, Allison; Balandier-Brown, Christine and Rea-Dickins, Pauline (2004), 'Young learners of foreign languages and their transition to the secondary phase; a lost opportunity?' *Language Learning Journal*, 30: 35–41.

Burstall, Clare; Jamieson, Monika; Cohen, Susan and Hargreaves, Margaret (1974), *Primary French in the Balance*, Slough: NFER.

Cameron, Lynne (2003), 'Challenges for ELT from the expansion in teaching children', *ELT Journal*, 57/2: 105–112.

Copland, Fiona and Enever Janet (2015), 'ELT Journal/IATEFL debate: Primary ELT does more harm than good', in Tania Pattison (ed.), *IATEFL 2014 Harrogate Conference Selections*, Faversham: IATEFL, pp. 73–76.

Coyle, Do; Hood, Philip and Marsh, David (2010), *CLIL: Content and Language Integrated Learning*, Cambridge: Cambridge University Press.

Cummins, James (1991),'Language development and academic learning', in Lilliam Malave, and Duquette, Georges (eds) *Language, Culture and Cognition*, Clevedon: Multilingual Matters, pp. 161–176.

Enever, Janet and Moon, Jayne (2009), 'New global contexts for teaching primary ELT: Change and challenge', in Janet Enever, Jayne Moon, and Uma Raman (eds), Young *Learner English Language Policy and Implementation: International Perspectives*, Reading: Garnet, pp. 5–20.

Garton, Susan; Copland, Fiona and Burns, Anne (2011), *Investigating Global Practices in Teaching English to Young Learners*. <http://iatefl.britishcouncil.org/2012/sites/iatefl/files/session/documents/eltrp_report_-_garton.pdf> [accessed 1 August 2014].

Graddol, David (2006), *English Next*. UK: British Council.

Halliwell, Susan (1992), *Teaching English in the Primary Classroom*, Harlow: Longman.

Hasselgren, Angela (2005), 'Assessing the language of young learners', *Language Testing*, 22: 337–354.

Hudelson, Sarah (1994), 'Literacy development of second language children', in Fred Genesee (ed.) *Educating Second Language children: The Whole Child, the Whole Curriculum, the Whole Community*, New York: Cambridge University Press, pp. 129–158.

Hunt, Marilyn; Barnes, Ann; Powell, Robert and Martin, Cynthia (2008), 'Moving on: The challenges for foreign language learning on transition from primary to secondary school'. *Teaching and Teacher Education*, 24/4: 915–926.

Johnstone, Richard (2009), 'An early start: What are the key conditions for generalized success?' in Janet Enever; Jayne Moon and Uma Raman (eds), *Young Learner English Language Policy and Implementation: International Perspectives*, Reading: Garnet Education, pp. 31–41.

Kachru, Braj (1985), 'Standards, codification and sociolinguistic realism: The English language in the Outer Circle' in Randolf Quirk and Henry Widdowson (eds), *English in the World: Teaching and Learning the Language and literatures*, Cambridge: Cambridge University Press, pp. 11–36.

Kersten, Kristin and Rohde, Andreas (2015), 'Immersion teaching in English with young learners', in Janice Bland (ed.), *Teaching English to Young Learners. Critical Issues in Language Teaching with 3–12 Year Olds*, London: Bloomsbury Academic, pp. 71–89.

Kubanek-German, Angelika (1998), 'Survey article: Primary foreign language teaching in Europe - trends and issues', *Language Teaching*, 31: 193–205.

Kuchah, Harry (2013), *Context-Appropriate ELT Pedagogy: An Investigation in Cameroonian Primary Schools*. Unpublished PhD thesis, University of Warwick.

Kuppens, Ari (2010), 'Incidental foreign language acquisition from media exposure', *Learning, Media and Technology*, 35/1: 65–85.

Landry, Rodrigue and Bourhis, Richard (1997), 'Linguistic landscape and ethnolinguistic vitality: An empirical study', *Journal of Language and Social Psychology*, 16/1: 23–49.

Lee, Wong Key (2009), 'Primary English language teaching in (ELT) in Korea: Bold risks on the National Foundation', in Janet Enever, Jayne Moon and Uma Raman (eds), *Young Learner English Language Policy and Implementation: International Perspectives*, Reading: Garnet, pp. 95–102.

Lefever, Samuel (2009) '"When I wanna be cool ..." English for Young Learners in Iceland', in Janet Enever, Jayne Moon and Uma Raman (eds), *Young Learner English Language Policy and Implementation: International Perspectives*, Reading: Garnet, pp. 103–112.

McKay, Penelope (2005), 'Research into the assessment of school-age language learners', *Annual Review of Applied Linguistics*, 25: 243–263.

Mourão, Sandie (2015a), 'English in pre-primary: The challenges of getting it right', in Janice Bland (ed.), *Teaching English to Young Learners. Critical Issues in Language Teaching with 3–12 Year Olds*, London: Bloomsbury Academic, pp. 51–69.

Mourão, Sandie (2015b), 'The potential of picturebooks with young learners', in Janice Bland (ed.), *Teaching English to Young Learners. Critical Issues in Language Teaching with 3–12 Year Olds*, London: Bloomsbury Academic, pp. 199–217.

Murphy, Victoria (2014), *Second Language Learning in the Early School Years: Trends and Contexts*. Cambridge Cambridge University Press.

Pinter, Annamaria (2006), *Teaching Young Language Learners*. Oxford: Oxford University Press.

Rich, Sarah (2014), *International Perspectives on Teaching English to Young Learners*, Basingstoke: Palgrave Macmillan.

Rixon, Shelagh (1992), 'State of the art article: English and other languages for younger children: Practice and theory in a rapidly changing world', *Language Teaching*, 25/2: 73–93.

Rixon, Shelagh (2000), 'Collecting eagle's eye data on the teaching of English to young learners: The British Council overview', in Jayne Moon and Marianne Nikolov (eds), *Research into Teaching English to Young Learners*, Pecs: University of Pecs Press, pp. 153–167.

Rixon, Shelagh (2012), *Beyond ABC: Investigating Current Rationales and Systems for the Teaching of Early Reading to Young Learners of English*. Unpublished PhD thesis, University of Warwick, 2012.

Rixon, Shelagh (2013), *British Council Survey of Policy and Practice in Primary English Language Teaching Worldwide*. <http://www.teachingenglish.org.uk/

article/british-council-survey-policy-practice-primary-english-language-teaching-worldwide> [accessed 1 August 2014].

Rogers, John (1982), 'The world for sick proper', *ELT Journal*, 36/3: 44–151

Sayer, Peter and Ban, Ruth (2014), 'Young EFL students' engagements with English outside the classroom', *ELT Journal*, 68/3: 321–329.

Singleton, David (1989), *Language Acquisition: The Age Factor*, Clevedon: Multilingual Matters.

Stokic, Lidvina and Mihaljevic Djigunovic, Jelena (2000), 'Early foreign language education in Croatia', in Marianne Nikolov and Helena Curtain (eds), *An Early Start: Young Learners and Modern Languages in Europe and Beyond*, Strasbourg: Council of Europe, pp. 41–50.

Vilke, Mirjana (1993), 'Early foreign language teaching in Croatian primary schools', in Mirjana Vilke and Yvonne Vrhovac (eds), *Children and Foreign Languages*, Zagreb: University of Zagreb, pp. 10–27.

3

English in Pre-primary: The Challenges of Getting It Right

Sandie Mourão

Introduction

The education of children from birth to the start of formal education is referred to as 'early childhood education' (UNESCO UIS 2012: 26) and educational programmes intended for children from age three to the start of primary education are more specifically referred to as 'pre-primary education'. The title of this chapter makes reference to this term (see also Ellis 2014) and discusses the second language education of children from three till around six years, depending on the age of entry into primary education.

A brief description of pre-primary education

Early childhood education varies across countries around the world regarding provision and accessibility mainly due to the absence of 'early childhood development policies, strategic plans and laws' (The Consultative Group 2013: 1). Its expansion since the 1970s runs parallel with the evolution of a female workforce (OECD 2014: 319), and though pre-primary education is the initial stage of 'organised instruction [and is] designed primarily to introduce children to a school-like environment' (OECD 2014: 324), in some cases it might include not only a focus on education during short periods of the day but also an element of care, extending provision to support parents' working hours.

According to World Bank data (2014), just over two-thirds of the world's countries stipulate that compulsory primary education begins at age six years,

20 per cent at seven years and the remaining at five years. Nevertheless, in most OECD countries children actually begin their education before they are five years old – 84 per cent of four-year-olds are enrolled in early childhood education, or in some cases, primary education programmes, rising to 89 per cent in European Union OECD countries (OECD 2014: 318). Compulsory pre-primary education exists from age three in Mexico and Israel; from age four in Luxembourg; from age five in Austria, Greece, Hungary, the Netherlands and Switzerland and from age six in Poland (OECD 2014: 328). In most countries provision is covered by both public and private services.

According to de Botton (2010: 7), early childhood education sits within two philosophical traditions based on 'two approaches' at different ends of a continuum: a teacher-led, education-focused approach related to school-readiness skills such as numeracy and literacy; and a child-directed, social, pedagogic approach, where attention is given to educational goals, play and interactivity with both pre-primary teachers and peers. This latter approach follows sociocultural theory, which includes the view of a child's development as a collective responsibility occurring in both formal and informal contexts. This results in an approach to learning where relationships between adults and children are fostered and encouraged, in order to develop a child's social and cognitive well-being. In practice most pre-primary programmes fall somewhere between the two extremes, though Nordic countries are well known for their child-directed, social pedagogic approach and the US for its education-focused approach (Miller and Almon 2009).

Languages at ever-earlier ages

It is well known that English is being introduced at ever-earlier ages and this 'enthusiasm for English learning is frequently cascading into Early Years teaching' (Rixon 2013: 13). On a European level, the most recent Eurydice report (2012) shows that by September 2015, just over a third of the European community will officially implement second or foreign-language teaching to children of six years and under. In the main, the chosen language is English. More precise figures for the rest of the world are a little more difficult to access. In Mexico, English has been mandatory in the final year of compulsory pre-primary education since 2010 (García and García 2011). However, even if teaching a second language (L2) is not mandatory, it is a frequent occurrence in pre-primary institutions and even a recommendation. Ellis (2015: forthcoming) affirms that, despite a non-existent national language policy, the French Ministry of Education encourages the teaching of a foreign language in preparation for more structured language learning at primary school. Research by Emery (2012), which involved nearly 2,500 teachers in forty-nine countries, revealed that 54 per cent of respondents stated children began English at six years or younger in their school. Yu and Ruan (2012) describe an 'English fever' hitting early childhood education in China, which is a direct response to 'the demand for a better educational experience for young children' (2012: 54) despite national policy initiating English in mid-primary. Similar information has been given in relation to South Korea, where a growing number of children are enrolled in fee-paying pre-primary establishments, some of which claim to be 'English kindergartens' (Song 2012: 40). In Lebanon English is the first foreign language taught from the age of four years old in 40 per cent of the pre-primary institutions where French was traditionally the option (Ghosn 2013: xxv). Research by Rokita-Jaśkow (2013) in Poland also confirms that L2 education is widespread in both state and private pre-primary establishments mainly due to parental pressure. Černá (2015) and Portiková (2015) report research related to the Czech Republic and Slovakia, respectively, which reflects similar indicatives. English is being taught in pre-primary institutions, often as a result of the influence parents wield upon decision makers both in relation to the provision of an L2 and regarding the choice of language. Edelenbos, Johnstone and Kubanek (2006) noted this had begun in the 1990s, a kind of 'parentocracy' (Enever 2007: 215).

Qualifications and competences for pre-primary English teachers

Implications of lowering the age with regard to English teacher qualifications and competences have been discussed in the context of primary language education (see Edelenbos, Johnstone and Kubanek 2006, Emery 2012, Enever 2011, Rixon 2015: 40–42), but as yet, very little has been written on this topic in relation to pre-primary education. Greater interest in early language learning at pre-primary level has naturally created a new demand for qualified English teachers but the recommended qualifications and competences are difficult to ascertain. European Commission guidelines (2011b: 17) highlight the fact that 'the qualification profile of staff working with young children in pre-primary settings has long been recognized as a critical factor for the quality of [these] settings and the children's experiences. This also holds true for those staff [...] who are supporting early language learning activities'. Naturally, it is noted that both pedagogical and language skills are essential. Teachers working with such young children require an understanding of the principles of pedagogy and child development as well as being sufficiently confident to speak fluently and spontaneously to children in the L2 using language considered suitable for this age group. Indeed, Hanušová and Najvar (in Černá 2015: 173) go so far as to state that contrary to general assumptions, 'the younger the child starting to learn an L2, the higher the importance of teacher qualifications'.

Together with qualifications in language and teaching, certain competences have been highlighted as important in English teachers of this age group. Pinthon (1979: 74) declares, 'a good teacher loves young children, is able to relate well to them, [and] knows how to create a relaxed atmosphere while motivating the children to learn.' Sofronieva (2015: 201) concludes that successful pre-primary language teacher skills involve 'being good communicators, respecting interpersonal distance, use of gaze, clear locution and combined verbal and gestural messages' and, finally, Fröhlich-Ward (1979: 30) describes a pre-primary language teacher as one that is 'dedicated to her [sic] job and to the children'.

Regarding pre-primary English teacher qualifications, Ioannou-Georgiou (2015) describes Cypriot pre-primary educators being given in-service training in English to become pre-primary English teachers, thus combining pedagogical and language skills. This is possible in Cyprus as a former British colony, where classroom teachers are considered fairly competent in English (Ioannou-Georgiou 2015: 98). Černá, on the other hand, reports that in the Czech Republic 'qualification requirements remain unspecified for pre-primary teachers of English' (2015: 174). Many teachers are external language tutors, meaning they are not permanent members of staff. This in itself has implications for programming and integrating language learning into a pre-primary project. Portiková (2015) describes a similar situation in Slovakia, where teachers of pre-primary English need only to have graduated from high school and possess a school-leaving examination in the target language. In her survey of school directors and language teachers in a small region of Slovakia, Portiková deplored the fact that just over a third of the seventy-three responding teachers did not even have this basic qualification (2015: 181).

Rokita-Jaśkow (2013: 235) provides quite different data that indicate over 43 per cent of the ninety teachers she surveyed in Poland had a first degree and 53 per cent had a master's degree – two-thirds had attended a course which included foreign-language methodologies for young learners and very young learners. These teachers had an average of five years teaching experience and over half were under twenty-five years of age. The profusion of young, inexperienced teachers in Rokita-Jaśkow's results supports the emerging trend in Emery's research with teachers of young learners, which indicates that 'more experienced teachers are teaching older learners [upper primary] and inexperienced teachers are teaching younger learners [pre-primary]' (Emery 2012: 12).

Practices and approaches

According to the European Commission, a review of practice undertaken by member states implementing language-learning projects shows that there is 'little evidence of agreed processes, uniformity of approach or established indicators of achievement in early language learning' (2011b: 14). Approaches are dependent upon the learning context, which will in turn affect teaching models and their learning objectives. Edelenbos, Johnstone and Kubanek (2006: 11) describe a variety of language-learning models that have also been observed in pre-primary education. These include the following:

- a language awareness model, which provides access to a number of languages and cultures in order to develop a plurilingual curriculum (see Lourenço and Andrade 2015)

- instructed foreign-language learning in a low-exposure context occurring once or twice a week (see McElwee 2015)

- an approach which brings the L2 and other learning areas together such as music (see Ioannou-Georgiou 2015)

- bilingual or partial immersion education (see K. Kersten 2015).

The European Commission highlights what they call 'proven orientations' (2011b: 8) for pedagogical processes: 'Language-learning activities should be adapted to the age of the learners and to the pre-primary context. Children should be exposed to the target language in meaningful and, if possible, authentic settings, in such a way that the language is spontaneously acquired rather than consciously learnt' (2011b: 17). A collection of 'Examples of Good Practice' (European Commission 2011a) is available to support these orientations and which are recognized, to a degree, in the few publications available that discuss this age group. Reilly and Ward (1997), Roth (1998) and Dunn (2012) advocate the inclusion of songs, rhymes, riddles and chants, craft activities, games and Total Physical Response activities, stories, project work, puppets and drama activities, all considered opportune for supporting spontaneous language acquisition and associated with early language learning.

Above all, we should be ensuring that activities take into consideration the educational attributes of pre-primary education. Despite the disparity of provision, we can assume these are shared characteristics worldwide, though interpreted by different cultural groups according to their own cultural meanings (Powell and David 2010). According to UNESCO, programmes in early childhood education are holistic in approach and support 'children's early cognitive, physical, social and emotional development' (2012: 26). The educational attributes are characterized:

by interaction with peers and educators, through which children improve their use of language and social skills, start to develop logical and reasoning skills, and talk through their thought processes. They are also introduced to alphabetical and mathematical concepts, and encouraged to explore their surrounding world and environment. Supervised gross motor activities (i.e. physical exercise through games and other activities) and play-based activities can be used as learning opportunities to promote social interactions with peers and to develop skills, autonomy and school readiness. (UNESCO-UIS 2012: 27).

The activities listed above (such as songs, games, stories and drama activities) will facilitate many of these attributes as long as there is a focus on the development of the whole child and the emulation of pre-primary practice, which remains 'qualitatively different' (European Commission 2011b: 14) to that of primary education – note the importance of 'play-based activities'. Pre-primary language learning should not 'foster languages as a specific subject but rather as a communication tool to be used in other activities' (2011b: 14). This should result in language learning becoming 'integrated into contexts in which the language is meaningful and useful, such as in everyday or playful situations' (2011b: 14). Here, we see reference to the concept of play-based activity once again, which thus far is rarely discussed in relation to pre-primary language learning (exceptions being Mourão 2014; Voise 2014; Mourão and Robinson, 2015; Robinson, Mourão and Kang 2015). I would like to continue this chapter by taking a closer look at the concept of play-based activity, its role in pre-primary language education and the challenges of taking play seriously in low-exposure language-learning contexts.

Play-based activities

Play is difficult to define: Moyles compares it to grasping bubbles 'every time there appears to be something to hold on to, its ephemeral nature disallows it being grasped' (2010: 5). We know it is a 'child's work' (Isaacs 1949: 9), but it is often contested as a serious approach to learning (E. Wood 2010). It has, however, been central in childhood education since the beginning of the twentieth century and is a 'powerful scaffold' to children's learning (Moyles 2010: 10).

Effective early years education programmes have been noted to combine the practice of adult-led and structured child-initiated activity (Kernan 2007: 12), ensuring that elements of playfulness exist in both scenarios. Child-initiated activity provides a child with 'the opportunity to explore materials and situations for oneself' (Moyles 1989: 14) and there is much evidence that through child-initiated play children become responsible for their learning; they experiment, make mistakes, exhibit choice and decide for themselves – in all they are respected as autonomous learners (Bruce 2011: 23–26).

Child-initiated and adult-led activities

A typical pre-primary room in many countries around the world, especially those that adopt a more child-directed, social, pedagogic approach to early years education, is open plan and it is divided into different *learning areas* or activity centres, providing opportunities for children to benefit from teacher-initiated group work as well as to have access to child-initiated 'potentially instructive play activities' (Siraj-Blatchford, Sylva, Muttock, Gilden and Bell 2002: 43). Learning areas furnish opportunities for structured child-initiated play and are influenced, for example, by the work of Ovide Decroly (1871–1932), who was one of the pioneers behind the idea of educational games, and Maria Montessori (1870–1952), whose approach involved creating environments specially adapted for children to develop a sense of responsibility and self-realization. Learning areas also draw on sociocultural theories where 'informal learning' (D. Wood 1988: 25) occurs as children play alone or with others and interact with the instructional materials they find there. Thus, learning is introduced, reinforced and/or extended, usually with little assistance from an adult. Effective educators create opportunities for children to learn by doing in the learning areas in the belief that, by interacting with their environment, children develop as autonomous and responsible learners.

Adult-led practices include teachers engaging with children in playful ways with the curriculum content (E. Wood 2010). This often occurs during circle time – whole-group gatherings where the children sit on the floor to listen to stories, sing songs and engage with the teacher in focused teacher-led activities that provide what Vygotsky referred to as opportunities for 'formal instruction' (D. Wood 1988: 25). Creating a balance between adult-led and child-initiated activity is a challenge felt by pre-primary educators and continues to be debated by scholars in the field (see e.g. Moyles 1989; Lindon 2001; E. Wood 2010).

Play in a low-exposure instructed foreign-language-learning context: Setting up an English learning area

As we have seen in the previous sections, in some countries English in pre-primary institutions is associated with a peripatetic teacher who visits children a couple of times a week, teaching English in short, isolated spurts of between thirty to forty-five minutes of activities. These activities are teacher-led out of necessity; they follow a well-used structure beginning with circle time and sometimes, when time allows, moving into table time. There is neither the time nor the inclination for incorporating child-initiated play. Nevertheless, it is still possible to incorporate child-initiated play into the children's daily activities if English is integrated into the children's learning context. Teacher-led activities occur during the weekly English sessions, with the addition of an English learning area (Mourão 2014), which is set up alongside the other learning areas in a typically open-plan pre-primary room.

An *English learning area* (ELA) contains resources associated with the English sessions and contributes to integrating English into the children's pre-primary day, but most importantly, an ELA ensures that children can engage in child-initiated play with and through English, if they want to. The setting up of an ELA requires collaboration between both the pre-primary educator and the English teacher. What is crucial in this approach is that both take the children's play in English seriously and work together as planners and mediators (Kernan 2007). The pre-primary educator plans and manages the ELA, either by creating a physical space in the classroom for the ELA or by ensuring the English resources are accessible to children during their pre-primary day. The educator is also responsible for planning time into the children's day for child-initiated play to occur, but as this is part of usual practice it requires little additional effort. The English teacher provides the resources for the ELA and is key as a mediator supporting children's development of the target language through teacher-led play during English sessions.

When a pre-primary educator and an English teacher collaborate, and both show an interest in the children's English-learning experience, children are highly motivated as they see that English is a valued part of their learning experience. Fröhlich-Ward (1979) describes the attitude of a pre-primary educator as affecting the success or failure of an early years language-learning project, and research into such collaborative practices has evidenced motivation in both the children and their parents (Rocha 2014; Mourão and Robinson 2015).

If the pre-primary educator is the English teacher, which may be the case in some countries, an ELA works in just the same way, with the educator becoming both mediator and planner. Additionally, if the English sessions are longer, thematic ELAs can be set up to enable children to engage in child-initiated play for a time during the English session. For example, an English picturebook area, an English flashcard game area, an English game area with board games and lotto sets and an English make-believe (role-play) area with props from favourite stories.

Circle time

Circle time, also referred to as carpet time or the morning/afternoon routine, is where whole-group activities take place. Children sit in a circle on a carpet to begin the morning, afternoon or day, or to listen to stories together. When beginning a session, circle time will include a number of routines – greetings, discovering who is at school and who is at home, asking about the weather, the days of the week, a birthday, talking about lunch time and sharing any news for the day. The pre-primary educator will incorporate songs and rhymes, tell a story and may even play a game or two as well as set up the day's activities.

Circle time forms an essential part of a pre-primary schedule as it supports the development of the whole child, for through these different activities children's personal and social skills are developed alongside other competences like maths, language and literacy, and gross and fine motor skills. For example:

- Children learn to wait their turn to speak, listen to others and sit still for a certain length of time.

- While counting how many children are missing, they are developing their notion of number and quantity and begin to understand the notion of time while talking about the days of the week.

- When saying a nursery rhyme, not only are they developing their phonological awareness, but they might also be using their hands and fingers and thus developing fine motor skills.

- While listening to and talking about a story, they are developing their listening and thinking skills as well as any number of other competences depending on the content of the story

It is for this reason that pre-primary English sessions often follow a circle time configuration. There is a focus on developing the whole child by emulating pre-primary practice; English is often a short session which also suits this configuration and contains routines and a focus on whole-group activities, all inherent to circle time.

A close look at routines and formats

Routines are extremely important for small children: the familiarity of routines enables them to feel safe and relaxed, which in turn directs and defines their behaviour. Succeeding in responding to a routine results in reduced instances when children feel out of control or at a loss, the structure behind the routines provides the boundaries children need to regulate their behaviour and a consequence is usually fewer instances of challenging behaviour for the educator. A predictable routine contributes to children becoming more responsible, independent and confident.

Language is part of the organization of routines, and their frequency and repetitive nature provide children with opportunities to predict, support their understanding as well as pick up language and build their vocabulary.

Bruner (1983: 45) describes these routine activities as an occasion for 'systematic use of language with an adult' and has called them 'closely circumscribed format(s)' (1983: 46). 'Formats' are made up of three essential components:

- a sequential structure 'and a set of realization rules' (1983: 46)

- clearly marked 'turn-taking roles' (1983: 47)

- a script-like quality that 'involves not only action but a place for communication that constitutes, directs and completes that action' (1983: 121).

Most routine activities typically found in pre-primary EFL classrooms contain these formats: they are the reason pre-primary English teachers are encouraged to use routines as their classroom management approach. Not only do they help children remain calm and thus enjoy English, they also support children's acquisition of the target language.

Formats in routine activities

To illustrate the idea of formats, Excerpt 1 is an example of a *Hello routine* in English. It is the transcription of a recording, which occurred after a group of twenty-five Portuguese children, aged five to six years old, had been exposed to approximately sixty hours of English over the previous twenty months. The context is typically low exposure and is led by an English teacher who visits the institution twice a week for thirty minutes.

Excerpt 1

Teacher: [To Filipa] It's your turn today!

Filipa: [Gets up, looks in the English box and finds the class puppet, Hoola; she places it on her hand, and looks at the class] Hello, good morning.

Class: Good morning.

Filipa: How are you?

Class: I'm fine thank you. What's the weather like today, Hoola?

Filipa: [Looks out of the window] It's cloudy.

These children proceeded with this routine independently of the teacher, for it contains the three components of a format: the sequential structure, which involved a child finding the English puppet, greeting her classmates and responding to their question about the weather; three clearly marked roles, that of the teacher who indicated who should be the puppet-holding child for that lesson, that of the child holding the puppet and that of the children; and a script-like exchange 'Hello, good morning!' 'Good Morning!' 'How are you?' 'I'm fine thank you.' 'What's the weather like today, Hoola?' 'It's [WEATHER]'. These children had been exposed to this particular format approximately thirty times in the previous year and confidently used the target language, with little or no prompting from their English teacher.

What is also evident in this excerpt is the use of formulaic language (Lightbown and Spada 2013: 218; see also S. Kersten 2015, this volume), which the children have memorized and are confident about using in context. 'What's the weather like today, Hoola?' is typical of an acquired stretch of unanalysed speech recognized by this community of learners. The children's pre-primary educator observed these children using this question playfully, outside of the English session, and enjoying the opportunity it gave them to engage in a dialogue in English for pleasure, especially when the weather was extreme, such as when very windy or stormy.

Formats in game-like activities

Exactly the same happens with the routine playful activities that take place during circle time. Resources like flashcards are used during circle time for different game-like activities. Children are exposed to the activity formats, with the English teacher mediating between the children and the English resources. During this time children naturally interact and play along, gradually noticing, picking up and understanding the structure, roles and script-like exchanges that define the activity format. The next section looks at a game-like activity played during circle time and analyses the format with a view to discussing how it supports target language use in an ELA.

Evidence of a format in teacher-led and child-initiated play

A favourite movement game during English circle time is *Listen and do*. It should be played at the beginning of a sequence of activities around a topic or theme (see Coelho and Mourão 2009), when children are getting to grips with a new set of lexical items and their related expressions. It involves the teacher asking the children to mime actions when they hear an instruction and is a fun game that supports memorization due to the use of the flashcard image, spoken word and movement. I observed this activity played by a group of five- to six-year-olds, after they had been learning English for eighteen months, for two sessions of thirty minutes per week. They were playing with clothes words and related expressions and their English teacher had shared a chant with them, before playing the *Listen and do* game. Here is an excerpt from the chant:

Brrr, It's cold!
Put on your hat
Brrr, it's cold!
Put on your scarf
Brrr, it's cold
Put on your gloves.
Umm much better! (Coelho and Mourão 2009: 45)

The chant serves to support the instructions of the game, where first the teacher places flashcards of clothes in a row and then gives instructions like 'Put on your hat'. The children mime putting on a hat and repeat the instruction. This particular activity is entertaining as it involves children miming putting on their clothes, pretending to get hot and then taking them all off again and pretending to get cold. They enjoy the pretence of feeling over-hot and then over-cold, and of course are exposed to the formula, 'put on your NOUN' repeatedly.

I observed that the children were already familiar with the format from previous exposure to the game, they knew the structure and the role elements of the format and they were getting to grips with the formulaic language related to this particular topic, 'Put on your NOUN'. The English teacher was careful to ensure that, after playing the game a couple of times, she invited a child to come to the front and be the leader and give the instructions. This is referred to by Bruner as the 'handover principle' (1983: 60), and it involves setting up an activity to facilitate a child's scaffolded entry to ensure their 'ineptitudes can be rescued or rectified by appropriate intervention'. The scaffold is removed little by little as the child demonstrates an ability to proceed alone. Confident children were very successful at giving instructions and even the lesser-confident children had a go.

Later, once the English session was over, I observed this same group of children playing in the ELA during child-initiated play moments, engaging with a number of different activities using the English resources they found there. I would like to share my observations of three children, Isabel, Pedro and Sara (all pseudonyms). During my observation of their child-initiated play, which lasted around ten minutes, they first read an English picturebook together, then took out the story cards belonging to the clothes topic (a story about a snowman getting dressed). They sequenced the story, retelling parts together, successfully repeating chunks of story language. Sara placed clothes flashcards alongside the story cards to emphasize the sequence. Once they had finished retelling the story, Pedro put the story cards away but left the clothes flashcards on the floor. Isabel, a confident child who often played teacher, or leader, in the ELA, placed the flashcards in a row, chanting the clothes words and imitating their English teacher's actions. Pedro and Sara sat back and watched. Excerpt 2 is a transcription of what happened next:

Excerpt 2

Isabel:	Put on your hat [mimes patting head]
Pedro & Sara:	[Mime patting their heads] hat
Isabel:	STOP!
Pedro & Sara:	[Freeze]
Isabel:	Put on your gloves!
Pedro & Sara:	[Mime putting on gloves] Gloves
Isabel:	You moved! [pointing at Pedro]
Pedro:	Mas eu estou a respirar (trans: *But I'm breathing*) [sits down]
Isabel:	Put on your coat!
Sara:	[Mimes putting on a coat] Coat
Pedro:	[Stands up]
Isabel:	Put on your scarf!
Pedro & Sara:	[Mime winding scarf around neck] Scarf, scarf, scarf.

The game stopped and the children went on to play something else.

We can see from this observation that these children are following the structure of a known game, *STOP!* They each have roles: Sara is the teacher and Pedro and Isabel are the students. There is a very clear script, 'Put on your NOUN', repeating 'NOUN', 'STOP!', 'You moved!' This latter exclamation is very much part of the circle time game, for the teacher, or child playing teacher, calls out 'You moved, sit down'.

In essence, therefore, a 'format is a routinized and repeated interaction in which [adults and children] *do* things [...] together using language' (Bruner 1983: 132, emphasis in the original). In the context of an English session, it enables the children during circle time to acquire the language of a topic through a familiar format. It is familiarity with the format that facilitates the handover of the activity, and it is the handover aspect of a format that is essential in supporting later child-initiated play, for both the leader and the led roles are being practised, allowing the formulaic language to be memorized as well. In the excerpt I shared with you, children engaged in the *Listen and do* game during circle time with their teacher and used the formulaic language they had acquired to play another game, *STOP!* in their ELA. This transfer of language from one context to another is clear evidence of language development and creativity supported by the existence of formats.

Children's activity in the ELA

STOP! is one of the many English games played in the ELA and anecdotal evidence over the last fourteen years, from educators in Portugal, Italy and Cyprus whom I have worked with, confirms that children imitate their English teacher and play circle-time games during child-initiated play. During naturalistic observations, while children were engaging in child-initiated play moments in the ELA, I also observed children imitating their English sessions (see Robinson, Mourão and Kang 2015). Younger children, aged four to five years old, tended to master the structure and roles of an activity's format, for example, the placing of flashcards and turn taking, before they mastered the script-like exchange. They were often heard saying the topic words in English, but rarely the formulaic language demonstrated in Excerpt 2. However, as we saw from the examples I have shared, older children confidently recreated the whole format, or creatively appropriated formulaic language to suit their needs during child-initiated play moments in the ELA.

Each group of children differs in their favourite English games and activities; from my own observations and collected anecdotal evidence, these include dialogues with a puppet or puppets, a wide variety of games (many involving flashcards), looking at books, chanting songs and rhymes and telling stories, as well as inventing games. Children actively use the language of a topic as well as formulaic language from the teacher-led activities: for example, 'Let's play...' 'Your turn!' 'Raise your hand!' 'What's missing?' 'They're the same' and 'Help please' (the latter a request the children are encouraged to use if they cannot remember something in English). Children have been observed correcting each other, reminding each other of English words and expressions and actively helping each other to play in English. The L1 is used too, but tends to be during moments of conflict or when trying to organize a game or an activity. All pre-primary educators I have worked with over the years describe their children showing an enormous amount of motivation to play in English.

Implications for pre-primary language learning

The implications based on what I have shared on incorporating play into pre-primary language-learning programmes are far reaching. The fact that provision for child-initiated play is largely ignored in published materials for this age group, as well as emerging evidence that English teachers tend to be peripatetic with little training in child pedagogy, together with little motivation to remain in the field of early childhood education, implies that practice requires reconsiderations on many levels.

As English teachers, we need to be aware of what constitutes an activity, be it routine or game-like. The understanding of the structures, roles and script-like exchanges that are inherent to activity formats will help teachers set up and plan for learning, which can be extended through child-initiated play. Teachers need to be conscious of and consistent in their use of language during circle time, so that children can easily pick up and imitate the target language. In addition, allowing for the handover aspect of an activity provides opportunities for children to become leaders and recognizes the sociocultural learning theories that support an approach which enables children to learn from adults *and* more able peers. This may be alien to many English teachers who come to the classroom with the belief that children learn English through interaction with the English teacher only.

Another challenge involves the language teacher, when peripatetic, working together with the educator to support the introduction of child-initiated play in English. In the years I have been working with ELAs, it has not always been easy to convince the educators of the validity of an ELA: until they actually see how children use this additional area and the benefits it brings to the children's use of the target language. When space is limited, a mobile area has been created (e.g. a box or boxes for the English resources), which can be placed on a shelf. The resources are then taken out and used on the carpet or on a table during children's free play. Working together means that educators and English teachers need to be clear about their roles as planners and mediators, and understand that both are responsible for the children's development in and through English.

A further challenge is related to this and involves the need to obtain or create materials to place in an ELA. Many teachers depend upon publishers to provide the materials they use in their lessons, though some make their own, but in both cases anecdotal evidence suggests English teachers reuse the same set of materials with different groups of children. Materials made for, or used in, an ELA have to stay there for a considerable period of time. They have to be duplicated if they are needed by the English teacher with another group of children. There is no solution other than an acceptance that the extra work involved brings huge potential benefits to the children's learning experience. There are, nevertheless, ways of involving children in the creation of materials. They can colour images that later become flashcards, and they consequently love using them due to their personal investment. They can also create their own games, something many of the educators I have worked with like to do with their groups of children.

Finally, I wish to highlight the perception of play in some settings. As I have outlined at the beginning of the chapter, early childhood education sits within two philosophical traditions – a teacher-led, education-focused approach related to school readiness skills and a child-directed, social, pedagogic approach, where attention is given to educational goals, play and interactivity with educators, teachers and peers. ELAs will, understandably, be easier to set up and flourish in those settings that believe in a child-directed, social pedagogic approach to educating children – I would go so far as to say they only succeed in these settings.

I began my chapter by describing the diverse provision of pre-primary education around the world and it is no surprise that there is an absence of guidelines for an appropriate EFL pedagogy in a pre-primary context. Language learning tends to be approached from the teacher-led, education-focused perspective related to school readiness skills and ignores the focus on play-based activities for learning opportunities highlighted by UNESCO. If we are seeing additional languages being taught in an increasing number of early years settings, in particular in low-exposure contexts, it is vital that we respect how children learn, and emulate pre-primary approaches. Planning for child-initiated play should be part of our early years English programmes, for it is essential in the creation of a rich learning environment that integrates another language into everyday learning and results in the other language being meaningful, useful and playful for pre-primary children. It is vital we get it right from the start.

References

Bruce, Tina (2011), *Early Childhood Education* (4th edn), London: Hodder Education.

Bruner, Jerome (1983), *Child's Talk: Learning to Use Language*. New York: Norton.

Černá, Monika (2015), 'Pre-primary English language learning and teacher education in the Czech Republic' in Sandie Mourão and Mónica Lourenço (eds), *Early Years Second Language Education: International Perspectives on Theories and Practice*, Abingdon: Routledge, pp. 165–176.

Coelho, Daniela and Mourão, Sandie (2009), *Little Hoola Teachers' Guide*, Porto: Porto Editora.

de Botton, Oli (2010), *Effective Early Childhood Education Programmes: Case Studies*, Reading: CfBT Education Trust. <http://cdn.cfbt.com/~/media/cfbtcorporate/files/research/2010/r-early-childhood-programmes-case-study-2010.pdf> [accessed 5 March 2015].

Dunn, Opal (2012), *Introducing English to Young Children: Spoken Language*, Glasgow: North Star.

Edelenbos, Peter; Johnstone, Richard and Kubanek, Angleika (2006), *The Main Pedagogical Principles Underlying the Teaching of Languages to Very Young Learners. Languages for the Children of Europe: Published Research, Good Practice and Main Principles*, Brussels: Eurostat.

Ellis, Gail (2014), '"Young Learners": Clarifying our terms', *ELT Journal* 68/1: 75–78.

Ellis, Gail (2015), 'A short, in-service training course for pre-school teachers in France', in Victoria Murphy and Maria Evangelou (eds), *Early Childhood Education in English for Speakers of Other Languages*, London: British Council.

Enever, Janet (2007), 'Yet another early start language policy in Europe: Poland this time!', *Current Issues in Language Planning*, 8/2: 208–221.

Enever, Janet (ed.) (2011), *ELLiE: Early Language Learning in Europe*, London: The British Council.

Emery, Helen (2012), *A Global Study of Primary English Teachers' Qualifications, Training and Career Development. ELT Research Papers*, London: The British Council.

European Commission (2011a), *Examples of Good Practice*, Brussels: European Commission <http://ec.europa.eu/languages/policy/language-policy/documents/early-language-learning-handbook_en.pdf> [accessed 26 November 2014].

European Commission (2011b), *Language Learning at Pre-primary School Level: Making It Efficient and Sustainable. A Policy Handbook*, Brussels: European Commission. <http://ec.europa.eu/languages/policy/language-policy/documents/early-language-learning-handbook_en.pdf> [accessed 26 November 2014].

Eurydice (2012), *Key Data on Teaching Languages at School in Europe*, Brussels: Education, Audiovisual and Culture Executive Agency.

Fröhlich-Ward, Leonora (1979), 'Environment and learning', in Reinhold Freudenstein (ed.), *Teaching Foreign Languages to the Very Young*, Oxford: Pergamon Institute of English, pp. 21–29.

García, Noemi and García, Juan M. M. (2011), *Programa Nacional de Inglés en Educación Básica. Segunda Lengua: Inglés*, Cuauhtémoc: Coordinación Nacional de Inglés.

Ghosn, Irma-Kaarina (2013), *Storybridge to Second Language Literacy*. Charlotte, NC: Information Age Publishing.

Isaacs, Susan (1949), *The Nursery Years: The Mind of the Child from Birth to Six Years*, London: Routledge & Kegan Paul.

Ioannou-Georgiou, Sophie (2015), 'Early language learning in Cyprus: Voices from the classroom', in Sandie Mourão and Mónica Lourenço (eds), *Early Years Second Language Education: International Perspectives on Theories and Practice*, Abingdon: Routledge, pp. 95–108.

Kernan, Margaret (2007), *Play as a context for early learning and development. A research paper*, Dublin: NCCA, <http://www.ncca.ie/en/Curriculum_and_Assessment/Early_Childhood_and_Primary_Education/Early_Childhood_Education/How_Aistear_was_developed/Research_Papers/Play_paper.pdf> [accessed 24 November 2014].

Kersten, Kristin (2015) 'Bilingual pre-primary schools: Language acquisition, intercultural encounters and environmental learning', in Sandie Mourão and Mónica Lourenço (eds), *Early Years Second Language Education: International Perspectives on Theories and Practice*, Abingdon: Routledge, pp. 29–45.

Kersten, Saskia (2015), 'Language development in young learners: The role of formulaic language', in Janice Bland (ed.), *Teaching English to Young Learners. Critical Issues in Language Teaching with 3–12 Year Olds*, London: Bloomsbury Academic, pp. 129–145.

Lightbown, Patsy and Spada, Nina (2013), *How Languages Are Learned* (4th edn), Oxford: Oxford University Press.

Lindon, Jennie (2001), *Understanding Children's Play*, Cheltenham: Nelson Thornes.

Lourenço, Mónica and Andrade, Ana Isabel (2015), 'Languages and diversity in pre-primary education: Towards a broader and integrated approach', in Sandie Mourão and Mónica Lourenço (eds.), *Early Years Second Language Education: International Perspectives on Theories and Practice*, Abingdon: Routledge, pp. 120–136.

68   TEACHING ENGLISH TO YOUNG LEARNERS

McElwee, James (2015), 'Introducing French to pre-primary children in the North East of England: The Narrative Format approach', in Sandie Mourão and Mónica Lourenço (eds.), *Early Years Second Language Education: International Perspectives on Theories and Practice*, Abingdon: Routledge, pp. 109–119.

Miller, Edward and Almon, Joan (2009), *Crisis in the Kindergarten: Why Children Need to Play in School*, College Park, MD: Alliance for Childhood. <http://files. eric.ed.gov/fulltext/ED504839.pdf> [accessed 26 November 2014].

Mourão, Sandie (2014), 'Taking play seriously in pre-primary English classes', *ELT Journal*, 63/3: 254–264.

Mourão, Sandie and Robinson, Penelope (2015), 'Facilitating the learning of English through collaborative practice', in Victoria Murphy and Maria Evangelou (eds), *Early Childhood Education in English for Speakers of Other Languages*, London: British Council.

Moyles, Janet (1989), *Just Playing? The Role and Status of Play in Early Childhood Education*, Milton Keynes: Open University Press, pp. 1–15.

Moyles, Janet (2010), 'Introduction', in Janet Moyles (ed.), *The Excellence of Play* (3rd edn), Maidenhead: Open University Press, pp. 1–15.

OECD (2014), *Education at a Glance: OECD Indicators*, OECD Publishing. <http:// www.oecd-ilibrary.org/education/education-at-a-glance-2014_eag-2014-en> [accessed 25 November 2014].

Pinthon, Monique (1979), 'The key to success: The teacher', in Reinhold Freudenstein (ed.), *Teaching Foreign Languages to the Very Young*, Oxford: Pergamon Institute of English, pp. 71–75.

Portiková, Zuzana (2015), 'Pre-primary second language education in Slovakia and the role of teacher training programmes', in Sandie Mourão and Mónica Lourenço (eds), *Early Years Second Language Education: International Perspectives on Theories and Practice*, Abingdon: Routledge, pp. 177–188.

Powell, Sacha and David, Tricia (2010), 'Play in the early years: The influence of cultural difference', in Janet Moyles (ed.), *The Excellence of Play* (3rd edn), Maidenhead: Open University Press/McGraw-Hill Education, pp. 244–258.

Reilly, Vanessa and Ward, Sheila (1997), *Very Young Learners*, Oxford: Oxford University Press.

Robinson, Penny, Mourão, Sandie and Kang, Nam-Joon (2015), *English Learning Areas in Preschool Classrooms: An Investigation of Their Effectiveness in Supporting EFL Development*, London: British Council.

Roth, Genevieve (1998), *Teaching Very Young Children*, London: Richmond Publishing.

Rixon, Shelagh (2013), *British Council Survey of Policy and Practice in Primary English Language Teaching Worldwide*, London: British Council.

Rixon, Shelagh (2015), 'Primary English and critical issues: A worldwide perspective', in Janice Bland (ed.), *Teaching English to Young Learners. Critical Issues in Language Teaching with 3–12 Year Olds*, London: Bloomsbury Academic, pp. 31–50.

Rocha, Carla (2014), *Collaborative Practices in 'Kiitos', A Pre-primary English Project in Ponte de Sor, Portugal*. [Presentation at International Conference: Language Learning 2–6: International Perspectives on Early Years Pluriligualism]. European University, Cyprus, 23–25 May 2014.

Rokita-Jaśkow, Joanna (2013), *Foreign Language Learning at Pre-primary Level. Parental Aspirations and Educational Practice*, Kraków: Wydawnictwo Naukowe Uniwerytetu Pedagogicznego.

Siraj-Blatchford, Iram; Sylva, Kathy; Muttock, Stella; Gilden, Rose and Bell, Danny (2002), *Researching Effective Pedagogy in the Early Years*. Research Report No. 356, London: Department of Education and Skills, HMSO <http://www.ioe.ac.uk/REPEY_research_report.pdf > [accessed 24 November 2014].

Sofronieva, Ekatarina (2015), 'Measuring empathy and teachers' readiness to adopt innovations in second language learning', in Sandie Mourão and Mónica Lourenço (eds), *Early Years Second Language Education: International Perspectives on Theories and Practice*, Abingdon: Routledge, pp. 189–203.

Song, Jae Jung (2012), 'South Korea: Language policy and planning in the making', *Current Issues in Language Planning*, 13/1:1–68.

The Consultative Group on Early Childhood Care and Development (2013), 'The Importance of Early Childhood Development to Education'. Prepared for the Global Meeting of the Thematic Consultation in the Post-2015 Development Agenda, Dakar, March 18–19, 2013. <http://www.beyond2015.org/sites/default/files/ECD-Education-Post-2015.pdf > [accessed 24 November 2014].

UNESCO-UIS (2012), *International Standard Classification of Education ISCED 2011*. Montreal: UNESCO Institute for Statistics. Available at <http://www.uis.unesco.org/Education/Pages/international-standard-classification-of-education.aspx> [accessed 19 August 2013].

Voise, Anne-Marie (2014), *English as a Foreign Language in French Pre-Primary Schools: A Focus on Oral Interactions* [Presentation at International Conference on Child Foreign Language Acquisition]. Facultad de Letras, Universidad de País Vasco, 16–17 October 2014.

Wood, David (1988), *How Children Think and Learn*, Oxford: Blackwell Publishers.

Wood, Elisabeth (2010), 'Developing integrated pedagogical approaches to play and learning', in Pat Broadhead; Justine Howard and Elisabeth Wood (eds), *Play and Learning in the Early Years*, London: Sage Publications, pp. 9–26.

World Bank (2014), 'Primary School Starting Ages (Years)'. <http://data.worldbank.org/indicator/SE.PRM.AGES> [accessed 25 November 2014].

Yu, Zhenyou and Ruan, Jiening (2012), 'Early childhood education in China', in Jiening Ruan and Cynthis, Leun, *Perspectives on Teaching and Learning English Literacy in China*, New York: Springer Dordrecht Heidelberg, pp. 51–66.

4

Immersion Teaching in English with Young Learners

Kristin Kersten
and Andreas Rohde

Introduction

In 2002, Marjorie Wesche questioned to what extent the original Canadian model of early immersion had stood the test of time. She concluded that the original model 'had the fundamentals right' and was still serviceable after all those years (Wesche 2002: 375). It has also served and informed European and other immersion programmes worldwide. However, not least due to organizational and logistic challenges as well as a lack of faith on the part of policymakers, the original idea of immersion and its related terminology have often been tampered with, leading to a multitude of different terms and programmes and sometimes making life difficult for the proponents of the original idea of immersion, for example, in Europe.

Terminological issues

Bilingual approaches to second or foreign language (L2)[1] acquisition, which rely on the concept of teaching content in L2, come under various terms, depending, for example, on diverse political contexts and pedagogical frameworks, which differ widely in their intensity, time of onset and practical applications. As the outcomes of bilingual-teaching programmes vary considerably with respect to such dissimilar implementations, the unfortunate effect is that research results are often interpreted without paying attention to the specific programme characteristics under which they were achieved. It is therefore necessary to clarify some terminology as a basis for the following considerations.

Although education in a foreign language can be considered 'as old as education itself' (Coyle, Hood and Marsh 2010: 2), the immersion programmes implemented in Canada in the 1960s are recognized as forerunners of immersion education as understood today (Cummins 2000) and have been subjected to extensive research for decades. The term *immersion* is used metaphorically for an intensive bilingual surrounding, a 'language bath' in which learners are immersed, that is surrounded by L2 as if immersed in water. In this context *immersion* is used for school programmes in which at least 50 per cent of the curriculum is taught in the foreign language for an extended period of time (Genesee 1987). Swain and Johnson (1997: 6–8) describe the core features of immersion programmes under the following headings:

1. L2 is a medium of instruction.

2. The immersion curriculum parallels the local L1 curriculum.

3. Overt support exists for L1.

4. The programme aims for additive bilingualism.[2]

5. Exposure to L2 is largely confined to the classroom.

6. Students enter with similar (and limited) levels of L2 proficiency.

7. The teachers are bilingual.

8. The classroom culture is that of the local L1 community.

When we refer to immersion programmes, we will use these features, including the intensity measure of 50 per cent of the curriculum, as defining criteria of immersion as the most intensive form within a continuum of Content and Language Integrated Learning (CLIL) programmes. CLIL has emerged within the context of European educational policies from the mid-1990s (see Bentley 2015, this volume, for a discussion of a number of CLIL scenarios). As an umbrella term (Mehisto 2011), 'CLIL' covers the whole range of different bilingual programmes with varying degrees of intensity in that it is 'a generic term and refers to any educational situation in which an additional language and therefore not the most widely used language of the environment is used for the teaching and learning of subjects other than the language itself' (Marsh and Langé 2000: iii). In Kersten and Rohde (2013a: 109), we argue that CLIL, *on a scale increasing in intensity*, can be considered to cover:

- strongly content-based sections within traditional FLT (see also Met 1999)

- single units, modules or projects carried out in the foreign language within other subjects, such as art or history (see also Burmeister and Massler 2010: 7, for whom the least intensive end of the CLIL continuum begins here)

- teaching of a single subject largely or entirely in the foreign language, typically for several years of schooling

- partial and full immersion programmes at the extreme end of the continuum.

Immersion programmes

Forms of immersion programmes

From the Canadian context, three main types of programmes have evolved: early immersion (onset in Grade 1, age 6), middle or delayed entry (Grade 4, age 9) and late entry (Grade 6 or 7, age 11–12). In Canada all three types begin with a monolingual phase in which most or all instruction is given through L2, which is French (Wesche 2002: 363, Cummins 2009). In addition, total and partial immersion programmes are distinguished. Total immersion refers to programmes in which L2 is used 100 per cent of the time for a number of years before being slightly reduced with the introduction of L1, whereas in partial immersion L1 is used for some of the subject matter teaching although, by definition, the share of L2 does not fall below the 50 per cent mark.

Immersion programmes can be further distinguished by the number of involved languages, such as *dual language*, two-way or reciprocal immersion (Baker 2011), where classrooms are composed of two groups of children, each speaking one of the involved languages as L1 and learning the other as L2. There are also *submersion* programmes (which can often be found in the US, or in the form of DaZ courses in Germany), where students with different L1s are learning the majority language. These programmes, however, have a high L2 competence as their aim, even at the cost of the children's L1, known as a *subtractive bilingual approach*. Strictly speaking, this type of programme aims to foster monolingualism rather than bilingualism. When it is assumed that students have attained sufficient L2 proficiency to follow instruction in that language, L1 instruction is discontinued and students are placed into mainstream classes taught exclusively in the majority language, which is often English (Cummins 2009: 161).

Apart from discussing immersion school programmes worldwide, in the following section, reference will also be made to studies carried out in preschool immersion programmes in Europe (K. Kersten, Rohde, Schelletter and Steinlen 2010a, K. Kersten 2015).

An overview of research carried out in early immersion

'In 1965, a well-researched experiment began in a St. Lambert, Québec kindergarten which was to help refine our understanding of how languages are learned and how they can be successfully taught' (Wesche 2002: 357). Despite other similar programmes that had been introduced in Europe earlier, for example, in Wales, Luxembourg and Catalonia, it was the Canadian programmes which were to have the strongest impact worldwide because they have been systematically evaluated over the last five decades (e.g. Cummins 2009, Möller 2013). The St. Lambert programme started with twenty-six children (Wode 2009: 41); today about 300,000 Canadian students currently participate in immersion programmes (Cummins 2009: 162). It should be explicitly stated here that the Canadian programmes are designed for L1 English-speaking learners in order to become proficient speakers of the dominant local language. They study French as L2 for cultural and occupational enhancement rather than out of necessity; thus additive bilingualism is the pronounced goal (Wesche 2002: 358).

Language and content learning

Laurén (1994: 4) states that Early French Immersion (EFI) may be the most effective means of school L2 instruction yet developed for majority language children. Wesche (2002: 360) summarizes the outcomes of EFI programmes as 'two for one', meaning that the EFI students achieve both a high level of L2 development and mastery of school subject matter which is equivalent to that of students studying the subject matter in their L1, English. She stresses, in addition, that English language development never stops during EFI and that three years of instruction entirely in French from kindergarten through Grade 2 produces no long-term negative effects on either English oral or literacy skills. She admits that EFI students do in fact experience a lag in standardized test performance on English literacy skills from the onset of EFI until English instruction is introduced after three years. This lag, however, is expected to be overcome within one year. After that, many EFI children even surpass children in the English-only programmes (Wesche 2002: 360). Turnbull, Lapkin and Hart (2001) note a lag in the Grade 3 EFI young learners' English literacy performance on Ontario provincial tests, but the literacy-test results which are reported for EFI young learners in Grade 6 are significantly higher than those of comparable students in English-language monolingual programmes (Lazaruk 2007: 614). Additionally, all types of French immersion programmes consistently lead to far stronger French proficiency in all skills than do forty minutes per day French setups (Wesche 2002: 361).

Research touching on the question of which levels of L2 proficiency can be achieved reveals that EFI students, unsurprisingly, display shortcomings when compared to native speakers of French. In general, at the end of Grade 6, the students' receptive skills in French are better developed than their productive skills. The significant gaps between the EFI students and native speakers in spoken and written French are particularly evident with respect to accuracy of grammar and vocabulary knowledge and use (Cummins 2009: 170–171). EFI students tend to use more restricted vocabulary, their skills are domain specific, they overuse high-frequency verbs and their L2 grammars are influenced by their L1 (Harley 1992: 180–181). On the discourse level, they rarely tend to initiate conversations in French, but rather use it reactively (Wesche 2002: 361). It is remarkable, however, that despite the frequent lack of wider contact with native speakers of French, the immersion students continue to progress towards native speaker norms throughout secondary school and do not display plateaus in their development (Harley 1992).

Both researchers and educators have sought to enhance teaching programmes through greater emphasis on speaking and writing activities as well as form-focused tasks (Wesche 2002: 362). A recent study of students' development of the German determiner phrase in an immersion programme in the US (Charlotte, NC), where subject matter is taught through German 90 per cent of the time, suggests that students fail to acquire the target-like inflected form of the determiner phrase (sequence of determiner-adjective-noun: nominative – *das große Haus* 'the big house'; genitive – *des großen Hauses* 'of the big house') even after being on the programme up to eight years (Schöneberger 2014). This may be (at least partly) accounted for by the programme not fostering any form-focused teaching whatsoever (see Lyster 2004). Immersion students' limitations, especially in L2 production, led Merrill Swain (1995) to formulate the *Output Hypothesis*. She suggested that only production (= output) really forces L2 learners to carry out full grammatical processing which most effectively enhances the students' development of L2 morpho-syntax.

One important question is whether there is a linear increase of L2 proficiency when the time of exposure to L2 is increased, and to what extent children enrolled in middle or late entry programmes are able to compete with the EFI children. In spite of the apparent advantages for EFI, many middle French immersion (MFI) and late French immersion (LFI) students catch up with EFI averages by Grade 8 on reading and written grammar measures. EFI students, however, tended to retain higher self-confidence than LFI students in their oral language abilities (Wesche 2002: 363). Reeder, Buntain and Takakuwa (1999) compared two groups of EFI students who received intensified teaching from Grade 4 to Grade 7, one group had had 80 per cent teaching in French, the other 50 per cent. The more intensive group scored better at descriptive writing but both groups showed the same results in narrative writing and reading comprehension. The authors conclude that after a certain threshold, increasing the time spent in L2 does not increase French proficiency (see also Lazaruk 2007: 611).

Harley (1998: 26) hypothesizes that EFI young learners acquire French through a lexical, memory-oriented approach in keeping with L1 and L2 acquisition in naturalistic settings, whereas LFI students use an analytical approach, although she also deems it possible that results are due to different teaching emphases rather than different starting ages (see also Lazaruk 2007).

Immersion programmes have been established worldwide for a number of decades, often following the Canadian example (overviews in Laurén 1994, Artigal 1997, Johnson and Swain 1997, Cummins 2009). It is important to note that the programmes may differ strongly from each other, depending on a number of factors, not least the sociolinguistic status of the involved languages and the expectations as to linguistic outcomes. Early immersion in Swedish, Finland's second official language (mainly in the Vaasa area), represents a similar context to Canada (Björklund 1997, Wesche 2002). In other countries, such as Australia, programmes fostering French, German and Hebrew highlight languages not officially spoken in Australia so that the students' (and their parents') motivation may differ from the Canadian setups (Clyne 2002). As English-language immersion programmes become attractive globally, there are potential problems due to 'the over-politicization of bilingualism at the expense of linguistic considerations' (Kuchah 2009: 91). A particularly disadvantageous situation is a combination of lack of vernacular language-arts support in contexts where there are many different local languages, together with inadequate English-language competence of the primary-school teacher due to hastily introduced programmes (see also Rixon 2015, this volume).

In Germany, a number of early immersion programmes were initiated with immersive L2 English input at preschool level, followed by primary school immersion, most notably in Kiel-Altenholz in the northernmost German state of Schleswig-Holstein. Unlike in EFI, English had a share of roughly 70 per cent in primary school, the remainder being dedicated to German language arts. English functional literacy was introduced at the end of Grade 2, following especially parents' fears that their children would be overwhelmed by two spelling systems at once. English oral proficiency was mainly measured with the help of the picture story 'Frog where are you?' (Mayer 1969). This was at a time when English had not been introduced as a school subject at elementary level (which happened in 2003 on a nationwide level), and thus there were no comparisons. Qualitative research, however, suggests that students steadily move towards standard language norms, not fossilizing at any point (Piske

2006). Subsequent quantitative studies confirm that students' skills in math and their L1 German do not suffer as a result of the L2 input. On the contrary, some students even tend to outperform the controls on a set of standardized tests (Zaunbauer, Gebauer and Möller 2013: 102).

Cognitive effects

While historically, despite Peal and Lambert's pioneer study (1962), bilingualism has frequently been regarded as disadvantageous or even detrimental, today '[c]ognitive research associates bilingualism with heightened mental flexibility and creative thinking skills, enhanced metalinguistic awareness, and greater communicative sensitivity' (Lazaruk 2007: 605). Recent studies have shown that students in immersion programmes may profit from the cognitive effects described above for children who grow up bilingually: Genesee, Tucker and Lambert (1975), for instance, found that children in immersion education show a higher communicative sensitivity in a task where they had to explain the rules of a game to blindfolded and non-blindfolded listeners. Nicolay and Poncelet (2013) carried out a study with eight-year-old French-speaking students with three years of experience in English partial immersion programmes in Belgium using a number of tests for verbal and non-verbal intelligence, attentional and executive function measure. As predicted, 'the immersion group performed better (more specifically, faster) than tho monolingual group on tasks assessing alerting, auditory selective attention, divided attention, and mental flexibility, but not on tasks assessing response inhibition' (p. 603), while no difference was found on an interference inhibition task.

On the other hand, a study by Carlson and Meltzoff (2008) in an immersion kindergarten was not able to detect cognitive differences between immersion children and monolingual children after six months; however, it is argued that the time of exposure was not long enough to reveal significant effects of immersion education (Nicolay and Poncelet 2013). This relates to Cummins' (1979) *threshold hypothesis*, which claims that the cognitive advantages of early bilingualism only emerge if a certain level of linguistic competence has been reached.

More recent results from studies in immersion education found support for this claim. In a study with Hispanic subjects in a 50 per cent English/ 50 per cent Spanish transitional primary programme, Hakuta and Diaz (1985) were able to show that the degree of bilingualism correlated with non-verbal cognitive abilities (i.e. non-verbal intelligence). The authors interpret their data in support of the assumption that a high degree of 'bilingualism fosters cognitive development' (Hakuta and Diaz 1985: 340) and is positively related to metalinguistic ability (Hakuta 1985). Diaz (1985, quoted in Hakuta, Ferdman and Diaz 1987) additionally reports stronger effects for beginning learners than for more advanced learners, concluding that 'some effects of bilingualism might occur as a result of the initial struggles and experiences of the beginning second-language learner' (Hakuta et al. 1987: 296), an effect which Nicolay and Poncelet (2013) corroborate, arguing for an effortful attention and training effect in that the 'immersion situation might train children to attain and/or maintain a high level of alertness, allowing them to react faster to environmental demands' (p. 604). Along the same lines, Bialystok and Barac (quoted in Nicolay and Poncelet 2013) found a longitudinal effect in immersion primary students' executive control, and Bialystok, Peets and Moreno (2014) describe a similar, gradually emerging positive effect on metalinguistic advantages over five years in a French immersion programme.

Thus, the degree of cognitive effects seems to depend on the degree of intensity of the bilingual experience: the greater the degree of bilingualism, the larger were the metalinguistic and cognitive effects observed (Bialystok, Craik, Green and Gollan 2009: 119, based on further studies carried out by Bialystok 1988, Bialystok and Majumder 1998, Luk 2008).

> Extending this pattern to education, it is reasonable to assume that there is a cumulative effect of learning language that, at least in the intense environment of immersion programs, confers some of the cognitive advantages on children even if they do not become highly fluent speakers. (Bialystok et al. 2009: 119)

At-risk learners

In Canada, at-risk learners have been studied in some detail since the 1970s. It could be shown that learners with below-average IQs, for example, had no disadvantage in immersion programmes compared to regular programmes (Genesee 1976). Bourgoin (2014) also finds no disadvantages for children with general learning difficulties. A recent study (Kruk and Reynolds 2012) reveals that learners with reading difficulties develop both a higher status of phonological awareness and a more rapid growth in reading comprehension than at programme entry. There are, however, as yet no studies including learners with dyslexia. In addition, there do not seem to be any studies investigating learners with autism or Down Syndrome in immersion setups (Piske 2013: 55).

Students who have dropped out of immersion programmes have been compared to students who stayed in the programmes despite their difficulties. Bruck (1985) identified a more negative attitude among dropout students with regard to education than for students remaining in the programme. In addition, the dropout students displayed the same problems in the regular programmes that they had experienced in immersion. Halsall (1994), however, concludes his overview by stating that it may well be advantageous, in individual cases, for students to discontinue immersion. Piske (2013) suggests that the study of dropout students has been controversial as the bulk of studies has been based on students' self-assessment and not on objective studies. More research is thus needed to corroborate the above findings, but the current results seem to indicate that students with special educational needs fare as well in immersion programmes as they do in mainstream schooling, and that there is thus no reason to deprive them from the beneficial effects of immersion teaching. Fortune (2011: 267) summarizes: 'Until we have strong evidence that shows that learners with certain language and/or learning disabilities are better served when schooled through one language only, there is no reason to deny the enrichment possibilities of an immersion education to any child.'

Bilingual preschools

Many immersion elementary programmes today are preceded by bilingual programmes for very young learners. Canadian schools often start at kindergarten level, while in European countries increasing numbers of bilingual preschools can be found. These preschool programmes are often referred to as immersion programmes although they do not involve any subject matter teaching. In fact, there is no formal teaching whatsoever. All the preschool routines are offered in L1 and L2 at the same time by two educators who are responsible for a group of children, the aim – as in the Canadian model – being a highly functional L2 proficiency and not standard grammatical accuracy (Fortune 2011: 267). The use of L1 and L2 by the educators follows the principle of *one person – one language* (de Houwer 2009).

The most comprehensive research study we are currently aware of, the ELIAS project, an EU-funded Comenius-project which ran from 2008 to 2010, investigated both receptive L2 English vocabulary and grammar growth in ten preschool immersion programmes in four European countries (seven in Germany, one each in Belgium and Sweden and one in England for comparisons) (K. Kersten et al. 2010a, see Rohde 2013, K. Kersten 2015 for a summary). In these countries English has a high cultural value but no official status. One central question of the project was whether the growth of linguistic proficiency correlated with both input quality (as measured by the newly developed instrument *Input Quality Observation Scheme, IQOS*) and input intensity (as measured by a formula calculated from the presence of kindergarten teachers, opening hours, teacher/child ratio). No correlation was found between input quality and receptive vocabulary growth; however, input quality correlated significantly with receptive grammar growth (Steinlen, Håkansson, Housen and Schelletter 2010a, Weitz, Pahl, Flyman Mattsson, Buyl and Kalbe 2010).

The studies within ELIAS also suggest that there are no deficits in the children's L1 in the case of German (this was not measured for Swedish and French), and, in addition, there were no significant differences with regard to the variables sex and migration background (Steinlen, Neils, Piske and Trumpp 2010b). A follow-up study involving the above-mentioned IQOS confirms the correlation between input quality and receptive grammar, whereas input intensity, including the mere time of exposure, correlates with receptive lexical development. Talking about and discussing L2 features (addressing metalinguistic issues) had no statistical effect on either grammar or vocabulary (Weitz 2014). The study was also able to show that the children exhibited a number of strategies of intercultural competence (Gerlich, H. Kersten, K. Kersten, Massler and Wippermann 2010) and showed environmental awareness in a *Green Immersion* preschool that took place in a zoo where nature topics were encountered in L2 (Thomas, Burmeister, Ewig, K. Kersten and Akerman 2010).

Implementation of immersion programmes: Practical and methodological issues

Programmes offering an early start, a high intensity of L2 contact and a high quality of language input (see 'Teaching principles' below) are good candidates for delivering successful content and L1 and L2 acquisition, as well as other cognitive benefits, yielding high levels of L2 competence and a strong motivation and satisfaction at the end of four years in primary school. As Lotta (aged 10), a Grade 4 German immersion student in a 70 per cent intensive immersion programme, puts it, when asked about her highlights and what role English played for her in school:

> A very big one, because it somehow slipped into my life, and I learn it since four years, and I will miss it at the new school. [...] I think, [...] my highlight was actually every single second in the school. [...] I will miss it, this atmosphere, and feeling confident in the class, and safe.

Organizational aspects

A number of aspects have been pointed out concerning the practical implementation of immersion programmes which need to be borne in mind to avoid unnecessary impediments especially for newly implemented programmes. The following list is based on summaries in K. Kersten (2010) and K. Kersten et al. (2010b, 2010c); see also Met and Lorenz (1997), Walker and Tedick (2000) and Hughes and Madrid (2011: 362–363).

1.   *Legal conditions/prerequisites:* The political aims and educational directives differ widely among countries, states and between different school forms (e.g. private and state schools) and need to be researched thoroughly before a programme is implemented.

2.   *Location and community:* The social and cultural structure of the catchment area influences the composition of the classes. The acceptance and support by the local community are vital for the success of a new programme, as are other bilingual institutions in the vicinity.

3.   *Cooperation and transition:* Programmes which result from special initiatives are frequently isolated islands in their educational systems and thus cannot guarantee a smooth transition from preschool to primary and secondary school. Classrooms have to cope with high language heterogeneity, and children might risk losing their acquired competences in the subsequent school. Close cooperation between the different partners is therefore highly recommendable from a very early stage in the implementation process (see Kersten and Rohde 2013a for an in-depth study on this issue).

4.   *The concept:* Each school has to make informed decisions on the selection of the language/s offered, the intensity of the L2 in the curriculum, the subjects taught in the L2 and the duration of the bilingual programme. Chapters 1–3 in this volume highlight influencing factors in young-learner L2 acquisition, which should be considered in each decision-making process.

5.   *Bilingual staff:* The selection of the staff touches on issues of language competence and pedagogical and methodological training in immersion-specific teaching strategies, which can and should be continually enhanced by additional in-service training. Non-native speakers of L2 need to have a very high competence in L2. If native speakers of L2, who convey language and culture in an authentic way, are chosen – a hotly debated issue in itself – questions of intercultural team building, differing educational backgrounds and philosophies, the distribution of responsibilities (which should be as evenly distributed among the staff as possible), the often highly problematic recognition of foreign certificates, language knowledge of the surrounding L1 and ensuing communication problems have to be taken into account. Additionally, special programmes are prone to attract attention by parents, school boards and the local press, which more often than not puts its sole focus on the L2 staff. Teams have to be prepared to deal with this imbalance in attention by valuing every contribution to the school programme in the same way.

6. *Selection of students:* Many schools (have to) decide on selecting students for the immersion programmes. Criteria for this selection process are a frequently discussed issue. As previously shown, however, it should be borne in mind that for most children with learning disabilities, the benefits of immersion teaching seem to outweigh negative effects, so that it is indeed 'difficult to argue in favor of whole program policies that would uniformly deny admission to any child' (Fortune 2011: 266).

7. *Additional time and finances:* In theory, immersion programmes embody a 'get two for the price of one' approach. Practice, however, often reveals that functional immersion programmes need highly committed teaching staff who are prepared to put in additional preparation time. Linguistically highly heterogeneous classrooms call for teaching materials that are adapted to all children's levels of language and content knowledge. Strategies of differentiation need to belong to the core repertoire of every immersion teacher. Also, following the recent debate on focus on form in immersion contexts (e.g. Lyster 2004), more and more schools decide to set apart additional time for language arts in L2. Some schools bring in additional pedagogic personnel or parent volunteers to assist in the classroom. All of these factors have to be taken into account when timetables and additional costs are calculated.

Teaching principles

The suggested teaching strategies or principles for the immersion classroom generally follow best practice models recommended for non-immersion L2 elementary school teaching (Burmeister 2006). As mentioned above, immersion as such does not represent a teaching method but is associated with a number of principles that have proved fruitful, the most important being holistic and interactive, hands-on classrooms and communicative language teaching (see Kersten and Rohde 2013b). Young learners should experience L2 as an instrument with the help of which they are able to express their own needs, ideas, attitudes and emotions, while being actively involved in meaningful tasks or problem-solving activities.

In immersion teaching the specific challenge is to convey content via L2. Therefore, the teacher has to make use of principles that enable the students to grasp the content despite the fact that it is presented in L2. One possible shortcoming of non-immersion L2 teaching is avoided by teaching compulsory subject matter content which inevitably makes the classroom interaction meaningful (Burmeister 2006: 204). Further principles which have proved to be of vital importance to make the subject matter comprehensible are, for instance:

1. *Scaffolding:* A scaffold can be described as situated help for the students, for example, making use of holistic linguistic structures (formulaic sequences or chunks), visual materials or signs and symbols for activities, the major idea being that 'with assistance, learners can reach beyond what they can do unaided' (Gibbons 2009: 15). Burmeister (2006) lists the recurrent weather routine with its fixed linguistic elements at the beginning of each science lesson as a scaffold (see also Massler and Ioannou-Georgiou 2010 and García and Beardsmore 2009: 329–331 for different types of scaffolds).

2. *Contextualization:* Teachers' L2 utterances are initially accompanied by physical actions and the students need more time than in their L1 to understand what the teachers' utterances exactly refer to. Therefore the teachers' main task is to embed each of their utterances in concrete situations which include a high amount of visualization through a host of different media, for example, pictures, realia as well as intonation, body language or mime (Burmeister 2006: 205).

3. *Multisensory learning:* This principle is an inherent trait of holistic learning. In immersion, however, it is even more significant. Burmeister (2006: 206) gives the example of a science class in which students cultivated their own plants by growing bean seeds (see Snow 1990 for hands-on activities; see also Bentley 2015, Bland 2015c and Tomlinson 2015, this volume)

4. *Negotiation of meaning:* 'In negotiating meaning, teachers and students endeavor to make themselves understood and to understand each other' (Met 1994: 167). It is vitally important for the students to engage in communication and to interact with both the teacher and their fellow students. The students negotiate meaning whenever there is something they have not as yet understood and when they ask their peers or are asked for a vocabulary item or for the meaning of an expression. Negotiation of meaning is believed to foster language acquisition because both linguistic and content information which is exchanged in negotiations is believed to be more deeply processed than if simply presented as facts to the students (Lamsfuß-Schenk 2007). Lyster (2004), however, suggests that negotiation of meaning has to allow for corrective feedback and that there should be a place for both form and meaning-focused negotiation in immersion as learners aged between seven and fourteen otherwise reach developmental plateau levels for some grammatical features.

Conclusion: A case for intensive bilingual approaches

If we want early language learning to be most effective, the factors discussed in this chapter have to be considered for implementation across the board. Even after decades of successful immersion teaching worldwide, we should not forget that immersion is still the exception among L2 teaching programmes. It is still struggling with recognition, organizational challenges and the fact that the rather imprecise application of the term 'immersion' to all kinds of bilingual or CLIL programmes is currently watering down, especially in the European context, what was once established as solid and conclusive results from decades of Canadian research. Our objective has to be to clarify the aims of immersion; the outcomes of different programmes need to be more clearly investigated. Last but not least, much more effort must be put into informing educational policymakers through systematic reviews of current research and the establishment of comprehensive programmes with a well-structured intensive bilingual approach.

Notes

1 In this chapter, no differentiation will be made between the terms 'second language' and 'foreign language'.
2 In additive programmes, proficiency in both L1 and L2 is promoted; L2 proficiency does not develop 'at the expense of the L1' (Swain and Johnson 1997: 7).

References

Artigal, Josep (1997), 'The Catalan immersion program', in Robert Johnson and Merrill Swain (eds), *Immersion Education. International Perspectives*, Cambridge: Cambridge University Press, pp. 133–50.
Baker, Colin (2011), *Foundations of Bilingual Education and Bilingualism*, Bristol: Multilingual Matters.
Bentley, Kay (2015), 'CLIL scenarios with young learners', in Janice Bland (ed.), *Teaching English to Young Learners. Critical Issues in Language Teaching with 3–12 Year Olds*, London: Bloomsbury Academic, pp. 91–111.
Bialystok, Ellen (1988), 'Levels of bilingualism and levels of linguistic awareness', *Developmental Psychology*, 24/4: 560–567.
Bialystok, Ellen and Majumder, Shilpi (1998), 'The relationship between bilingualism and the development of cognitive processes in problem solving', *Applied Psycholinguistics*, 19/01: 69.

Bialystok, Ellen; Craik, Fergus; Green, David and Gollan, Tamar (2009). 'Bilingual minds', *Psychological Science in the Public Interest* 10/3: 89–129.

Bialystok, Ellen; Peets, Kathleen and Moreno, Sylvain (2014), 'Producing bilinguals through immersion education: Development of metalinguistic awareness', *Applied Psycholinguistics*, 35: 177–191.

Björklund, Siv (1997), 'Immersion in Finland in the 1990s: A state of development and expansion', in Robert Johnson and Merrill Swain (eds), *Immersion Education. International Perspectives*, Cambridge: Cambridge University Press, pp. 85–102.

Bland, Janice (2015c), 'Drama with young learners', in Janice Bland (ed.), *Teaching English to Young Learners. Critical Issues in Language Teaching with 3–12 Year Olds*, London: Bloomsbury Academic, pp. 219–238.

Bourgoin, Renée (2014), 'Inclusionary practices in French immersion: A need to link research to practice', *Canadian Journal for New Scholars in Education*, 5/1: 1–11.

Bruck, Margaret (1985), 'Predictors of transfer out of early French immersion programs', *Applied Psycholinguistics*, 6/01: 39–61.

Burmeister, Petra (2006), 'Immersion und Sprachunterricht im Vergleich', in Manfred Pienemann, Jörg Keßler, and Eckhard Roos (eds), *Englischerwerb in der Grundschule. Ein Studien- und Arbeitsbuch*, Paderborn: Schöningh.

Burmeister, Petra and Massler, Ute (2010), 'Vorwort', in Ute Massler and Petra Burmeister (eds), *CLIL und Immersion: Fremdsprachlicher Sachfachunterricht in der Grundschule*. Braunschweig: Westermann.

Carlson, Stephanie and Meltzoff, Andrew (2008), 'Bilingual experience and executive functioning in young children', *Developmental Science*, 11/2: 282–298.

Clyne, Michael (2002), 'The Use of Community Resources in Immersion', in Petra Burmeister; Thorsten Piske and Andreas Rohde (eds), *An Integrated View of Language Development. Papers in Honor of Henning Wode*, Trier: WVT, pp. 399–408.

Coyle, Do; Hood, Philip and Marsh, David (2010), *CLIL: Content and Language Integrated Learning*, Cambridge: Cambridge University Press.

Cummins, Jim (1979), 'Linguistic interdependence and the educational development of bilingual children', *Review of Educational Research*, 49/2: 222–251.

Cummins, Jim (2000), *Immersion Education for the Millennium: What We Have Learned from 30 Years of Research on Second Language Immersion*, <http://carla.acad.umn.edu/cobaltt/modules/strategies/immersion2000.pdf> [accessed 28 August 2014].

Cummins, Jim (2009), 'Bilingual and immersion programs', in Michael Long and Catherine Doughty (eds), *The Handbook of Language Teaching*, Oxford, UK: Wiley-Blackwell, pp. 159–181.

de Houwer, Annick (2009), *Bilingual First Language Acquisition*, Bristol: Multilingual Matters.

Fortune, Tara (2011), 'Struggling learners and the language immersion classroom', in Diane Tedick, Donna Christian, and Tara Fortune (eds), *Immersion Education. Practices, Policies, Possibilities*, Bristol: Multilingual Matters, pp. 251–270.

García, Ofelia and Baetens Beardsmore, Hugo (2009), *Bilingual Education in the 21st Century: A Global Perspective*, Oxford: Blackwell.

Genesee, Fred (1976), 'The suitability of immersion programs for all children', *The Canadian Modern Language Review*, 32: 494–515.

Genesee, Fred (1987), *Learning through Two Languages: Studies of Immersion and Bilingual Education*, Cambridge: Newbury House.

Genesee, Fred; Tucker, Richard and Lambert, Wallace (1975), 'Communication skills of bilingual children', *Child Development*, 46/4: 1010–1014.

Gerlich, Lydia; Kersten, Holger; Kersten, Kristin; Massler, Ute and Wippermann, Insa (2010), 'Intercultural encounters in bilingual preschools', in Kristin Kersten, Andreas Rohde, Christina Schelletter and Anja Steinlen (eds), *Bilingual Preschools. Vol. I. Learning and Development*, Trier: WVT, pp. 136–76.

Gibbons, Pauline (2009), *English Learners, Academic Literacy, and Thinking: Learning in the Challenge Zone*, Portsmouth, NH: Heinemann.

Hakuta, Kenji (1985), 'Cognitive development in bilingual instruction', in National Clearinghouse for Bilingual Education (ed.), *Issues in English Language Development. Information Exchange*, Rosslyn, VA: Inter-America Research Associates, pp. 63–7.

Hakuta, Kenji and Diaz, Rafael (1985), 'The relationship between degree of bilingualism and cognitive ability: A critical discussion and some new longitudinal data', in Keith Nelson (ed.), *Children's Language*, Hillsdale, NJ: Lawrence Erlbaum Associates, pp. 319–44.

Hakuta, Kenji; Ferdman, Bernardo and Diaz, Rafael (1987), 'Bilingualism and cognitive development: Three perspectives', in Sheldon Rosenberg (ed.), *Advances in Applied Psycholinguistics*, Cambridge: Cambridge University Press, pp. 284–319.

Halsall, Nancy (1994), 'Attrition/retention of students in French immersion with particular emphasis on secondary school', *The Canadian Modern Language Review*, 50: 312–345.

Harley, Birgit (1992), 'Patterns of second language development in French immersion', *Journal of French Language Studies*, 2/02: 159–183.

Harley, Birgit (1998), 'The outcomes of early and later language learning', in Myriam Met (ed.), *Critical Issues in Early Second Language Learning. Building for our Children's Future*, Glenview: Scott Foresman – Addison Wesley, pp. 26–31.

Hughes, Stephen and Madrid, Daniel (2011), 'Synthesis of principles, practices and results', in Daniel Madrid and Stephen Hughes (eds), *Studies in Bilingual Education*, Bern: Peter Lang, pp. 351–63.

Johnson, Robert and Swain, Merrill (1997), *Immersion Education: International Perspectives*, Cambridge: Cambridge University Press.

Kersten, Kristin (2010), 'DOs and DON'Ts bei der Einrichtung immersiver Schulprogramme', in Christiane Bongartz and Jutta Rymarczyk (eds), *Languages Across the Curriculum. Ein Multiperspektivischer Zugang*, Frankfurt am Main: Peter Lang, pp. 71–92.

Kersten, Kristin (2015), 'Bilingual pre-primary schools: Language acquisition, intercultural encounters and environmental learning', in Sandie Mourão and Mónica Lourenço (eds), *Early Years Second Language Education. International Perspectives on Theories and Practice*, London: Routledge.

Kersten, Kristin; Rohde, Andreas; Schelletter, Christina and Steinlen, Anja (2010a), *Bilingual Preschools. Vol. I: Learning and Development*, Trier: WVT.

Kersten, Kristin; Fischer, Uta; Burmeister, Petra; Lommel, Annette; Schelletter, Christina; Steinlen, Anja and Thomas, Shannon (2010b), 'Immersion in primary school: A guide', <http://www.elias.bilikita.org/docs/guidelines_for_bilingual_primary_schools_e.pdf> [accessed 25 September 2013].

Kersten, Kristin; Drewing, Martina; Granados, Jessica; Leloux, Barbara; Lommel, Annette; Schneider, Anke and Taylor, Sarah (2010c), 'How to start a bilingual preschool: Practical guidelines', in Kristin Kersten; Andreas Rohde; Christina Schelletter and Anja Steinlen (eds), *Bilingual Preschools. Vol. II. Best Practices*, Trier: WVT, pp. 77–101.

Kersten, Kristin and Rohde, Andreas (2013a), 'On the road to nowhere?: The transition problem of bilingual teaching programmes from kindergarten to secondary education', in Daniela Elsner and Jörg-Ulrich Keßler (eds), *Bilingual Education in Primary School*, Tübingen: Narr, pp. 93–120.

Kersten, Kristin and Rohde, Andreas (2013b), 'Teaching English to young learners', in Anna Flyman Mattsson and Catrin Norrby (eds), *Language Acquisition and Use in Multilingual Contexts. Theory and Practice*, Lund: Lund University, pp. 107–121.

Kruk, Richard and Reynolds, Kristin (2012), 'French immersion experience and reading skill development in at-risk readers', *Journal of Child Language*, 39/3: 580–610.

Kuchah, Kuchah (2009), 'Early bilingualism in Cameroon: Where politics and education meet' in Janet Enever, Jayne Moon and Uma Raman (eds), *Young Learner English Language Policy and Implementation: International Perspectives*, Reading: Garnet Education, pp. 87–94.

Lamsfuß-Schenk, Stefanie (2007), *Fremdverstehen im bilingualen Geschichtsunterricht: Eine Fallstudie*, Frankfurt am Main: Peter Lang.

Laurén, Christer (1994), *Evaluating European Immersion Programs: From Catalonia to Finland*, Vaasa: Vaasan Yliopisto.

Lazaruk, Wally (2007), 'Linguistic, academic, and cognitive benefits of French immersion', *The Canadian Modern Language Review*, 63/5: 605–628.

Luk, Gigi (2008), *The Anatomy of the Bilingual Advantage in Executive Functions: Levels of Functional Use and Proficiency* Unpublished doctoral dissertation, Toronto: York University.

Lyster, Roy (2004), 'Research on form-focused instruction in immersion classrooms: Implications for theory and practice', *French Language Studies*, 14/3: 321–341.

Marsh, David and Langé, Gisella (eds) (2000), *Using Languages to Learn and Learning to Use Languages*. TIE-CLIL, Ministero della Pubblica, University of Jyväskylä and Milan Istruzione.

Massler, Ute and Ioannou-Georgiou, Sophie (2010), 'Best practice: How CLIL works', in Ute Massler and Petra Burmeister (eds), *CLIL und Immersion. Fremdsprachlicher Sachfachunterricht in der Grundschule*, Hannover: Westermann, pp. 61–76.

Mayer, Mercer (1969), *Frog, Where Are You?*, New York: Dial Books.

Mehisto, Peeter (2011), 'Complexity competence: A tool for co-constructing CLIL', in Daniela Elsner and Anja Wildemann (eds), *Sprachen lernen – Sprachen lehren. Perspektiven für die Lehrerbildung in Europa*, Frankfurt am Main: Peter Lang, pp. 121–41.

Met, Myriam (1994), 'Teaching content through a second language', in Fred Genesee (ed.), *Educating Second Language Children. The Whole Child, the Whole Curriculum, the Whole Community*, Cambridge: Cambridge University Press, pp. 159–82.

Met, Myriam (1999), *Content-Based Instruction: Defining Terms, Making Decisions: NFLC Reports*, Washington, DC: The National Foreign Language Centre <http://www.carla.umn.edu/cobaltt/modules/principles/decisions.html>, [accessed 25 Sep 2013].

Met, Myriam and Lorenz, Eileen (1997), 'Lessons from US immersion programs: Two decades of experience', in Robert Johnson and Merrill Swain (eds), *Immersion Education. International Perspectives*, Cambridge: Cambridge University Press, pp. 243–64.

Möller, Christine (2013), 'Zur Geschichte und Zukunft des bilingualen Unterrichts', in Anja Steinlen and Andreas Rohde (eds), *Mehrsprachigkeit in bilingualen Kindertagesstätten und Schulen. Voraussetzungen-Methoden-Erfolge*, Berlin: Dohrmann Verlag, pp. 14–30.

Nicolay, Anne-Catherine and Poncelet, Martine (2013), 'Cognitive advantage in children enrolled in a second-language immersion elementary school program for three years', *Bilingualism: Language and Cognition*, 16/03: 597–607.

Peal, Elizabeth and Lambert, Wallace (1962), *The Relation of Bilingualism to Intelligence*, Washington, DC: American Psychological Association.

Piske, Thorsten (2006), 'Zur Entwicklung der Englischkenntnisse bei deutschsprachigen Immersionsschülerinnen und –schülern im Grundschulalter', in Norbert Schlüter (ed.), *Fortschritte im frühen Fremdsprachenlernen – Ausgewählte Tagungsbeiträge Weingarten 2004*, Berlin: Cornelsen, pp. 206–212.

Piske, Thorsten (2013), 'Immersion für Kinder mit Lernschwierigkeiten und für Kinder nicht-deutscher Muttersprache: Chance oder Risiko', in Anja Steinlen and Andreas Rohde (eds), *Mehrsprachigkeit in bilingualen Kindertagesstätten und Schulen. Voraussetzungen-Methoden-Erfolge*, Berlin: Dohrmann Verlag, pp. 45–59.

Reeder, Kenneth; Buntain, Jennifer and Takakuwa, Mitsunori (1999), 'Intensity of L2 instruction and biliterate proficiency in the intermediate years of a French immersion program', *Canadian Modern Language Review*, 56/1: 50–72.

Rixon, Shelagh (2015), 'Primary English and critical issues: A worldwide perspective', in Janice Bland (ed.), *Teaching English to Young Learners. Critical Issues in Language Teaching with 3–12 Year Olds*, London: Bloomsbury Academic, pp. 31–50.

Rohde, Andreas (2013), 'Bilinguale Vorschul- und Kindergartenerziehung', in Wolfgang Hallet and Frank Königs (eds), *Handbuch Bilingualer Unterricht. Content and Language Integrated Learning*, Seelze: Klett Kallmeyer, pp. 60–66.

Schöneberger, Christiane (2014), *Grammar Growth in Child L2 German. Investigating DP Development in an Immersion Setting: Unpublished Doctoral Thesis*, University of Cologne: Köln.

Snow, Marguerite (1990), 'Instructional methodology in immersion foreign language education', in Amado Padilla, Halford Fairchild, and Concepcion Valadez (eds), *Foreign Language Education. Issues and Strategies*, Newbury Park, Calif: Sage Publications, pp. 156–171.

Steinlen, Anja; Håkansson, Gisela; Housen, Alex and Schelletter, Christina (2010a), 'Receptive L2 grammar knowledge development in bilingual preschools', in Kristin Kersten; Andreas Rohde; Christina Schelletter and Anja Steinlen (eds), *Bilingual Preschools. Vol. I. Learning and Development*, Trier: WVT, pp. 69–100.

Steinlen, Anja; Neils, Katharina; Piske, Thorsten and Trumpp, Christian (2010b), 'SETK 3-5: A developmental language test on German for 3 to 5-year-old children', in Kristin Kersten; Andreas Rohde; Christina Schelletter and Anja Steinlen (eds), *Bilingual Preschools. Vol. I. Learning and Development*, Trier: WVT, pp. 119–35.

Swain, Merrill (1995), 'Three functions of output in second language learning', in Guy Cook, Barbara Seidlhofer, and Henry Widdowson (eds), *Principle and Practice in Applied Linguistics. Studies in Honour of H. G. Widdowson*, Oxford: Oxford University Press, pp. 125–144.

Swain, Merrill and Johnson, Robert (1997), 'Immersion education: A category within bilingual education', in Robert Johnson and Merrill Swain (eds), *Immersion Education. International Perspectives*, Cambridge: Cambridge University Press, pp. 1–16.

Thomas, Shannon; Burmeister, Petra; Ewig, Michael; Kersten, Kristin and Akerman, Suzanne (2010), 'Green Immersion', in Kristin Kersten; Andreas Rohde; Christina Schelletter and Anja Steinlen (eds), *Bilingual Preschools. Vol. I. Learning and Development*, Trier: WVT, pp. 177–212.

Tomlinson, Brian (2015), 'Developing principled materials for young learners', in Janice Bland (ed.), *Teaching English to Young Learners. Critical Issues in Language Teaching with 3–12 Year Olds*, London: Bloomsbury Academic, pp. 279–293.

Turnbull, Miles; Lapkin, Sharon and Hart, Doug (2001), 'Grade 3 immersion students' performance in literacy and mathematics: Province-wide results from Ontario (1998–99)', *The Canadian Modern Language Review. Special Issue*, 58: 9–26.

Walker, Constance and Tedick, Diane (2000), 'The complexity of immersion education: Teachers Address the Issues', *The Modern Language Journal*, 84/1: 5–27.

Weitz, Martina (2014), *Die Rolle des L2-Inputs in bilingualen Kindergärten. Inputqualität als potentieller Einflussfaktor auf den frühen L2-Erwerb: Identifikation, Beobachtung und Analyse verschiedener Struktur- sowie Prozessvariablen: Unpublished Doctoral Dissertation*, University of Cologne: Köln.

Weitz, Martina; Pahl, Svenja; Flyman Mattsson, Anna; Buyl, Aafke and Kalbe, Elke (2010), 'The input quality observation scheme (IQOS): The nature of L2 input and its influence on L2 development in bilingual preschools', in Kristin Kersten; Andreas Rohde; Christina Schelletter and Anja Steinlen (eds), *Bilingual Preschools. Vol. I. Learning and Development*, Trier: WVT, pp. 5–44.

Wesche, Marjorie (2002), 'Early French immersion. How has the original Canadian model stood the test of time?', in Petra Burmeister, Thorsten Piske and Andreas Rohde (eds), *An Integrated View of Language Development. Papers in Honor of Henning Wode*, Trier: WVT, pp. 357–79.

Wode, Henning (2009), *Frühes Fremdsprachenlernen in bilingualen Kindergärten und Grundschulen*, Braunschweig: Westermann.

Zaunbauer, Anna; Gebauer, Sandra and Möller, Jens (2013), 'Bilinguale Grundschulen: Auswirkungen auf das Sachfachwissen am Beispiel Deutsch und Mathematik', in Anja Steinlen and Andreas Rohde (eds), *Mehrsprachigkeit in bilingualen Kindertagesstätten und Schulen. Voraussetzungen-Methoden-Erfolge*, Berlin: Dohrmann Verlag, pp. 96–106.

5

CLIL Scenarios with Young Learners

Kay Bentley

What is CLIL in young-learner education?

In order to examine content- and language-integrated learning scenarios with young learners, this chapter first opens with a definition of Content and Language Integrated Learning (CLIL), and then provides a brief history related to young-learner CLIL contexts. Key issues at the heart of primary CLIL are explored along with planning and assessment for primary CLIL. This is followed by an examination of the differences between the implementation of CLIL programmes where young learners study curricular subjects through the medium of a non-native language and the emergence of a scenario where sections in primary ELT coursebooks are entitled 'CLIL'. The chapter ends with a description of European CLIL primary scenarios and examples of what teachers of young learners say about teaching CLIL.

The definition of CLIL has evolved since the acronym was first used in 1994 to describe educational practice in European primary and secondary schools 'where teaching and learning take place in an additional language' (Coyle, Hood and Marsh 2010: 3). In Marsh's (2000: 3) introductory text on CLIL, he stated, 'What CLIL can offer to youngsters of any age, is a natural situation for language development which builds on other forms of learning. This natural use of language can boost a youngster's motivation and hunger towards learning languages.' By 2006, CLIL was recognized as 'an innovative methodological approach of far broader scope than language teaching' (Eurydice 2006: 7). What is significant about CLIL is that in the acronym, content was placed before language. This reflects the fact that the subject content determines the choice of language, whether with a lexical, grammatical or functional focus, used to teach subject matter, as well as the language which learners use in order to communicate what they know about curricular content. Language for learning about curricular subjects such as geography or art involves a combination of

- subject-specific vocabulary, for instance sets of lexical items related to habitats or colours

- academic vocabulary in order to, for example, classify and compare animals or types of art

- grammatical categories, for instance, forms of the simple present tense and

- discourse functions, such as giving opinions about a photograph and justifying them: We *think it's an Arctic ecosystem because of the snow and the polar bear. Our group thinks the painting is dark because it's a cloudy day.*

What differentiates primary CLIL from primary English language teaching (ELT) is 'the planned pedagogic integration of contextualised content, cognition, communication and culture into teaching and learning practice' (Coyle et al. 2010: 6).

The rise of CLIL in primary schools

In the decade following 1994, a CLIL approach for young learners was implemented across Europe in a diversity of mainstream and pilot programmes. These include the Ministry of Education and British Council programme in Madrid, 1996, the Madrid Comunidad preschool and primary bilingual programmes for three- to twelve-year-olds from 2004 and a primary CLIL programme promoted by the Ministry in Slovakia in 2003. Furthermore, from 2004 to the present, an increasing amount of research undertaken in primary CLIL classrooms has been published using both quantitative and qualitative data. This research includes findings about CLIL in young-learner contexts from Belgium (Van de Craen, Mondt, Allain and Gao 2007), from Finland (Jäppinen 2008), from the Basque Country, where English is a third language taught through CLIL (Ruiz de Zarobe and Lasagabaster 2010), and from Slovakia (Pokrivčáková 2013). According to Coyle et al. (2010: viii), 'Spain is rapidly becoming one of the European leaders in CLIL practice and research.' This observation applied to both primary and secondary CLIL contexts. In addition to published research related to primary CLIL contexts, an increasing number of CLIL primary coursebooks, several primary CLIL resource books and online materials have been produced for CLIL teachers. But what exactly is a CLIL approach and what are the CLIL-specific challenges surrounding it?

In a CLIL approach, most primary programmes implemented by countries, regions or even at an individual-school level use subject content from the national, regional or school curriculum as a starting point for planning learning outcomes for CLIL courses, modules and lessons. This is the case whether young learners are:

- studying one-third and up to 40 per cent of the curriculum, such as science, social science, art, music or physical education (PE), through the medium of a non-native language, as in Madrid Comunidad

- studying three subjects such as science, art and geography for up to seven hours a week, as in regions of Italy, or

- studying only a module – part of one curricular subject such as PE, maths or music – for 10–12 per cent of the curriculum, as in some primary schools in Catalonia.

In 2013 the Dutch Ministry of Education proposed a new policy which 'allows any primary school to offer up to 15 per cent of their curriculum in a second language, being English, French or German' (Albregt 2014: 24). Primary CLIL is also taught through languages other than English. For example, CLIL through the medium of French is known as EMILE (Enseignement d'une Matière par l'Intégration d'une *Language* Etrangère)

Key Concepts in Primary CLIL

Although CLIL may be implemented in a variety of ways, there are key concepts related to a CLIL approach which should be evident in all primary CLIL lessons. In order to examine some of these concepts, the 4Cs Framework – content, communication, cognition and culture (Coyle 1999) – will be used to exemplify how this framework is helpful in understanding effective CLIL practice. *Content*, or subject knowledge learning, involves knowledge, skills and understanding. *Communication* has been described as 'learning to use language and using language to learn' (Coyle et al. 2010: 54), but what does this mean in practice? For young learners, communication, as in foreign-language lessons, tends to involve more oral than written work at the start of CLIL. However, learners in all CLIL subjects need to produce subject-specific vocabulary: word-level output including chunks and formulaic sequences, then simple sentences to define, describe and comment on subject-specific concepts. Later, as young learners deepen their subject knowledge and language skills, communication is required at text level so that they can develop subject literacy. Examples include giving a sequence of instructions in PE, recounting stages in experiments, describing details in artwork and writing short explanations of how water changes state. At text level, young learners in CLIL contexts need to read and to produce a far wider range of *non-fiction* genres than in EYL contexts where young learners are more likely to focus on songs, poetry, drama and narrative.

Coyle's third 'C', *cognition*, recognizes that for CLIL to be effective, young learners need 'to create new knowledge and develop new skills through reflection and engagement in higher-order as well as lower-order thinking [. . .] whatever their age or ability' (Coyle et al. 2010: 54). CLIL teachers must therefore analyse the cognitive demands of subject tasks to ascertain what kind of thinking is involved: is it lower-order processing such as recalling the names of 2D shapes and identifying them; or is it higher-order processing, such as evaluating how well they have drawn 2D shapes and thinking creatively about how they could make repeated patterns with them? Teachers can then consider the language needed to accomplish each task. Content, communication and cognition are therefore interrelated. The fourth 'C', *culture*, does not refer to learning about topics such as festivals or types of food eaten in different countries, although these may be part of understanding our multicultural world. Rather, in CLIL, culture encompasses 'intercultural understanding and global citizenship' (Coyle et al. 2010: 41) and what it means to be a responsible, respectful citizen with an understanding of self, others and the needs of the planet (see also Driscoll and Simpson 2015, this volume).

A further key concept which is important for effective CLIL practice is how young learners can develop basic interpersonal communicative skills (BICS) as well as cognitive academic language proficiency (CALP) (Cummins 2001: 64). Mostly, young learners are timetabled to have English language lessons in addition to CLIL lessons such as science, geography or art; and in some instances, all three subjects may be connected by one topic area such as 'weather'. To become fluent, young learners need both basic communicative skills in order to collaborate in pair or group work tasks and they also need some academic language to express subject concepts. The former could involve everyday language to turn take, agree or disagree about what types of weather are shown in pictures; the latter, content-obligatory words, phrases and sentences to express knowledge of types of weather and differences in weather.

In addition to the 4Cs Framework, BICS and CALP, another key concept in CLIL, although contentious in some contexts, valid in others, is learners' use of some L1 when they respond. This tends to occur more frequently in the first two years of CLIL programmes. Interaction using both the non-native language mixed with some L1 is considered a 'characteristic of successful CLIL programmes' (Navés 2009: 34). This is because teachers are 'allowing learners to respond in a variety of ways [...] in early stages'. When learners respond using both English and L1, the reason may be that they are attempting to process new subject concepts as well as new subject language. Allowing some switching between languages is believed to be more than translating because it can develop ideas, organize thinking and help learners clarify understanding of new subject knowledge. Researchers document examples of oral code switching in the classroom. For example, from a primary science class with Spanish speakers:

Teacher: This tree is bigger. That tree is smaller.
Pupil: (Under breath) Yes, this tree is *grander*. (checking concept in L1)

And from a primary maths class when it is particularly challenging for primary learners to communicate numbers in a non-native language:

Pupil: I have *veinticinco* (25) *y* I need *dos mas*. [...] I only have
                 veintitres now [...]. I need *dos*! (quoted in García 2009: 7)

CLIL teachers should be aware that there are times during a lesson when young learners are more likely to use both languages and they should plan for this. For example, at the start when activating learners' prior knowledge of subject content, when comparing and contrasting new subject-specific vocabulary as a means of helping learners make links and when conducting a plenary at the end of a lesson to consolidate or check what has been learned. Furthermore, teachers should observe when and why young learners switch languages and understand that learners 'are gradually expected to respond only in the target language once they show enough command of it' (Navés 2009: 34).

Planning and assessment in primary CLIL

Planning for CLIL is complex, takes longer than planning for ELT lessons and causes teachers concern. But planning for CLIL lessons is vital. To quote Miranda and García, two primary CLIL PE teachers, 'teachers were going to cope with new scenarios, [and] planning acquired major importance' (cited in Dafouz-Milne and Guerrini 2009: 34). The 4Cs Framework – content, communication, cognition and culture, as detailed above – is a useful tool for teachers when planning for CLIL. The teachers must first decide on the subject content learning outcomes their pupils are working towards achieving. Plans then focus on choice of a sequence of tasks to achieve the learning outcomes and analysing the cognitive demands of those tasks. Next, plans need to address language input from the teacher, book or digital resources, and this input needs to be linked to learner output. For instance, in an art lesson, are young learners going to talk about primary and secondary colours ('Red and yellow make orange'); are they testing and commenting on mixes of different colours ('This orange paint has got a lot of yellow in it. Let's put more red in it. Look! Now it's dark orange. It's beautiful...') or are they evaluating the effectiveness of different colours they have used in a painting? In addition, support strategies need to be planned so that young learners can communicate in a range of general and academic language appropriate for the curricular subject as well as the age and stage of the young learners. Examples include putting forward ideas about how to solve a number problem, asking questions about a science experiment and expressing uncertainties about how people lived 500 years ago. In addition, in European contexts, CLIL teachers are required to plan for competency-based education, which includes assessment of competences such as digital competence, learning strategies, sociocultural and civic competence, cultural expression and intercultural learning.

A primary CLIL approach promotes learning by doing, active and cooperative learning, which demands development of both communicative and cognitive processes. In general, the higher the cognitive demand of a CLIL task, the more advanced the grammar required for young learners to communicate their knowledge and ideas. For example, although lower-order thinking processes such as recalling parts of a plant require young learners to produce relatively technical vocabulary such as soil, roots, stem, leaves and petals, it may only entail use of the simple present tense. However, when young learners are developing higher-order thinking processes such as analysing and evaluating, for example, the best positions for plants to grow, use of more advanced grammar, such as the modals 'could', 'might' or 'will', is required to talk about possible locations to set up the experiment: 'We could put plant 1 in the cupboard and plant 2 near the window'; 'Plant 3 might grow well on this table'; and to predict outcomes: 'We think plant 2 will grow the most'. In order to achieve tasks such as these, young learners in CLIL contexts are likely to need an abundance of support and 'rich contextual background [...] making language explicit' (Gibbons, 2008: 10). In the plant examples, a visual of a labelled plant, sentence starters or gap-fills such as: 'We think the plant will grow best in/on/next to the _____' can be offered. At a further stage, young learners may need support to describe how a plant grows. This could be in the form of a language frame with time or sequencing connectors so learners can then communicate the explanation of a life cycle with confidence. In CLIL lessons, young learners need to understand the concept of the life cycle of a plant (science content) and they also need to think like scientists by predicting, observing and recording findings of experiments (science content and language). In addition, in effective CLIL teaching, teachers facilitate 'noticing of problematic and relevant language forms [. . . and provide. . .] examples of correct and relevant language forms' (De Graaf, Koopman, Anikina and Westhoff 2007: 609). CLIL primary teachers, however, should avoid 'using error correction procedures typically found in the foreign language lesson or by giving exercises that require the application of language knowledge rather than subject knowledge' (Rowe and Coonan 2012: 3).

Assessment in primary CLIL approaches is inseparable from planning. In other words, when teachers plan content and language-learning outcomes, assessment focuses on how far learners have achieved these outcomes. A common question from CLIL primary teachers is: 'Do we assess content and language or only content?' This question misrepresents the challenges and complexity of CLIL and how assessment works on multiple levels. There may be instances when CLIL teachers do decide to focus on assessing understanding of content only. For example, a music teacher could ask young learners to circle the correct number of beats in a bar after they have listened to some music, or learners doing maths in CLIL could be asked to tick the even numbers in a list. However, if CLIL teachers are expected to develop learners' communicative and cognitive skills and learning strategies, they need to assess these by conducting systematic, formative assessment, in other words, learning-oriented assessment. This sees 'assessment practices as integrated into teaching, and oriented, not towards a statement of level, but towards enhanced learning' (Kiely 2009: 3). In formative assessment, CLIL teachers determine young learners' strengths and weaknesses in their understanding of subject concepts as well as their abilities to communicate those concepts in a non-native language. The challenge for CLIL teachers is evident, as Kiely (2009: 3) explains: 'For example, if a child in a primary-school assessment task in geography performs poorly, is it because of her limited understanding of the geography concepts or details, because she has not understood the question or because she cannot express her understanding clearly?'

In addition, teachers are expected to assess young learners' attitudes towards learning while they monitor content and language learning. Examples of how learners can be assessed in primary CLIL contexts are shown in the tables below. Teachers decide which learners to assess in a particular lesson, and when they see evidence of achievement of the learning outcomes, record a date. Further comments on individual progress can be added post lesson.

Over a school year, teachers should record evidence of progress in achieving CLIL outcomes for each child (see Table 5.1).

Table 5.1 Communicative skills (adapted from Bentley 2010: 86)

Name	Date	Date	Date	Date
Can...				
Respond to closed questions about a science topic?				
Ask closed questions about a science topic?				

Cognitive skills

Name	Date	Date	Date	Date
Can...				
Understand how to add numbers between 10 and 100?				
Evaluate how well he/she can add numbers between 10 and 100?				

Learning to learn

Name	Date	Date	Date	Date
Can...				
Work systematically?				
Cooperate with others in a group?				

Besides teacher assessment, young learners in CLIL lessons should be encouraged to self- and peer-assess as well as review their learning. For example, Spanish learners using *Essential Science 4 Activity Book* (Santillana 2006b) complete 'can do' statements such as: 'I can talk about what plants need.' 'I can classify food into groups.' 'I can name the parts of the digestive system.' 'I can describe how blood circulates around the body' (2006: 2). Young learners who use *The Thinking Lab Science* reflect on subject concepts by summarizing what they have learned about each part of a topic. For example, after learning about elements in a forest, learners do a gap-fill writing task entitled, 'We have learned that... ' and then complete sentences such as, 'A habitat is _____. The forest is a _____ because _____.' (Maldonado Martín, Bergadá Llobet, Carillo Monsó, Jové Roda and Olivares Aguilar 2012: 10). Finally, summative assessment, 'which usually takes place at the end of a school term or school year [...] and may be based on results of internal or external tests, or on a teacher's summative decisions after observations of the child's performance made during the year' (McKay 2006: 22), should contain a range of task types to accommodate needs of different learners rather than, for example, a page of multiple-choice questions.

Different CLIL scenarios

In addition to primary CLIL programmes in which the subject content taught relates directly to the L1 subject curriculum, and where input develops learners' knowledge of cognitively challenging subject concepts, ELT publishers have started including CLIL pages, sections or topics within primary (circa 5–12-year-olds) and lower-secondary (12–14-year olds) English language coursebooks. The aim of this scenario is to encourage English language teachers to use subject materials as a means of helping children and young teenagers learn language through cross-curricular input. The following quotations are from covers of ELT coursebooks which promote CLIL in primary lessons: 'A CLIL feature in every unit, focusing on core subjects such as science and maths' (House and Scott 2012), and in lower-secondary lessons: 'CLIL (Cross-curricular learning) in Maths, Geography, Music, Science and Information Technology' (Puchta and Stranks 2008). However, these CLIL cross-curricular pages and CLIL features are one-off subject topics within a language syllabus, often selected to present grammar such as superlative forms, for example, by comparing famous waterfalls in a primary context, or presenting a biology topic in order to draw a bar chart and then describe the data shown in the form of an informal diary. Such subject concepts presented in ELT coursebooks do not develop learners' understanding of scientific, mathematical, geographical or historical concepts in any depth because they are not expanded upon in later units in the coursebook, nor developed in subsequent levels of the same course. Rather, subject topics are used to stimulate production of accurate and fluent language planned around a grammar syllabus. Input to develop topics from science such as 'food types', from history 'cities old and new', from geography 'geographical features of South America' or from maths 'number challenges' is usually graded according to Common European Framework of Reference for Languages (CEFR) levels. Although these 'CLIL topics' may present subject concepts, they lack the range of subject-specific and academic vocabulary to explore and communicate ideas about science and history to match what young learners would do in subject lessons learned through CLIL.

Table 5.2 illustrates differences between an animal topic for young learners from extracts in an ELT coursebook and the same animal topic presented in a young-learner CLIL science coursebook.

Table 5.2 Comparison of coursebook materials for primary ELT and CLIL

Primary ELT coursebook for 8- to 9-year-old young learners (House and Scott 2012: 43–50)	CLIL science coursebook for 8- to 9-year-old young learners (Santillana 2006a: 14–19)
Topic Title: Amazing Animals	Topic Title: Animals
Sample Tasks	Sample Tasks
1 Look at the pictures (*5 animal photographs*) and answer the questions. What animals do you see? Which of these animals fly?	1 Compare (*4 animal photographs with labels*) How are these animals similar? How are they different? Put the animals into two groups.
2 Sing the song. Listen and point. (*Song about types of animals and body parts*)	2 Read. We can classify animals using different criteria. (*Explanatory text: classification of animals using different criteria with key science vocabulary in bold*)
3 Play a guessing game. Has it got fur? Yes, it has. It's a bear. Yes, it is. (*5 animal photographs*)	3 Look. A fish. The shape of fish helps them to move quickly through water. (*Labeled diagramme of fish*)
4 Listen to the story. (*Story in cartoon form about ants and an anteater*) Find the objects and say the number. (*6 drawings from story*)	4 What do animals eat? Look. (*Photograph of animals*) What is the pony eating? Name three other animals that eat plants? Do dogs eat plants?
5 Listen and say the correct number. (*5 boxes with three numbered cartoon animals in each box*) Play the True or False game Girl A: Bear 1 has got the biggest nose. Girl B: Wrong. Bear 3 has got the biggest nose.	5 Read. (*Explanatory text about herbivores, carnivores and omnivores and two photographs with captions*) Make more sentences. Change the underlined words. Bears are omnivores. (substitution)

Primary ELT coursebook for 8- to 9-year-old young learners (House and Scott 2012: 43–50)	CLIL science coursebook for 8- to 9-year-old young learners (Santillana 2006a: 14–19)
Topic Title: Amazing Animals	Topic Title: Animals
Sample Tasks	Sample Tasks
6 Make questions and ask your classmate. Does an ant live in the sea? Yes, it does. No, it doesn't. *(Substitution table: Does a/an + animal + eat/live + noun or noun phrase)*	6 How are animals born? Look. *(Labeled photographs of 4 animals)* Look at these photos. How do these animals look after their babies?
7 Listen and point. Read the words out loud. *(2 boxes with drawings of 4 words with different final consonant clusters: -nt and –st)*	7 Vertebrates and invertebrates Compare. Match the skeletons to the animals. Are the skeletons similar? *(3 animal photos + 3 labeled skeletons)*
8 Read the sentences. What words can you replace with 'it' or 'they'? *(4 sentences with nouns to substitute with pronouns)*	8 Invertebrates *(4 photographs of invertebrates, labeled insect and three explanatory texts: 1. How invertebrates protect their bodies 2. Insects 3. Insect life)*
9 Use the chart to ask questions and guess the animal. *(10 small animal photographs and binary identification key with yes/no questions)* Choose an animal category and make a poster.	9 Apply your knowledge. Differences between animals What characteristics to those groups of animals have? Decide and tick. Then draw an insect and a fish. *(Lateral identification key – 4 columns with types of animals, 7 rows with facts e.g. They breathe air. – Learners tick boxes.)*
Activity book	Project
Choose two different types of animals and write about them. *(Animal: . . . Type of animal: . . . It lives . . . . . .)*	Project: Animal index cards *(Name of animal: . . . Animal group: . . . Description (what it looks like, size etc.). . . Eating habits (omnivore, carnivore…). . ., Normal habitat (country, type of environment)*
Level 4	Level 4
No further development of animal topic	Learning about life cycles of vertebrates and invertebrates

As Table 5.2 illustrates, the approach to learning about animals is different. In the ELT book, young learners first activate prior knowledge of animal names and animal movements, a task which demands the lower-order cognitive processes of identifying and recalling, while the task in the CLIL book develops the more demanding processes of comparing, contrasting and then classifying. In Tasks 2 and 4 in the ELT book, young learners sing and then read a cartoon about animals. Both activities provide enjoyment while learners are developing listening and reading skills. In Task 2 in the CLIL book, young learners develop reading skills to understand the criteria for classifying animals. The latter is an important skill in science so here learners develop subject literacy. The guessing game in the ELT book presented in Task 3 and the true/false game in Task 5 enable learners to work in pairs in order to develop oral skills while also revisiting topic vocabulary and consolidating production of positive and negative forms of the simple present. In contrast, CLIL Tasks 3, 7 and 8 involve learners in looking at labelled diagrams of a fish, animal skeletons and an insect to understand how they move. Unlike the ELT matching in Task 4, where learners match words from the text with drawings of them in order to check comprehension of vocabulary, in CLIL matching Task 7, learners match animal photographs with skeletons, therefore content knowledge rather than knowledge of the meaning of words is tested. In Tasks 6, 7 and 8 in the ELT book, learners practise accuracy of grammar and lexical items: in Task 6 interrogative, affirmative and negative forms of the present simple are practised; in Task 7 differentiating final consonant clusters in familiar vocabulary is required; in 8 substituting nouns with pronouns is called for. In Task 6, a substitution table is provided to encourage accuracy. In contrast, all CLIL tasks have key science vocabulary written in bold so learners focus on understanding subject-specific words, and in Task 5, the provision of a sentence with underlined nouns and adjectives helps learners understand which words to substitute when they communicate animal facts. Although both books are aimed at learners of the same age and at the same stage of learning, in CLIL Task 4, it is assumed in the question, 'What is the pony eating?', that learners understand the use of the present continuous form.

Further differences are noticeable in the reading tasks. In the ELT unit, apart from the song and story, there is not much text to read and what is presented is written in sentences rather than in paragraphs. However, in the CLIL unit, most reading involves learners in understanding non-fiction explanatory texts. This is more challenging, yet matches what learners would be reading if the science topic were presented in L1. It is noticeable that in Task 9 in both books learners are required to understand and then use an identification key to consolidate learning, but again there are differences.

The key in the ELT book is a binary one with yes/no questions and with all answers provided. Learners simply match answers written in words to pictures of animals. On the other hand, the CLIL book presents a lateral key, which involves reading and then ticking sentences according to criteria given for different animals. In the CLIL task, learners therefore apply their knowledge of a science topic while in the ELT task, learners recall knowledge of animal vocabulary. As with the opening tasks, the cognitive processes demanded by the closing tasks are different: ELT Task 9 demands the lower-order thinking skills of comparing and identifying, while CLIL Task 9 demands the higher-order thinking skills of analysing and applying knowledge. The CLIL thinking task is in fact stated in the rubric: 'Apply your knowledge' and again encourages young learners to think like scientists. The follow-up writing tasks in the ELT activity book and in the CLIL project continue to exemplify the difference between ELT and CLIL: the former demands communication of basic knowledge about animals, the latter requires deeper, more detailed knowledge of them. Finally, Level 4 of the ELT coursebook lacks any topic which builds upon learners' knowledge of animals presented in Level 3, whereas Level 4 of the CLIL book ensures learners will progress to understanding the deeper science topic of life cycles of vertebrates and invertebrates.

CLIL scenarios in Europe

In addition to the considerable differences between CLIL and the ELT subject topics presented primarily as a means of developing language skills, it is widely acknowledged that there are different varieties of CLIL practised around the world. It is also recognized that there is a need for examining these variations to learn from existing practice as well as trying out new ideas to see what can be achieved, even when there is a lack of resources. Four different CLIL young-learner scenarios are therefore presented here to examine variations, practice and resources. CLIL teachers from three of the four scenarios – Lombardy, Madrid Comunidad and Catalonia – teach part of the core L1 subject curriculum through English, while teachers of young learners in Austria 'follow the initiatives of head teachers and staff [... as...] national programmes have not been in operation there yet' (Bärnthaler 2014: 19).

Table 5.3 shows responses from teacher trainers about how primary CLIL is implemented in four different European regions. In the case of Catalonia, only one subject specialism is highlighted from many subjects taught through CLIL in this region.

Table 5.3 Different CLIL scenarios in Europe. The data was kindly provided by teacher trainers Evelin Fuchs (Austria), Catherine Shaw (Italy), Maribel Pareja Moreno (Madrid Comunidad) and Josep Coral (Catalonia).

	Austria: Styria CLIL started in 2009 in Graz	Italy: Lombardy British Council pilot project in six schools from 2009	Spain: Madrid Comunidad CLIL established in 2004	Spain: Catalonia CLIL established in 1999
Who are the teachers? What is the training?	Class teachers with B2 or C1 English level who have done CLIL training in Graz. CLIL teachers with 'good command of English' and class teachers planning and working together without official courses or training.	Generalist primary teachers with minimum B2 English level or English specialists who teach bilingual subjects. One British Council (BC) language assistant in each of the six pilot schools. BC training, in-service sessions and observations.	Primary foreign-language specialists with Linguistic Certificate for bilingual teaching. C1 level of English or an equivalent degree. Training by Comunidad and summer courses to fit the wide needs of primary teachers.	PE (Physical Education) specialist teachers with minimum B2 English level. Training – by Catalan Department of Education and intensive 10-week Primary CLIL course in Britain.
Who are the learners?	6–10-year olds in primary 10–15-year olds in secondary	6–11-year olds	3–12-year olds	9–12-year olds

	Austria: Styria CLIL started in 2009 in Graz	Italy: Lombardy British Council pilot project in six schools from 2009	Spain: Madrid Comunidad CLIL established in 2004	Spain: Catalonia CLIL established in 1999
Which subjects are taught?	Primary: sports, music, arts, science and sometimes some maths. Secondary: mainly sports, biology, geography, music and arts.	Cross-curricular approach combining art, geography, science and literacy. Some schools teach maths, PE or history.	Natural and Social Sciences (geography and history) and at least one other subject from Visual Arts, PE, Music or education for citizenship.	Physical Education. (Most other subjects are also taught through a CLIL approach except Catalan and Spanish languages.)
How many lessons and for how long each week? What % of the curriculum?	No regulations, the teachers decide. For example, some teachers do CLIL 3 to 4 lessons a week. Sometimes teachers decide only to do 1 out of 3 lessons in CLIL.	7–9 hours of Italian curriculum, which is up to 25% of the teaching hours a week.	At least one-third and up to 40% of the curriculum. Lessons are between 45 minutes and 1 hour.	Grades 4–5: three 50-minute lessons a week, i.e. 10% of the curriculum. Grade 6: three 60-minute lessons a week, i.e. 12% of curriculum. Time allocated to CLIL varies from school to school.

	Austria: Styria CLIL started in 2009 in Graz	Italy: Lombardy British Council pilot project in six schools from 2009	Spain: Madrid Comunidad CLIL established in 2004	Spain: Catalonia CLIL established in 1999
What materials are used?	Although there are books on the market, teachers create their own materials and use the internet as a main resource.	Teachers create and share their materials using the internet and key CLIL resource books. Stories and non-fiction texts are used for developing literacy and cross-curricular projects.	Digital resources from Madrid Comunidad and when possible, teachers make and share resources. Publishers' books with extra materials and ideas for using ICT, planning lessons and worksheets.	PE is a hands-on subject but books are used to facilitate communication of integrated motor and language skills. Workbooks provide pre-teaching and scaffolding of new language. Teachers also create materials.
How are learners assessed?	Legislation states students can do exams in German. When exams are in English in secondary schools, the students' command of English isn't assessed, only the content. Some primary teachers use summative and formative assessment, e.g. self-assessment with feedback.	Formative (self and peer) and summative assessment (where content knowledge and language are assessed separately). Teachers design their own tests.	Regional Board of Education evaluates primary students in years 2, 4, 6 through external tests from Trinity College London and Cambridge English Language Assessment. Teachers carry out formative assessment of subject and language learning every term (3 per year).	Self and peer formative assessment of cooperative learning. Summative assessment by teacher of motor, communicative, cognitive, personal and social development. External assessment of PE in CLIL by Catalan Government.

	Austria: Styria CLIL started in 2009 in Graz	Italy: Lombardy British Council pilot project in six schools from 2009	Spain: Madrid Comunidad CLIL established in 2004	Spain: Catalonia CLIL established in 1999
Main challenges for teachers	In primary, command of English and developing materials. The shift from being a language teacher to a content and language teacher. In lower-secondary, materials and time.	Teachers' English level and confidence in their ability. Finding and creating materials (time). Teaching content to children with little or no previous experience of English and who in first year cannot write. Assessment	Introducing new methodology to develop CLIL, e.g. using ICT and implementing cooperative, project-based learning. Taking into account student diversity so they all have the opportunity to meet the demands of CLIL.	Use of balanced tasks that include language and PE without slowing down the pace of a game or a drill. When no book is used, planning and scaffolding tools to achieve motor and language goals.
Main challenges for learners	Code switching at the beginning. 'I haven't seen real challenges for children because they love working in English' (teacher trainer).	Language production and everyday communication. Children in upper primary are strong code-switchers.	Using language such as giving opinions and expressing ideas as well as basic communication. To develop autonomy and curiosity for CLIL.	To articulate difficulties when comprehension is difficult. To incorporate English in oral interaction while playing.

Challenges teachers and learners face in primary CLIL

As can be seen from the table above, there are considerable variables involved in CLIL programmes: who teaches CLIL, subjects learned, how much CLIL is taught, use of formative and summative assessment. However, when the challenges faced by teachers are examined, some similarities appear. These include the difficulties learners face to produce language for CLIL, the lack of appropriate materials and the difficulties teachers have in finding appropriate resources to suit input of subject content in a non-native language as well as content to suit the ages and stages of their learners. It is acknowledged that 'CLIL teachers from around the world [...] require more examples of good teaching practice, more tailor-made teaching materials and more CLIL training' (Pokrivčáková 2013: 69). The lack of materials is a critical matter because it has been found that in CLIL contexts 'there is a clear link between appropriate materials and curriculum and student academic outcome' (Navés 2009: 33). One way forward is to do what the Catalan PE specialist and trainer did, which was to write and publish his own books for PE in primary CLIL, such as *Physical Education Year 5. P.E. World 5* (Coral 2013).

In addition to the challenges CLIL materials present, primary teachers new to CLIL, for example, during their first two years of teaching, generally report challenges related to their own language level. Examples are seen in Table 5.4.

Table 5.4 Challenges reported by primary teachers new to CLIL

CLIL Subject	Challenges: primary teachers new to CLIL
Art	To feel comfortable with my language
Music	Speaking in English for all the lessons
PE	Improving my English for PE
Science	Learn more English and improve my lexis in specific topics
All subjects	Update my level of English for teaching CLIL

However, primary teachers with three or more than three years' experience of teaching CLIL tend to report challenges related to teaching new subject concepts, especially when teaching science in the top grades of primary, as Table 5.5 shows.

Table 5.5 Challenges reported by experienced primary CLIL teachers

CLIL Subject	Challenges: experienced primary CLIL teachers
Art	Some ideas are difficult to explain in English. Pupils have to make an extra effort to understand. It is also much more difficult for them to produce language.
Geography	Getting learners to really understand what they are learning.
Music	We have to know a lot about our subject, have good knowledge of the content and how to teach it.
Science	Teaching science in upper levels because the content is more difficult and intense.
Science	Because of the difficult content, pupils don't have a clear idea of some concepts. Many are difficult to explain.
Science	Making an effort to translate and explain ideas clearly and accurately so pupils can understand new concepts in a foreign language.
All subjects	To know a lot about our subjects, to have good knowledge of the content and the methodology we use.

It is evident that teachers with longer experience of CLIL are less concerned about their own language levels for teaching CLIL subjects and more concerned about how to teach tricky subject concepts. Teachers' feedback on their experiences of teaching CLIL to young learners has an important implication for training. English language specialists know which areas of grammar are tricky for young learners, such as understanding and producing the continuous aspect and modal verbs, and most trainers can demonstrate a range of scaffolding strategies to show teachers how to support students in acquiring new language. But, it is vital that CLIL trainers and teacher educators also know which are the tricky subject concepts in each subject area and at what stage to teach them. Deep knowledge of subject content, especially in upper primary and lower secondary levels, is essential not only to develop learners' understanding of content but also to help develop learners' subject literacy across the curriculum. But what is also evident is the 'generally positive attitude of teachers and learners towards CLIL' (Pokrivčáková 2013: 69).

In conclusion, as a result of acknowledgement that CLIL can play a central role in education for the twenty-first century, and because of the increased demand for CLIL primary teachers in Europe and elsewhere, it is essential that teachers start teaching CLIL with knowledge and understanding of key concepts associated with a CLIL approach as well as knowledge of how to teach tricky subject concepts and that they have the language competence to do this. Teachers will also benefit from being aware of a range of CLIL scenarios so they can learn from other countries, other regions and other CLIL colleagues, can share materials and consider ways to assess CLIL in different primary contexts. Through achieving these goals, teachers' motivation and enthusiasm for teaching CLIL will be boosted.

References

Albregt, Frank (2014), 'CLIL Country Profile, Netherlands', in *CLIL Policy and Practice: Competence-Based Education for Employability, Mobility and Growth*, Italy: British Council, p. 24.

Bärnthaler, Andreas (2014), 'CLIL Country Profile, Austria', *CLIL Policy and Practice: Competence-Based Education for Employability, Mobility and Growth*, Italy: British Council, p. 19.

Bentley, Kay (2010), *The TKT Course CLIL Module*, Cambridge: Cambridge University Press.

Coral, Josep (2013), *Physical Education Year 5. P.E. World 5, Student's Book*. Zaragoza: Edelvives.

Coyle, Do (1999), *Content and Language Integrated Learning Motivating Learners and Teachers*, Nottingham: University of Nottingham. <http://blocs.xtec.cat/clilpractiques1/files/2008/11/slrcoyle.pdf> [accessed 23 March 2014].

Coyle, Do; Hood, Philip and Marsh, David (2010), *CLIL*, Cambridge: Cambridge University Press.

Cummins, Jim (2001), *Negotiating Identities: Education for Empowerment in a Diverse Society*, Los Angeles: Californian Association for Bilingual Education.

Dafouz-Milne, Emma and Guerrini, Michelle (2009), *CLIL across Educational Levels*, Madrid: Richmond.

De Graaf, Rick; Koopman, Gerrit Jan; Anikina, Yulia and Westhoff, Gerard (2007), 'An observation tool for effective L2 pedagogy in Content and Language Integrated Learning', *International Journal of Bilingual Education and Bilingualism*, 10/5: 603–624. <http://www.unifg.it/sites/default/files/allegatiparagrafo/20-01-2014/de_graaff_et_al_an_observation_tool_for_effective_l2_pedagogy_in_clil.pdf> [accessed 5 September 2014].

Driscoll, Patricia and Simpson, Helen (2015), 'Developing intercultural understanding in primary schools', in Janice Bland (ed.), *Teaching English to Young Learners. Critical Issues in Language Teaching with 3–12 Year Olds*, London: Bloomsbury Academic, pp. 167–182.

Eurydice (2006), Content and Language Integrated Learning (CLIL) at School in Europe.

García, Ofelia (2009), *Reimagining Bilingualism in Education for the 21st Century*, NALDIC Conference Keynote Presentation. <http://www.naldic.org.uk/Resources/NALDIC/Professional%20Development/Documents/NQ7.2.3.pdf> [accessed 30 March 2014].

Gibbons, Pauline (2008), 'More than just good practice', *NALDIC Quarterly*, 6/2 <http://www.naldic.org.uk/Resources/NALDIC/Professional%20Development/Documents/NQ6.2.3.pdf> [accessed 2 August 2014].

House, Susan and Scott, Katharine (2012), *English Ladder, Pupils Book 3*, Cambridge: Cambridge University Press.

Jäppinen, Aini Kristiina (2008), 'Thinking and content learning of mathematics and science as cognitional development in CLIL: Teaching through a foreign language in Finland', *Language and Education*, 19/2: 148–168. <http://www.tandfonline.com/doi/abs/10.1080/09500780508668671#preview> [accessed 31 March 2014].

Kiely, Richard (2009), *CLIL – The Question of Assessment*. <http://www.developingteachers.com/articles_tchtraining/clil1_richard.htm> [accessed 2 August 2014].

Maldonado Martín, Natàlia; Bergadá Llobet, Rosa; Carrillo Monsó, Núria; Jové Roda, Lídia and Olivares Aguilar, Pilar (2012), *The Thinking Lab Ecosystems: Keeping the Balance*, Madrid: Cambridge University Press.

Marsh, David (2000), *Using Languages to Learn and Learning to Use Languages*. <http://www.tieclil.org/html/products/pdf/%201%20UK.pdf> [accessed 30 March 2014].

McKay, Penny (2006), *Assessing Young Language Learners*, Cambridge: Cambridge University Press.

Navés, Teresa (2009), 'Effective Content and Language Integrated Learning (CLIL) programmes', in Yolanda Ruiz de Zarobe and Rosa Maria Jiménenz Catalán (eds), *Content and Language Integrated Learning*, Bristol: Multilingual Matters.

Pokrivčáková, Silvia (2013), *CLIL Research in Slovakia*, Hradec Králové: University of Hradec Králové Press.

Puchta, Herbert and Stranks Jeff (2008), *More! 2 Student's Book*, Cambridge: Cambridge University Press.

Rowe, Jan and Coonan Mary (2012), *Some Foreign Language Issues in Primary CLIL: The teacher's voice*, International Conference The Future of Education. <http://www.pixel-online.org/edu_future/common/download/Paper_pdf/ITL08-Coonan.pdf> [accessed 5 September 2014].

Ruiz de Zarobe, Yolanda and Lasagabaster, David (eds) (2010), *CLIL in Spain: Implementation, Results and Teacher Training*, Cambridge: Cambridge Scholars Publishing.

Santillana (2006a), *Essential Science*, Madrid: Santillana Educación.

Santillana (2006b), *Essential Science 4 Activity Book*, Madrid: Santillana Educación.

Van de Craen, Piet; Mondt, Katrien; Allain, Laure and Gao, Ying (2007), 'Why and how CLIL works. An outline for a CLIL theory', *Vienna English Working Papers, CLIL Special Issue 2*, 6/3: 70–78. <http://www.multilingualresearchunit.be/wp-content/uploads/2013/06/Viewz2007.pdf> [accessed 21 June 2014].

6

Task-Based Learning with Children

Annamaria Pinter

Introduction

Task-based learning in different variations has become very popular indeed all over the world in English language teaching although often there is 'a gap between pedagogic policy and classroom practice' (Garton, Copland and Burns 2011: 6). Task-based language learning is regarded as more meaningful, more communicative and more purposeful than 'traditional' learning that relies on mechanical exercises, rote learning and the PPP (Presentation/ Practice/Production) lesson structure. In task-based lessons learners are likely to engage with the learning materials more enthusiastically and thus develop their language skills more efficiently. Although there is a growing body of research about task-based learning for younger learners, most of what has been written about language tasks concerns adult learners, so we still know very little about how children of different ages in different formal or informal learning contexts engage with and benefit from language tasks and how these tasks are actually used in classrooms. This chapter aims to review what we know from both research and practice about the benefits of task-based language learning with children. The chapter also discusses task design issues for young learners and highlights ways in which tasks may be incorporated into language classrooms. The chapter concludes with issues and priorities for future research.

Research tasks and younger learners

Language-learning tasks have been defined and used in various different ways both in the more practical teacher development literature and in the academic research literature (e.g. Skehan 1996, Ellis 2003, Nunan 2004, Willis and Willis 2007, Samuda and Bygate 2008). Language-learning tasks, historically, grew out of the communicative language teaching approach (the CLT approach) and thus they share concerns with CLT about the importance of meaning, genuine communication and real-life-like experiences in the classroom. Tasks are often contrasted with more rigid language exercises that lack tangible purpose and appeal. The underlying principle behind both CLT and task-based learning is that authentic learner interaction, motivated engagement and purposefulness are important in making progress in language learning. Kumaravadivelu (2006: 66) suggests that tasks are in fact an 'offset of CLT'. Samuda and Bygate (2008: 69) in their comprehensive overview of definitions conclude that a task is 'a holistic activity which engages language use in order to achieve some non-linguistic outcome while meeting a linguistic challenge, with the overall aim of promoting language learning through process or product or both.'

For example, a typical task might be to find five differences between two similar pictures. Learner A has a version of a picture and Learner B has the same picture but with five differences. They cannot look at each other's pictures but instead by describing them and asking and answering questions about them, they jointly identify the five differences. This is a classic speaking task that involves two-way communication and it has a clear non-linguistic goal, which is to find the differences and solve the puzzle. If it is played in a classroom where several pairs of students are carrying it out at the same time, it can be set up as a competitive task. There will be a winning pair, those who are the first to identify the five differences correctly.

Within SLA research, tasks have been used as elicitation tools for data collection to answer questions about features of talk that emerge as a result of using certain types of tasks. Researchers have used tasks to explore how speakers negotiate meaning when there is a communication breakdown, or how they compensate for gaps in their knowledge by employing different communication strategies, such as compensatory strategies. Those researchers interested in language processing have looked at how learners' L2 fluency, accuracy and linguistic complexity might be affected when working with different types of tasks. Such research is also aimed at identifying patterns in learners' output related to different types of language tasks. One popular area within this research domain is exploring the effect of planning time and task repetition. Given the opportunity to repeat a task or to have some time to plan what one is going to say is likely to enhance the performance, for example, in terms of the speaker's fluency, grammar or choice of words and phrases.

Much of this adult-focused research is conducted in the psycholinguistic tradition (see e.g. Bygate 1999, Skehan and Foster 1999) focusing on large numbers of participants and often comparing several tasks, or examining the effect of particular variables such as planning time, interlocutor type or learners' familiarity with the task. These studies report trends and general patterns based on large data sets, using statistical analyses, and they do not focus on the unique features of individual performance. On the other hand, sociocultural perspectives reject the idea that tasks determine patterns of output but instead they emphasize how individuals approach and make sense differently of the same task. These studies are more qualitative in nature and are focused on fewer learners. In this qualitative research tradition, tasks have been used to explore the nature of collaborative dialogue that emerges from task-based interactions as learners work together on joint problem-solving tasks, talking through aspects of language they are not sure about, scaffolding each other's output or externalizing their knowledge for consolidation (e.g. Ohta 2001, Swain and Lapkin 2003).

Most published studies with children in the domain of English as a second language (ESL) in the task-based literature have been an extension of adult studies and have tended to focus on children's abilities to negotiate meaning on classic gap tasks. All these studies have confirmed that ESL children are able to work with and benefit from tasks even though the exact benefits may be different from adults. For example, Oliver (1998, 2002) compared the interactions of children (aged eight to thirteen) and adult dyads (pairs) and found that they differed in the number of negotiation strategies that were used. Young learners employed far fewer comprehension checks than did adults and tended to rely heavily on self- and other-repetition. This was interpreted as a developmental effect, in that young learners might be more concerned with constructing their own meaning than clarifying meaning for their partner. In Oliver's studies the children employed a variety of negotiation strategies. Non-native speaker pairs (NNS–NNS) produced more clarification requests than their native speaker–non-native speaker (NS–NNS) counterparts and more occurrences of negotiation of meaning in NNS–NNS dyads were found than in NS–NNS dyads. This was because in the NS–NNS dyads the NS were considered to be 'experts' whereas in NNS–NNS dyads children saw each other as joint problem solvers. In another study Mackey, Oliver and Leeman (2003) found that twenty-four dyads of young ESL learners (NNS–NNS pairs) produced significantly more modified output than the twenty-three adult NNS–NNS pairs. This means that when they negotiated meaning with each other not only did they manage to overcome the communication breakdown but on top of that they also corrected each other, which led to improved/modified language output. Also, the amount of negative feedback and the opportunities to use feedback were comparable between the two groups, suggesting that children were able to modify their output by directly making use of feedback from their peers.

In some studies adult interlocutors interacted with children using various tasks. Mackey and Oliver (2002) studied twenty-two young ESL learners (aged eight to twelve) interacting in dyads with adult NS, performing five different communication tasks. Their results indicated that young learners who were provided with interactional feedback, in other words the adult NS reformulated input and targeted new language at the children's specific needs, showed greater improvement in English question formation than those who interacted with the adults but did not receive such targeted feedback. This study was replicated in Singapore by Mackey and Silver (2005) with twenty-six young Chinese learners (aged six to nine) and reported similar positive results between the provision of interactional feedback and L2 development of question forms.

Just like in the literature on adult students, different variables that are likely to influence the task-based performance are often isolated and placed under scrutiny in an experimental research design. Such a variable is, for example, familiarity with task content. In Mackey, Kanganas and Oliver's study (2007: 306) children were shown to be willing to take more linguistic risks when they were familiar with the content of a task. They negotiated more meaning and produced more modified output when working with familiar tasks, as opposed to new, unfamiliar tasks. While this literature on task-based learning, which is largely based on experimental studies with ESL as opposed to EFL children, is immensely informative, findings will have to be taken cautiously when interpreted for EFL contexts where language levels and exposure to English are very different indeed.

Some more qualitative studies have also been undertaken indicating that children are able to scaffold/support each other in dialogic tasks even in EFL contexts but such peer-scaffolding differs from teacher–learner scaffolding (e.g. Guk and Kellogg 2007). In another study Pinter (2005) showed that Hungarian ten-year-old children were able to support each other with peer-correction at a very low level of competence and they also got better at paying attention to each other through repeating versions of a 'spot the differences' task. Similarly, in a Canadian ESL classroom (Gagne and Parks 2013), Grade 6 children were observed providing varied scaffolding to peers as they worked with cooperative tasks such as jigsaw tasks.

Pedagogic tasks and young learners

The discussion has so far been focused on academic research on tasks as elicitation tools which serve as a means of data gathering. Teachers, of course, are mostly concerned with tasks as vehicles for meaningful learning and practice in classrooms. While in reality these two orientations need not be in opposition with one another, many writers find it useful to differentiate between research tasks (as elicitation tools in research) and pedagogic tasks as 'workplans' (Ellis 2003) that teachers plan and implement in order to challenge traditionally PPP-oriented structures of teaching. Task-based sessions are usually broken into three stages: pre-task, during task and post-task phases. According to Willis (1996) the pre-task phase is devoted to an initial exploration of the topic. The teacher might pre-teach some new language or play a recording of others doing the task. Then the main task phase contains different sub-phases, such as the students working in pairs or groups solving a problem and then putting a report together for the whole class to listen to. Finally, in the post-task phase there is a focus on form and some language analysis and awareness raising about language structures that emerged as problematic during the task phase. Different authors describe the task cycle slightly differently and offer different frameworks for task types (see e.g. Nunan 2004).

One popular framework is that proposed by Willis and Willis (2007). In addition to specifying text-based tasks, Willis and Willis (2007) talk about generating tasks based on topics such as 'Travel' or 'Pets'. The following types of tasks are suggested: listing, ordering and sorting, matching, comparing, problem solving, sharing personal experience, project and creative tasks. The authors suggest that a particular topic might run for several lessons and will involve a sequence of different tasks. The task cycle described earlier may take shape based on a concrete topic: 'Volcanoes'. The teacher might start by showing some pictures of volcanoes and eliciting personal comments from the class about their experience and their knowledge about volcanoes. Then subsequent tasks might involve *listing* features of volcanoes, *labelling* a cross-section of a volcano, then *comparing* different volcanoes, *making quizzes* about them or *writing creative stories* about them. Task-based teaching always begins with a preparation and priming pre-task phase (where the teacher introduces the topic, and sometimes new vocabulary), then during the target task phase the learners undertake tasks such as a class survey or a project, and finally, there is an opportunity to reflect and focus on form. Such delayed focus on form is argued to be more beneficial than focusing on form upfront, since the learners can see how the need arose for the use of those forms and the language is both contextualized and personalized.

One way to think about classroom tasks/pedagogic tasks for young learners is that they can be the same as those designed for adults. For example, the above-mentioned Willis and Willis (2007) categories can be used in children's classrooms as well with appropriate content. Cameron (2001: 32), writing about tasks for young learners, recommends a three-stage approach, as recommended with adult learners. Task implementation for children involves the pre-task phase, the target task phase and the follow-up phase, but Cameron also stresses the need to balance 'task demands' and 'task supports'. The difference between task demands and task supports is the space for growth and opportunity to learn (Cameron 2001: 22–25).

Cameron (2001) further highlights that tasks for children should have coherence and unity, meaning and purpose, a clear language-learning goal, a beginning and an end, and they should involve the learners actively. Legutke, Müller-Hartmann and Schocker-von Ditfurth (2009: 38–43) similarly suggest that tasks for children should be challenging, should promote active, playful and creative participation, and confidence and willingness to take risks. Tasks may have the potential to contribute to developing learners' autonomy and responsibility through choice and repetition. Tasks for children will also integrate different language skills. In addition to the four skills (speaking, listening, reading and writing) other activities might include miming, role playing, drawing, cutting out and crafting. Legutke et al. illustrate these task characteristics with an example where a teacher introduces a picturebook to a class of young learners (see Mourão 2015b, for an extensive discussion of the potential and challenges of picturebooks with young learners).

More fluid pedagogic tasks for children are often reminiscent of language games. Indeed studies that have explored games with children also report higher levels of engagement and motivation and they emphasize the importance of the primacy of meaning over form and a genuine purpose. In one recent study, Dourda, Bratitsis, Griva and Papadopoulou (2014) examine a complex online game where young learners in a CLIL (content and language integrated learning) classroom in Greece work together to solve a set of problems. As they play the game and look for clues, they come across phrases that they can make sense of in context, and because of the repetitive nature of game-playing moves, they have a good chance of learning some new language. They progress to higher and higher levels in the game over the course of several lessons. The study indicates that the children are deeply engaged and motivated, which is always an aim when working with tasks. Complex online games are difficult to incorporate into everyday teaching, but even a simple, everyday game such as the well-known 'Simon says' (a Total Physical Response game suitable for the youngest children where they follow instructions and mime actions but only if the instruction was prefaced by the words 'Simon says') displays features of a communicative task in that the game is meaning focused, there is a clear goal that is non-linguistic (the aim is to try not to be caught out) and yet it provides useful language practice in listening and following instructions, from very basic to potentially quite complex (see Bland 2015c: 229).

Van Gorp and Bogaert (2006: 82) suggest that learners need motivation to invest their energies in a task; in other words, tasks need to inspire young learners to work with the language. The challenge is to design tasks that children want to complete: learners work in groups and try to work out solutions to problems that interest them. For example, Van Gorp and Bogaert mention that mysterious problem-solving tasks might be attractive to children, such as 'Strange footprints have been found near a bed of lettuce. Someone has eaten the lettuce. Do the footprints belong to a mole?' (2006: 83).

Another idea is to embed tasks within a story, such as, for example, transporting children into various periods of history and getting them to solve a puzzle in each historical era. While the tasks are motivating and fun, they also link to target curricular goals. Since the language use grows out of the puzzle or the problem, learning happens by confronting gaps between the young learners' existing linguistic repertoire and what emerges as a need/gap while talking about the puzzle with others. Different learners may run into different challenges and in small groups there may be a wide array of opportunities for each learner to benefit from this type of task work. Tasks like these inherently elicit interaction and feedback, and peers can add to each other's motivation to tackle the task. Peers can also act as sounding boards for ideas and opinions and can push their partners to produce cognitively and linguistically modified, better-quality output. Van Gorp and Bogaert (2006: 97) also note that the roles that children take up, their relative status in the group, their personalities, the extent to which they are willing to cooperate and support each other and their interpretation of the task are so influential that the same task performance in two different groups always results in two different stretches of interaction. So, consequently, the teacher's role in monitoring and facilitating the task-based work is essential.

Task demands and difficulty

How should teachers select tasks for their learners? What challenges or demands are hidden in different tasks? These could be linguistic demands, social demands, cognitive or metacognitive demands. Does the task require, for example, that two learners work together and exchange information? If yes, at least two issues seem important. Do the children have relevant language to activate in order to communicate their content and do they have the required maturity as speakers to package their information, listen carefully to their partner and monitor the task performance? Children should be able to ask themselves questions like this: Do I understand what my partner is saying? Should I check/ask the same question again if I did not quite understand what was said? What is important information and what is not? How do we know we are doing well so far with this task? What do we do if we get stuck?

Robinson (2001: 30) discusses three different types of difficulties with tasks. The first group of variables relates to cognitive factors and these refer to attentional, reasoning and memory demands. The more complex the information you need to remember and justify, for example, the harder the task. Task difficulty is also related to how much practice children may have with a task. If you repeat the same task several times or get time dedicated for planning, the task becomes easier and more familiar.

The second category of difficulties comprises interactive factors such as whether the task is closed or open (i.e. there is only one answer versus various answers), two-way or one-way (i.e. both partners talk or only one partner talks and the other one listens) and what the relationship is like between the learners. In the case of children, one consequence of this is that friends who are comfortable with each other and who can work with a familiar task will find their experience easier.

The final category of difficulties includes confidence, motivation, anxiety, intelligence, aptitude and cognitive style. These are learner attributes that are hard to change; thus, an anxious, less-motivated learner will find the same task harder than a learner who is relaxed, happy and confident, ready to take risks. This is why teachers of young learners need to cultivate a positive and relaxing learning environment in order to reduce the possibility of negative attitudes.

When designing or selecting tasks, teachers need to analyse which features of the task represent specific difficulties, and whether it might be necessary or possible to adapt the task so that the children are better supported. For example, many speaking tasks, such as 'telling a story' or 'describe and draw' tasks, require a good grasp of referencing, which means differentiating carefully between various items or elements in the task (Yule 1997: 38). If the story is about a group of people or animals, it will be important to make reference to them in a way that is unambiguous to the listener as to which character is being talked about. But even in a simple 'spot the differences' task, it is important to locate and refer to an item correctly, especially if there are several similar items within the picture. During the task performance it is also important to monitor progress strategically depending on the task demands. A whole set of basic social skills (such as how to work well in pairs, how to listen to one another, how to ask for clarification, how to collaborate) is also necessary for most pair and small group tasks, and typically younger children need a great deal of support with these challenges.

Table 6.1 summarizes some inherent difficulties in four classic tasks and Table 6.2 suggests possible ways in which the task can be made easier.

Table 6.1 Examples of difficulties in four tasks

TASK 1 *Spot the differences*	TASK 2 *Write a story together*	TASK 3 *Describe and draw*	TASK 4 *Tell a story based on pictures*
Find five differences between the two pictures (A and B) of the same castle. You can talk together but cannot look at each other's pictures.	Listen to a story and take notes. Then together with your friend, reproduce the story as close to the original as possible.	Learner A draws a picture of a playground but does not show it to learner B. Learner B asks questions so that he/she can reproduce the same picture.	Look at the five pictures and tell the story.
A two-way gap task	A collaborative writing task (dictogloss)	A one-way gap task	A monological task
Difficulties:	Difficulties:	Difficulties:	Difficulties:
• Establishing what the other learner has or does not have. • Asking clarification questions and insisting on accuracy. • Realizing that the differences need to be carefully tallied.	• Brainstorming content and language together. • Listening to and evaluating each other's ideas. • Making decisions about who is writing, what to look up in the dictionary and what to ask the teacher. • Working through a draft. • Noticing mistakes and making improvements.	• Describing the picture in sufficient detail so that the listener can make sense of it. • Sorting out misunderstandings, e.g. by paraphrasing. • Listening carefully and responding to questions. • Using effective communication strategies to compensate for lack of language.	• Setting the scene and introducing the characters. • Structuring the plot step by step, making sure there is a beginning, a middle and an ending. • Judging the right amount of information required from the listener's point of view.

Table 6.2 Examples of support/adaptation in the four tasks

TASK 1 *Spot the differences*	TASK 2 *Write a story together*	TASK 3 *Describe and draw*	TASK 4 *Tell a story based on pictures*
Find five differences between the two pictures (A and B) of the same castle. You can talk together but cannot look at each other's pictures.	Listen to a story and take notes. Then together with your friend, reproduce the story as close to the original as possible.	Learner A draws a picture of a playground but does not show it to learner B. Learner B asks questions so that he/she can reproduce the same picture.	Look at the five pictures and tell the story.
A two-way gap task	A collaborative writing task (dictogloss)	A one-way gap task	A monological task
Support/adaptation: • Include fewer differences. • Include fewer items and thus less referential challenge. • Remind the children to search systematically. • Remind the children to count the differences.	Support/adaptation: • Provide some notes from the oral storytelling. • Brainstorm some key phrases from the story as a whole class activity. • Check first drafts and give feedback. • Discuss good strategies together before writing begins. • Provide dictionaries. • Get children to work in bigger groups first to share writing plans.	Support/adaptation: • Specify how many items the picture needs to contain. • Specify the level of detail needed in locating items. • Remind children of key clarification questions they can use. • Take out location and just include isolated numbered items.	Support/adaptation: • Brainstorm main ideas and phrases together as a class. • Put the pictures in the correct order. • Use fewer pictures. • Provide a skeleton text. • Give planning time. • Get children to plan in pairs or groups. • Use a story with a simple plot and fewer characters.

While it is important for teachers to think carefully about the difficulties tasks entail, it is also important not to underestimate what children can do in contexts that make sense to them even with very little language. Some research suggests that task-based learning is in fact possible with children who are complete beginners and thus have no knowledge of L2 at all. A study conducted with six-year-old Japanese children with no prior knowledge of English (Shintani 2012) indicates that meaning-focused input-based tasks (such as 'listen and do' tasks) are possible to implement at very low levels of proficiency and indeed children learn new language effectively if the task is repeated and thus allows for multiple exposure to the same language/language chunk. In Shintani's study the teacher used a mixture of Japanese and English (L1/L2) to give the instructions to begin with and then gradually reduced the use of L1 as the children began to be able to respond to the task, first non-verbally and then with some basic unanalysed L2 chunks (Shintani 2012).

Teachers and task-based learning

Tasks, although extremely popular with teacher educators and widely recommended, can also be a source of concern for teachers. Butler (2011) reports that in Asian classrooms, where large classes are the norm, teachers lack confidence to work with tasks. In addition, when children see little relevance of English to their own lives with hardly any opportunities for real interactions outside classrooms, engaging with genuine communication and experiencing authentic language practice are often less attractive than in ESL contexts.

Deng and Carless (2009) explored the extent to which primary English teachers' practice in China reflected principles of task-based language teaching (TBLT) and they found very limited evidence of task-based practice. Teachers are not in favour of it, and task-based teaching is perceived as too complicated. Butler (2011) comments that TBLT remains an unresolved issue in many parts of Asia, for example, because it is difficult to reconcile it with the exam culture.

Carless (2002, 2004) explored the implementation of TBLT in Hong Kong elementary schools and identified some common problems in classrooms where teachers were implementing task-based learning. These issues include difficulties in maintaining discipline during the task cycle, learners' excessive use of their mother tongue and a large variety across the board in terms of production of the target language. Teachers did not truly believe in task benefits and did not fully understand tasks. There were serious time constraints in the timetable and some teachers therefore did not even attempt time-consuming tasks or tasks that did not match the more traditional textbooks. Many teachers also stated that there were no adequate resources in their schools to plan for task-based teaching. In a further paper Carless (2009) suggests that perhaps it might be advisable to productively combine PPP and TBLT in a way that teachers can minimize the limitations that PPP may have, instead of completely dismissing it. This is a measured and balanced suggestion that takes into account the social realities of particular contexts.

Future directions: Context and technology

Most current EFL materials incorporate some form of task-based learning or games for children. In some current course materials online activities are becoming common. For example, children might be asked to select a picture and describe it by recording their own voice and upload this spoken performance to a website (e.g. *Fotobabble*). This is a meaningful monologic task that is highly motivating because children can choose their own pictures and they describe something that is personally relevant and meaningful to them. Before uploading the spoken text file, children are likely to practise their monologues several times to be able to upload a polished version. When all children in the class have uploaded their descriptions, a further sub-task may be for each learner to choose two to three favourite descriptions and give feedback to peers. This is purposeful and meaningful learning with a clear goal and since individual choices are made, the task is also motivating.

Information and Communication Technology (ICT) and online materials offer some new ways in which children can learn from tasks. In fact recent research (Pellerin 2014) suggests that even very young learners are able to make use of advanced ICT technology in classrooms and can create their own meaningful tasks. Pellerin (2014: 4) suggests that 'the issue of task-based language learning linked with the use of these new touch screen and mobile technologies in the primary language classroom (children aged 5–12) is very much under-explored'. Individual tasks created by children represent a more dynamic concept of task and authenticity. An example cited by Pellerin is a task that two Grade 1 learners initiated while playing with their puppets. They acted out a dialogue using the puppets and then decided to record their puppet show on the class tablet computer. Other children liked this idea so they took turns to record different puppet shows which then generated meaningful and truly authentic practice, and served as authentic listening material for the entire class. The whole experience increased their motivation, and the frequent listening and viewing allowed these children to have some rich language practice, but also to begin to reflect on their own strengths and weaknesses as learners. Seeing yourself on the screen can provide that distance you need to enhance reflective skills. Handling the tablet computer and being able to make original recordings also gives children some control over their learning. Once young learners have ownership and control over a task, they will be motivated to invest into it.

More research is needed in the future with children as task users and even task creators in language classrooms, especially in EFL classrooms. More empirical evidence is also needed through longitudinal studies about how tasks of all kinds actually work, what language output they help to activate and what children feel or think about them. The majority of task research has targeted task outcomes as a result of design and much less has been done about the context of unique classrooms where task performances are shaped by the interaction between task and context. In this respect Batstone (2012) calls for a more context-embedded approach to TBLT, documenting what actually happens to task performances over long periods of time, across several lessons and units of learning. Research has started to explore what teachers know and think about tasks but we know virtually nothing about children's own views and interpretations of tasks. Some new innovative methodologies are needed to tackle this since children's perspectives are lacking in EFL/ESL (Pinter 2014). For example, we need research into children's insights about what tasks they enjoy and why, how they collaborate using different interactive tasks and what they think they can learn from them.

References

Batstone, Rob (2012), 'Language form, task-based language teaching, and the classroom context', *ELT Journal*, 66/4: 459–467.

Bland, Janice (2015c), 'Drama with young learners', in Janice Bland (ed.), *Teaching English to Young Learners. Critical Issues in Language Teaching with 3–12 Year Olds*, London: Bloomsbury Academic, pp. 219–238.

Bygate, Martin (1999), 'Task as the context for the framing, re-framing and unframing of language', *System*, 27: 33–48.

Butler, Yuko Goto (2011), 'The implementation of communicative and task-based language teaching in the Asia-Pacific region', *Annual Review of Applied Linguistics*, 31: 36–57.

Cameron, Lynne (2001), *Teaching Languages to Young Learners*, Cambridge: Cambridge University Press.

Carless, David (2002), 'Implementing task-based learning with young learners', *ELT Journal*, 56: 389–396.

Carless, David (2004), 'Issues in teachers' re-interpretation of a task-based teaching in primary schools', *System*, 31: 485–500.

Carless, David (2009), 'Revisiting the TBLT versus P-P-P debate: voices from Hong Kong', *Asian Journal of English Language Teaching*, 19: 49–66.

Deng, Chunrao and Carless, David (2009), 'The communicativeness of activities in a task-based innovation in Guangdong, China', *Asian Journal of English Language Teaching*, 19: 113–134.

Dourda, Kyriaki; Bratitsis, Tharrenos; Griva, Eleni and Papadopoulou, Penelope (2014), 'Content and language integrated learning through an online game in primary school: a case study', *The Electronic Journal of E-learning* 12/3: 243–258.

Ellis, Rod (2003), *Task-Based Language Learning and Teaching*, Oxford: Oxford University Press.

Gagné, Nathalie and Parks, Susan (2013), 'Cooperative learning tasks in a Grade 6 intensive ESL class: the role of scaffolding', *Language Teaching Research*, 17/2: 188–209.

Garton, Susan; Copland, Fiona and Burns, Ann (2011), *Investigating Global Practices in Teaching English to Young Learners*. <http://www.teachingenglish.org.uk/publications/global-practices-teachingenglish-young-learners> [accessed 1 October 2014].

Guk, Iju and Kellogg, David (2007), 'The ZPD and whole class teaching: teacher-led and student-led interactional mediation of tasks', *Language Teaching Research*, 11: 281–299.

Kumaravadivelu, B (2006), 'TESOL methods: changing tracks, challenging trends', *TESOL Quarterly*, 40: 59–81.

Legutke, Michael; Müller-Hartman, Andreas and Schocker-von Ditfurth, Marita (2009), *Teaching English in the Primary School*, Stuttgart: Klett Lerntraining.

Mackey, Alison; Kanganas, Alec Peter and Oliver, Rhonda (2007), 'Task familiarity and interactional feedback in child ESL classrooms', *TESOL Quarterly*, 41/2 285–321.

Mackey, Alison and Oliver, Rhonda (2002), 'Interactional feedback and children's L2 development', *System* 30/4: 459–477.

Mackey, Alison; Oliver, Rhonda and Leeman, Jennifer (2003), 'Interactional input and the incorporation of feedback: an exploration on NS-NNS and NNS-NNS adult and child dyads', *Language Learning*, 53/1: 35–66.

Mackey, Alison and Silver, Rita Elaine (2005), 'Interactional tasks and English L2 learning by immigrant children in Singapore', *System*, 33/2: 239–260.

Mourão, Sandie (2015b), 'The potential of picturebooks with young learners', in Janice Bland (ed.), *Teaching English to Young Learners. Critical Issues in Language Teaching with 3–12 Year Olds*, London: Bloomsbury Academic, pp. 199–217.

Nunan, David (2004), *Task-Based Language Learning*, Cambridge: Cambridge University Press.

Ohta, Amy Snyder (2001), *Second Language Acquisition Processes in the Classroom*, Mahwah, New Jersey: Lawrence Erlbaum Associates.

Oliver, Rhonda (1998), 'Negotiation of meaning in child interaction', *Modern Language Journal*, 82: 372–386.

Oliver, Rhonda (2002), 'The patterns of negotiation for meaning in child interactions', *Modern Language Journal*, 86: 97–111.

Pellerin, Martine (2014), 'Language tasks using touch screen and mobile technologies: reconceptualising task-based CALL for young learners', *Canadian Journal of learning and Technology*, 40/1: 1–23.

Pinter, Annamaria (2005), 'Task repetition with 10-year old children', in Corony Edwards and Jane Willis (eds), *Teachers Exploring Tasks in English Language Teaching*, Basingstoke: Palgrave Macmillan, pp. 113–126.

Pinter, Annamaria (2014), 'Child participant roles in applied linguistics research', *Applied Linguistics*, 35/2: 168–183.

Robinson, Peter (2001), 'Task complexity, task difficulty and task production: exploring Interactions in a componential framework', *Applied Linguistics*, 22: 27–57.

Samuda, Virginia and Bygate, Martin (2008), *Tasks in Second Language Learning*, Basingstoke: Palgrave Macmillan.

Shintani, Natsuko (2012), 'Repeating input-based tasks with young beginner learners', *The RELC Journal*, 43/1: 39–51.

Skehan, Peter (1996), 'A framework for the implementation of task-based instruction', *Applied Linguistics*, 71/1: 38–62.

Skehan, Peter and Foster, Pauline (1999), 'The influence of task structure and processing conditions on narrative retellings', *Language Learning*, 49/1: 93–120.

Swain, Merrill and Lapkin, Sharon (2003), 'Talking it through: two French immersion learners' response to reformulation', *International Journal of Educational Research*, 37: 285–304.

Van Gorp, Koen and Bogaert, Nora (2006), 'Developing language tasks for primary and secondary education', in Kris Van den Branden (ed.), *Task Based Language Education from Theory to Practice*, Cambridge: Cambridge University Press, pp. 76–105

Willis, Jane (1996), *A Framework for Task-Based Learning*, Harlow: Addison Wesley Longman.

Willis, David and Willis, Jane (2007), *Doing Task-Based Teaching*, Oxford: Oxford University Press.

Yule, George (1997), *Referential Communication Tasks*, Mahwah, New Jersey: Lawrence Erlbaum Associates.

7

Language Development in Young Learners: The Role of Formulaic Language

Saskia Kersten

Introduction

Formulaic language not only plays an important role in second language (L2) development but also represents one of the most challenging areas a learner has to master. Wray (2002: ix) even goes so far as to state that it may be 'the biggest stumbling block to sounding nativelike' for 'L2 learners of intermediate and advanced proficiency'. This chapter outlines the role of formulaic language in L2 development, discusses some of the reasons why it may be regarded to be such an obstacle, argues for an inclusion of formulaic language in English classes aimed at young learners and, finally, makes some suggestions of how formulaic language can be incorporated in the (primary) school syllabus.

Second language development

Traditionally, learning a language was seen as consisting of two components: learning the words and learning the rules that explain how to combine them. That vocabulary and grammar are often treated as two distinct entities in language teaching may in part be because '[t]raditional structural analysis displays how words are combined to make grammatical phrases', but overlooks the fact that there are some word combinations that form 'multi-word composites' (Erman and Warren 2000: 30), which often have a meaning and function that are not the same as the sum of the meaning and function of the discrete parts.

For many decades, linguistic analysis and theory was heavily influenced by Chomsky's theory of language. His emphasis on the creativity of language, that is, that every sentence is generated by slotting words into the syntactic structure, meant that idiomatic expressions were seen as idiosyncrasies of language, because they do not follow the rules of generation, which in this framework are believed to be innate (for a more detailed discussion of creativity in the Chomskyan sense and other types of creativity, e.g. in the language of literature, see Hoey 2005; for the relation of formulaic language, creativity and language play in L2 learners, see Bannard and Lieven 2009, Bell 2012, Bland 2013).

The ubiquity of formulaic language

Modern technology has made it possible to search large collections of authentic language data (corpora) for patterns of use, and thus corpus linguists have been able to show that language users make use of prefabricated language far more often than previously thought. This has led to the assumption that language is predominantly 'lexically driven with the resultant concept of "lexico-grammar"' (Schmitt, Dörnyei, Adolphs and Durow 2004: 55).

These studies have shown that a large part of language used in spoken and written discourse appears to be formulaic. In the *Longman Grammar of Spoken and Written English*, Biber, Johansson, Leech, Conrad and Finegan (1999) report that 20 per cent of academic prose and 28 per cent of spoken discourse consist of lexical bundles, which are 'recurring sequences of three or four words' (Biber et al. 1999: 451). Erman and Warren (2000: 31) investigated combinations 'of at least two words favored by native speakers' and found that the average proportion of prefabricated language in texts is 55 per cent. Generally, 'conversations exhibit a greater proportion of prefabricated language than does written language, but that difference is not as great as expected' (Erman and Warren 2000: 51). One reason for this reliance on formulaic language is that, because it represents 'single choices' (Sinclair 1991: 110), it lowers the processing burden of both the speaker and the listener.

Sinclair (1991) proposes that language users have two principles at their disposal, the *idiom principle* and the *open-choice principle*. The open-choice principle allows anyone to produce and comprehend utterances they have never encountered before, in short, to create utterances from scratch by creating sentences using lexical items and syntactic rules (Sinclair 1991: 114). The other principle that humans can employ when communicating is the idiom principle. Here, speakers rely heavily on prefabricated language: 'the principle of idiom is that a language user has available to him or her a large number of semi-preconstructed phrases that constitute single choices, even though they might appear to be analysable into segments' (Sinclair 1991: 110).

As the capacity of our working memory is limited, formulaic sequences are the more economical and, therefore, 'prevalent mode of language processing' (Rott 2009: 406). When producing or comprehending language, formulaic language is produced more fluently (Boers and Lindstromberg 2009, Wood 2010) and processed more rapidly (Underwood, Schmitt and Galpin 2004, Conklin and Schmitt 2008, Conklin and Schmitt 2012).

In addition to easing the processing load in both language production and comprehension, Wray (2002) also proposes that formulaic language promotes the speaker's and hearer's interests. 'One effective tool for drawing others into behaviors beneficial to us is to employ word strings that are in current use in our community' (Wray 2012: 231). Formulaic language can be used to manipulate the hearer and the situation, for instance, by using 'pragmatic prefabs' such as turn-regulators (*Well . . . I think . . . Can I just say this. . .*) which are employed to organize a conversation, allocating whose turn it is to speak and whose it is to listen (Erman and Warren 2000: 43). Formulaic sequences are also employed to establish group identity, for example, by using group-specific and/or culture-specific phrases (Wray 2002: 90). In short, formulaicity in language is ubiquitous and multifaceted.

Defining formulaic language: An attempt

Formulaic language has been called many things in the literature. The most common terms used to describe language that is prefabricated are *chunk, multiword unit/multiword expression, prefabricated language* (or *prefab*), *collocation,* (*routine*) *formula* and *morpheme-equivalent unit* (MEU), to name but a few (for an exhaustive list and more information on terminology, see e.g. Wray 2002, 2009, Wood 2010). In this chapter, the terms *formulaic sequence/ language, prefabricated language, chunk, multiword expression/string* and *phrase* are used synonymously.

Wray (2002: 9) gives the following working definition of what she regards to be a formulaic sequence:

> a sequence, continuous or discontinuous, of words or other elements, which is, or appears to be, prefabricated: that is, stored and retrieved whole from memory at the time of use, rather than being subject to generation or analysis by the language grammar.

In their definition of the term *prefab*, Erman and Warren (2000: 31) focus on another feature: 'A prefab is a combination of at least two words favoured by native speakers in preference to an alternative combination which could have been equivalent had there been no conventionalization.' Formulaic sequences are not only stored in the mental lexicon as single units; they also represent the preferred choice over other potential ways of expressing the same idea, for example, when telling the time. 'Instead of saying *it's twenty to six* one might say [...] *It's six less twenty; It's two thirds past five*' (Pawley and Syder 1983:197–198), but one does not.

The role of context

Formulaic language is also context dependent, which means it is more likely to occur in a given context, forming part of the pragmatic competence, which 'accounts for the speaker's ability to continue to access these forms as pre-assembled chunks, ready for a given functional use in an appropriate context' (Nattinger and DeCarrico 1992: 13). Politeness, for example, is commonly linked to very specific formulas that depend on the situation, in fact so much so that children are reminded to use these politeness markers by yet another formula: *What's the magic word?*

Idioms and other chunks

The most discussed form of formulaic language is the idiom, because for most idioms it is virtually impossible to guess what the overall phrase means, even if every individual word that occurs in the phrase is known. The example *kick the bucket* illustrates why: depending on how the sequence is processed, the hearer interprets the sequence differently. The first option is to arrive at the meaning of the overall phrase *John kicked the bucket* by looking at the meaning of the individual parts and the underlying syntax. In this scenario, there is an actual bucket that John's foot (or possibly another part of his anatomy) made contact with, propelling it forwards. The second (and more likely) interpretation is the holistic interpretation: a euphemism for dying. It is this second option, interpreting the sentence holistically following the idiom principle (Sinclair 1991), that L2 learners, even very proficient ones, have most problems with, both when listening to and producing L2. Prodromou (2008: 43) calls this the 'idiomatic deficit'.

Idioms, which are fully fixed expressions, are not the only type of formulaic language. Many formulaic expressions have open slots that can be filled with different items, although what can be used in these slots may be limited by certain constraints. For example, when inviting someone to a wedding or a party (the latter being a more likely occurrence in the life of young learners), there are certain phrases that can be used to express the invitation: *I/We (would like to) (cordially) invite you to (attend) the/our/my party/reception...* As can be seen in this example, there is a degree of variability in this formulaic expression; it is only semi-fixed.

Frequency-based measures of formulaic language

A purely frequency-driven approach to the investigation of formulaic language is adopted by Biber et al. (1999) and Biber, Conrad and Cortes (2004) among others. These multiword units, called *lexical bundles*, 'are defined simply as the most frequent recurring lexical sequences in a register' (Biber et al. 2004: 376). The lexical bundles can be subdivided according to length, for example, three-word lexical bundles or four-word lexical bundles. The bundles are not necessarily complete, that is, the actual formulaic sequence may consist of more than the three words that constitute the lexical bundle, for example, *what I want to* and *to talk about is* are treated as two separate lexical bundles, although they could both be part of a larger formulaic expression (Biber et al. 2004: 386). In addition, the 'frequency cut-off used to identify lexical bundles is somewhat arbitrary' (Biber et al. 2004: 376). Following a definition based on frequency means that other forms of formulaic language, for example idioms, are not necessarily regarded as lexical bundles, because they are relatively infrequent (Moon 1998).

Collocations are yet another type of formulaic language, 'the occurrence of two or more words within a short space of each other in a text' (Sinclair 1991: 170) with a higher frequency than predicted by chance. The definition for what exactly a collocation is varies, however, depending on what is considered to be a 'short space', whether the two words have to be consecutive and many other possible criteria (Nesselhauf 2004).

In summary, how formulaicity is defined depends in part on what is focused on in any given study, because there are so many facets to formulaicity that it is difficult to find an all-encompassing definition (for a more detailed discussion, see e.g. Read and Nation 2004, Wray 2009, Wray 2012).

The acquisition of formulaic language in young L2 learners

Many studies investigating the acquisition of formulaic language in L2 learners focus on intermediate or advanced learners, most of them students in tertiary education (see e.g. Nesselhauf 2003, Lindstromberg and Boers 2008a, Prodromou 2008, Erman 2009; see also studies in Schmitt 2004, Corrigan, Moravcsik, Ouali and Wheatley 2009). Myles, Hooper and Mitchell (1998) investigate the role of rote-learned chunks in secondary school students during their first two years of learning French, and Smiskova, Verspoor and Lowie (2012: 141) look at 'conventionalised ways of saying things' in the L2 development of Dutch learners aged thirteen and find that it is the 'beyond-word-level notions' that learners 'express awkwardly'.

Wray (2002: chapter 9) reports the findings of a number of studies on L2 acquisition of very young and young learners in a variety of contexts. Most of these studies were undertaken in the 1970s and the 1980s, and the young learners acquired the L2 predominantly in naturalistic or immersion contexts. The children made use of formulaic sequences extensively, particularly in the very early stages of L2 acquisition: 'As control of language increased, the formulaic sequences which formed the basic currency of interaction were used more creatively. They were added together, or embedded into novel structures, to make new or better utterances' (Wray 2002: 169).

There seems to be a paucity of studies that focus on young learners in a classroom context in particular, which is surprising, because the notion that young L2 learners rely on formulaic language in the first phases of their L2 development is often stressed (see e.g. Wray 2002, McKay 2006). However, the argument that these imitated chunks of language directly repeated from the input are only the first step that soon makes way for other, more complex processing strategies has also been put forward. 'The debate centres on whether learners gradually "unpack" the initially unanalysed utterances […], or whether they merely drop such rote-learned utterances from their speech repertoire as their creative, rule-governed competence develops along a different route' (Myles et al. 1998: 327). Myles et al. (1998: 358) come to the conclusion that there may be 'a two-way process' at work; 'the use of formulaic language therefore has a role beyond that of facilitating entry into communication and speeding up production'.

McKay (2006: 37) suggests that teaching learners based on a strict division of rules and words may result in them becoming 'tongue-tied and anxious trying to construct a sentence in their head based on the rules they have learned', stating that this may be particularly true for young learners who have yet only limited metalinguistic ability. Instead, they should have the opportunity to acquire a 'formulaic system developed through language use opportunities' (McKay 2006: 37). These language-use opportunities, which can also be called usage events, not only result in the learners being able to accumulate a large number of memorized strings they can reuse as the need arises but also feed the language acquisition process.

Usage-based linguistic approaches to language learning

In a usage-based framework of language development (see e.g. Tomasello 2003 for first language (L1) development and Eskildsen 2009 for L2 development), all linguistic symbols are seen to be form-meaning mappings.

In contrast to the field of generative linguistics, which views grammar as being innate, usage-based approaches to L1 and L2 development hold that rules are abstracted solely from the input using general learning principles (Littlemore 2009, for a more general discussion of why 'language is not innate', see Evans 2014). Both L1 and L2 learning occur through usage events, which are 'situated instances of the language user either understanding or producing language to convey particular meaning in a given communicative situation' (Tyler 2012: 33). In usage-based approaches, language acquisition is exemplar based: 'It is the piecemeal learning of many thousand constructions and the frequency-biased abstraction of regularities within them' (Ellis 2002: 143).

Following Nattinger and DeCarrico (1992) and Myles et al. (1998) in their assumption that there is dynamic interplay between formula and creativity, Eskildsen (2010: 338) states that usage-based linguistics can account 'for the gradual evolution of formulas into increasingly more productive structures'. He particularly stresses the role of semi-fixed expressions. In the context of L1 development, Bannard and Lieven (2009) point out that children reuse multiword units from their input, which in turn give rise to complex grammatical knowledge. They use the 'traceback method' to 'identify novel utterances and to find their possible basis in what the child has said or heard before' (Bannard and Lieven 2009: 309). They argue that, as an inventory of exemplar-based constructions with open slots is acquired, these form networks, which in turn allow the development of more abstract constructions and categories (Bannard and Lieven 2009: 308).

Teaching language to young learners: The role of semi-fixed expressions

In a classroom context, new vocabulary is often introduced using flashcards or realia. The teacher shows the item in question and says *This is a(n)* _____. As the learners listen to this string repeatedly with the open slot filled with a number of different items (e.g. *girl, dog, pineapple, table, book, heart, ball, egg,* etc.), the learner's mind can form an abstraction based on the repetition and variation encountered so far, for example, *This is a(n)* NOUN. Whether it is *a* or *an* depends on the phonology of the following item, which is another rule that is abstracted from the input after encountering enough variations of this semi-fixed expression. And as the learners are exposed to even more varied language, they then realize that other words can be slotted in as well, for example, adjectives preceding the noun. Again, there are certain constraints limiting the material that can be used to fill the open slot, which they also become aware of.

In her book *Formulaic Language and the Lexicon*, Wray (2002: chapter 11) outlines a model for the acquisition of formulaic language in L2 learners, differentiating between very young learners, who are still at the early stages of L1 acquisition as well. For this group of learners, 'language is primarily employed for socio-interactional functions (in the widest sense), word strings are broken down only as necessary' (Wray 2002: 203). At this stage, children are also still preliterate. Being able to read may have an impact on how formulaic language is perceived and processed.

Young learners, who already attend primary school and are thus in the process of literacy development, will start to break down chunks more readily. 'The further a child is into the school system, the more he or she will be encouraged, through reading and writing, to examine language as a succession of words, rather than just trusting the socio-interactional effect of whole memorised sequences' (Wray 2002: 205). This may partly be due to the acquisition of literacy skills, during which children become familiar with the notion of words as individual units, which leads to their becoming aware of the fact that longer sequences could potentially be broken down and analysed. But this awareness that memorized sequences have the potential to be used as a quarry or template for new language (see Bland 2015a) can also be influenced by the cognitive style of the learner, the sibling constellation at home and parental education, to name but a few factors (Wray 2002: 116–117). Playing naming games may also have an effect, as the semi-fixed sequence *What's this? It's a(n)* _____, for example, can be used to highlight nouns in the input.

As argued above, treating vocabulary as atomic, that is focusing on individual words rather than chunks, often in the form of vocabulary lists consisting of single items either with their translation equivalent or with a short L2 definition, can also potentially hinder the recognition that words also form chunks of language.

The noun problem

Although making single items in the input more salient can trigger the acquisition process, this needs to be balanced with raising the awareness that words also form semi- or fully fixed combinations. L2 coursebooks tend to view vocabulary as consisting of single words only, rather than prefabricated expressions, in some cases even to the extent of providing vocabulary lists in which L2 words are presented as being translation equivalents of L1 words (S. Kersten 2010). This atomic perspective on vocabulary is not conducive to making learners aware of the fact that words very rarely occur in isolation, thus not raising their awareness of underlying patterns of formulaicity.

Young learners in particular are often taught a large number of nouns, because they are easily illustrated and explained. What they frequently lack, however, are the means to put the vocabulary they know into a meaningful context. Communicative situations, meaningful interaction with peers and teachers and repeated recycling of vocabulary in different contexts have been shown to foster vocabulary acquisition and heighten self-reported vocabulary knowledge in young learners (S. Kersten 2010).

Secondary school teachers sometimes say that all children learn in primary school is nouns without the means to put them together into sequence. Although this may not be true for the majority of primary-school classrooms, there is a grain of truth in it. As argued above, however, the answer is not necessarily to teach grammatical rules explicitly, but rather expose learners to semi-fixed expressions, giving them the opportunity to develop more abstract notions of language. Young learners need to encounter both single lexical items and prefabricated language chunks to become successful language learners.

The importance of repetition and variation

Abstraction is not a process that follows a single exposure to any given phrase or sentence, but is rather dependent on the frequency of occurrence of certain strings in the input (Ellis 2002, Larsen-Freeman 2002, Ellis and Ferreira-Junior 2009, Ellis, O'Donnell and Römer 2013). This unpacking, or analysing, of formulaic language into its components, which then leads to an abstraction of the underlying construction with all its constraints as well as the acquisition of its parts, can only happen if the learners are repeatedly exposed to the formula and its variations: 'Learning, memory, and perception are all affected by frequency of usage: the more times we experience something, the stronger our memory for it, and the more fluently it is accessed. The more times we experience conjunction of features, the more they become associated in our minds' (Ellis et al. 2013: 31).

In L1 and naturalistic L2 acquisition, this is bound to happen, because learners are exposed to a large amount of input (see K. Kersten and Rohde 2015, this volume). In classroom-based L2 development, however, this is not always the case (Enever 2015: 26). Ellis (2002: 173–174) states that frequency of occurrence is not the only factor affecting acquisition, and stresses that evidence showing that learning is based on frequency, which is implicit learning, 'do[es] not deny a role for explicit instruction, the efficacy of which is now well established. Language acquisition can be speeded up by explicit instruction' and that '[t]he initial registration of a language representation may well require attention and conscious identification'.

As already discussed above, learners in a classroom-based setting are far less likely to encounter strings often enough to facilitate acquisition. Based on an analysis of teacher talk, Horst (2010: 177) found that 'the teacher speech proved to be long on richness [...] but short on redundancy, with few words recycled often enough to be remembered' (see also Meunier 2012). Instead, '[i]n the early stages of learning categories from exemplars, acquisition might thus be optimized by the introduction of an initial, low-variance sample centered upon prototypical exemplars' (Ellis et al. 2013: 33).

Here, the use of picturebooks, with their often highly repetitive content, seems to be one of the suitable ways to meet this requirement of familiarizing learners with authentic language which is also rich in formulaic language, fairly restricted and repetitive. In addition, the stories in picturebooks often employ certain recurring chunks that have a specific function in the story, thereby also exposing learners to the way in which formulaic sequences can be used to structure a text and/or fulfil a socio-interactional function. Bland (2013: 152) highlights yet another benefit of formulaic sequences employed in picturebooks, folk stories and nursery rhymes, because these can also foster the development of intercultural communicative competence, as some formulas are culture-specific. How politeness is expressed, for example, varies from culture to culture, as do the formulas one employs. One culture may have a formulaic expression closely associated with a particular routine or ritual, while another may not. For example, there may be a ritualized start of a family meal, which differs (or may not even exist) from culture to culture, even within one speech community, as it depends on religion, ethnicity, social class and so forth.

Formulaic language is also encountered in songs, rhymes, dialogues and classroom language (Cameron 2001: 50), but in an institutional setting, where the foreign language is used in classroom situations only and most formulas are not encountered frequently enough for the learner to extract and abstract the constraints a formulaic sequence is subject to, explicit teaching may be the best way to impart this particular kind of knowledge.

Raising learners' awareness

It has been proposed that awareness-raising techniques can be used to alert learners to the fact that formulaic language both exists and is often 'linguistically motivated' (Condon 2008, Lindstromberg and Boers 2008a, 2008b, Boers and Lindstromberg 2009). Linguistic motivation can be found in the etymology of the chunk, its meaning and/or its form, anything that led to this particular chunk becoming accepted conventional usage in a given speech community (Boers and Lindstromberg 2009: 15).

One type of motivation can often be found in binomials, 'phrases of the form A and B' (Boers and Lindstromberg 2009: 71–72): 'For example, the institutionalized word order in such expressions may reflect the chronology of events in the real world, as in *crash and burn, spit and polish, kiss and tell'* (Boers and Lindstromberg 2009: 72). Another motivating factor frequent in binomials is alliteration, '28% of English *binomial* idioms alliterate and/or rhyme (*chop and change, fair and square, spick and span*)' (Boers and Lindstromberg 2009: 114).

In their book *Teaching Chunks of Language*, aimed at teenagers and young adults, although some of the activities could be adapted to suit younger learners, Lindstromberg and Boers (2008b) include a number of activities and worksheets that encourage learners to notice the underlying sound patterns which can occur in chunks, often in the form of alliterations. In an activity aimed at pre-intermediate learners, they suggest that film titles are often alliterative, citing *Bend It like Beckham, Beauty and the Beast* and *Dirty Dancing* as examples, among others (Lindstromberg and Boers 2008b: 78). Experiments showed that patterns of sound repetition have a mnemonic effect (Lindstromberg and Boers 2008a). An example of sound repetition in chunks more suited for young learners is, for example, the text of the picturebook *Superworm* (Donaldson and Scheffler 2013), in which 'Superworm is super-long, Superworm is super-strong' and 'the bees are feeling bored today'. In addition, Superworm is also described as 'fat and firm' by a hungry crow who is about to eat him. The sound repetition employed by the authors can help highlight the underlying formulaicity.

The argument behind these awareness-raising activities is that it is impossible to teach all existing chunks; therefore, making examples particularly salient in the input is thought to foster the acquisition and reuse of chunks. Boers, Eyckmans, Kappel, Stengers and Demecheleer (2006) show that adult learners of English who were made aware of the formulaic language in their input were judged to be more orally proficient than their peers who had been taught the same content in a more traditional approach in which grammar and lexis are separated.

Salience is a key feature of vocabulary acquisition, because to be able to acquire any given vocabulary item, be it individual words or multiword expressions, the learners have to notice the item in the input: 'Noticing [...] is an active process in which learners become aware of the structure, notice connections between form and meaning, but do not themselves manipulate the language' (Cameron 2001: 109). If a vocabulary item is the novel item in an already familiar formulaic sequence, it becomes salient, because it is new information filling an open slot, making it more likely to be noticed. This avoids the pitfall of de-contextualizing new vocabulary items, as is sometimes done when introducing new vocabulary (Nation 2001).

One recurring theme in the definitions of formulaic language is the notion that formulaic sequences are often linked to a particular pragmatic use, that they are often situation-dependent (Coulmas 1979, Nattinger and DeCarrico 1992, Wray 2002, Wood 2010). This is another area in which young learners may benefit from explicit teaching, because one of the deficits of even very proficient L2 users is that they lack awareness of what language is appropriate in a given situation. If register awareness is raised in the early stages of L2 development, this problem may be overcome.

From a learner perspective, explicitly taught formulas are useful not only because they aid fluency but also because they offer reliable routines in known situations that can even take the form of 'phrasal teddy bears' (Ellis 2012: 17).

Ideas for teaching formulaic language to young learners

Although an in-depth discussion of how to teach formulaic language would be beyond the scope of this chapter, this section tries to give the reader at least an idea of how formulaic language can be incorporated into a primary-school classroom. In line with Ellis et al. (2013), the language employed in this exercise is very limited. It is aimed at young learners at A1 level of learning English.

As an example, the beginning of *Little Red Riding Hood* in the version from *Children's Hour with Red Riding Hood and Other Stories* (Piper 1922, available on Project Gutenberg) is used (see Figure 7.1).

1   There was once a sweet little maid who lived with her father and mother in a pretty

2   little cottage at the edge of the village. At the further end of the wood was another

3   pretty cottage and in it lived her grandmother.

4   Everybody loved this little girl, her grandmother perhaps loved her most of all and

5   gave her a great many pretty things. Once she gave her a red cloak with a hood

6   which she always wore, so people called her Little Red Riding Hood.

    [...]

7   'Who is there?' called the grandmother.

8   'Little Red Riding Hood,' said the wicked wolf.

9   'Press the latch, open the door, and walk in,' said the grandmother.

FIGURE 7.1 Extract from *Little Red Riding Hood*.

The story begins with the common formulaic sequence *There was once*, which signals to the reader (or listener) that the following is a fairy story; it has the function of signalling the genre of the subsequent text. In the following six lines, the word *little* is repeated in different contexts: *a sweet little maid* (line 1), *a pretty little cottage* (lines 1–2), *this little girl* (line 4) and also the protagonist's name *Little Red Riding Hood* (line 6). This allows the reader to understand which words collocate with *little*. In addition, *little* is also used in conjunction with *pretty*, once in the phrase *a pretty little cottage*, which is repeated in the expression *another pretty cottage* (lines 2–3). *Pretty* is also repeated in *a great many pretty things*. This repetition of the same lexical items in variation gives examples of the contexts in which they can occur in and thus helps the young learner acquire the meaning and the formulas it occurs in.

In line 7, the grandmother uses the common formulaic sequence that is employed when enquiring who is at the door: *Who is there?* The wolf throughout the fairy tale is described as *wicked*, another example of alliteration and an expression which has become a formula in itself to denote an abstract villainous character.

The following dialogue sequence allows the learner to encounter and, subsequently, to internalize the underlying structure of how reported speech is presented in English. Every utterance is followed by a verb for speaking (*call* and *say*), the definite article, because both participants in the conversation are known, and a noun, or, in the case of the wicked wolf, an adjective followed by a noun. This pattern is repeated throughout the story, sometimes in variation, sometimes using the exact same form, thus providing the pattern of repetition and variation discussed above.

The way the grandmother tells the wicked wolf how to enter the cottage is also repetitive, because, although the words themselves are not repeated, the underlying construction of a command is: *Press the latch* and *open the door* (line 9). Later on in the story, of course, the well-known dialogue between Little Red Riding Hood and the wicked wolf is also highly formulaic. Little Red Riding Hood uses the structure *What big _____ you have, Grandmother* and the wolf answers *All the better to _____ you with, my dear*. These formulas lend themselves to follow-up activities in which the learners can manipulate the formulas and experiment with other nouns and verbs that can be used to fill the slots in these semi-fixed chunks.

Little Red Riding Hood ends with the fairy tale formula of *and they lived happily ever after*, which, together with the formulaic beginning, frames the text and functions as an indicator of the genre and signals the end of the narrative.

The above examples are only a few of the formulaic sequences that can be found in this particular text; there are many more, which are often repeated in this text or other fairy tales, for example *X and X*, as in *father and mother* (or *mother and father), brother and sister, king and queen* and many more. In addition, fairy tales often contain expressions which give an indication of chronology, expressing, for example, periods of time that have elapsed, such as *a short while later, not long after, at the end of X years* or *at the end of that time*, to name but a few.

Using fairy tales or other stories presents learners with language that is both repetitive and varied, allowing them to encounter chunks of language embedded in meaningful context and with a variety of functions, both pragmatic and narrative.

Conclusion

This chapter has argued that second language development can greatly benefit from the formulaic language that is learned implicitly or taught explicitly. Chunks of language do not only seed L2 acquisition; their mastery is also a factor in the success of language learning. In addition, formulaic language has a dual function: it is not only what is learned but also what gives rise to the development of new language competence.

Exposing young learners to formulaic language from the very start will give them the building blocks to express themselves quite fluently even in the early stages of their L2 development, hopefully leading to an increase in motivation. For the acquisition of single lexical items, formulaic language can be used as a backdrop highlighting novel language items, thus making them more noticeable and fostering their acquisition.

Instead of just focusing on the rules underlying language on the one hand and individual words on the other, successful language development in young learners hinges on a balanced mix of single and multiword items.

References

Bannard, Colin and Lieven, Elena (2009), 'Repetition and reuse in child language learning', in Roberta Corrigan; Edith Moravcsik; Hamid Ouali and Kathleen Wheatley (eds), *Formulaic Language Volume 2: Acquisition, Loss, Psychological Reality, and Functional Explanations*, Amsterdam: Benjamins, pp. 299–321.
Bell, Nancy (2012), 'Formulaic language, creativity, and language play in a second language', *Annual Review of Applied Linguistics*, 32: 189–205.
Biber, Douglas; Conrad, Susan and Cortes, Viviana (2004), 'If you look at...: Lexical bundles in university teaching and textbooks', *Applied Linguistics*, 25: 371–405.

Biber, Douglas; Johansson, Stig; Leech, Geoffrey; Conrad, Susan and Finegan, Edward (1999), *Longman Grammar of Spoken and Written English*, Harlow: Pearson Education.

Bland, Janice (2013), *Children's Literature and Learner Empowerment: Children and Teenagers in English Language Education*, London: Bloomsbury Academic.

Bland, Janice (2015a), 'Grammar templates for the future with poetry for children', in Janice Bland (ed.), *Teaching English to Young Learners. Critical Issues in Language Teaching with 3–12 Year Olds*, London: Bloomsbury Academic, pp. 147–166.

Boers, Frank; Eyckmans, June; Kappel, Jenny; Stengers, Hélène and Demecheleer, Murielle (2006), 'Formulaic sequences and perceived oral proficiency: putting a lexical approach to the test', *Language Teaching Research*, 10: 245–261.

Boers, Frank and Lindstromberg, Seth (2009), *Optimizing a Lexical Approach to Instructed Second Language Acquisition*, Basingstoke: Palgrave Macmillan.

Cameron, Lynne (2001), *Teaching Languages to Young Learners*, Cambridge: Cambridge University Press.

Condon, Nora (2008), 'How cognitive linguistic motivations influence the learning of phrasal verbs', in Frank Boers and Seth Lindstromberg (eds), *Cognitive Linguistic Approaches to Teaching Vocabulary and Phraseology*, Berlin: Mouton de Gruyter, pp. 133–158.

Conklin, Kathy and Schmitt, Norbert (2008), 'Formulaic sequences: Are they processed more quickly than nonformulaic language by native and nonnative speakers?', *Applied Linguistics*, 29: 72–89.

Conklin, Kathy and Schmitt, Norbert (2012), 'The processing of formulaic language', *Annual Review of Applied Linguistics*, 32: 45–61.

Corrigan, Roberta; Moravcsik, Edith; Ouali, Hamid and Wheatley, Kathleen (eds) (2009), *Formulaic Language Volume 2: Acquisition, Loss, Psychological Reality, and Functional Explanations*, Amsterdam: Benjamins.

Coulmas, Florian (1979), 'On the sociolinguistic relevance of routine formulae', *Journal of Pragmatics*, 3: 239–266.

Donaldson, Julia and Scheffler, Axel (2013), *Superworm*, London: Alison Green.

Ellis, Nick (2012), 'Formulaic language and second language acquisition: Zipf and the Phrasal Teddy Bear', *Annual Review of Applied Linguistics*, 32: 17–44.

Ellis, Nick (2002), 'Frequency effects in language processing: A review with implications for theories of implicit and explicit language acquisition', *Studies in Second Language Acquisition*, 24: 143–188.

Ellis, Nick and Ferreira-Junior, Fernando (2009), 'Construction learning as a function of frequency, frequency distribution, and function', *The Modern Language Journal*, 93: 370–385.

Ellis, Nick; O'Donnell, Matthew and Römer, Ute (2013), 'Usage-based language: Investigating the latent structures that underpin acquisition', *Language Learning*, 63: 25–51.

Enever, Janet (2015), 'The advantages and disadvantages of English as a foreign language with young learners', in Janice Bland (ed.), *Teaching English to Young Learners. Critical Issues in Language Teaching with 3–12 Year Olds*, London: Bloomsbury Academic, pp. 13–29.

Erman, Britt (2009), 'Formulaic language from a learner perspective: What the learner needs to know', in Roberta Corrigan; Edith Moravcsik; Hamid Ouali and Kathleen M. Wheatley (eds), *Formulaic Language Volume 2: Acquisition, Loss, Psychological Reality, and Functional Explanations*, Amsterdam: Benjamins, pp. 324–346.

Erman, Britt and Warren, Beatrice (2000), 'The idiom principle and the open choice principle', *Text*, 20: 29–62.

Eskildsen, Søren (2009), 'Constructing another language: Usage-based linguistics in second language acquisition', *Applied Linguistics*, 30: 335–357.

Evans, Vyvyan (2014), *The Language Myth: Why Language Is Not an Instinct*, Cambridge: Cambridge University Press.

Hoey, Michael (2005), *Lexical Priming: A New Theory of Words and Language*, London: Routledge.

Horst, Marlise (2010), 'How well does teacher-talk support incidental vocabulary acquisition?', *Reading in a Foreign Language*, 22: 161–180.

Kersten, Kristin and Rohde, Andreas (2015), 'Immersion teaching in English with young learners', in Janice Bland (ed.), *Teaching English to Young Learners. Critical Issues in Language Teaching with 3–12 Year Olds*, London: Bloomsbury Academic, pp. 71–89.

Kersten, Saskia (2010), *The Mental Lexicon and Vocabulary Learning: Implications for the Foreign Language Classroom*, Tübingen: Narr.

Larsen-Freeman, Diane (2002), 'Making sense of frequency', *Studies in Second Language Acquisition*, 24: 275–285.

Lindstromberg, Seth and Boers, Frank (2008a), 'Phonemic repetition and the learning of lexical chunks: The power of assonance', *System*, 36: 423–436.

Lindstromberg, Seth and Boers, Frank (2008b), *Teaching Chunks of Language: From Noticing to Remembering*, London: Helbling Languages.

Littlemore, Jeannette (2009), *Applying Cognitive Linguistics to Second Language Learning and Teaching*, Basingstoke: Palgrave Macmillan.

McKay, Penny (2006), *Assessing Young Language Learners*, Cambridge: Cambridge University Press.

Meunier, Fanny (2012), 'Formulaic language and language teaching', *Annual Review of Applied Linguistics*, 32: 111–129.

Moon, Rosamund (1998), *Fixed Expressions and Idioms in English: A Corpus-based Approach*, Oxford: Clarendon Press.

Myles, Florence; Hooper, Janet and Mitchell, Rosamond (1998), 'Rote or rule? Exploring the role of formulaic language in classroom foreign language learning', *Language Learning*, 48: 323–364.

Nation, Paul (2001), *Learning Vocabulary in Another Language*, Cambridge: Cambridge University Press.

Nattinger, James and DeCarrico, Jeanette (1992), *Lexical Phrases and Language Teaching*, Oxford: Oxford University Press.

Nesselhauf, Nadja (2003), 'The Use of Collocations by Advanced Learners of English and Some Implications for Teaching', *Applied Linguistics*, 24: 223–242.

Nesselhauf, Nadja (2004), *Collocations in a Learner Corpus*, Amsterdam: Benjamins.

Pawley, Andrew and Syder, Frances (1983), 'Two puzzles for linguistic theory: Native like selection and native like fluency', in Jack Richards and Robert Schmidt (eds), *Language and Communication*, London: Longman, pp. 191–226.

Piper, Watty (ed.) (1922), *Children's Hour with Red Riding Hood and Other Stories*, available on Project Gutenberg, http://www.gutenberg.org/files/11592/11592-h/11592-h.htm [accessed 16 November 2014]

Prodromou, Luke (2008), *English as a Lingua Franca: A Corpus-Based Analysis*, London: Continuum.

Read, John and Nation, Paul (2004), 'Measurement of formulaic sequences', in Norbert Schmitt (ed), *Formulaic Sequences: Acquisition, Processing and Use*, Amsterdam: Benjamins, pp. 23–35.

Rott, Susanne (2009), 'The effect of awareness-raising on the use of formulaic construction', in Roberta Corrigan; Edith Moravcsik; Hamid Ouali and Kathleen Wheatley (eds), *Formulaic Language Volume 2: Acquisition, Loss, Psychological Reality, and Functional Explanations*, Amsterdam: Benjamins, pp. 405–422.

Schmitt, Norbert (ed.) (2004), *Formulaic Sequences: Acquisition, Processing and Use*, Amsterdam: Benjamins.

Schmitt, Norbert; Dörnyei, Zoltán; Adolphs, Svenja and Durow, Valerie (2004), 'Knowledge and acquisition of formulaic sequences: A longitudinal study', in Norbert Schmitt (ed), *Formulaic Sequences: Acquisition, Processing and Use*, Amsterdam: Benjamins, pp. 55–86.

Sinclair, John (1991), *Corpus, Concordance, Collocation*, Oxford: Oxford University Press.

Smiskova, Hana; Verspoor, Marjolijn and Lowie, Wander (2012), 'Conventionalized ways of saying things (CWOSTs) and L2 development', *Dutch Journal of Applied Linguistics*, 1: 125–142.

Tomasello, Michael (2003), *Constructing a Language: A Usage-Based Theory of Language Acquisition*, Cambridge, MA: Harvard University Press.

Tyler, Andrea (2012), *Cognitive Linguistics and Second Language Learning: Theoretical Basics and Experimental Evidence*, New York: Routledge.

Underwood, Geoffrey; Schmitt, Norbert and Galpin, Adam (2004), 'The eyes have it: An eye-movement study into the processing of formulaic sequences', in Norbert Schmitt (ed), *Formulaic Sequences: Acquisition, Processing and Use*, Amsterdam: Benjamins, pp. 153–171.

Wood, David (2010), *Formulaic Language and Second Language Speech Fluency: Background, Evidence and Classroom Applications*, London: Continuum.

Wray, Alison (2002), *Formulaic Language and the Lexicon*, Cambridge: Cambridge University Press.

Wray, Alison (2009), 'Identifying formulaic language: Persistent challenges and new opportunities', in Roberta Corrigan; Edith Moravcsik; Hamid Ouali and Kathleen Wheatley (eds), *Formulaic Language Volume 1: Distribution and Historical Change*, Amsterdam: Benjamins, pp. 27–51.

Wray, Alison (2012), 'What do we (think we) know about formulaic language? An evaluation of the current state of play', *Annual Review of Applied Linguistics*, 32: 231–254.

8

Grammar Templates for the Future with Poetry for Children

Janice Bland

Introduction

> *King's Cross!*
> *What shall we do?*
> *Leave him alone*
> *For a minute or two. (Farjeon 1999: 138)*

This extract from a poem by Eleanor Farjeon, a well-known writer for children, can serve as a neat illustration of the potential value of poetry for foreign-language classrooms that are both creative and competence oriented: (1) as a mnemonic that may be particularly useful in classroom rituals, (2) as support for affective learning and intercultural insight and (3) as a grammar template for the future.

1. As a mnemonic: the rhythm and the rhyme of poetry function as memory aids. In this example the play on words (King's Cross as the London railway station, as well as an angry royal person), in addition to the rhythm and rhyme, is memorable. As a template this can function usefully and humorously in classroom management situations, whenever a child behaves in a short-tempered way: Sue's cross! What shall we do? *Leave her alone for a minute or two.*

2. Lines of poetry can transmit cultural knowledge by allowing the young learner to enter a different storyworld. The humour, excitement or tension of lines of poetry can support affective learning, learning that is pleasurable, relaxed or energized, depending on the poem. Farjeon uses intertexuality to enrich her poem, the lines in this brief example refer to King's Cross Station, a major London railway terminus. Of course the young learners will probably be familiar with the secret King's Cross Station Platform 9 ¾, which features in the *Harry Potter* books. 'All poetry is magic' writes poet Charles Causley (1974: 15): 'Its hints, suggestions, the echoes it sets off in the mind, [...] all join up with the reader's thoughts and feelings and make a kind of magical union.'

3. Lines of poetry can provide linguistic patterns as a grammar template for the future. In most contexts where English is learned as a foreign language in formal classroom settings, the instruction takes place in an input-limited environment, which means the young learners will not be able to invoke their implicit learning mechanisms (see Introduction to the volume). An extreme restriction of input is typical of EFL in primary schools, due to lack of time in the curriculum and also frequently due to lack of fluency on the part of the teacher (see Enever 2015: 22–23). The young learner encounters a limited soundtrack of linguistic experience. In addition, the children are not able to add input autonomously unless, for example, they have access to English-language movies or TV outside school with subtitles in the mother tongue, a powerful and cognitively active kind of exposure (Lindgren and Muñoz 2013: 122), or until they can read fluently, and have manageable and motivating children's books in English at their disposal, which is seldom the case in school settings (Krashen and Bland 2014: 8–9). Most secondary school students, on the other hand, are able to employ some explicit language-learning mechanisms to support their learning. Thornbury refers to 'slow-release grammar' (2009: 4), suggesting that the lexical patterns and grammatical categories acquired unanalysed by young learners – for example through poetry – may still be available to them as meaningful illustrative exemplars when they are introduced to pedagogical grammar rules in the secondary school. The above example, 'King's Cross', spotlights the genitive – Ben's cross, Baby's cross, Mum's cross, etc. – making this grammatical category salient. It also models the very useful language: What shall we do? Leave him/her alone! For a minute or two ...

These everyday chunks, or formulaic sequences, could become immediately available for regular classroom discourse.

Listening to stretches of spoken language is of enormous importance to the young learner, who may be silently absorbed. The teacher (also secondary school teachers) must avoid slipping into the mother tongue in the urgency of the moment when organizing and managing young learners. Management situations usually require formulaic language, which 'plays an important role in second language development' (S. Kersten 2015: 129). Having studied early French immersion programmes, Harley (1998) suggests that young learners acquire second language (L2) through a memorizing, lexical approach, in contrast to a more analytic approach of late immersion students (see also K. Kersten and Rohde 2015: 76). We should trust the young learners' tolerance of ambiguity, their growing receptive and interpretative abilities, to understand chunks of language and follow the 'recommendations of researchers and child language acquisition specialists that language instruction for young learners should focus on exposure to more extended stretches of spoken language, to discourse at sentence and whole-text level' (Campfield and Murphy 2013: 2). Through salience, repetition and exaggerated prosodic features in performance, the latent structures, lexical patterns and grammatical units within playful language can stimulate the emergence of grammar.

Repetition, repetition, repetition

According to linguist Jean Aitchison (1994: 16), 'In one sense, the whole of linguistics can be regarded as the study of repetition, in that language depends on repeated patterns.' A major part of the value of poetry for young learners of English is found in this very repetition, for a number of reasons:

- Repetitive rituals characterize the child's environment.

- Language and language acquisition rely on repeated patterns.

- The patterned language of children's culture supports functional literacy (learning to read and write).

- Art can be described as patterned cognitive play.

- Literature is characterized firstly by repetition then by deviation, both of which can create salience.

- Play is itself endlessly repeated because it is pleasurable as well as educational.

Aitchison states that 'repetition skulks under numerous different names, one might almost say aliases, depending on who is repeating what where' (1994: 15). She goes on to include the following aliases in her list of repetitions:

> When parrots do it, it's parrotting [sic].
> When advertisers do it, it's reinforcement.
> When children do it, it's imitation. [. . .]
> When novelists do it, it's cohesion.
> When poets do it, it's alliteration, chiming, rhyme, or parallelism.
> When priests do it, it's ritual. (Aitchison 1994: 15)

The above list is abridged; however, one kind of repetition that is missing even from Aitchison's complete list is

> When teachers do it, it's recycling.

In addition to recycling as repetition, it has been noted that the entire language environment of early childhood, including children's literature, is repetitive and playful, and in this sense closer to poetry than to information texts (Rosenblatt 1982: 271, Bland 2013, chapter 5).

Protoconversations

Protoconversations refer to chant-like, prosodically rich and patterned child-directed speech. As an expression of the child–adult relationship they deeply engage the partners: rhythmical repetition emotionally involves infants while attuning them to a discourse partner. Vigorous nursery rhymes, with their thumping, tapping and bouncing rhythms abound in children's culture: 'Children's responses to poetry are innate, instinctive, natural – maybe it starts in the womb, with the mother's heartbeat? Children are hard-wired to musical language – taking pleasure in the rhythm, rhyme, repetition and other patternings of language that are a marked feature of childhood' (Styles 2011). This leads on to children's natural affinity with poetry: 'Poetry is never better understood than in childhood, when it is felt in the blood and along the bone' (Meek 1991: 182). Protoconversations are routines that 'use eyes and faces, hands and feet, voice and movement, these protoconversations consist of rhythmic, finely attuned turn-taking and mutual imitation, involving elaboration, exaggeration, repetition, and surprise, with each partner anticipating the other's response so as to coordinate their emotions in patterned sequence' (Boyd 2009: 97).

Using poems and rhymes with young language learners ensures that pronunciation and prosodic features (pitch, tempo, volume, rhythm and intonation) are taken up pleasurably, with singsong ease; and when the rhyme is used as a ritual, it is an expression of the classroom community. Language patterns or chunks can be noticed within this protoconversational context, for the salient stress and rhythm and repetitive exposure allow time for processing and help children perceive syntactic phrase boundaries (Campfield and Murphy 2013: 12). Rhythmical movement and also frequently physical contact are involved, promoting relaxation and trust. A significant observation in the context of L2 acquisition is that the 'delight in rhyming [...] seems to peak at around age eight' (Crystal 1998: 172), the age at which children are often already learning English as a foreign language. Functional literacy has also been shown to be supported by the mnemonic patterning of children's culture, such as the pulsating rhythm and rhyme, onomatopoeia with its echoes from the outside world, the vowel and the consonant repetition of assonance and alliteration. A longitudinal study has shown that 'informal experience with [...] linguistic routines such as nursery rhymes does play a considerable role in preparing children for learning how to read and write' (Bryant, Bradley, Maclean and Crossland 1989: 418–419), by developing children's phonological sensitivity to the component sounds in words (rhyme and phoneme detection) and drawing attention to the recurrence of patterns and grapheme-phoneme correspondences.

Fairy tales, cumulative picturebooks and above all nursery rhymes and poems abound in strong sound patterning: dynamic rhythm and rhyme, parallelism, assonance, alliteration, onomatopoeia and refrains. These delight children and are memory anchors at the same time. Listening to stories, participating in nursery rhymes, playground rhymes and poetry are therefore supremely useful activities for incidental language learning. Additionally, rhythmical repetition is hypnotic, for adults as well as for children. For centuries chants have been used to enchant audiences and gatherings.

Classroom recycling has various guises, such as revisiting, echoing, chorusing and repeating. Further, young learners often actively engage with input through individual murmured echoing or *intra*personal communication (like the whispered private speech of very young children acquiring their first language). Despite the vital importance of multiple exposures to new language material, language teachers are often far too uneasy or unaware with regard to the need for repetition. Having analysed a 121,000-word corpus of teacher talk with adult English as a second language (ESL) learners, Horst (2010: 177) reports 'few words recycled often enough to be remembered'. Lack of repetition and lack of perceptual salience are problematic particularly (but not only) with younger learners, who must largely rely on the teacher for their language input, for supportive language modelling and verbal scaffolding.

Fortunately, teachers and young learners readily accept the repetition and rehearsal (another kind of repetition) required to learn poems by heart and recite them dramatically in chorus. Young learners not yet literate in the foreign language must learn poems initially by listening, and an important support for the memorization process is the echo technique. Teachers can even encourage children to pretend they really are in a cave, asking them to echo each line three times, gradually reducing the volume to a whisper (*diminuendo*). Alternatively, it is pleasurable for children to chant dialogues rhythmically – one side of the classroom answering the other side, the boys answering the girls or the eight-year-olds answering the nine-year-olds – rehearsing language and dramatic routines using body language, gestures and facial expression, also participating in energetic communal interaction: turning, jumping, stretching and bumping.

Patterned cognitive play

All kinds of art, but particularly narrative art, have been defined as patterned cognitive play (Boyd 2009: 80–98). With reference to neuroscience, Boyd maintains that humans have evolved 'pattern-matching neural processing' (2009: 134). Poems and nursery rhymes are highly patterned, due to their singsong rhythms, rhymes, alliteration and regular personifications. No doubt also for this reason they appeal so intensely to primary-aged children as they are one of the important ways to satisfy the *cognitive need for pattern* of this age group. The larger-than-life characters become lifelong friends and the rhythms become enduringly familiar melodies.

> Hey diddle, diddle!
> The cat and the fiddle,
> The cow jumped over the moon;
> The little dog laughed
> To see such sport,
> And the dish ran away with the spoon.

This favourite nursery rhyme succeeds, in its few brief catchy lines with a total of thirty words, not only to create a vivacious personification of the animals, the musical cat, sportive cow and the humorous dog, but also invites the listener to infer a love story to the dish and the spoon. Illustrators invariably depict them as running away hand in hand, and the moon is traditionally given a laughing face. Personification is a potent tool that recurs as a pattern in literature for the young: emotional engagement is achieved and the inexplicable comes alive. Clearly visualization, in the sense of creating mental images while listening or reading, is strongly supported. This is an important introduction to the skill of creating a mental model of a storyworld, which is the essence of reading literature meaningfully.

The recent Children's Laureate, Michael Rosen, has created his own version of 'Hey Diddle Diddle', which is identical to the traditional rhyme except for the last line: 'And the dish ran away with the *chocolate biscuits*' (Rosen 2000: 10). This is an invitation and challenge to young readers to copy the rhyme into their portfolios, making up and illustrating their own final line, for example:

- And the dish ran away with the *jar of honey.*
- And the dish ran away with the *wobbly jelly.*
- And the dish ran away with the *gingerbread man.*

Or the young writers may be invited to find an alternative rhyming word:

- And the dish ran away with the *raccoon/ baboon/ with a balloon/ in the afternoon.*

In this way, traditional rhymes can be creatively reworked (especially when food is involved) as a support for children's reading and writing. The nursery rhyme *Old Mother Hubbard* tells a sad little tale of empty cupboards and hunger:

Old Mother Hubbard
Went to the cupboard
To get her poor dog a bone.
When she got there,
The cupboard was bare,
And so the poor dog had none.

Once again, alternative final lines can be invented, for example:

When she got there,
The cupboard was bare,
So she summoned a pizza by phone.

Or

So they had a McChicken at home. So they ordered fish and chips by phone.

In a multicultural classroom, the children will certainly be able to think of many alternative takeaways. Children's appetite for food and for love, as well as for pattern – their pattern-matching neural processing – is expertly expressed in the following poem, Brian Patten's 'Squeezes':

We love to squeeze bananas,
We love to squeeze ripe plums,
And when they are feeling sad
We love to squeeze our mums. (Patten 1999: 100)

This is another poem that can take its place happily in classroom management situations, contributing to affective learning, when weary young learners need stirring up or cheering up. I suggest reciting together both Patten's original, and an alternative version with the final last line:

We love to squeeze our chums.

No child needs prompting to act out the real world of friendship, by seizing their chums and giving them a hug.

Mini storyworlds: Essential context for affective learning and intercultural insight

The previous section emphasized that repetition is essential for language learning and discussed the usefulness of poetry in this respect. Repetition is also characteristic of play, 'Play's compulsiveness ensures the repetition that allows time to reconfigure minds and bodies. [...] Through overlearning actions, we can take them to a new level of control and flexibility [...] ' (Boyd 2009: 180). Make-believe is the natural continuation and further development of individual child play, taking place with school-aged children mostly in the social sphere. Performance of poetry mirrors children's make-believe games, as long as the rhymes and poems tell stories that the young learners can picture in their minds. This section illustrates how the storyworlds of narrative poems give the new language patterns a meaningful context: 'The contextualization of vocabulary is vital, even from the earliest stages. [...] [L]exical items should be stored [in the mental lexicon] in a meaningful way, i.e. in connection with other related words and in a specific context' (Hutz 2012: 111).

Smith (2000: 16) considers the 'virtuoso marriage of form and content is not unusual in nursery rhymes, and must be part of their strength and appeal'. Nonsense words in poetry are additional fun, as in 'Hey Diddle Diddle', with lines that 'glitter with rhyme and alliteration' (Smith 2000: 16), but alongside the fun of language, poetry for children should create a coherent mini fantasy storyworld or reflect the child's own world. This is particularly important in the foreign-language classroom with school-aged children. Mere rhythm and rhyme without a story attached to it (however inventive and bizarre) comes across as mechanical jingle and meaningless – except, for example, as skipping and counting out rhymes, which have a functional purpose in skipping and chasing games. It is, however, frustrating to try and act out rhymes without a mini storyworld and nearly impossible to learn them by heart; young learners are not able to create a mental model of the storyworld when there is none to imagine.

Guy Cook (2000) emphasizes the need for a much stronger play element in language learning, not only for young learners. Cook notes 'it is the bizarre and unusual uses of language which, outside the classroom, seem to capture attention, take on importance, and remain in the mind' (Cook 2000: 169).

Many rhymes demand to be acted out, for example, 'Five Little Soldiers Standing in a Row', with three children playing the soldiers that stand up straight and two children playing soldiers lounging about. Another child, the 'captain', marches up to the two relaxing 'soldiers', and of course they jump to attention 'as quick as a wink'. Children enjoy performing or rehearsing disobedience as well as obedience to authority, and as the story of the rhyme suits children's natural make-believe, they find the rhyme easy to memorize and pleasurable to act out:

> Five little soldiers standing in a row,
> Three stood straight,
> And two stood – so.
> Along came the captain,
> And what do you think?
> They ALL stood straight,
> As quick as a wink. (traditional)

Nursery rhymes have stood the test of time, over generations parents have remembered them from their own childhoods and passed them on to their children, which supports David Crystal's claim that 'Everyone, regardless of cognitive level, plays with language or responds to language play' (Crystal 1996: 328).

Poets who write for children often emulate the successful combination of language play and strong rhythm, colourful characters and vibrant storyworld that characterizes long-lasting anonymous nursery rhymes. The following poem has a clear storyworld, one that most primary-aged children are able to relate to. Young learners whom I have taught have recited this poem back to me as adults, as it caught their imagination and stayed with them over the years:

> Mummy, mummy, sweet as honey,
> Busy as a bee,
> Buzzing off to earn some money,
> Buzzing home to me. (Anholt and Anholt[1] 1998)

Dividing the class into bees and children enlivens the poem and concentrates attention. The 'bees' provide a soft buzzing chorus, an *ostinato*, watch the drama the other children are acting out and wait their turn. The remaining young learners play the children who recite the poem and one of them plays 'mummy'. The class first needs to negotiate what mothers do that keeps them busy at home, such as cooking, gardening, writing emails, hanging up washing, unpacking shopping, tidying away toys, filling in forms, etc. The 'mummy' mimes a household chore as the first two lines are recited, moves away to the door on the third line, then on the fourth line buzzes back to the young learners reciting the poem, choosing and embracing her 'child' (who becomes the next 'mummy'). The excitement of being chosen to star in the next round is an aspect of the compulsiveness of games that supports learning through repetition: overlearning actions and language. At the same time, the children are incidentally learning pronunciation ('busy' does *not* rhyme with 'buzzing'), interesting similes (sweet as honey, busy as a bee) and onomatopoeia (buzzing), which can lay the groundwork of literary competence.

A simile is a comparison between two different things and is a common literary device in poetry. The following poem is shaped by a humorous extended comparison between Scotland and England, possibly an interesting subject for the EFL classroom as stereotyping is avoided. The lines are taken from an autobiographical, uncharacteristically playful poem by the English Romantic poet John Keats. Despite the naughtiness of the boy in 'A Song about Myself', the poem ends quietly and contemplatively; the story seems to illustrate the proverb 'the grass is always greener on the other side of the fence'. It might appeal to the imaginations of older primary students or lower secondary, as the poet died tragically young, at the age of twenty-five, and yet his (more complex) major works have since been recognized as among the finest English poems ever written.

> There was a naughty boy,
> And a naughty boy was he,
> He ran away to Scotland
> The people for to see –
> There he found
> That the ground
> Was as hard,
> That a yard
> Was as long,
> That a song
> Was as merry,
> That a cherry
> Was as red
> As in England –
> So he stood in his shoes
> And he wondered,

He wondered,
He stood in his
Shoes and he wondered. (from 'A Song about Myself', John Keats 1818)

This is a poem for wondering, listening and thinking, not acting out. If it catches
the children's imagination, they may like to copy it into their portfolio – copying
down interesting texts is a potent learning strategy, for it can give the children
confidence that they can act autonomously and take ownership of their learning.
The young learners could illustrate the poem with the outline of Great Britain –
England, Scotland and Wales, or the UK – Great Britain and Northern Ireland.

Transmitting cultural knowledge with poems

Great Britain is the largest island in Europe and the ninth-largest island in
the world, so it is not surprising that the sea features in many poems that
originated there. This little poem is evocative of draughty old houses on the
coast of the windy and stormy North Atlantic Ocean.

I know a house, and a cold old house,
A cold old house by the sea.
If I were a mouse in that cold old house
What a cold, cold mouse I'd be! (anonymous)

After learning the poem using the echo technique, the children can have fun
performing it. One half of the class performs the whistling wind, while the
other half recites the poem in unison – not forgetting to shiver, of course.
British family holidays frequently take place by the sea, on sandy or pebbly
beaches. The seaside can be very windy, so most British children are used
to sand in their clothes and shoes, sand in their eyes and sand in their
sandwiches, as the following lines from a longer poem by Judith Nicholls
demonstrate:

We've crisps with sand
and cake with sand –
it's grand with lunch or tea –
crunch it up,
enjoy it, love,
at least we're by the sea! (Nicholls 2000: 76)

No wonder Margaret Meek (1988: 17) calls British sea bathing children's
'annual endurance test'. Some poems are humorously anarchical. In the

following one it is Daddy who suffers from too much sand (burying fathers in the sand is fun even on cold and windy beaches).

> Daddy at the seaside,
> Daddy in the sun,
> Daddy on a surfboard,
> Daddy having fun.
> Daddy getting buried
> In sand up to his chin –
> 'Help!' he yells.
> 'Please dig me out
> Before the tide comes in!' (Anholt and Anholt[2]: 1998)

When there are lines of direct speech in a poem, as in this case, these can be performed by a group of young learners or an individual volunteer.

From anarchy to empathy

A flirtation with anarchy is typical for humorous and nonsense literature (Goldthwaite 1996: 15). This reflects children's position in the family and in the classroom – they are learning to fit in but also testing the boundaries. Subversive children's literature often parodies conventional heavily didactic and sentimental children's stories.

> Thank you for your photo,
> I think it's very nice.
> I've put it in the attic
> To scare away the mice. (anonymous)

Children's own invented rhymes are usually subversive and challenge authority; they are attractive to young learners because they belong to the children, not the adults. Some will be keen to learn the following rhyme by heart or write it in their portfolio just because it is so cheeky.

> Two little kids in a flying saucer
> Flew around the school one day.
> They looked to the left and right a bit,
> And couldn't bear the sight of it,
> And then they flew away! (anonymous)

The subject matter of this little poem could be introduced as a picture dictation. The teacher can invite the young learners to draw the outline of their school and the teacher describes school children running around in the scene – for example, they are playing football, skipping, playing chase, sitting on a bench and reading – the young learners draw the picture according to the teacher's description. Finally the teacher tells the children to draw a flying saucer hovering over the school. The teacher can bring a saucer to the classroom and fly it around the classroom, or draw a UFO on the blackboard to support comprehension. The young learners draw two little kids inside their flying saucer, and colour them green, red or whatever colour they choose. In this way the teacher can set the scene before telling the above rhyme. Setting the scene is a very important pre-task for poems and stories, and the picture-dictation method often allows the teacher to introduce the most important new vocabulary quite incidentally. The humour of children's culture and children's literature is also seen as an empowering and meaningful element: 'The best antidote to the anxieties and disasters of life is laughter; and this children seem to understand almost as soon as they are born. If laughter is lacking, they create it; if it is offered to them, they relish it' (Opie 1992: 14).

All primary children enjoy the joke of the following kind of rhyme. The 'insiders' chorus the narrating lines, beginning 'I went up one pair of stairs'. The newcomers to the poem who are to be tricked (e.g. a visiting teacher or parent) are invited to chorus 'Just like me' after each line:

I went up one pair of stairs.
Just like me.
I went up two pairs of stairs.
Just like me.
I went into a room.
Just like me.
I looked out of a window.
Just like me.
And I saw a monkey.
Just like me. (anonymous)

Humour is one of the most inviting and therefore important ingredients in children's literature (Tabbert and Wardetzky 1995: 3). When the storyworld is topsy-turvy and inventive, the creativity of the pattern-seeking reader/ listener is exercised. When the storyworld is implausible and bizarre the imagination is exercised, as in the following little poem:

As I was going out one day
My head fell off and rolled away.
But when I saw that it was gone,
I picked it up and put it on. (anonymous)

Poetry offers the young-learner classroom language-rich input. The little verse above consists of just two sentences, but five extremely useful phrasal verbs: 'go out', 'fall off', 'roll away', 'pick up' and 'put on'. The usage-based linguistic approach to L2 development (see S. Kersten 2015: 134–135) suggests that experience of template-like exemplars in a supportive context results in language emergence over time. Additionally, the ability of poems to highlight language – making its usage salient and memorable, for example, 'my head fell off' – is an important support for L2 acquisition. Limericks too offer humour and brevity and encourage performance with expressive prosodic features, and are easily memorized by young learners who do not yet read fluently – due to their strong rhythm:

> There was a young man of Bengal,
> Who was asked to a fancy dress ball.
> He murmured: 'I'll risk it
> And go as a biscuit'.
> But a dog ate him up in the hall. (anonymous)

The first two lines offer a relative clause and passive voice, which will remain initially unanalysed and latent in young-learner contexts. However, children may find the lexical patterns 'fancy dress ball' and 'go as a biscuit' immediately useful. Finally, 'I'll risk it' could be considered a valuable template and helpful exemplar of the use of the future, which may be unpacked when the young learners are ready to acquire this structure: 'I'll risk it. I'll go as a vampire.'

As well as anarchy, the storyworld of poetry often encourages empathy, which is an important ingredient of intercultural learning. Empathy helps children view the world through the eyes of others and moves them towards flexibility of perspective. The persona of a poem, the 'I' who speaks the lines, may be a lively, a mischievous or a contemplative child, with whom the young learners may both identify and feel empathy. The following lines are taken from a longer poem, 'First and Last', by June Crebbin; in this case the persona is a quieter child who would rather 'stay by the wall' and who chooses 'to be last in the line':

> I like to be first in the playground,
> I like to stand by the tree,
> I like to imagine that all this space
> Belongs entirely to me. (Crebbin 2000: 25)

Poetry makes language salient through its appeal to the emotions and the magnetism of its repetitions ('I like to … ' in the poem above), its rhythms and rhymes: 'Poetry is an intense form of language. It can be simultaneously personal and universal. It enlarges the sympathies, helps us understand ourselves better, gives us the pleasure of vicarious experience and offers us insights about being human. It provides a way of working out feelings, giving order to experience by reducing it to manageable proportions' (Styles 2011). Salient, evocative language and moving, musical repetition are the highly important ingredients that make poetry memorable.

Grammatical categories acquired as a template for the future

Recent psycholinguistic and corpus linguistic investigations into young children's first language acquisition suggest that 'the children are picking up frequent patterns from what they hear around them and only slowly making more abstract generalizations as the database of related utterances grows' (Ellis 2002: 169). The usage-based model of language acquisition stipulates that, in their first language, children's ability to create their own grammatically well-formed utterances emerges over time from the tremendous wealth of input they receive. In L2 acquisition, the input is, of course, usually severely limited and the progress is consequently very slow. The rhymes and poems in this chapter can nonetheless help young learners acquire an inventory of grammatical categories and lexical patterns, which are important even though these are not yet analysed in the primary school.

Usage-based approaches to L2 acquisition emphasize the role of input, and the importance of frequency of exposure: 'Learning, memory and perception are all affected by frequency of usage: the more times we experience something, the stronger our memory for it, and the more fluently it is accessed' (Ellis, O'Donnell and Römer 2013: 31). However, the input must also be varied in semantic scope, as learner productivity – the discovery of grammatical categories and unpacking of lexical patterns – is due to type rather than token frequency (Ellis et al. 2013: 31). The simple repetition of the same brief poem, rhyme or song does not support type frequency, but reiterates the self-same tokens or reoccurrence of words. This is useful too, for young learners need consistency and routines, as well as salience and frequency (Murphy 2014: 13). However, the morphemes, words and lexical patterns should reappear in different contexts. Otherwise the 'repeating after the teacher', which is a favourite activity in many primary language classrooms worldwide (Garton, Copland and Burns 2011: 12), can too easily become meaninglessly mechanical. Myles, Hooper and Mitchell (1998: 359) have shown how the young learners in their study, who had initially acquired formulaic sequences as unanalysed wholes, 'did use the formulas as a database for hypothesis testing'. Thus rich input in the wider context of classroom discourse is of central importance, for it will allow the young learners to experience richer linguistic breadth to scaffold language development.

The poems introduced in this chapter have included negatives, imperatives, interrogatives, infinitives, comparatives, conditionals, modal verbs, relative clauses, phrasal verbs, many prepositional phrases, formulaic sequences generally, idiomatic language, future, genitive and passive, and numerous examples of present and past tenses. The aim is for young learners to add many unanalysed exemplars of grammatical categories and lexical patterns to their repertoire of language. These are acquired as templates and hopefully in future reactivated. With sufficient input, children may infer productive patterns, and, as in first language acquisition, increased command of language may emerge. Moreover, it is to be expected that pedagogical grammar rules learned in the secondary school will be more effective and meaningful when language students already have a repertoire of lexical patterns and grammatical categories as illustrative exemplars, for 'the rule is an artefact of the pattern-based learning, rather than the underlying source of learning' (Schmitt and Carter 2004: 14).

Whole-body repetition, whole-body classroom rituals

The centrality of repetition in language learning has been highlighted in this chapter. A major advantage of performing poems in primary school is that the repetition is both natural and pleasurable, and poetry offers 'the kinesthetic bounce of repetition and surprise' (Coats 2013: 133). The following poem can be practised in a tactile and whole-body fashion. The storyworld is easily visualized, and the alliteration, personification and direct speech draw the young learners into the pretty green garden.

> I saw a slippery, slithery snake
> Slide through the grasses,
> Making them shake.
> He looked at me with his beady eye.
> 'Go away from my
> Pretty green garden', said I.
> 'Sssss', said the slippery, slithery snake,
> As he slid through the grasses,
> Making them shake. (anonymous)

In order to practise the poem until all the young learners have learnt it by heart, the teacher invites the children to form a circle, standing close together around the pretty green garden. All the children stand facing in the same direction, with their hands on the back of the child in front. Their hands perform the slippery, slithery movements of the snake on the child's back in front of them, and shake the shoulders of the child on the words 'Making them shake'. Gestures that illustrate 'beady eye', 'go away' and 'sssss' accompany the next lines. Finally, the children perform the snake movements of the last two lines on the back of the child in front. Reciting a poem in a circle in this participatory way can also fulfil the function of an end-of-class ritual over a number of weeks.

Similarly, the following rhyme combines meaningful and tuneful language as an opportunity for a whole-body classroom ritual. At the beginning or end of the English lesson, the young learners can transform from silent 'paper and string' (the children crouching on the ground) to a kite that flies (the children dancing with their arms and bodies, but attached to the ground by the string), then back to the ground as silent string and paper:

A kite on the ground
is just paper and string
but up in the air
it will dance and sing.
A kite in the air
will dance and will caper
but back on the ground
it's just string and paper. (anonymous)

Conclusion

It has been shown in this chapter that the pulsating and salient language of poetry helps young learners develop phonological and grammatical sensitivity. I have also emphasized that children experience a sensory pleasure in meaningful repetition, such as rhythmical chanting, rehearsing and repeated performance. However, this approach is very different from that of the pattern drill of the audio-lingual method, which was based on behaviourist theory. For I have discussed in this chapter the importance of context, meaning and storyworlds that allow young learners to create mental representations of the language in the poems. This aspect was missing from the soul-less mechanical pattern drills of the past. Young learners' language learning requires patterns with an emphasis on meaning: 'Mindful repetition in an engaging communicative context by motivated learners' (Ellis 2002: 177, emphasis in the original). Lexical patterns and grammatical categories can be a template for the future, as long as they are *contextualized and meaningful*, as they are, for example, in well-chosen poetry for children.

Notes

1 'Mummy, mummy, sweet as honey' © 1998 Catherine and Laurence Anholt. From *Big Book of Families*. Reproduced by permission of Walker Books Ltd. London SE11 5HJ www.walker.co.uk.

2 'Daddy at the seaside' © 1998 Catherine and Laurence Anholt. From *Big Book of Families*. Reproduced by permission of Walker Books Ltd. London SE11 5HJ www.walker.co.uk.

References

Aitchison, Jean (1994), '"Say, say it again Sam": The Treatment of Repetition in Linguistics', in Andreas Fischer (ed), *Repetition*, Tübingen: Narr, pp. 15–34.

Anholt, Catherine and Anholt, Laurence (1998), *Big Book of Families*, London: Walker Books.

Bland, Janice (2013), *Children's Literature and Learner Empowerment. Children and Teenagers in English Language Education*, London: Bloomsbury.

Boyd, Brian (2009), *On the Origin of Stories: Evolution, Cognition, and Fiction*, Harvard: Harvard University Press.

Bryant, Peter; Bradley, Lynette; Maclean, Moira and Crossland, John (1989), 'Nursery rhymes, phonological skills and reading', *Journal of Child Language*, 89/16: 407–428.

Campfield, Dorota and Murphy, Victoria (2013), 'The influence of prosodic input in the second language classroom: Does it stimulate child acquisition of word order and function words?', *Language Learning Journal*, DOI: 10.1080/09571736.2013.807864.

Causley, Charles (ed) (1974), *The Puffin Book of Magic Verse*, London: Puffin.

Coats, Karen (2013), 'The meaning of children's poetry: A cognitive approach', *International Research in Children's Literature* 6/2: 127–142.

Cook, Guy (2000), *Language Play, Language Learning*, Oxford: Oxford University Press.

Crebbin, June (2000), 'First and last', in June Crebbin (ed), *The Puffin Book of Fantastic First Poems*, London: Puffin.

Crystal, David (1996), 'Language play and linguistic intervention', *Child Language Teaching and Therapy*, 12: 328–344.

Crystal, David (1998), *Language Play*, London: Penguin Books.

Ellis, Nick (2002), 'Frequency effects in language acquisition: A review with implications for theories of implicit and explicit language acquisition', *Studies in Second Language Acquisition*, 24/2: 143–188.

Ellis, Nick; O'Donnell, Matthew and Römer, Ute (2013), 'Usage-based language: Investigating the latent structures that underpin acquisition', *Language Learning*, 63: 25–51.

Enever, Janet (2015), 'The advantages and disadvantages of English as a foreign language with young learners', in Janice Bland (ed), *Teaching English to Young Learners. Critical Issues in Language Teaching with 3–12 Year Olds*, London: Bloomsbury Academic, pp. 13–29.

Farjeon, Eleanor (1999), *Blackbird Has Spoken: Selected Poems for Children*, London: Macmillan.

Garton, Susan; Copland, Fiona, and Burns, Anne (2011), *Investigating Global Practices in Teaching English to Young Learners*. <http://iatefl.britishcouncil.org/2012/sites/iatefl/files/session/documents/eltrp_report_-_garton.pdf> [accessed 11 September 2014].

Goldthwaite, John (1996), *The Natural History of Make-Believe*, New York: Oxford University Press.

Harley, Birgit (1998), 'The outcomes of early and later language learning', in Myriam Met (ed), *Critical Issues in Early Second Language Learning. Building for Our Children's Future*, Glenview: Scott Foresman – Addison Wesley.

Horst, Marlise (2010), 'How well does teacher-talk support incidental vocabulary acquisition?', *Reading in a Foreign Language*, 22: 161–180.

Hutz, Matthias (2012), 'Storing words in the mind: The mental lexicon and vocabulary learning', in Maria Eisenmann and Theresa Summer (eds), *Basic Issues in EFL Teaching and Learning*, Heidelberg: Winter, pp. 105–117.

Kersten, Kristin and Rohde, Andreas (2015), 'Immersion teaching in English with young learners', in Janice Bland (ed), *Teaching English to Young Learners. Critical Issues in Language Teaching with 3–12 Year Olds*, London: Bloomsbury Academic, pp. 71–89.

Kersten, Saskia (2015), 'Language development in young learners: The role of formulaic language', in Janice Bland (ed), *Teaching English to Young Learners. Critical Issues in Language Teaching with 3–12 Year Olds*, London: Bloomsbury Academic, pp. 129–145.

Krashen, Stephen and Bland, Janice (2014), 'Compelling Comprehensible Input, Academic Language and School Libraries', *Children's Literature in English Language Education*, 2/2: 1–12.

Lindgren, Eva and Muñoz, Carmen (2013), 'The influence of exposure, parents and linguistic distance on young European learners' foreign language comprehension', *International Journal of Multilingualism*, 10/1: 105–129.

Meek, Margaret (1988), *How Texts Teach What Readers Learn*, Stroud: Thimble Press.

Meek, Margaret (1991), *On Being Literate*, London: Bodley Head.

Murphy, Victoria (2014), *Second Language Learning in the Early School Years: Trends and Contexts*, Oxford: Oxford University Press.

Myles, Florence; Hooper, Janet and Mitchell, Rosamond (1998), 'Rote or Rule? Exploring the role of formulaic language in classroom foreign language learning', *Language Learning*, 48: 323–364.

Nicholls, Judith (2000), 'Picnic', in June Crebbin (ed), *The Puffin Book of Fantastic First Poems*, London: Puffin.

Opie, Iona (1992), 'Introduction', in Iona Opie and Peter Opie (eds), illus. Sendak, Maurice, *I Saw Esau*, London: Walker Books, pp. 11–14.

Patten, Brian (ed) (1999), *The Puffin Book of Utterly Brilliant Poetry*, London: Puffin Books.

Rosen, Michael (2000), 'Hey Diddle Diddle', in June Crebbin (ed), *The Puffin Book of Fantastic First Poems*, London: Puffin.

Rosenblatt, Louise (1982), 'The Literary Transaction: Evocation and response', *Theory into Practice*, 21/4: 268–277.

Schmitt, Norbert and Carter, Ronald (2004), 'Formulaic sequences in action', in Norbert Schmitt (ed), *Formulaic Sequences*, Amsterdam: John Benjamins, pp. 1–22.

Smith, Vivienne (2000), 'Give Yourself a Hug. Reading between the rhymes', in Holly Anderson and Morag Styles (eds), *Teaching through Texts*, London: Routledge, pp. 13–28.

Styles, Morag (2011), *The Case for Children's Poetry*. University of Cambridge. <http://www.cam.ac.uk/research/discussion/the-case-for-children's-poetry> [accessed 17 November 2014].

Tabbert, Reinbert and Wardetzky, Kristin (1995), 'On the success of children's books and fairy tales: A comparative view of impact theory and reception research', *The Lion and the Unicorn*, 19/1: 1–19.

Thornbury, Scott (2009), 'Slow-release grammar', *English Teaching Professional*, 09/61: 4–6.

9

Developing Intercultural Understanding in Primary Schools

Patricia Driscoll
and Helen Simpson

Introduction

The rise of English as an international language for popular culture, technology, the internet, research, commerce and banking (Nuffield 2000, Crystal 2003, British Academy 2011) has created the need for an unprecedented number of individuals from non-English-speaking countries to learn the language. In secondary schools, English is acknowledged as a key skill and is the main language other than the national language taught in schools (European Commission 2012). The rapid increase of early language-learning programmes has been stimulated predominantly by the need to learn English and to raise levels of linguistic competence by the end of schooling (Edelenbos, Johnstone and Kubanek-German 2006; Enever and Moon 2008).

In England, early language learning springs from similar instrumental aspirations of equipping citizens with the necessary skills to operate globally in the twenty-first century (DfES 2002). The Nuffield Foundation's investigation of the language capability of the UK found that 'English alone is not enough' for economic growth, and the chronic shortage of usable language skills leaves the country vulnerable in an increasingly competitive world (Nuffield Foundation 2000: 14). There are considerable differences in educational policy in the four countries of the UK and this chapter focuses centrally on policy and practice in England. The evidence and discussion, however, have broader implications and relate to early language learning and developing intercultural understanding in general.

Findings from a recent study of the languages most needed in the UK (British Council 2014) suggest that a much wider range of languages will be needed in the future to preserve economic well-being. The report lists the most important languages associated with UK exports, these include Arabic, Mandarin and Portuguese, as well as German, Spanish and French, which are predominantly taught in English schools. Importantly, the report argues for the need to balance economic priorities with cultural, intellectual, individual and societal non-market factors (2014). It specifically draws attention to a position paper published by the British Academy (2011), which makes a powerful case for the importance of developing greater intercultural understanding for economic as well as societal reasons.

Tinsley (2013) presents a range of evidence about the benefits of intercultural as well as linguistic skills in her recent examination of the current demand and supply of language skills in the UK. She also argues for the personal and societal value of developing a global mindset and a willingness and ability to manage complex intercultural relationships when abroad as well as at home. Fostering an open mindset, developing tolerance, cultural sensitivity and an acceptance and understanding of diversity in increasingly multilingual and multicultural societies are essential features in preparing young people for a future which is not confined by local, regional or national borders. Schools play a crucial role in preparing learners for their future lives; arguably it is an essential part of their core purpose.

Education cannot be justified purely in terms of future attainment. Cregan and Cuthbert (2014: 4) question the term 'child' in relation to the notion of the global child and argue that at the simplest level a child 'is a young human being [...] in the stage of life known as childhood', which should be respected. They are not simply adults-in-waiting. Alongside preparing future citizens, primary schools also play a key role in educating children in the broadest sense, by providing a wide variety of experiences to enable them to thrive as children, as well as the adults they will become. Children's own perceptions about what is significant in their lives are also important. According to Robin Alexander (2010), there is limited evidence reported that relates to pupils' views of the purpose of primary schooling. The evidence presented in the Cambridge Primary Review (Alexander 2010: 20) suggests that pupils predominantly view primary schools as places to prepare them for their future work. In addition, pupils consider that schools provide important contexts for social mixing and making friends, and spaces to learn how to generally conduct themselves outside of the home. Understanding and accepting cultural and social diversity and gaining insights into the nuances of one's own cultural identity are key features of learning about the complexity of social and cultural interaction and the etiquette of social conduct.

We argue in this chapter that in general, intercultural understanding is marginalized in language lessons even though many teachers believe that culture is a key component of learning a foreign language. We begin the chapter by defining culture and the importance of cultural learning within foreign languages. We present recent evidence of intercultural learning in primary schools, locating the discussion within the policy framework at the time the research was conducted. Finally we consider the potential of a more holistic cross-curricular approach that extends the dynamics of intercultural understanding across the whole school and the wider curriculum with the child and not the symbolic 'stranger' or 'foreigner' (representative of foreign cultures) at the centre of learning.

Defining culture

Culture is an all-encompassing and complex concept with a wide range of different types of definitions. According to Woodgate-Jones and Grenfell (2012: 333), 152 definitions of culture existed by the early 1950s, to include 'the arts [...] human knowledge, beliefs, behaviour, shared attitudes, values, goals, practice, and traditions' but, they argue, the concept has developed since then. Culture is, therefore, everywhere. It is tangible in the form of visual arts, music and literature and visible in the everyday behaviours, routines and rituals of people; it is also embedded within the pattern of invisible codes which influence our beliefs, deeds, way of life, perceptions of our heritage and the vision of our future. Wedell and Malderez (2013: 31) describe culture as 'a socially shared, underlying, often "taken-for-granted" system of "rules" which guide and control social behaviour, and which are very strongly held and affectively charged'. To develop an awareness of the forces which have such a powerful effect on one's own identity and the identity of others is an important step in self-discovery and understanding the communities in which we live.

Through a patchwork of emotional, physical and cognitive, active and passive experiences, we both absorb and actively learn about the attitudes, beliefs, values and behaviour of a particular group. Adapting to different macro-cultures within a society is part of being human, and children from an early age begin to learn how to modify their behaviour and respond in different settings both within and outside of the home. Once at school and frequently before, they begin to learn how to interact with different groups and that there exist rules of conduct which they may or may not understand, and which at times may be contradictory, but which can command sanctions if contravened. They absorb culture as they go about their daily lives and learn how to modify and adapt their behaviour as they interact with the range of people they encounter.

By learning to look critically at the dominant discourses that surround them and by beginning to analyse the dynamics of culture from an early age, children can develop an appreciation and respect for the diversity within their own culture. Schools, through the curriculum, play a part in offering children opportunities to feel a sense of belonging to a regional or national group. Reflecting upon and analysing culture does not undermine feelings of belonging; rather it has the potential to create curiosity about the world, raise questions about the simple notion of 'us' and 'them' and promote a sense of global identity.

Intercultural learning within foreign languages

The importance of the cultures and context associated with foreign or second language learning is emphasized by Kramsch (1993: 1), who argues that 'culture in language learning is not an expendable fifth skill, tacked on', but rather it is fundamental in achieving communicative competence and an essential part of learning another language. Understanding cultural conventions of interaction and rules of social engagement, therefore, is considered essential to minimize the potential for offense or miscommunication.

Johnstone (2009: 38) reminds us that we are now in the third wave of implementing early language learning: with the first wave starting in the 1960s, the second in the mid-1980s and the third wave in recent times. Over this period language teaching has changed radically and with it the role and status of cultural and intercultural learning. Fluent communication, as the ultimate aim of language learning, swept across much of foreign and second language pedagogy from the 1980s, with the communicative language teaching (CLT) approach (Littlewood 1981). CLT focuses on setting up communicative activities for practical communication in the classroom. Learners are encouraged to interact in the target language about matters which interest them and engage in role-play scenarios in simulated 'real-life' situations with the view that they will be able to apply their knowledge and skills when communicating outside of the classroom and in the target country. Grenfell (2000: 24) argues that the national curriculum and public examinations were designed according to the principles of CLT which placed the learner as a tourist or host by reinforcing the prominence of personal communication in 'authentic' learning situations.

Culture can be incorporated into classroom-based learning through the teacher, through interaction with others and through resources. Technological advances in teaching materials from the 1980s to the present day have allowed teachers to provide learners with vicarious experiences of 'real life' cultural images and scenes of native speakers interacting. Teachers can exploit these visual images and creatively enhance teaching and learning so the language is modelled within a cultural frame. Non-specialist primary teachers, however, may have limited, if any, personal experience of countries where the target language is spoken, and may lack the knowledge to explore culture in any depth (Driscoll, Earl and Cable 2013). Curriculum time for primary languages is also relatively short in England, with the majority of language lessons taught once a week for thirty or forty-five minutes (Wade and Marshall 2009). As a consequence, irrespective of teachers' subject knowledge when cultural references are made, they tend to be brief, leaving little time for analysis or discussion about cultural identity (Driscoll et al., 2013).

The Common European Framework (CEFR) (Council of Europe 2001), a curriculum guidance resource used extensively across Europe and beyond, strongly advocates the importance of intercultural knowledge and skills within effective communication. The concept of intercultural competence developed extensively by Michael Byram (1989, 1997), underpins how intercultural understanding is conceptualized in the CEFR. His model of the five *savoirs* encompasses the knowledge, skills, behaviours and attitudes needed to interact with those from other cultures and the ability to de-centre and understand other cultures and one's own through the eyes of someone from another culture. The *savoirs* include:

- *Savoir être* – attitudes of curiosity and openness: 'the kind of learner who notices and asks questions, who expresses wonder and interest in other people's behaviours and beliefs, rather than rejection and disgust' (Byram and Doyé 1999: 142).

- *Savoirs* – knowledge of self, other and individual and societal interaction.

- *Savoir comprendre* – skills of interpreting: 'the ability to take a person's school report and not just translate it but explain the significance of what is written, how it relates to the education system' (Byram and Doyé 1999: 142).

- *Savoir apprendre/faire* – skills of discovery and interaction.

- *Savoir s'engager* – critical cultural awareness, which calls for reflection and analysis within an educational framework.

Byram's model of the skills, knowledge and understanding required for intercultural competence is also evident in the national strategy, *Languages for All: Languages for Life* (DfES 2002), which set out a vision for lifelong language learning starting in primary school, over a decade ago. The strategy extends the cultural dimension in languages to include global citizenship and social cohesion, highlighting the importance of understanding different perspectives and cultures with the view to breaking down *'barriers of ignorance and suspicion'* (DfES 2002: 13). Through developing a more explicit understanding of their own culture and language, and the culture and language of those around them, children can learn to appreciate and value diversity while appreciating a sense of their own uniqueness. The concept of 'otherness', therefore, becomes a normal part of the local as much as the national and international.

Hennebry (2014: 141) compares the ways in which culture is included in the national curricula of languages in five countries. The comparison demonstrates that although culture manifests itself in different ways in different curricula, the aims and objectives in the majority of cases tend towards a conceptualization of culture as intercultural communicative competence. Hennebry argues that these include comparing and appreciating the similarities and differences between the home and target culture, developing a critical cultural awareness about one's own and other cultures and valuing the perspective of others. The comparison focuses on secondary-school education, but nonetheless it gives an insight into the concept of culture within these national policies.

Language learning in primary school

Byram and Doyé (1999: 141) suggest that there are aspects of intercultural competence that can be pursued easily in the primary school. They contend that primary schools are well placed to cultivate attitudes of openness and curiosity (*savoir être*) and develop positive attitudes towards the people who live in the countries where the target language is spoken. They also highlight the potential for reinforcing primary children's knowledge of their own culture through contrast (*savoirs*), by comparing the similarities and differences between cultural habits and traditions, as children are being socialized into their own environment. In addition, children can also gain insights into their own cultural identity. Furthermore, they argue that knowing how to elicit information (*savoir apprendre*) is a basic learning strategy, and as such, it is a fundamental aspect of primary education.

The Key Stage 2 Framework for Languages (DfES 2005), a curriculum resource to help teachers plan languages, provides detailed learning objectives and a wide range of suggestions for teaching activities addressing children from the age of seven to eleven. The Framework is designed with three core strands – Oracy (listening and speaking), Literacy (reading and writing) and

Intercultural Understanding (IU), and two strands which are designed to cut across the core strands – Knowledge about Language (KAL) and Language Learning Strategies. The IU Strand provides a loose structure for progression as broad cultural concepts are revisited at increasingly complex levels. Cultural objectives are also embedded within the KAL Strand in order to help children develop insights into the nature of language and recognize its cultural value in that language does not always have a direct equivalent, and therefore communication is not simply a matter of translation. The KAL Strand also offers suggestions of how to reinforce children's understanding of their own language while learning another language by comparing patterns in language structure and the roots of words. The KAL Strand thereby incorporates language awareness within the language-learning experience. The Framework was a key part of government policy until it was archived in 2011.

Language awareness

Children bring a wide range of language experiences and skills to the classroom and it is from this starting point that teachers begin to develop their oracy and literacy skills. A language awareness approach to language learning offers opportunities for children to reflect on the nature of language and see the relationship that exists between languages, thereby learning more about their own language. Language awareness can develop linguistic and cultural sensitivity which allows learners to perceive language as a product of and part of culture. Rather than focusing on one foreign language with the view to developing competence, language awareness can offer children opportunities to encounter different languages and help them identify patterns and make important connections between languages.

Eric Hawkins has written extensively about the benefits of language awareness (1984, 1991). He contends that language awareness programmes provide a positive foundation for subsequent foreign-language learning, stimulate an interest in linguistic and cultural differences and help learners with poor communication skills. He also argues (1991: 228) that language awareness provides a bridge that connects the many languages in the classroom including the language of instruction, mother tongue, foreign, community and heritage languages. This approach is therefore considered a good base for plurilingual programmes. *L'Eveil aux Langues dans l'école primaire* (EVLANG) project, for example, was designed as an 'awakening' to languages and implemented in five countries. Candelier (2003) reported that through the project learners developed a greater openness to linguistic and cultural diversity.

Recent evidence

A three-year longitudinal study in forty primary schools in England (Cable, Driscoll, Mitchell, Sing, Cremin, Earl, Eyres, Holmes, Martin and Heins 2010), which investigated the influence and impact of the Key Stage 2 Framework on practice, provides robust evidence about cultural learning associated with foreign-language learning. Data were collected through interviews with head teachers, teachers and pupils and yearly observations of language classes for a period of three years. Specifically designed instruments were created to assess learner attainment in listening, speaking, reading and writing in eight of the forty schools.

In over half of the schools visited, teachers and head teachers in the study spoke with strong conviction about the importance of providing children with opportunities to develop tolerance and empathy, an interest and acceptance of diversity and a sense of the wider world. Yet despite a clear commitment to promote a global mindset and recognition of the importance of intercultural understanding, evidence of practice was found in less than a quarter of lessons. Teachers generally made brief cultural references when teaching the language, such as information about the weather or common traditions in the target country. On occasion, children were exploring their own culture or the lifestyles of others within their own communities, but examples such as these were rare in lessons. In contrast, teachers frequently compared grammatical structures between English and the foreign language and many reported that learning a foreign language had enhanced children's general awareness of language. Some teachers, especially in multilingual schools, reported that foreign languages were a means to raise children's awareness of the social and cultural value of language through comparing structures and exploring the roots of words (Cable et al., 2010).

An increasing number of whole-school events, which offered opportunities to develop children's cultural understanding, took place over the three years of the study. Functions such as international book events portraying picturebooks, poems, fables, folk tales and other texts from around the world provided dynamic opportunities for language and cultural awareness and learning about the world (Cable et al., 2010). Cultural themes were also emphasized in whole-school assemblies and language days where each class prepared materials, food and emblems associated with another country. These opportunities for cultural learning tended to be stimulated by foreign-language learning in the school but there were no indications of direct links with cultural or linguistic objectives in lessons.

Children were able to discuss basic information about the European country where the language is spoken, for example, the culture of Spain rather than Spanish-speaking countries in South America. Factual information about other countries tended to be drawn from multimedia resources which increased substantially over the three years of the study. Many children indicated that they had not learnt very much about the people who live in the countries where the target language is spoken during lessons, and what they did know had been shared mainly by teachers who had personal experience of the target countries.

In line with other research (Muijs, Barnes, Hunt, Powell, Arweck, Lindsay and Martin 2005, Edelenbos, Johnstone and Kubanek-German 2006, Barton, Bragg and Serratrice 2009), children's attitudes were very positive about learning the language. Indeed, 80 per cent of children reported that they were interested in knowing more about the people and way of life and almost all children expressed a desire to visit the country. This curiosity and openness towards the people of the target countries and enthusiasm about knowing and understanding more about the world could be conceptualized as the initial stages of *savoir être*. Overall, however, children tended towards generalizations about 'the French' or 'Spanish people' although some of the older children (ages nine to eleven) contested the sweeping statements made by their peers about a national group. Furthermore, some teachers in multicultural schools indicated that languages had made a difference to their children's developing appreciation and respect for diversity. Discussions, reflections or analysis about the influence of culture on children's own and others' lives were not observed by the research team. Further research is clearly needed about the more complex elements of *savoir* and *savoir être* outlined by Byram (1997). Evidence is very limited about how teachers develop learners' curiosity and openness, and which types of activities and tasks are most effective for children of different ages in helping them develop skills to 'step into another's shoes' or understand the complexity of intercultural interaction. Equally, little is known about whether the skills of eliciting information (*savoir apprendre*) extend to learning more about the nuances of cultural diversity as suggested by Byram and Doyé (1999).

A few schools employed foreign-language assistants who contributed to children's knowledge and understanding about cultural life abroad. Several schools also organized visits and exchanges so children experienced for themselves interaction with native speakers. In approximately half of the schools, teachers organized email exchanges so children could communicate directly with their peers in other countries. Some teachers also shared curriculum resources, designing units of work together for children in two cultural settings to share learning tasks. These activities highlight the common ground between learners from different countries as well as their differences, as children can see first-hand that to a large extent, as pupils, they have similar roles and responsibilities at school. Schools also share common features: knowledge and skills are broadly conceptualized in subject disciplines, the teacher undertakes the management of teaching and learning and the learners' role is to engage.

Evidence suggests limited cultural learning within language lessons, however schools in this study tended to celebrate cultures outside of language lessons in the wider curriculum of the school. Teachers' vision of preparing children for a global world and their aims to develop a greater acceptance of diverse ways of thinking and behaving could be witnessed across these whole-school activities and events, connecting language learning naturally and seamlessly to themes underpinning global citizenship.

Statutory status for languages in primary schools

The national curriculum, implemented from September 2014 (DfE 2013), raised the status of foreign languages to a statutory subject for all pupils in Key Stage 2 (seven to eleven) for the first time in England. It is too early to predict the impact of this new policy on practice, but the new curriculum hails some significant changes to the foreign-language curriculum. The new programme of study begins with a position statement regarding culture, but culture is not mentioned again in the aims, objectives or content for primary schools and it is only mentioned briefly, with reference to reading literary texts for learners aged eleven to thirteen in Key Stage 3.

Unlike curricula in other European countries referenced by Hennebry and discussed earlier in the chapter, the new curriculum does not draw directly upon the concept of intercultural competence. The lack of emphasis on culture marks a radical shift from the notion of IU in the languages strategy (DfES 2002) and from the importance of intercultural insights in a multicultural and internationally connected world outlined in previous national curricula (DfE 1999). The solitary mention of culture in the new curriculum is as follows: 'Learning a foreign language is liberation from insularity and provides an opening to other cultures. A high-quality languages education should foster pupils' curiosity and deepen their understanding of the world' (DfE 2013: 193).

The diminished scope of culture within the new curriculum is disappointing and represents a lost opportunity, particularly now, as languages are finally a legal requirement in English primary schools. Rather than statutory status increasing the potential for cultural exposure in language lessons, practice may well decrease, with the weakened steer from policymakers and as curriculum time remains limited. Creative solutions are needed if children are to develop the intercultural knowledge, skills, attributes and mindset for the global world of the twenty-first century.

One potential solution is to draw upon teachers' commitment to promote cultural learning (Cable et al. 2010) and build upon the growing portfolio of whole-school events, visits and exchanges that teachers are organizing in schools. Key cultural themes or concepts could be identified, such as empathy or an appreciation of heritage, as a basis for whole-school planning. Starting from the child's own cultural experiences, teachers could plan systematically to explore these concepts within subject areas and across all cultural activities in the school. Long-term cross-curricular planning would ensure that specific cultural themes are revisited in increasingly sophisticated ways from the beginning of primary school until the end with clear overarching learning intentions which make strong connections between English, foreign, community and heritage languages. Rather than ad hoc activities, space could be created for cultural development where children flourish and work together and benefit from a joined-up and coherent educational offer tailor-made for their age group and interests.

Languages as part of the whole curriculum

Culture is explicitly referenced in a number of curriculum subjects. To construct a cultural programme which cuts across subjects connecting different aspects of culture into a coherent whole is relatively straightforward. A traditional view of high culture is proposed in the Art and Design Technology curriculum that promotes knowledge about great artists and designers and how they have shaped the heritage of the country as well as their contribution to the creativity of the nation. Making direct links to art in countries where the target language is spoken is relatively easy. The legacy of Greek or Roman culture in relation to art, architecture and literature throughout history to the present day is referenced in the programme of study for History. Linking art to language awareness and the legacy of Latin within many languages could be a recurrent theme planned for children within several subjects over a period of time. Culture is also conceptualized as an understanding about the changing ways of life and the changing beliefs of people over time, from the Stone Age onwards. Learning and understanding about the ways of the people at some prior time and developing empathy towards them is not dissimilar to the understanding required to analyse, interpret and reflect upon different cultures at home and abroad in the present day. Equally, learning about artists, designers and architects from around the world is an important part of learning about any country, including the target country. Designing and planning a cultural theme on empathy, which could be explored in many ways across different subject areas, would help reinforce children's learning. Within the English curriculum, culture is referenced through reading a range of fiction from the national literary heritage and traditional stories, as well as books, poems and songs from other cultures and traditions. A cross-curricular approach to culture is not possible without effective professional development both for practitioners and for student teachers. We have insufficient evidence of effective practice in teacher education in how to develop teachers' IU and help them to challenge issues which lead to stereotypes, prejudice and racism.

'Liberation from Insularity' (DfE 2013: 193), quoted in the previous section, is not just an aim for language learning. It reflects the broader purpose of schooling in offering 'moral, cultural, mental [...] development' and to prepare students for their future lives (DfE 2013: 5). Ofsted, the national monitoring body for schools in England, in a positive move echoes this broader purpose of education which cannot be simply defined subject by subject. Their remit of inspection includes the quality and overall effectiveness of cultural development in schools (Ofsted 2014: 36). Although the measurement of cultural learning implies a commodification of culture, it also raises the importance of cultural development in schools and highlights the need for schools to focus on the quality of their provision across subjects, in their approach to global learning and in light of their international profile. Aims of cultural awareness and intercultural sensitivity are closely interconnected to those of global learning through discussions about identity and stereotypes, equality and diversity. The Maastricht Declaration of Global Education, for example, contends that education 'opens people's eyes and minds to the realities of the world' (O'Loughlin and Wegimont 2003: 13). Hunt (2012) found in her study of global learning in 217 primary schools across England that schools expressed their aims in relation to developing rights, responsibilities and values, followed by developing an interest in other countries and cultures and broadening pupils' horizons (Hunt 2012: 29).

Martin (2007: 164) suggests that it is not necessary for young children to understand where people and places are in order to think and care about them. While this is an interesting proposition, children most certainly need concrete examples and activities to learn. Over recent years the strong influence from policy for IU within language learning (DfES 2002, 2005) has prompted a greater focus on good-quality resources, particularly with multimedia commercial materials. With ongoing technological advances, teaching resources will undoubtedly improve enabling easy contact across the world from classroom to classroom offering all manner of exciting cultural and linguistic experiences for children (see Cutrim Schmid and Whyte 2015, this volume). Language teachers with cultural and intercultural skills themselves have an important role to play in leading a cultural learning programme across the curriculum and in supporting their colleagues in cultural initiatives. There is no quick fix to developing intercultural understanding at any age but it makes sense to start early as children begin to explore their own identity within the social context of schooling.

Conclusion

This chapter has explored teaching IU within foreign languages. We have considered findings from a three-year study which documented cultural and intercultural understanding associated with languages against the backdrop of policy guidance. Through languages, primary schools are increasingly providing whole-school cultural activities and international opportunities. These rich opportunities offer a platform to develop IU but there is limited evidence to suggest that schools plan a cohesive cultural programme with clear conceptual goals and strategies even though many primary teachers believe that intercultural learning is at the heart of the languages curriculum.

We argue that an intercultural programme of learning needs to be started early, when children are young and encountering the rules, behaviours and codes of conduct in the world away from their parents and carers. Children begin to appreciate in the early stage of schooling that they are members of a group outside of their immediate experience. As young learners progress through primary schools, they acquire a greater understanding of the subtle rules which govern the parameters of acceptability within the society to which they belong. Just as language awareness can improve a learner's understanding of their own language, intercultural learning has the potential to deepen an appreciation of and respect for diversity within one's own culture and that of others. A positive way forward in order to maximise opportunities for cultural development and experiences offered to primary children is the use of long term planning with clear learning objectives associated with cultural concepts and themes, that can be woven through the subject curriculum, the wider curriculum and school events.

References

Alexander, Robin (ed.) with Doddington, Christine; Frey, John; Hargreaves, Linda and Kershner, Ruth (2010), *The Cambridge Primary Review Research Surveys*, London: Routledge.

Barton, Amanda; Bragg, Joanna and Serratrice, Ludovica. (2009) '"Discovering Language" in primary school: An evaluation of a language awareness programme', *Language Learning Journal*, 37/2: 145–164.

British Academy Policy Publication (2011), *Language Matters More and More*. <http://www.britac.ac.uk/policy/Language_Matters_More_And_More.cfm> [accessed 15 July 2014].

British Council (2014), *Languages for the Future. Which languages the UK Needs Most and Why*, UK: British Council. http://www.britishcouncil.org/sites/ britishcouncil.uk2/files/languages-for-the-future.pdf [accessed 3 December 2014].

Byram, Michael (1989), *Cultural Studies in Foreign Language Education*. Clevedon: Multilingual Matters.

Byram, Michael (1997), *Teaching and Assessing Intercultural Communicative Competence*. Clevedon: Multilingual Matters.

Byram, Michael and Doyé, Peter (1999), 'Intercultural competence and foreign language learning in the Primary school', in Patricia Driscoll and David Frost (eds), *The Teaching of Modern Foreign Languages in the Primary School*. London: Routledge, pp. 138–151.

Cable, Carrie; Driscoll, Patricia; Mitchell, Rosamund; Sing, Sue; Cremin, Theresa; Earl, Justine; Eyres, Ian; Holmes, Bernardette; Martin, Cynthia with Heins, Barbara (2010), *Languages Learning at Key Stage 2: A Longitudinal Study Research Report No. 198*, London: DCSF. <https://www.gov.uk/government/ publications/languages-learning-at-key-stage-2-a-longitudinal-study-final- report> [accessed 17 June 2014].

Candelier, Michel (2003). *L'Eveil aux Langages à l'Ecole Primaire*. Brussels: de Boeck and Larcier.

Council of Europe/Council for Cultural Cooperation (2001), *Common European Framework of Reference for Languages: Learning, Teaching, Assessment*. Cambridge: Cambridge University Press.

Cregan, Kate and Cuthbert, Denise (2014), *Global Childhoods – Issues and Debates*. London: Sage Publications Ltd.

Crystal, David (2003), *English as a Global Language* (2nd edn), Cambridge: Cambridge University Press.

Cutrim Schmid, Euline and Whyte, Shona (2015), 'Teaching young learners with technology', in Janice Bland (ed.), *Teaching English to Young Learners. Critical Issues in Language Teaching with 3–12 Year Olds*, London: Bloomsbury Academic, pp. 239–259.

Department for Education (2013), *National Curriculum in England: Framework for Key Stages 1–4* <https://www.gov.uk/government/publications/national- curriculum-in-england-framework-for-key-stages-1-to-4/the-national-curriculum- in-england-framework-for-key-stages-1-to-4> [accessed 8 September 2014].

Department for Education and Skills (2002), *Languages for All: Languages for Life, a Strategy for England*. Nottingham: DfES Publications.

Department for Education and Skills (2005), *Key Stage 2 Framework for Languages*. Nottingham: DfES Publications.

Department for Education and Employment and Quality and Curriculum Authority (1999), *National Curriculum Programme of Study and Attainment Targets, Handbook for Teachers Key Stage 1 and 2*, <https://www.education.gov.uk/ publications/eOrderingDownload/QCA-99-457.pdf> [accessed 7 June 2014].

Driscoll, Patricia; Earl, Justine and Cable, Carrie (2013), 'The role and nature of the cultural dimension in primary modern languages', *Language, Culture and Curriculum*, 26/2: 146–160.

Edelenbos, Peter; Johnstone, Richard and Kubanek-German, Angelika (2006), *The main pedagogical principles underlying the teaching of languages to very young learners. Languages for the Children of Europe: Published Research, Good Practice and Main Principles*. Final Report of the EAC, 89/04 Brussels: European Commission.

Enever, Janet and Moon, Jayne (2008), *A Global Revolution? Teaching English at Primary School*, https://www.teachingonglish.org.uk/sites/teacheng/files/ MoonEneverBCpaper.pdf [accessed 17 July 2014].

European Commission (2012), *First European Survey on Language Competences: Final Report*. Brussels: European Commission.

Grenfell, Michael (2000), 'Modern languages beyond Nuffield and into the 21st Century', *Language Learning Journal*, 22: 23–29.

Hawkins, Eric (1984), *Awareness of Language*. Cambridge: Cambridge University Press.

Hawkins, Eric (1991), *Modern Languages in the Curriculum* (2nd edn). Cambridge: Cambridge University Press.

Hennebry, Mairin (2014), 'Cultural awareness – Should it be taught? Can it be taught?' in Patricia Driscoll; Ernesto Macaro and Ann Swarbrick (eds), *Debates in Modern Languages Education*, London: Routledge, pp. 135–139

Hunt, Frances (2012), *Global Learning in Primary Schools in England: Practices and Impacts, Research Paper No. 9*, Development Education Research Centre, Institute of Education, London <http://www.ioe.ac.uk/ GlobalLearningInPrimarySchools.pdf> [accessed 15 August 2014].

Johnstone, Richard (2009), 'An early start: What are the key conditions for generalised success?' In Janet Enever, Jayne Moon and Uma Raman (eds), *Young Learners English Language Policy and Implementation: International Perspectives*, Reading: Garnet Publishing, pp. 31–41.

Kramsch, Claire (1993), *Context and Culture in Language Teaching*, Oxford: Oxford University Press.

Littlewood, William (1981), *Communicative Language Teaching*, Cambridge: Cambridge University Press.

Martin, Fran (2007), 'The Wider World in the Primary School', in David Hicks and Cathie Holden (eds), *Teaching the Global Dimension, Key Principles and Effective Practice*, Oxon: Routledge, pp. 164–175.

Muijs, Daniel; Barnes, Ann; Hunt, Marilyn; Powell, Bob; Arweck, Elizabeth; Lindsay, Geoff and Martin, Cynthia (2005), *Evaluation of the Key Stage 2 Language Learning Pathfinders*. London: DfES.

Nuffield Foundation (2000), *Languages: The Next Generation Final Report of the Nuffield Languages Inquiry*. London: The Nuffield Foundation.

Ofsted (2014), *School Inspection Handbook* <http://www.ofsted.gov.uk/ sites/default/files/documents/inspection–forms-and-guides/s/School%20 inspection%20handbook.pdf> [accessed 15 August 2014].

O'Loughlin, Eddie and Wegimont, Liam (eds) (2003), *Global Education in Europe to 2015, Strategy, Policies and Perspectives, Outcomes and Papers of the Europe-wide Global Education Congress, Maastricht, the Netherlands, 15–17 November 2002*, North-South Centre of the Council of Europe: Lisbon <http:// www.coe.int/t/dg4/nscentre/Resources/Publications/GE_Maastricht_Nov2002. pdf> [accessed 12 November 2014].

Tinsley, Teresa (2013), *Languages: The State of the Nation Demand and Supply of Language Skills in the UK.* London: British Academy.

Wade, Pauline and Marshall, Helen, with O'Donnell, Sharon (2009), *Primary Modern Foreign Languages Longitudinal Survey of Implementation of National Entitlement to Language Learning at Key Stage 2.* Research report No. RR127. London: DCSF.

Wedell, Martin and Malderez, Angi (2013), *Understanding Language Classroom Contexts: The starting point for change,* London: Bloomsbury.

Woodgate-Jones, Alex and Grenfell, Michael (2012), 'Intercultural Understanding and primary-level second language learning and teaching', *Language Awareness,* 21/4: 331–345.

10

Oral Storytelling in the Primary English Classroom

Janice Bland

Introduction

This chapter is about oral storytelling in the language classroom. As we shall see, sharing stories is central to humankind. Stories, or narratives, help us learn from experience and to Currie 'it does not seem at all exaggerated to view humans as narrative animals, as *homo fabulans* – the tellers and interpreters of narrative' (2011: 6). Stories allow us to use our imagination to possibly engender new options and hopefully act with foresight, 'to explore our own mind and the minds of others, as a sort of dress rehearsal for the future' (Cron 2012: 9). Thus this chapter will touch upon issues that have a wide relevance for education. Authors, unsurprisingly, have also observed the apparent human predisposition for storying: 'stories appear to be there because stories are a pervasive and perpetual human characteristic, like language, like play' (Byatt 2004) and Le Guin writes: 'For the story – from *Rumpelstiltskin* to *War and Peace* – is one of the basic tools invented by the mind of man, for the purpose of gaining understanding. There have been great societies that did not use the wheel, but there have been no societies that did not tell stories' (1985: 31). Of old, storytellers were our teachers, we learn from stories in complex ways and we can pass learning on as teacher-storytellers: 'There are lots of things that are vital to being human. Things like food, culture, warmth. The things that are most vital, and most easy to overlook, are stories. [...] People that think stories aren't important – aren't as important as breathing, aren't as important as warmth, aren't as important as life – are missing the point' (Gaiman 2014).

We know that children need rich high-quality language input, which well-told stories can offer, for second language (L2) teaching to play to their strengths – particularly their aural perception and their ability to learn implicitly. The other side of the coin is that minimal exposure in an input-limited, formal instructional setting, with the few contact hours taken up by explicit language-teaching activities, will remove any advantages children have as *young* learners (see research reported in García Mayo and García Lecumberri 2003). As Kieran Egan (1986: 22) maintains on teaching in the primary school, 'focus on what they most obviously *can* do, and seem able to do best' (emphasis in the original).

It is therefore disappointing that the advice of teacher educators deeply involved in teaching observation and action-researchers with sometimes decades of highly valuable experience with storytelling in language teaching (recent publications Wright 2009, Ellis and Brewster 2014, Heathfield 2014) is largely ignored according to Garton, Copland and Burns: 'One very noticeable absentee from the list of frequently used activities is storytelling. [...] This is surprising given their [stories] importance in the young learner literature, particularly in books which provide practical advice to teachers' (2011: 12). It must therefore be concluded that pre-service teacher education does not yet sufficiently provide teachers with the tools to become teacher-storytellers.

Oral stories versus picturebooks

The main concern of this chapter is oral storytelling. Therefore some distinctions and definitions, which have often been blurred in the literature on teaching young learners, should be clarified at the outset. Narrative plays a major role in our lives, also beyond the age of twelve and into adulthood, in the form of movies, television, news reportage or stories 'carefully arranged so that the most newsworthy piece of information comes first, thus "hooking" the reader into reading further' (Crago 2011: 209), biographies, crime novels, historical fiction, celebrity stories, anecdotes of all kinds – the list is endless. For young language learners, picturebooks and oral stories are probably the dominant narrative forms, and as the children get older film, digital media, comics, graphic novels and finally novels may play an increasingly important role, ideally also outside the school setting. If children have unlimited access to English-language out-of-school environments, narrative can play an enormous role in their L2 acquisition (see Enever 2015: 26), for the efficacy for L2 acquisition of extensive reading (see Krashen 2004, 2013) and extensive listening (Mason and Krashen 2004, Mason 2013) has been thoroughly researched (Hoey 2015).

Film, picturebooks, comics and graphic novels are multimodal texts in that they tell their stories through the modes of pictures and verbal text, and audio in addition in the case of film. As multimodal texts they communicate as a synthesis of signs. The teacher might choose to show a film without the pictures or without the sound, and invite the children to predict, but in the end would want to show and allow the children to enjoy the complete work. Aidan Chambers (2011: 162) made the point that 'books that are worth bothering with at all are worth [. . .] rereading'. Picturebooks that are worth bothering with are literary texts, and the best are a *Gesamtkunstwerk*. The young learners need to have the opportunity to read the pictures and enjoy the carefully orchestrated layout – their multimodal nature is an excellent introduction to literature (see Bland 2013, Mourão 2013, 2015b). There are abundant picturebooks that are 'worth bothering with', and in the L2 classroom we should choose among these for the children's literary apprenticeship.

Oral stories, in contrast, are stories that have traditionally been told by word of mouth, with, these days, many retellings in written form and remediations in digital form or film. Short oral tales are, for example, fables, fairy tales, legends, myths and folk tales from around the world. One of the defining characteristics of what was once *only* oral literature is that there is no one 'correct' or authoritative version; 'there is no such thing as a definitive version' (Zipes 2004: 118). Nonetheless most stories from folk literature now have a written expression – to name just a few: the versions of Aesop fables, Anansi and Nasreddin trickster tales, the numerous versions of fairy tales by the Brothers Grimm, as well as the ubiquitous Disney versions in books and film. On the one hand, I suggest we impoverish the classroom if we omit traditional fairy tales altogether and allow the globally popular Disney versions to eclipse all other versions, a phenomenon known as Disneyfication due to the 'saccharine, sexist, and illusionary stereotypes of the Disney-culture industry' (Zipes 2007: 25). On the other hand, in these days of English as a global language and multicultural classrooms, clearly we should include stories from around the world in our storytelling.[1] Teachers can search for inspiration from a treasure trove of tales recorded, for example, by the Story Museum: 'Every young human who grows up hearing and telling, reading and writing stories gains access to a lifetime of treasures' (2014).

Despite the omnipresence of pictures and print or digital media in our lives, orally transmitted stories have an important role to play, particularly for children who are not yet fluent readers. According to Ong

sound enters deeply into human beings' feel for existence, as processed by the spoken word. For the way in which the word is experienced is always momentous in psychic life. The centering action of sound (the field of sound is not spread out before me but is all around me) affects man's sense of the cosmos. (2002: 71)

Teachers should be aware of the 'centering action of sound' and support the rapt attention that storytelling can induce. I have seen this many times in my observations of teaching practice; it can be magical. In the young-learner classroom, the cinema circle, or semicircle around the teacher, provides comfortable whole-group togetherness without the paraphernalia of desks, pencil cases and school bags to distract from a trance-like immersion in a well-told story. Fifty English language teachers in Slovenia who taught children aged from eight to nine years took part in a study on their use of storytelling, and reported that narratives are 'a good source of language and a springboard for follow-up activities, as well as generating a relaxed and safe learning environment. Having pupils seated on the floor, in the form of a semi-circle, further contributes to the pleasant atmosphere in the classroom' (Dagarin Fojkar, Skela and Kovač 2013: 26).

Oral storytelling is flexible and can and should be moulded to the particular audience. This is a different performance act from the sharing of a picturebook, for in the case of picturebook storytelling the book itself and the pictures (which have another kind of magical power) can arrest and focus the children's attention through their continuous and repeated presence. Storytelling is also different from acting, for when acting the children and teacher-in-role (see Chapter 12) feel the emotions of the characters. However, when the teacher is storytelling 'while we may sometimes become a character and show their emotion, for the most part we are aiming to pass an emotion out to our audience – to make them feel it' (Tisdall 2013: 37). This chapter will also be examining the role of the teacher as oral storyteller – for it is the teacher who decides the form of each retelling, shaping the story to the audience, encouraging a response and perhaps introducing a new element without disturbing the template-like building blocks of storytelling.

Children do have a pre-existing story template, as do we all, suggesting once again that humans have evolved as *homo fabulans*, or indeed as a 'storytelling animal' (Gottschall 2012). The template includes '*a logically linked series of events*, a structure that includes *a beginning, a middle and an end, characters who remain the center of attention throughout*, and to whom the story happens, and *a resolution that offers some form of resolution or release*' (Crago 2011: 211, emphasis in the original). Booker Prize winner Antonia Byatt (2004) writes of a 'narrative grammar' of our minds: 'An all-important part of our response to the world of the tales is our instinctive sense that they have rules.'

Therefore Cameron has rightly criticized the texts in English as a Foreign Language (EFL) coursebooks that are called 'stories' when they do not adhere to the archetypal story template: 'Most often they lack a plot; instead of setting up a problem and working towards its resolution, the characters just move through a sequence of activities. Teachers should not assume that such non-stories will capture children's imagination in the same way that stories can do' (2001: 162). Non-stories do not play to the children's strengths, for children have a desire 'to find and construct coherence and meaning' (Cameron 2001: 159). In fact this is *exactly* what stories can offer according to Gale and Sikes: 'Narratives provide links, connections, coherence, meaning, sense' (2006).

Orality and oracy

The language teacher as storyteller needs an awareness of the mode of *orality*, which will be introduced next. *Oracy*, on the other hand, as the development of spoken language, is an important aspect of language teaching to young learners generally:

> While *oracy*, a term coined in recent decades, has been used almost exclusively in educational settings to describe students' oral language as something to be developed or improved – like literacy or numeracy – *orality* [...] is a much older and broader term referring to the overall use of spoken language, especially in a culture. Oracy is a word used to name a skill; orality is a mode. (Bomer 2010: 205–206)

Perhaps the most important aspect of orality has been termed as 'methods of remembering' (Bomer 2010: 207). This is crucial for the storyteller as well as the audience and is extremely relevant for language teaching. Patterned language is also to be found in literary texts such as novels, picturebooks and poems – however, patterning is the *essence* of oral storytelling. The following categories can be identified:

> *Repetitive, patterned language*: Repetition is important for the (teacher-)storyteller and crucial for the listener (especially when the story is in a foreign language). Patterned language refers to both phonological and semantic levels: 'heavily rhythmic, balanced patterns, in repetitions or antitheses, in alliterations and assonances, in epithetic and other formulary expressions' (Ong 2002: 34). Repetition of sounds and meanings is also a poetic characteristic of written narrative (Bland 2013: 156–187).
>
> *Formulaic language*: The best-known formulas of fairy tales are 'Once upon a time' and 'They lived happily ever after'. However, a great deal more formulaic language can be discovered in oral tales – see

the analysis of a passage from *Little Red Riding Hood* in this volume (S. Kersten 2015: 140–142). A rich use of epithets is also formulaic, for example wicked witch, little cottage and big bad wolf. Well-known examples from written texts are the Cheshire Cat, the yellow-brick road and the Wild Wood.

Additive language and an avoidance of complex sentences: This is clearly important for language teaching, for complex sentences (sentences which contain subordinate clauses) are difficult for young learners. Expert children's literature authors also make use of the additive characteristic of oral tales, as the multiple 'ands' in this extract from *The Firework-Maker's Daughter* show:

And her throat was parched and her lungs were panting in the hot air, and she fell to her knees and clung with trembling fingers as the stones began to roll under her again. [. . .] up and up, until every muscle hurt, until she had no breath left in her lungs, until she thought she was going to die; and still she went on. (Pullman 1995: 68–69)

Stock characters, repeated themes and settings: Oral tales cannot sustain the complexity of written literature with regard to characterization, setting and theme. Familiar stock characters, iconic settings with few details and recurrent themes and triples (such as three brothers or sisters, three wishes, three attempts) are the conventions of oral tales. This characteristic helps young learners predict and activates their prior knowledge on the creatures of tales, like dragons, monsters and trolls. It also compels children to listen carefully to confirm or disprove their hypotheses and it helps them notice new ideas.

Participants interact: Because oral storytelling relies on the 'building blocks of oral composition' (Garner 2005: 411), audience participation is anticipated. Listeners are attuned to the story template and ready-made structural units, as outlined above. Teachers should make use of these expectations. Although a storyteller reacts flexibly to the needs of the audience, the standard story patterns and formulaic language, including the well-known fairy tale refrains, remain unchanged. Referring to oral storytelling, Bauman (2005: 420) suggests that the 'collaborative participation of an audience is an integral component of performance as an interactional accomplishment'.

The hunt for meaning

According to Lisa Cron, who discusses the importance of stories for humankind in her book on narrative writing, stories train the imagination to mentally represent alternative visions for the future. In the past, as in the present, this may have been crucial for our survival: 'story is what enabled us to imagine what might happen in the future, and so prepare for it' (Cron 2012: 1). Boyd argues that 'art in general and storytelling in particular are also adaptations in our species. Far from being ornaments, they too, often, become a pivot of human lives' (2009: 35). With reference to neuroscience, Boyd suggests that telling stories is adaptive human behaviour that tones neural wiring, rehearses cumulative creativity and offers advantages for human survival. He writes: 'Humans uniquely inhabit the "cognitive niche": we gain most of our advantages from intelligence. We therefore have an appetite for information, and especially for pattern, information that falls into meaningful arrays from which we can make rich inferences' (Boyd 2009: 14).

Because ideas become virtually real to us in stories – to discover and reflect upon as outlined above – storytelling is arguably the most powerful educational tool. Storytelling not only supports empathy and creativity but also trains our thinking: 'Childhood play and storytelling for all ages engage our attention so compulsively through our interest in event comprehension and social monitoring that over time their concentrated information patterns develop our facility for complex situational thought' (Boyd 2009: 49). As a species 'we're wired to hunt for meaning in everything' (Cron 2012: 27), and our storytelling is a way of achieving this. The stories we tell to children in the EFL classroom are intrinsically motivating; they are often connected to 'the warmth of early childhood experiences' (Cameron 2001: 160).

Michael Morpurgo, award-winning author of children's literature, locates the importance of stories in the area of intercultural understanding, 'without stories, and without an understanding of stories, we don't understand ourselves, we don't understand the world about us. And we don't understand the relations between ourselves and those people around us. Because what stories give us is an insight into ourselves, a huge insight into other people, other cultures, other places' (Morpurgo 2014). Boyd confirms the prosocial nature of sharing stories, which spread 'prosocial values, the likeliest to appeal to both tellers and listeners. It develops our capacity to see from different perspectives, and this capacity in turn both arises from and aids the evolution of cooperation and the growth of human mental flexibility' (Boyd 2009: 176). There are, as we have seen, many arguments in favour of storytelling, both for second language acquisition and for wider educational goals, particularly empathy and intercultural understanding. In the next section the implementation of stories with young learners is considered in more detail.

Storytelling in the classroom

In foreign-language teaching, stories should be shared over several lessons, with possibly as many as nine steps to the storytelling (see further below). In the first few steps, there is no doubt that the teacher plays the central role in the telling. In fact the teacher's input is crucial generally for the teaching of young learners in most countries: 'In the many countries where little contact with English outside school is readily available, it is the teacher who is the major source and catalyst for children's development in English' (Rixon 2015, 42).

Teacher-storytellers

For vivid multisensory storytelling, the words are not the only consideration (Wright 2013); special clothing such as a story jacket, puppets, sound effects, props or realia can be helpfully involved. However, the art of what I will call *creative teacher talk* is undoubtedly the area that needs most attention. The teacher-storyteller employs a varied paralanguage involving expressive prosodic features (pitch, tempo, volume, rhythm – including dramatic pauses), exuberant intonation, gasps and, where suitable, even sighs. Some storytellers employ exaggerated gesture and facial expressions, while others have a quieter style. This will also depend on the story and the age of the young learners; the younger the child, the more the storytelling (and classroom discourse generally) should resemble repetitive child-directed speech. Storyteller Heathfield (2014: 14) advises making good use of direct speech, 'so you can play with the characters' voices and mannerisms'. As Thornbury (2002: 20) indicates, 'The average classroom L2 learner will experience nothing like the quantity nor the quality of exposure that the L1 infant receives (. . .) Moreover, the input that infants receive is tailored to their immediate needs – it is interactive, and it is often highly repetitive and patterned – all qualities that provide optimal conditions for learning.'

Inexperienced teachers lack a repertoire of ritualized language and have some difficulty in using patterned language, similar to child-directed speech, in an impromptu yet cunningly regulated way. Frequent storytelling will supply this practice and also enrich the classroom discourse; therefore teachers should avoid the expediency of reading aloud simplified stories. Simplified stories do not normally offer sufficient language patterning with connectedness and salience through phonological and semantic repetition (Bland 2013: 8). Good-quality authentic children's literature *is* well written: 'A writer's use of language is central to the quality of a book, and so it is no coincidence that good quality children's stories also offer language learning opportunities' (Cameron 2001: 179). However, as previously mentioned, sharing picturebooks with young learners is a different method and will be discussed in the next chapter. With regard to the older children in the target age range of this book (eleven- and twelve-year-olds), in some contexts the children might have sufficient competence to follow read-alouds of good-quality chapter books. These are books written for native-speaker children who can manage to read extended prose. In consideration of the short attention span of young readers, the books are divided into short chapters – and this is convenient for reading aloud in the classroom too. Although they usually have some illustrations, the story is told entirely in prose and not in pictures. Thus, unlike picturebooks, the illustrations are not an essential component of the narrative. An example is Philip Pullman's *The Firework-Maker's Daughter*, which was quoted in the section on orality and oracy on page 188.

However, for most young learners, chapter books are still too challenging. Moreover oral storytelling, without a script, could provide teachers with the routine they need to spontaneously produce chant-like, highly repetitive discourse to support the children's emerging L2. This could be a move in the direction of 'generalized success', which according to Johnstone (2009: 31) 'implies achieving success not only with expert teachers working in favourable circumstances but also with "ordinary" teachers working in "ordinary" circumstances, which may be far from ideal' (see also Enever 2015: 22–26). All storytellers need practice and need to employ repetition as Ong (2002: 40) has identified: 'it is better to repeat something, artfully if possible, rather than simply to stop speaking while fishing for the next idea'. A marvellous expediency, also borrowed from professional storytellers, is to learn certain rituals by heart. For example, each story in the enchanting television series *The Storyteller* begins: 'When people told themselves their past with stories, explained their present with stories, foretold the future with stories, the best place by the fire was kept for the storyteller' (Jim Henson Company 2005), which seems to promise magic and mystery, and thus motivates for the coming story.

One of the most important features of oral storytelling is eye contact. Oral stories evolve as they pass from storyteller to teacher-storyteller; they are moulded to each new audience and retelling, and this is only possible if the teacher is in contact with the audience. Through eye contact the teacher can check that the children are following where the story takes them, with the result that the 'listener's brain is as active as the storyteller's and is, in fact, telling and anticipating the story *internally* along with [the teacher]' (Heathfield 2014: 10, emphasis in the original). Creative teacher talk involves an enhanced dynamic to suit the story, and phonological intensity with vividly orchestrated stress, pitch, tempo, volume and rhythm. However, the story progress can be adjusted, as long as the basic template is maintained. Where necessary the teacher can elaborate, with a slower speech rate, different gestures, additional contextual cues, comprehension checks, clarification requests, repetition and paraphrase.

In summary, story*telling* gives the teacher authorial power to suit the story to the audience: 'telling a story should be used more often in the young learner classroom, as it offers a shared social experience and creates a relaxed classroom atmosphere. Furthermore, it is easier to verify pupils' understanding of a story while telling the story, and it is also easier to adapt the language or speed of delivery' (Dagarin Fojkar, Skela and Kovač 2013: 26). The rewards are more confidence for the teacher and pleasurable extensive listening for the children. Extensive listening is highlighted by Tomlinson (2015: 283) and Mason (2013), whose studies have produced impressive results: 'The finding that story-listening is as effective as or more effective than traditional methods is encouraging. Stories are far more pleasant and engaging than traditional instruction, and students can gain other aspects of language from stories, as well as knowledge' (2013: 28). Repetition, however, remains key. Elley (1989: 174) explored the significant vocabulary gains children achieved incidentally through listening to stories and found the frequency of repetition to be a feature that predicted which words would be acquired. Therefore the next section will consider the variety of different steps that are possible in oral storytelling.

Story steps with *Three Billy Goats Gruff*

The following introduces nine storytelling steps that might be undertaken with children who have as yet little English. Listening comprehension and oracy skills require *extensive* practice; 'over a series of lessons, possibly as many as eight or twelve, the children will come back to the story three or four times. During this period, their initial receptive understanding of the story will be scaffolded in order to enable them to act out and re-tell the story, to explore relevant issues it raises, and to personalise and transfer some of the language it contains to their own lives' (Read 2008: 7). This approach (see Figure 10.1) emphasizes that storytelling is a method that involves recycling over several lessons, allowing the children to participate while the teacher supports their contribution by recasting when necessary – remodelling their language in well-formed language chunks. Thus storytelling practises both comprehension fluency: engaging with extended stretches of creative teacher talk, and speaking: 'Children encounter English through talk and practise English through talk, and literacy skills can be developed through talk, for example by using rhymes and stories as entry points to written English. [...] children are well-equipped to rely on oral language; after all, this is what they have been doing since birth. They will hear differences in the spoken language that older learners will find less noticeable' (Cameron 2003: 108–109).

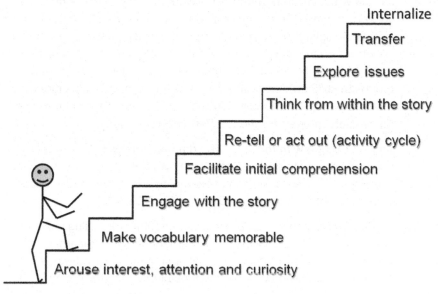

FIGURE 10.1 Scaffolding through story and drama (Read 2008: 7).

I have chosen as my exemplar the well-known tale *Three Billy Goats Gruff.* Some of the steps described below include drama strategies, and these are described in detail in Chapter 12 on drama with young learners (Bland 2015c), also with reference to *Three Billy Goats Gruff.* There is a recorded storytelling of *Three Billy Goats Gruff* made available by the Oxford-based Story Museum, which can be accessed, together with a written version and a story map, at http://www.storymuseum.org.uk/1001stories/detail/83/the-three-billy-goats-gruff.html. A recorded version is very useful for teacher preparation. However, as explained earlier, the first and second storytelling (Steps 4 and 5 below) should be live, with eye contact and the ability to react to the audience. Any version of the tale can be altered to suit the age and competence of the class, except for the building blocks of oral composition, such as *Once upon a time*, and in this story the refrains *trip-trap, trip-trap, trip-trap* across the bridge as well as the troll's question to each goat: *Who's that trip-trapping across my bridge?* Billy goats are male goats (a female is a nanny goat); the fearful troll can, of course, be a female troll.

Step 1. *Arouse interest, attention and curiosity*: Where do goats live? What do they eat? Do you know any stories about goats? What is a troll? What does a troll look like? (Some children may be aware that goats, like deer, in fact prefer shrubs to grass.)

Step 2. *Make vocabulary memorable*: The picture-dictation method can allow the children to form a network of associations around new vocabulary while the teacher sets the scene for the story. The teacher dictates a picture to the young learners, including any new language important for the story (e.g. mountain or hill, river, grass, bridge, troll, billy goat, horn), while touring the class and interacting with groups of children. Alternatively, the teacher can draw a picture on the blackboard and let the children guess. Wright (1994) includes very many useful models for the teacher's own drawings.

Step 3. *Engage with the story*: The drama strategy *Whoosh!* is an excellent way to engage with any as yet unknown story in the classroom. This is explained and exemplified with *Three Billy Goats Gruff* in Chapter 12 on drama (Bland 2015c: 233–234).

Step 4. *Facilitate initial comprehension*: The first storytelling should now be easy to follow. With encouragement, the young learners will spontaneously join in the refrains that are repeated three times *trip-trap, trip-trap, trip-trap* and *Who's that trip-trapping across my bridge?*

Step 5. *Retell the story*: The teacher retells the story and the children all join in the refrains. The children might act the swinging bridge: little swings for Little Billy Goat Gruff, swinging more with Middle Billy Goat Gruff and wider swings for Big Billy Goat Gruff.

Step 6. *Think from within the story*: The drama strategies conscience alley and collective role play are explained and exemplified with *Three Billy Goats Gruff* in Chapter 12 on drama (2015c: 234–235). These allow the young learners to use their own ideas and language. This valuable stage takes up time, because the children often need language support to express their ideas in English.

Step 7. *Explore issues*: Three billy goats cross the bridge in the story – three is a magical number in fairy tales. How many stories can the children name that feature three sisters or brothers, three friends, three actions …? The maxim: *If at first you don't succeed, try, try again* might be taught and discussed.

Step 8. *Transfer*: The story map provided by the Story Museum, available at http://www.storymuseum.org.uk/1001stories/

upload_files/map_pdf_83.pdf, could be used as an opportunity for motivated creative writing using one or two speech bubbles. Motivated creative writing is exemplified with *Three Billy Goats Gruff* in Chapter 12 on drama (Bland 2015c: 230–232).

Step 9. *Internalize*: The children might hot-seat the teacher (Bland 2015c: 236). This gives them much-needed practice in asking questions. If the teacher plays the troll, for instance, the children might ask: *Is your home under the bridge? What is your everyday food? Have you got a family? Can you swim?* The young learners can prepare the questions first in pairs (think, pair, share strategy), while the teacher tours the classroom. When answering in role, the teacher should optimally provide a useful language model, for in the nine-step lesson series described here this is the final opportunity to recycle vocabulary and stretches of language from the story.

Conclusion

This chapter has illustrated the important role of oral storytelling on many levels, for L2 acquisition, for participation in an activity that is prosocial, deeply satisfying and probably vital to humans and for education in the wider sense of developing connected thinking and empathy. Importantly, stories train the imagination to mentally represent alternative visions for the future, for the story 'is not just some casual entertainment; it reflects a basic and powerful form in which we make sense of the world and experience' (Egan 1986: 2). Teachers are encouraged to develop their creative teacher talk skills, by engaging in oral storytelling; for according to Showalter (2003: 79), 'Teaching is itself a dramatic art and it takes place in a dramatic setting.' Finally, learners deserve some relaxation and pleasure in the school setting, which stories for children promise: 'We fill our heads with improbable happy endings, and are able to live – in daydreams – in a world in which they are not only possible but inevitable' (Byatt 2004).

Notes

1 Stories from around the world, with audio recordings, may be found on the following websites: http://www.storymuseum.org.uk/stories/audio-stories/ and http://www.worldstories.org.uk.

References

Bauman, Richard (2005), 'Performance', in David Herman; Manfred Jahn and Marie-Laure Ryan (eds), *Routledge Encyclopedia of Narrative Theory*, Oxford: Routledge, pp. 419–421.

Bland, Janice (2013), *Children's Literature and Learner Empowerment. Children and Teenagers in English Language Education*, London: Bloomsbury.

Bland, Janice (2015c), 'Drama with young learners', in Janice Bland (ed.), *Teaching English to Young Learners. Critical Issues in Language Teaching with 3–12 Year Olds*, London: Bloomsbury Academic, pp. 219–238.

Bomer, Randy (2010), 'Orality, literacy, and culture: Talk, text, and tools in ideological contexts', in Dominic Wyse, Richard Andrews and James Hoffman (eds), *The Routledge International Handbook of English, Language and Literacy Teaching*, London: Routledge, pp. 205–215.

Boyd, Brian (2009), *On the Origin of Stories: Evolution, Cognition, and Fiction*, Harvard: Harvard University Press.

Byatt, Antonia (2004), 'Happy ever after', *Guardian*, 3 January 2004. <http://www.theguardian.com/books/2004/jan/03/sciencefictionfantasyandhorror.fiction> [accessed 25 October 2014].

Cameron, Lynne (2001), *Teaching Languages to Young Learners*, Cambridge: Cambridge University Press.

Cameron, Lynne (2003), 'Challenges for ELT from the expansion in teaching children', *ELT Journal*, 57/2: 105–112.

Chambers, Aidan (2011), *Tell Me. The Reading Environment*, Woodchester: Thimble Press.

Crago, Hugo (2011), 'Story', in Philip Nel and Lissa Paul (eds), *Keywords for Children's Literature*, New York: New York University Press, pp. 207–213.

Cron, Lisa (2012), *Wired for Story*, Berkeley: Ten Speed Press.

Currie, Mark (2011), *Postmodern Narrative Theory* (2nd edn), London: Macmillan.

Dagarin Fojkar, Mateja; Skela, Janez and Kovač, Pija (2013), 'A study of the use of narratives in teaching English as a foreign language to young learners', *English Language Teaching*, 6/6: 21–28. http://www.ccsenet.org/journal/index.php/elt/article/viewFile/27258/16551 [accessed 27 November 2014].

Egan, Kieran (1986), *Teaching as Storytelling*, Chicago: University of Chicago Press.

Elley, Warwick (1989), 'Vocabulary acquisition from listening to stories', *Reading Research Quarterly*, 24: 174–187.

Ellis, Gail and Brewster, Jean (2014), *Tell It Again! The Storytelling Handbook for Primary Teachers* (3rd edn), London: British Council. <http://www.teachingenglish.org.uk/article/tell-it-again-storytelling-handbook-primary-english-language-teachers> [accessed 27 November 2014].

Enever, Janet (2015), 'The advantages and disadvantages of English as a foreign language with young learners', in Janice Bland (ed.), *Teaching English to Young Learners. Critical Issues in Language Teaching with 3–12 Year Olds*, London: Bloomsbury Academic, pp. 13–29.

Gaiman, Neil (2014), <http://www.storymuseum.org.uk/about-us/testimonials/> [accessed 26 November 2014].

Gale, Ken and Sikes, Pat (2006) *Narrative Approaches to Education Research.* <http://www.edu.plymouth.ac.uk/resined/narrative/narrativehome.htm> [accessed 26 November 2014].

García Mayo, Maria and García Lecumberri, Maria Luisa (eds) (2003), *Age and the Acquisition of English as a Foreign Language*, Clevedon: Multilingual Matters.

Garner, Lori Ann (2005), 'Oral-formulaic theory', in David Herman; Manfred Jahn and Marie-Laure Ryan (eds), *Routledge Encyclopedia of Narrative Theory*, Oxford: Routledge, pp. 410–411.

Garton, Susan; Copland, Fiona, and Burns, Anne (2011), *Investigating Global Practices in Teaching English to Young Learners.* <http://iatefl.britishcouncil.org/2012/sites/iatefl/files/session/documents/eltrp_report_-_garton.pdf> [accessed 1 October 2014].

Gottschall, Jonathan (2012), *The Storytelling Animal. How Stories Make Us Human*, New York: Houghton Mifflin Harcourt.

Heathfield, David (2014), *Storytelling with Our Students: Techniques for Telling Tales from around the World*, Peaslake: Delta Publishing.

Hoey, Michael (2015), 'Old approaches, new perspectives: The implications of a corpus linguistic theory for learning the English language (and the Chinese language, too)', in Tania Pattison (ed.), *IATEFL 2014 Harrogate Conference Selections*, Faversham: IATEFL, pp. 12–20.

Jim Henson Company (2005), *The Storyteller*, <http://www.goodreads.com/quotes/283681-when-people-told-themselves-their-past-with-stories-explained-their> [accessed 17 November 2014].

Johnstone, Richard (2009), 'An early start: What are the key conditions for generalized success?' in Janet Enever; Jayne Moon and Uma Raman (eds), *Young Learner English Language Policy and Implementation: International Perspectives*, Reading: Garnet Education, pp. 31–41.

Kersten, Saskia (2015), 'Language development in young learners: The role of formulaic language', in Janice Bland (ed.), *Teaching English to Young Learners. Critical Issues in Language Teaching with 3–12 Year Olds*, London: Bloomsbury Academic, pp. 129–145.

Krashen, Stephen (2004), *The Power of Reading. Insights from the Research* (2nd edn), Portsmouth, NH: Heinemann.

Krashen, Stephen (2013), 'Free reading: Still a great idea', in Janice Bland and Christiane Lütge (eds), *Children's Literature in Second Language Education*, London: Bloomsbury Academic, pp. 15–24.

Le Guin, Ursula (1985), *Language of the Night. Essays on Fantasy and Science Fiction*, New York: Berkley Books.

Mason, Beniko (2013), 'Efficient use of literature in foreign language education free reading and listening to stories', in Janice Bland and Christiane Lütge (eds), *Children's Literature in Second Language Education*, London: Bloomsbury Academic, pp. 25–32.

Mason, Beniko and Krashen, Stephen (2004), 'Is form-focused vocabulary instruction worth while?', *RELC Journal*, 35/2: 179–185.

Morpurgo, Michael (2014), <http://www.storymuseum.org.uk/about-us/testimonials/> [accessed 26 November 2014].

Mourão, Sandie (2013), 'Picturebook: Object of discovery', in Janice Bland and Christiane Lütge (eds), *Children's Literature in Second Language Education*, London: Bloomsbury Academic, pp. 71–84.

Mourão, Sandie (2015b), 'The potential of picturebooks with young learners', in Janice Bland (ed.), *Teaching English to Young Learners. Critical Issues in Language Teaching with 3–12 Year Olds*, London: Bloomsbury Academic.

Ong, Walter (2002), *Orality and Literacy*, London: Routledge, pp. 199–217.

Pullman, Philip (1995), *The Firework-Maker's Daughter*, London: Corgi Yearling Books.

Read, Carol (2008), 'Scaffolding children's learning through story and drama', *Children & Teenagers: Young Learners and Teenagers SIG Publication, IATEFL*, 08/2: 6–9.

Rixon, Shelagh (2015), 'Primary English and critical issues: A worldwide perspective', in Janice Bland (ed.), *Teaching English to Young Learners. Critical Issues in Language Teaching with 3–12 Year Olds*, London: Bloomsbury Academic, pp. 31–50.

Showalter, Elaine (2003), *Teaching Literature*, Oxford: Blackwell.

Story Museum (2014), < http://www.storymuseum.org.uk/stories/stories/why-stories-matter/> [accessed 26 October 2014].

Thornbury, Scott (2002), *How to Teach Vocabulary*, Harlow: Pearson Longman.

Tisdall, Polly (2013), 'Affecting the audience', in Amy Douglas and Graham Langley (eds) *Pass It On. A Resource for Teaching Storytelling with Young People*, Birmingham: Traditional Arts Team, pp. 36–37.

Tomlinson, Brian (2015), 'Developing principled materials for young learners of English as a foreign language', in Janice Bland (ed.), *Teaching English to Young Learners. Critical Issues in Language Teaching with 3–12 Year Olds*, London: Bloomsbury Academic, pp. 279–293.

Wright, Andrew (1994), *1000 + Pictures for Teachers to Copy* (2nd edn), Harlow: Pearson Longman.

Wright, Andrew (2009), *Storytelling with Children* (2nd edn), Oxford: Oxford University Press.

Wright, Andrew (2013), 'Stories as symphonies', in Janice Bland and Christiane Lütge (eds), *Children's Literature in Second Language Education*. London: Bloomsbury Academic, pp. 205–217.

Zipes, Jack (2004), *Speaking Out. Storytelling and Creative Drama for Children*. New York: Routledge.

Zipes, Jack (2007), *When Dreams Came True. Classical Fairy Tales and Their Tradition* (2nd edn). New York: Routledge.

11

The Potential of Picturebooks with Young Learners

Sandie Mourão

Picturebooks: A definition

Picturebooks have been used in primary English Language Teaching (ELT) methodologies for over four decades (Ghosn 2013a). They are referred to as 'storybooks' (Ellis and Brewster 2014, Ghosn 2013a), 'real books' (Cameron 2001, Dunn 1997–2004, Machura 1991, Mourão 2003) and real picturebooks (Dunn 2003). More recently the term 'authentic children's literature' (Ghosn 2013a) has also been used, and for language-learning purposes it is authenticity that is key in the definition of a picturebook, in particular authenticity of the words found alongside the pictures (Ghosn 2013a). But, defining picturebooks merely as authentic materials does them a huge injustice, as does an overemphasis on the words they contain. To discuss this further I would like to begin by looking at a definition of a picturebook and unravelling it. A definition which is used widely in the field of children's literature comes from Bader:

> A picturebook is text, illustrations, total design; an item of manufacture and a commercial product; a social, cultural, historic document; and foremost, an experience for a [reader]. As an art form it hinges on the interdependence of pictures and words, on the simultaneous display of two facing pages, and on the drama of the turning page. On its own terms its possibilities are limitless. (Bader 1976:1)

Bader uses the compound noun, picturebook, reflecting the 'compound nature of the artefact itself' (Lewis 2001a: xiv). 'Picturebook' is the spelling we see in the more academic publications dealing with this form of literature in language education (Bland 2013; Bland and Lütge 2013; Birketveit and Williams 2013). Now, let us unravel the definition.

Unravelling the definition

The pictures and the words

Picturebooks contain pictures and the words, which when seen together produce a whole that 'is more than the sum of its parts' (Nodelman 1988: 200). A picturebook is thus dependent upon pictures and words together to create meaning: it is the 'interdependence' of what the pictures show and the words tell (Lewis 2001b) that makes picturebooks so special. This interdependence creates a picture–word dynamic ranging from a simple showing and telling of the same information to a more complex showing and telling of different, even contradicting information. This variation in picture–word dynamic can be seen within a single picturebook, demonstrating how flexible they are in nature. Pictures and words provide readers with information 'by means of its own specific forms, and independently' (Kress and van Leeuwen 1996: 17), and we read both modes. It is for this reason that I have placed 'reader' in Bader's definition above. Her original referred to 'child', but it is now well established that picturebooks are not just for children and can be enjoyed by readers of all ages (Beckett 2013).

Picturebooks at the simple end of the continuum give our younger learners confidence to listen to an English picturebook being read to them, but these picturebooks also encourage passivity, for little effort is needed to understand the picturebook. At the complex end of the picture–word dynamic, pictures and words interact with each other, either wholly or partially, filling each other's gaps or creating their own (Nikolajeva and Scott 2006). These are more sophisticated, often multilayered picturebooks that provide multiple opportunities for interpretation, promoting discussion and language use. By using these types of picturebooks we are encouraging more active learners (Baptista 2008: 4).

Generally in English language teaching the teacher selects and uses picturebooks that contain a simple picture–word relationship, with illustrations that synchronize (Ellis and Brewster 2014: 18) with the text providing a secure, supportive learning context. The focus is more on the words, a stance which is typical in ELT (Bland 2013: 31), often working with concept books that contain predictable and repetitive, sometimes cumulative refrains, and pictures that please the eye but give little extra information. Confirmation of this comes from three studies that questioned teachers about the picturebooks they used most often in class (Mourão 2010, Schaefer 2010, Soares 2011).[1] The three sets of results show that the most popular picturebooks fall at the simpler end of the picture–word dynamic. Table 11.1 shows that two titles appear in all three lists, *The Very Hungry Caterpillar* (Carle) and *Brown Bear, Brown Bear, What Do You See?* (Martin Jr and Carle).

Table 11.1 Top three picturebooks used by teachers in three different studies.

Schaefer (2010)	Mourão (2010)	Soares (2011)
The Very Hungry Caterpillar (n 19)	*The Very Hungry Caterpillar* (n 13)	*The Very Hungry Caterpillar* (n 15)
Elmer's Colours (n 6)	*Brown Bear, Brown Bear What Do You See?* (n 8)	*Brown Bear, Brown Bear What Do You See?* (n 10)
Brown Bear, Brown Bear What Do You See? (n 4)	*The Gruffalo* (n 6)	*The Enormous Turnip* (n 9)

Why are these titles so popular? As well as covering learning items and themes you would find in typical English-language programmes (colours, animals, days of the week, food and life cycles), there are published materials (see Ellis and Brewster 2014) as well as many online resources which help teachers use these titles successfully. But most importantly, the pictures and words are at the simpler end of the picture–word dynamic. Children look at the illustrations and the meaning is immediately apparent. These picturebooks are firm favourites with both L1 and L2 teachers, and Ghosn describes the *The Very Hungry Caterpillar*, in particular, enabling 'a wise [L2] teacher [to] select the instructional objectives according to the curriculum but allowing also for children's individual interests to be addressed' (2013a: 57). This is important in language learning and in particular with younger learners, but not the sole reason for including picturebooks in our planning.

Titles at the complex end of the picture–word dynamic are far less frequently used in our classrooms; however, the pictures and words often leave readers with gaps for personal interpretations and our students can become involved in a more critical and questioning approach to learning. These texts 'challenge young learners to search for, and in the classroom negotiate for, understanding and meaning' (Bland 2013: 32) and provide realistic opportunities for interaction and talk, instinctive in children at this age (Halliwell 1992: 5). Such picturebooks often move beyond the typical thematic language of our primary classes and cover more challenging topics; they are also more suitable for older primary children.

Examples are *Something Else* (Cave and Riddell), related to accepting difference, *Is It Because?* (Willis and Ross), clearly but carefully expounding on bullying, *Piggybook* (A. Browne), dealing with equality in the home and *Susan Laughs* (Willis and Ross), which is a sensitively created picturebook which prompts discussion around disability. Ghosn (2013b) provides further examples of picturebooks which support development of moral reasoning, emotional intelligence and empathy and Dolan (2014) highlights picturebook titles which support development of learners' intercultural understanding. These are all topics we should be including in our language classrooms, and picturebooks can help us do this.

And the design?

Bader's definition includes design alongside pictures and words. The design of a picturebook, that is the parts of the book considered peripheral in most literature, is deliberately put to use, so that a picturebook becomes an integrated whole. Publishers bring together the skills of the illustrator, author, editor and designer to make use of the book's format and its peritextual features – those parts of a text which 'surround it and extend it, precisely in order to present it' (Genette, 1997: 1). These are the front and back covers, the endpapers,[2] title pages and copyright and dedication pages. Illustrations, in particular, 'overflow' (Díaz Armas 2006) into all parts of the picturebook enabling an illustrator to use the whole book for narrative significance. For pre-primary learners, the endpapers in *Brown Bear, Brown Bear, What Do You See?* (Martin Jr & Carle) provide information that supports retelling the picturebook, as they depict strips of coloured tissue paper in the sequence of the animals as they appear in the story. When retelling this picturebook it is impossible to miss out these pages, as children want to chant the colours and together recall which animals they represent. For older primary learners, the endpapers in an entertaining semi-factual picturebook, *Mythological Monsters* (Fanelli), serve to entice the reader to go back and forth within the book to confirm what they have seen, in such a way that they are very much part of the active picturebook experience. The front endpapers contain quirky ink drawings of monsters placed as though in a notebook and with spaces for the reader to write their names underneath. As readers we are encouraged to ask ourselves, before we begin, if we know these monsters. The back endpapers include illustrations and questions, as though to test the reader once they have finished the book.

By skipping over these parts of a picturebook in our classes, we may be omitting information that contributes to the meaning-making process we engage in while reading and sharing a picturebook. In neglecting the peritextual features we also omit the use of metalanguage for talking about and discussing these parts (Mourão 2013), such as cover, endpapers and title page. If we, as teachers, naturally comment and model noticing as we share these parts of a picturebook, we can instil a curiosity in our students which will result in discovery and enjoyment in using these features to make meaning. Students will naturally put the metalanguage to use and also improve their understanding of how picturebooks work, which in turn will promote development of visual literacy and learning to look, an often forgotten learning strategy.

A social, cultural, historic document

Picturebooks cover a variety of socially, culturally and historically appropriate material for the language classroom dealing with a myriad of themes, and of course bringing the cultures of many Englishes to our classrooms through the words and pictures they contain. This makes them an excellent springboard for expanding students' understanding of a topic as well as motivating and supporting them to look beyond their own worlds and positively experience others. For the younger learner, however, many cultural nuances go unnoticed unless teachers ensure their responses are scaffolded. There are titles that, in showing us more through the pictures than the words, provide opportunities to develop critical thinking and discussion; Bland refers to these as picturebooks with 'an implicit sociocultural agenda' (2013: 59). *Handa's Surprise* (E. Browne) not only features wild animals and exotic fruits but also enables children to experience and thus talk about other cultures through the beautiful illustrations of Handa's home village and the Kenyan landscape. With careful support from the teacher, children can be helped to understand that Handa's world is different and will therefore have different kinds of opportunities.

Piggybook (A. Browne), a title for children in the upper young-learner age range, is a picturebook that could be shared while talking about families and daily routines. The simple verbal text is deceptive, for the complex picture–word dynamic leaves telling gaps between the two modes. Children understand what the words are saying but have to think about what is shown in the illustrations and piece the puzzle together; in so doing they are encouraged to reconsider male/female roles at home and in society. By using these types of picturebooks we are giving our students the tools to begin challenging social constructs.

Picturebooks are far more than *just* authentic texts. They provide affordances for authentic L2 use through interpretation of the books' pictures, words *and* design, as these elements come together to produce a visual-verbal narrative that FL teachers sometimes take for granted to be led by the words. I hope I have provided evidence that this is not the case. Additionally there is a belief that picturebooks are for the very young learner, yet I have given several examples of titles that are appropriate for children of nine years old and above. It is with this definition of picturebooks that I move on to the second part of this chapter, which includes a discussion around four different picturebooks for children ranging from three to twelve years. I have chosen these picturebooks for the affordances they provide learners for language use, based on their more complex picture–word dynamic.

The untapped potential for L2 use

Head, Shoulders, Knees and Toes... a picturebook for pre-primary children

The first picturebook is one for pre-primary children and an age-old favourite. With three- and four-year-old children the board book *Head, Shoulders, Knees and Toes...* (Kubler 2003) can be used and shared when singing the traditional song of the same name. As the very young learners look at the book, chanting the words of the song they know, they see the many illustrations of small children touching the different parts of their bodies. In this sense the picturebook supports the children's understanding of the body words – the illustrated children touch their heads, and soft toys fall and bump their heads – but the illustrations go further than merely confirming understanding of the well-known song.

Figure 11.1 shows Opening 4,[3] a double-page spread that depicts a part of the song 'And eyes and ears and mouth and nose'. The illustrations do not show (stereo)typically pale-skinned, blond-haired children. In this picturebook there are children of colour, Asian children, Hispanic children with black hair, fair-skinned children with red hair, children with straight hair, curly hair and no hair. This picturebook belongs to a collection of specially designed and illustrated traditional rhymes and songs, which depicts a multicultural array of children. Books like this act as mirrors, enabling children to see themselves in the pages, and as windows, so they can see what others are like too (Botelho and Rudman, 2009).

and ears   and mouth

FIGURE 11.1 *Opening 4 of* Head, Shoulders, Knees and Toes... *by Annie Kubler. Reproduced by kind permission of Child's Play (International) Ltd. © 2003 Child's Play. All Rights Reserved.*

Additionally, in the illustration we can see objects that make noises on the left hand, verso page; and on the right hand, recto page, the child's food and drink are at her feet. Children naturally comment on illustrations, so a comment from a child, even if it is in their own language, about the maracas, for example, can be rephrased into English, 'Yes, we can hear maracas *with our ears'*. This leads naturally into talking about senses, a topic which is included in early-years learning objectives. For some teachers, moving away from the verbal text might be frightening, but this represents the very essence of response to literature (Rosenblatt 1995, Iser 1978), in particular visual literature (Sipe 2000). Read (2006: 17) has documented the importance of such responses providing the 'joint construction of discourse' and Mourão (2012) highlights the importance of accepting a learner's personal interest by following child-initiated talk around a picturebook and provides empirical evidence that children's L1 utterances when rephrased into L2 by a teacher can support L2 development.

Yo! Yes?[4] a picturebook for middle primary children

Yo! Yes? (Raschka 1993) is a great favourite with children who are familiar with the notion of friendship groups and being left out. It was a Caldecott Honor book, which is a highly prestigious American picturebook award. The children will be curious about the silver medal which is clearly visible on the front cover (see Figure 11.2), and the teacher should refer to this in the booktalk.

As a picturebook, its simplicity is deceptive. There are just thirty-four words, with one or two words seen on each page placed above apparently hastily charcoal-drawn and watercoloured illustrations. The combination of image and word is superb. It is a simple story – two boys meet, they talk and become friends. But that very short summary ignores the visual impact of each page and double spread. Chris Raschka uses a large handwritten font for each punctuated utterance and it becomes as much part of the image as his vibrant depictions of the two boys, one African American, the other white Caucasian.

In the paperback edition I have, the dedication and copyright page come after the title page, which is uncommon. The illustrations are already showing us how the boys meet, by chance as they pass in the street. When we turn the page we see a large arresting *'Yo!'* and Raschka's figures ooze unspoken communication. The white boy's posture, with simple charcoaled eyes and mouth, together with the small-size reply, *'Yes?'*, conveying the depths of uncertainty he is feeling.

FIGURE 11.2 *Front cover of Yo! Yes? by Chris Raschka, Scholastic Inc./ Orchard Books. Copyright © 1993 by Chris Raschka. Reprinted by permission.*

Each page and spread continues in this way, a visual dialogue between the two boys, where we read the words, the punctuation and their postures as one whole visual communicative act. The two boys remain centred on their respective pages, their feet anchoring them to the spot, but their bodies lean forwards or backwards; their arms out or folded in over their chests; their heads up or down. The background in light washes, starting with a greeny blue at the beginning of the book and moving through pinky red, orangey yellow and finally a glowing bright yellow, represents the emotions on each page. And each figure is outlined by this wash, as though in a spotlight, a spotlight for each boy – visually it both unites and separates them on the page – they are both boys, yet different.

With each utterance and pose, we learn the problem. The white boy has no friends. The black boy cannot believe it. And so he offers his own friendship – his chest is proudly stuck out towards the white boy, he points at the bull's eye-like circle on his T-shirt. The white boy's reaction confirms the doubt we already feel inside... friends? But after some thought, with the background washes moving through pink to yellow, the white boy gleefully decides that he will accept the offer of friendship. The big handwritten word, 'Yes!', almost squashes him with its weight. On the next opening the boys are together, the white boy has crossed over to the other side of the double spread, walking to the left with his newfound friend. They are joyous, holding hands and the white spotlight is on both of them, no longer separate, uniting the two boys. The bright yellow wash in the background emphasizes their happiness and the words 'Yo! Yes!', both beginning with 'y', unite them too... rolling off our tongue as we read them out loud.

But that is not the end, there is one final page. They are very happy, jumping up out of the page, up and over the word, *'Yow!'* They are no longer anchored to the bottom of the page, but free to leap and loop. Free to be friends, black or white. When you reread this picturebook, your students will be ready with that *'Yow!'*, no matter how old they are.

Yo! Yes? in the classroom

This picturebook will be retold many times and enjoyed by learners. Having encountered the book once, learners can be encouraged to think about the boys – what each looked like, what was he wearing, what did they think he was like? How were the boys different? How were they the same? These are a mixture of open and closed questions generating language related to clothes, physical descriptions, personalities and emotions which can lead nicely into discussing how we choose our friends, what we do with our friends and even what friendship is. Themes of diversity and tolerance will emerge, which can be expanded upon if the teacher feels it is necessary.

An additional activity is one related to punctuation. The visual cohesion of word, punctuation and illustration means that dramatic activities lend themselves well to playing with the words. It is easy to demonstrate that punctuation can make a difference, even through a single word – 'Me?' 'Me!' 'Me.', which are all visible in the verbal and visual texts of this picturebook. Learners enjoy saying words and short expressions in different ways – a great favourite is playing around with the expression 'I love you'.

Once the punctuation symbols used in the book have been understood, a class of around thirty pupils (any larger makes visibility of the picturebook difficult) can be split in half, each group reading a character's words in a kind of choral reading. Young learners should be encouraged to say their lines with as much emotion as possible, using voice, facial expression and body language. Anecdotal evidence has shown that children use 'Yo!' and 'Yow' in the playground, with much hilarity.

'Yo!' is an informal greeting commonly associated with American English and Rap music, and learners may well already be familiar with it. An extension activity could involve discovering other informal greetings in their own country and language(s), discussing when they are used and why and then compare these with other informal greetings in English-speaking countries, such as 'Hi there!', 'Hiya!', 'Hey!' and 'Watcha!' Learners can write new dialogues incorporating these newly learned greetings, then act them out them in pairs. The importance of focusing on one's own culture as well as looking at others produces an intercultural awareness based on 'Knowledge, awareness and understanding of the relation (similarities and distinctive differences) between the "world of origin" and the "world of the target community" ' (Council of Europe 2001: 103). Additionally, a follow-up activity could involve looking at different ways people greet each other around the world. If learners have family or know people from/in other countries, they can ask about the different ways they greet and bring the information back to the classroom. It is fairly easy to google world greetings and together practise them with each other, discussing how we feel and our expectations, especially in relation to our own forms of greeting, both formal and informal.

Wolves,[5] a picturebook for older primary children

Wolves (Gravett 2005) has been labelled postmodern (Mackey 2008) – a picturebook that emphasizes such things as pastiche, parody, bricolage, irony and playfulness, which according to Dresang 'are related to the ambiguity and fragmentation of postmodernism in society' (2008: 44). The design and layout is due to the *mise-en-abyme* device – a book within a book, for as readers we hold the very book being read by the rabbit protagonist. Different verbal text styles are used – a factual description and a disclaimer – and readers are given the possibility of 'multiple readings and meanings for a variety of audiences' (Anstey 2002: 447). *Wolves* is non-fiction made fiction; fantasy and references to reality coexist on its pages (Hall 2008:140). From reading the verbal text we learn about wolves. The words tell us how they live (in packs), where they live (in the Arctic Circle, forests, woodlands and near civilizations), what they look like (they have bushy tails, claws and forty-two teeth) and what they eat (meat in the form of large and small animals). The visual text shows us the journey a little rabbit makes to the library, to borrow a book about wolves. This visual quickly takes over and leaves the fairly banal description of a wolf to one side, as the wolf in the illustrations becomes a real-life wolf and the rabbit becomes his real-life dinner.

The peritextual features of *Wolves* form unclear boundaries between what is part of the narrative and what is not. The endpapers are pastiche in style: typical of old, antique books, buff brown with a pattern of angular lines. After reading the story and returning to these endpapers they no longer represent arbitrary marks, but remind us of claws and scratches. The copyright and title page show a hessian doormat, one we would expect to find directly beneath the letter box in our front door. The publisher details are shown on a postcard and the title information is conveyed in the form of a flyer from the 'West Bucks Public Burrowing Library' (the verbal text is full of rabbit-related puns). In the following openings, a rabbit is shown visiting a library and selecting a book about wolves. A close-up of the book, followed by the very same endpapers we have just seen (only this time there is an old-fashioned library card there for us to actually remove and give to the librarian), enables us to

FIGURE 11.3 Wolves *Opening 12. Text and illustration copyright © Emily Gravett 2005. First published by Macmillan Children's Books, a division of Macmillan Publishers 2005.*

feel we really are beginning the book again. Only then do we begin the story as such, and see the rabbit intently reading his library book, literally walking into his own story, oblivious to what is going on around him.

As the rabbit reads we see the wolf he is reading about leave the pages to become a real-life wolf. The rabbit continues, engrossed as he walks unknowingly past the wolf's feet, up his tail, onto his back and over his nose. There is a moment of panic when the rabbit has just read what the wolf eats, and we see him silhouetted between the wolf's eyes, balanced on the wolf's nose (see Figure 11.3). When we turn the page the illustration is of the book's red, cloth cover all scratched and tattered and a bit of ripped paper tells us that the wolf also eats '… rabbits'. Shocked? Turning the page again and we find a disclaimer announcing that not only is the book fictional, but no rabbits were eaten while making the book! It announces there is an alternative ending for 'more sensitive readers' (Opening 14). Rabbit and wolf are shown eating a jam sandwich together (Opening 15) – the illustration is made of ripped bits of drawing, as though Gravett has collected the pieces after the terrible rabbit-eating event and made it all better. And of course they live happily ever after. So, for a while we are happy that the wolf is vegetarian and does not eat rabbits, but upon turning the page again there is yet another ending: we are back in rabbit's house, but the doormat is now covered in mail. This page is a treasure trove of rabbit puns, for example, a Chinese restaurant called '*Burrowed Wok*', offering 'FREE Lawn Crackers' and 'FREE Morning Dew'. There is also a letter from the library, which we can actually take out of the envelope and read. It tells us the book is overdue. Does this mean rabbit did not get home after all? We are left wondering… and much discussion ensues among any group of children that this picturebook is shared with.

When reading a book like this with young learners, they are being given access to three different texts: the visual, the verbal and the text created by the combination of the two, the one we construct as readers. We could say *Wolves* is a 1+1=3 picturebook. It is a picturebook that needs to be read and reread. Children will request that it be left in their classroom or library, so they can browse through it, take out the library card, read the letter from the library and look closely at every detail.

Wolves in the classroom

The picturebook *Wolves* is very useful to support or extend Content and Language Integrated Learning (CLIL) lessons linked to the topic of food chains, for example. However, it is my view that the pleasure of sharing such a magical picturebook with young learners is what makes this a worthy text for English as a Foreign Language (EFL) classes. It should be read to children for the simple enjoyment of sharing the visual jokes – a socially enriching encounter, which is also important for fostering a positive language-learning experience.

Voices in the Park, a picturebook for (in most contexts) younger secondary learners

Voices in the Park (A. Browne 1999) is another postmodern picturebook. It shows and tells four different perspectives of a visit to a city park. Each perspective comes from a different character, and as in many of Browne's books these characters are zoomorphic, with human bodies and ape heads. Each voice is shown in a different font (see Figure 11.4, the voice of Charles), which adds to the visual dimension of this particular mode of communication. There is Charles and his upper-class mother, with their pedigree Labrador, Victoria; and there is Smudge, her out-of-work Dad and their mongrel dog, Albert. The children and dogs play together; the adults keep to themselves. You may already have noticed the pun in the dogs' names, referring readers to Queen Victoria and Prince Albert. This description of the characters also hints at themes found within the narratives: these include perceived social class, loneliness and friendship. Four different seasons represent each character, prompting us to question the time span within the narrative, and though each narrative is linear and sequential, within each narrative the illustrations create bridges linking the characters and events and forcing the reader to fill gaps and find the pieces to complete the puzzle in an attempt to understand the whole story.

THIRD VOICE

I was at home on my own again. It's so boring. Then Mummy said that it was time for our walk.

There was a very friendly dog in the park and Victoria was having a great time. I wished I was.

FIGURE 11.4 Voices in the Park *Opening 7. Text and illustration copyright © Anthony Browne, Random House. Reprinted by permission.*

The verbal text is simple and accessible for A2-level learners, but it is Browne's illustrations and surreal visual content that make this a challenging picturebook. Gorillas appear as statues (comically as a cupid on one page), trees look like apples and pears and lamp posts have crowns, repeated images of the grumpy mother's hat are seen in lamp posts, trees, clouds and shadows (see Figure 11.4). There are pages with visual divides, associating dark skies with a solitary Charles and sunny sides and flowering plants with an outgoing Smudge. Victoria and Albert are seen constantly in the background, enjoying being dogs, running and playing, oblivious to class differences. There are many intertextual connections to films, art and literature: there is a Santa Claus and a King Kong; Edvard Munch's *The Scream* is an advertisement in the newspaper Smudge's Dad is reading; on the way to the park there is a Rembrandt self-portrait and a Mona Lisa painting. Thus, this picturebook provides numerous opportunities for developing aesthetic understanding and the all-important ability to connect with, and recognize, references to other texts. It also provides an alternative support for learners to think about using *voice* in their own writing and, no less important, it helps them develop an understanding of multiple points of view. Finally Browne's creativity invites readers to add their own ideas to the four interconnected tales, providing a legitimate route to authentic talk.

Voices in the Park in the classroom

The main activity I would like to pursue with this picturebook is authentic talk, and it is important to let learners decide what *they* want to talk about. To do this successfully the 'Tell me' approach (Chambers 1983) is a useful guide, as it involves helping students decide together what can be talked about, enabling more authentic and natural participation. I suggest a sequence of activities being guided by the following stages (Mourão 2011: 14):

Stage 1: Reading and rereading

Reading involves first predicting what the book is about, individually or in groups, if possible using written notes to support post-reading discussion. Once the book has been read, learners talk about their predictions, in pairs or small groups. Rereading the book one more time, at least, is essential to give learners time to reconsider what they saw and heard during the telling.

Stage 2: Thinking and rethinking

Thinking and rethinking involve learners considering four different questions ideally with a class set of picturebooks: *Was there anything you liked about this book? Was there anything you disliked about this book? Was there anything that puzzled you? Did you notice any patterns or connections to real-life experiences?* This latter question can result in comparisons and discussions around socioculturally related themes.

Stage 3: Discussion

Discussion follows with learners commenting on and justifying what they have said in response to the questions. Discussion should come naturally, as the topics are those that have been highlighted as being most interesting by the learners themselves. The 'Tell me' approach provides opportunities for discussion and challenges the learners to think and write 'for real'. Teachers become mediators through the open-ended questions they ask, generated from the questions the students pose. According to Chambers (1983: 81–82), the teacher's role as scaffolder is crucial and involves:

- bringing the readers back to the original text by asking: *How do you know that?*

- being ready to ask general questions which will help develop talk

- being ready to ask book-specific questions

- summing up what seems to have been said so that everyone has a chance to remember and which helps the discussion find a destination.

In addition to using English for a purpose, young learners are also learning to look, and in focusing on the visual all students are being given an equal opportunity to interpret and talk about what they see. This approach does not focus *on* language, but on interpretation *through* language. It may therefore be necessary to help students with certain phrases so that they can feel confident when discussing – phrases related to predicting, verifying, comparing, extending, appreciating and wondering may be usefully highlighted. Even in the most fully developed CLIL and immersion approaches (see Bentley 2015, K. Kersten and Rohde 2015), this kind of literacy teaching will still be necessary, if English is not to be downgraded to a mere teaching medium.

Voices in the Park is a complex, thought-provoking picturebook. It tackles a topic that is both relevant and non-existent in ELT materials. It also supports the development of visual and critical literacy and thinking skills due to the open-endedness of the narrative. There is no key with the right answers for teachers, for the children decide what they think the significances are.

Closing comments

The objective of this chapter was to provide the reader with a fuller understanding of the picturebook as a form of children's literature, to expand and develop young learners' use of English, through enabling authentic responses. I chose a definition which highlights that picturebooks contain pictures *and* words and both should be used for the creation of meaning, alongside the book's design features. I have also provided evidence that picturebooks are social, cultural, historic documents, which require serious consideration.

With a picturebook, the potential for language learning arises from the active engagement that takes place between learner and book, which results in participation with and use of language. There is nothing fixed about this affordance; it is dependent upon the learners and their own personal experience as they interact within a meaning-making experience. With picturebooks, young learners are given a multitude of opportunities to use language that represents the pictures and the words and the interpretations created from the two modes coming together. Birketveit and Williams (2013: 11) describe English as 'a school subject with a vast potential for variation, underpinned by a wide variety of engaging, exciting and wonderful stories and genres to choose from'. In using engaging picturebooks, the children's aesthetic, cultural, cognitive and emotional development can be simultaneously supported alongside their language and literacy development.

Notes

1 Mourão (2010) used an online discussion list to collect data from twenty-six teachers worldwide; Schaefer (2010) questioned forty-six teachers in Germany and Soares (2011) questioned thirty teachers in Portugal.

2 Endpapers are the first and last pages in a picturebook. In a hardback book they are pasted down onto the inside of the cover, serving the function of holding the book together. If they are significant to the visual narrative they are often included in a paperback edition.

3 Openings are referred to in picturebooks as they do not have page numbers. Openings are two facing pages and are counted from the title page of the picturebook.

4 For those readers who do not know this picturebook, they can read a blog post which discusses this picturebook in detail: http://picturebooksinelt. blogspot.pt/2010/11/about-being-friends.html [accessed 22 March 2015].

5 For those readers who do not know this picturebook, they can read a blog post which discusses this picturebook in detail: http://picturebooksinelt. blogspot.pt/2011/01/emily-gravetts-wolf.html [accessed 19 August 2014].

Bibliography

Browne, Anthony (2008), *Piggybook*, London: Walker Books.
Browne, Anthony (1999), *Voices in the Park*, London: Picture Corgi Books.
Browne, Eileen (1994), *Handa's Surprise*, London: Walker Books.
Carle, Eric (2002), *The Very Hungry Caterpillar*, London: Picture Puffin.
Cave, Kathryn and Riddell, Chris (2011), *Something Else* London: Picture Puffin.
Donaldson, Julia and Scheffler, Axel (1999), *The Gruffalo*, Oxford: Macmillan Children's Books.
Gravett, Emily (2006), *Wolves*, London: Macmillan Children's Books.
Martin Jr, Bill and Carle, Eric (1995), *Brown Bear, Brown Bear, What Do You See?* London: Puffin Books.
Fanelli, Sara (2006), *Mythological Monsters*, London: Walker Books.
Kubler, Annie (2001), *Head, Shoulders, Knees and Toes*. Swindon: Child's Play.
McKee, David (1994), *Elmer's Colours*, London: Andersen Press.
Raschka, Chris (2007), *Yo! Yes!* New York: Scholastic.
Ross, Tony (2008), *Is It Because?* London: Andersen Press.
Willis, Jeanne and Ross, Tony (2011), *Susan Laughs*, London: Andersen Press.

References

Anstey, Michèle (2002), 'It's not all black and white: Postmodernist picturebooks and new literacies', *Journal of Adolescent & Adult Literacy*, 44: 444–457.
Bader, Barbara (1976), *American Picturebooks from Noah's Ark to the Beast Within*, New York: Macmillan Publishing Company.
Baptista, Adriana (2008), 'Texto e imagem: um mais um igual a outro', pp. 1–17. <http://195.23.38.178/casadaleitura/portalbota/bo/documentos/ot_texto_e_imagem_c.pdf> [accessed 7 December 2014].
Beckett, Sandra (2013), *Crossover Picturebooks: A Genre for All Ages*, New York: Routledge.
Bentley, Kay (2015), 'CLIL scenarios with young learners', in Janice Bland (ed.), *Teaching English to Young Learners. Critical Issues in Language Teaching with 3–12 Year Olds*, London: Bloomsbury Academic, pp. 91–111.
Birketveit, Anna and Williams, Gweno (eds) (2013), *Literature for the English Classroom*, Bergen: Fagbokforlaget.
Bland, Janice (2013), *Children's Literature and Learner Empowerment*, London: Bloomsbury Academic.
Bland, Janice and Lütge, Christiane (eds) (2013), *Children's Literature in Second Language Education*, London: Bloomsbury Academic.
Botelho, Maria José and Rudman, Masha (2009), *Critical Multicultural Analysis of Children's Literature: Mirrors, Windows, and Doors*, Abingdon: Routledge.
Cameron, Lynne (2001), *Teaching Languages to Young Learners*, Cambridge: Cambridge University Press.
Chambers, Aiden (1983), *Tell Me. Children Reading and Talk*, Gloucester: Thimble Press.

Council of Europe (2001), *Common European Framework of Reference for Languages: Learning, Teaching, Assessment*, Cambridge: Cambridge University Press.

Díaz Armas, Jesus (2006), 'El contrato de lectura en el álbum: Paratextos y desbordamiento narrativo' *Revista: Primeras Noticias*, 222: 33–40.

Dolan, Anne (2014), 'Intercultural education, picturebooks and refugees: Approaches for language teachers', *Children's Literature in English Language Education Journal*, 2/1: 92–109

Dresang, Eliza (2008), 'Radical change theory, postmodernism, and contemporary picturebooks', in Laurence Sipe and Sylvia Pantaleo (eds), Postmodern Picturebooks: Play Parody and Self Referentiality, New York: Routledge, pp. 41–54.

Dunn, Opal (1997–2004), *REAL BOOK News* <http://www.teachingenglish.org.uk/article/real-books> [accessed 10 December 2014].

Dunn, Opal (2003), 'REALpictureBOOKS – An additional experience in English', in Sandie Mourão (ed.), *Current Practices: A Look at Teaching English to Children in Portugal. Book of Proceedings, APPI & IATEFL 1st Young Learner Conference*, Lisbon: APPI. pp. 106–114.

Ellis, Gail and Brewster, Jean (2014), *Tell It Again! The Storytelling Handbook for Primary Teachers* (3rd edn), London: British Council. <http://www.teachingenglish.org.uk/article/tell-it-again-storytelling-handbook-primary-english-language-teachers> [accessed 13 August 2014].

Genette, Gerrard (1997), *Paratexts: Thresholds of Interpretation*. Cambridge: Cambridge University Press.

Ghosn, Irma-Kaarina (2013a), *Storybridge to Second Language Literacy. The Theory, Research and Practice of Teaching English with Children's Literature*, Charlotte, NY: Information Age Publishing.

Ghosn, Irma-Kaarina (2013b) 'Humanizing Teaching English to Young Learners with Children's Literature', *Children's Literature in English Language Education*, 1/1: 39–57.

Hall, Christine (2008), 'Imagination and multimodality: Reading, picturebooks and anxieties about childhood', in Laurence Sipe and Sylvia Pantaleo (eds), *Postmodern Picturebooks: Play Parody and Self Referentiality*, New York: Routledge, pp. 131–148.

Halliwell, Susan (1992), *Teaching English in the Primary Classroom*, London: Longman.

Iser, Wolfgang (1978), *The Act of Reading*, London/Henley: Routledge & Kegan Paul.

Kersten, Kristin and Rohde, Andreas (2015), 'Immersion teaching in English with young learners', in Janice Bland (ed.), *Teaching English to Young Learners. Critical Issues in Language Teaching with 3–12 Year Olds*, London: Bloomsbury Academic, pp. 71–89.

Kress, Gunther and van Leeuwen, Theo (1996), *Reading Images: The Grammar of Visual Design*, London: Routledge.

Lewis, David (2001a), *Reading Contemporary Picturebooks: Picturing Text*. Abingdon: RoutledgeFalmer.

Lewis, David (2001b), 'Showing and telling: The difference that makes a difference', *Reading: Literacy and Language*, 35/3: 94–98

Machura, Ludmilla (1991), 'Using literature in language teaching', in Christopher, Brumfit; Jayne Moon and Ray Tongue (eds), *Teaching English to Children*, London: HarperCollins Publishers. pp. 67–80.

Mackey, Margaret (2008), 'Postmodern picturebooks and the material conditions of reading', in Laurence Sipe and Sylvia Pantaleo (eds), *Postmodern Picturebooks: Play Parody and Self Referentiality*, New York: Routledge, pp. 103–116.

Mourão, Sandie (2003), *Realbooks in the Primary Classroom.* Southam: Mary Glasgow Scholastic.

Mourão, Sandie (2010) Unpublished text retrieved from http://groups.yahoo.com/group/younglearners/message/12859

Mourão, Sandie (2011), 'Demystifying the picturebook', *IN English: The British Council Magazine for Teachers of English in Lusophone Countries*, pp. 11–15. <http://issuu.com/britishcouncilportugal/docs/inenglishdigital_01> [accessed 21 August 2014].

Mourão, Sandie (2012), *English Picturebook Illustrations and Language Development in Early Years Education*, Unpublished PhD Thesis, University of Aveiro, Portugal.

Mourão, Sandie (2013), 'Picturebook: Object of discovery', in Janice Bland and Christiane Lütge (eds), *Children's Literature in Second Language Education.* London: Bloomsbury Academic, pp. 71–84.

Nikolajeva, Maria and Scott, Carol (2006), *How Picturebooks Work*, Abingdon: Routledge.

Nodelman, Perry (1988), *Words about Pictures. The Narrative Art of Children's Picture Books*, Athens, Georgia: University of Georgia Press.

Read, Carol (2006), 'Supporting teachers in supporting learners', in Janet Enever and Gisela Schmid-Schönbein (eds), *Picture Books and Primary EFL Learners*, Munich: Langenscheidt. pp. 11–21.

Rosenblatt, Louise (1995), *Literature as Exploration.* New York: Modern Language Association of America.

Schaefer, Annett (2010), *Investigating the use of songs, rhymes and stories in primary EFL teaching.* Paper presented at the Children's Literature in Language Education Conference – from Picture Books to Young Adult Fiction, February 2010, Hildesheim University, Germany.

Sipe, Laurence (2000), 'The construction of literary understanding by first and second graders in oral response to picture storybook read-alouds', *Reading Research Quarterly*, 35/2: 252–275.

Soares, Helena (2011), *Ler para aprender: As histórias como ponto de partida para a aprendizagem do Inglês no 1º ciclo do Ensino Básico.* Unpublished MA dissertation, ESEIP, Porto.

12

Drama with Young Learners

Janice Bland

Introduction

Drama in the language classroom is like a magical box of tools; the more you take out of it, the more you find inside for future use. I have observed hundreds of primary-school lessons in my role as pre-service teacher educator in Germany. One of the most enjoyable and effective warming-up sessions that I have witnessed – stirring the young learners up for an active English lesson – was a versatile role-play activity. The teacher had a box of finger puppets: there were fairy-tale figures, monsters, wild animals and farm animals, mythical characters and easily identifiable professionals such as firefighters, police officers and doctors. The children were given one finger puppet each for the warming-up phase, and took on that role as they moved around the classroom. They moved from partner to partner, conversing with other characters, while practising, consolidating, expanding and transferring to each new partner and context the language they had so far acquired.

This regularly repeated activity allows the children to interact with different characters, and the following levels of holistic language learning are involved:

- The cognitive level of suitable language choice is practised while children negotiate and infer meanings. Formulaic sequences can be employed such as: Who are you? I'm a crocodile/ witch/ clown. Where do you live? In the river, forests, city ... Do you like swimming/ riding a broomstick/ playing tricks?

- The sociological dimension of language learning is practised, as the young learners must find and exchange partners. They listen to their partner's questions and respond, taking turns at asking questions. This supports awareness that language is social interaction.

- The affective dimension of language learning is practised. The young learners are energized to speak in role and there are many incentives to talk; they take pleasure in becoming different characters and on the simplest level they are encouraged to change perspective.

- The physiological dimension of holistic language learning is practised. The children move around the classroom as they communicate; they use actions, gestures and facial expressions.

Following this effective and lively beginning, the young learners can settle down to a concentrated phase of English.

As language learning worldwide involves ever-younger learners, the craft repertoire of the language teacher must continually develop. Including drama as a language-learning method will help perpetuate the advantages of younger second language (L2) learners, as listed, for example, in Saville-Troike (2006: 82). These advantages include brain plasticity (helpful for the acquisition of target phonology), non-analytical processing mode (helpful for the acquisition of language chunks holistically), fewer inhibitions (helpful for taking risks) and weaker group identity (helpful for acquiring intercultural competence), and they are best exploited in naturalistic language-learning settings, such as drama offers. Drama provides an opportunity both to nurture the global and holistic cognitive style of the younger learner and to support and value less-analytic secondary-school learners, whose cognitive style is often undervalued in mainstream schooling.

The value of drama is multilayered: it can be used as a brief interactive warming-up activity, as the example above demonstrates, or as a task-based project that lasts many weeks. On the one hand drama methodology is seen to comprise improvisational drama processes involving whole-body spontaneous response, and on the other hand, play scripts as literary texts to be learned by heart and acted out. This highlights the difficulty of developing a coherent rationale for the use of educational drama. Nevertheless, as Moses Goldberg (1974: 4), an influential drama educator, has argued, both what he calls 'creative dramatics' (without a script) and 'recreational drama' (scripted drama) have the aim of 'the development of the whole child through a group process'. Goldberg also stresses that the term 'recreation' is not meant to signal drama as a diversion activity but as one that allows for the re-creation of the self (1974: 5). In the English as a Foreign Language (EFL) classroom, both scripted and unscripted drama have the potential to provide multisensory clues to meaning – much effective drama work involves multiple overlapping sensory systems – and both give students the opportunity to learn to trust and enjoy their linguistic resources and extend their repertoire. Whereas scripted drama offers opportunities for *motivated reading*, unscripted drama can provide opportunities for *motivated creative writing*. Thus, both scripted and unscripted drama should have a place in the EFL classroom.

Drama is embedded language learning

Sociocultural theory in L2 learning is a research framework that pays attention to the role of social context and *collaborative* dialogue: language performance is jointly constructed. Thus language is dynamically co-constructed in contexts and is not static and unchanging. It is crucially important that young learners can take on various roles from the outset of language learning, not only the role of 'being questioned by the teacher'. In drama, the context is always central, not isolated linguistic sign making such as a single verbal utterance, and thus the potential of multiple meanings and the sociocultural context are naturally and authentically involved. Contextualizing make-believe comes naturally to children; it provides them with their vital and authentic learning environment. When taken into the EFL classroom, drama consequently shares the underlying principle behind task-based learning, which is 'that authentic learner interaction, motivated engagement and purposefulness are important in making progress in language learning' (Pinter 2015: 114). Drama is sociocultural interaction that utilizes numerous semiotic systems simultaneously. Kramsch writes of the linguistic sign as 'one of many kinds of signs that can be created and perceived by the senses, be they verbal, acoustic, visual, olfactory, touch-related. Even silences or blank spaces on a page can be made into signs' (2000: 134). So, for instance, drama usually involves the following:

- The linguistic or verbal system – this can include spoken dialogue, shouting or whispering, or a written script and stage directions.

- The visual system – this can include pictures that inspire a role play; while a dramatized story can include scenery, masks, stage make-up and costumes.

- The touch-related system – this can include physical contact, glove puppets, finger puppets, realia or symbolic props.

- The gestural system – this includes facial expressions, body language, dance and stillness.

- The audio system – this includes prosodic features (patterns of intonation, stress, pitch, tempo, volume and rhythm), sound effects, music and silence.

- The spatial system – this includes the set, as well as the positioning of interlocutors/ characters to each other and to the audience.

This complex combination of semiotic systems in drama processes bears a resemblance to the interactive language play of children, with its vocal-visual and vocal-tactile choreography (Crystal 1998: 164). The link between the rich semiotics of drama and children's play is echoed in the polysemic word 'play', which also refers to a stage play. As children are extremely involved in learning through imitation and playful experimentation, the sociocultural context is central to their L2 acquisition. Learning another language, according to Kramsch (2000: 139–140), can be considered 'another way of creating, conveying, and exchanging signs, not primarily of acquiring new grammatical and lexical tools that are then put to use in a social context'.

Humanistic learning

Drama is a holistic method, both in the sense of whole language – learning whole language in context and usage-based (see S. Kersten 2015) – and holistic in the sense of the whole person – or *humanistic learning*. Drama, in the first sense, as discussed above, avoids decontextualized language that is abstracted from any sociocultural context. Drama thus avoids mono-dimensional activities, for example filling gaps in worksheets, which inhibit multisensory encounters with language. In the second sense, drama aims to achieve 'learning as a whole person, with body, mind, and emotions in harmony with one another' (Stevick 1980: 11). Young learners can identify with their language learning – so achieving a positive mindset – if they can emotionally engage with it. Many scholars consider the affective dimension of central importance in language teaching (see e.g. Jane Arnold, Gertrude Moskowitz, Mario Rinvolucri, Earl Stevick and Brian Tomlinson).

Stevick, writing from the perspective of humanistic language-learning theory (1980: 4), declared that for L2 teaching 'success depends less on materials, techniques and linguistic analyses, and more on what goes on inside and between the people in the classroom'. Working towards a whole-group goal, such as a performance, promotes group cohesion, students' self-confidence and self-esteem. Working on a play together supports a motivating classroom environment:

One of the most salient features of the classroom environment is the quality of the relationships between the class members. The quality of teaching and learning is entirely different depending on whether the classroom is characterized by a climate of trust and support or by a competitive, cutthroat atmosphere. (Dörnyei 2007: 720)

Commonly recognized categories of motivation are, for example, *intrinsic* (young learners are often considered to be motivated from within to learn), *instrumental* (the learner wants to do well in a test, move to a better school and so forth), *integrative* (the learner is interested in interacting with another culture) and *resultative* (the learner is motivated by language-learning success). However, Dörnyei (2007) reminds us that the classroom environment also plays a strong role in motivation. Working with drama in the EFL classroom – through group work and drama processes as well as with the aim of performance – helps fulfil most of the criteria for a *motivating classroom environment* listed in Dörnyei. These include: proximity, contact and interaction; the rewarding nature of group activities; investing in the group; extracurricular activities, whereby 'students lower their "school filter" and relate to each other as "civilians" rather than students' and also cooperation towards common goals (2007: 721–722).

Children show us their active way of learning: they play games, they play roles, they observe, they listen, they imitate and they try out. And this, like all child's play, belongs to the really serious stuff of life. Since drama can be seen to provide many of the conditions for play activity, it is widely advocated by many young-learner practitioners and has historically occupied an important position in young-learner pedagogy in many countries. Despite this, however, the role of drama in English for young learners (EYL) is often given little systematic focused attention by teacher educators, and suitable material to promote drama is sparse. To Bolton and Heathcote (1998: 159), 'there appears to be evidence of much talk but little practice.' This echoes the mismatch or gap that exists generally between pedagogic theory and classroom practice in teaching English to young learners, as Garton, Copland and Burns have observed (2011: 6). Yet the usefulness of drama encompasses literacy as well as oracy. Thus the next section considers scripted drama, and opportunities for *motivated reading*. The following section will focus on unscripted drama, opportunities for *creative writing* and improvised drama processes.

Scripted drama

In order to consider how scripted drama can achieve motivated reading in EFL, it should first be considered how drama scripts can be employed with young learners who are *not yet* readers of English. Becoming acquainted with the sound patterns and meanings of a script, even a very short one, should take place in steps over several meetings with the text, approaching and consolidating the meaning gradually, before the children are given the script to read themselves. This is how young children learn meaning in their mother tongue: first by guessing or predicting, then by (self)questioning and approximating a meaning and finally clarifying. In acquiring the first language (L1), this process takes place orally. It must also take place orally initially in the L2 classroom setting; it is now well established that well-developed oracy supports literacy (Wells 2009).

Acquiring target phonology

Children's play scripts consist of dialogue to be performed; in order to appeal to the children authentically they should reflect the playful linguistic manifestation of children's oral culture (Bland 2015a). Furthermore a patterned, rhythmical text best serves the literacy apprenticeship of young EFL learners, as rhyme and alliteration are a superb aid in mastering reading (Bryant, Bradley, MacLean and Crossland 1990). In the L2 classroom, a recording of the play script or dialogue, that the children may listen to while miming actions or colouring an illustration of the setting or characters, at the same time whispering along with the text, can be a tremendous support. It has been noted earlier that one of the advantages of young language learners includes brain plasticity. This helps young learners in the acquisition of the L2 sound system (Johnstone 2002: 12), including 'not only the pronunciation of individual sounds but also patterns of intonation'. For this, however, the children need suitable input, with a good model of the pronunciation and intonation of English, and not all teachers of young learners will feel confident to provide this. In addition, as Długosz (2000: 289) notes, a 'very short book and its recording can also be read and listened to at home. The increased frequency and amount of contact directly affects the retention of words and grammatical constructions in long-term memory'.

Primary-school children are open to puzzles and riddles (Tomlinson 2015: 286) as well as rhyme and rhythm. If this openness is encouraged, the young learners may become adventurous foreign-language learners. According to research reported in Saville-Troike (2006: 89), imaginative, empathetic, self-confident, risk-taking, adventuresome and tolerant-of-ambiguity personality traits correlate with success in L2 learning. With suitable input, young learners can acquire authentic, idiomatic English as they are generally tolerant of ambiguity. Whereas older learners who are in an analytic processing mode may find formulaic sequences or multiword units, like 'Let's have a go' (in the script excerpt below) puzzling to analyse and therefore difficult, younger learners tend to pick them up as wholes unquestioningly, as young children do in L1 acquisition. The following is from a mini-play for the primary EFL classroom written largely in rhythm and rhyme, *Valentine's Day* (Bland 2009).

Alex:	Can you do it?
Mark:	I don't know.
David:	Is it easy?
Alex:	I hope so.
Mark:	Right. We'll try.
David:	Let's have a go!
Lena:	Help! It's no good! I don't know!
	I'll never understand!
Scarlet:	Don't worry! Come here! Let's see!
	Let me give you a hand! (2009: 6)

This excerpt can be rehearsed as a mini-drama on the topic of supporting each other. If shared with young learners who as yet read very little in English, perhaps around the age of eight, it is advisable to divide even this very short excerpt into two scenes, for a brief drama activity in two separate lessons. The second part – beginning with 'Help!' – could be introduced in four steps as follows:

- The first step is intensive listening as the teacher recites.

- The second step is echoing around the classroom, with a different young learner speaking each brief sentence (Come here! Let's see! and so forth). The teacher initially ignores the fact that in the play script – which the children don't yet see – the lines are spoken by only two children, Lena and Scarlet. The four-line rhyme has eight mini-sentences, and breaking the lines up in this way ensures a rapid succession of turns. After perhaps three or four repetitions of the rhyme, every child in the class has spoken a few words out loud.

- The third step is to divide the class into two groups – one group is Lena and one is Scarlet – and rehearse the rhyme as if with two voices in a chorus dialogue. The children have fun in trying to keep up a rhythmical tempo. At the same time, the meaning should also be rehearsed, by encouraging a dramatic performance of the lines with suitable gestures, facial expressions and intonation. This adds the important element of 'story', which otherwise is missing as this rhyme is excerpted from a play script. The thematic emphasis is on being brave and having a go. Almost without noticing it, the children are acquiring target phonology while repeating and learning the lines by heart. Of course, if the young learners are preparing a performance of a complete mini-play, working on brief individual scenes over several lessons, they are even more motivated to rehearse: 'repetition inherent in and necessary to memorisation can become tiresome, whereas the objective at the end of drama work – acting – transforms repetition into the challenge of rehearsing and improving one's performance' (Serrurier-Zucker and Gobbé-Mévellec 2014: 16).

- The fourth step is pair work. The children rehearse in pairs and are encouraged to perform in front of the class, for even a mini performance adds creative tension and encourages self-confidence and adventurousness, which are supportive of L2 learning. As temporally spaced repetition is essential for long-term retention, the third and fourth steps should be repeated in future lessons. Furthermore, the young learners should, after working on a mini-scene as above, have access to the written script to support their memory.

Useful formulaic phrases in the above lines from *Valentine's Day*, apart from the helpful recycling of chunks like *Can you do it?* and *Let's see!*, are the negatives: *I don't know* and *Don't worry!* These will introduce the children to new functional communicative opportunities. The teacher can try to introduce negatives into the classroom discourse, to help the children collect this pattern, too. *Everybody look at the blackboard, please. Don't look out of the window. Don't run please! Don't forget to do your homework. Don't shout please. Don't forget to go into the fresh air and play.* Repetitive classroom-management discourse of this kind is extremely supportive of L2 acquisition (see also Mourão 2015a: 59–63).

Motivated reading

Children learn best when they are scarcely aware they are learning, for example, through drama, as a kind of extended play. Drama can support all language skills, including reading. It is now widely accepted that primary-school EFL learners should have the opportunity to read familiar texts in English, such as reading a picturebook, when they have already heard the story and shared the pictures several times in class. Reading in the foreign language is not only one of the basic skills, but it is additionally – particularly with regard to English – a crucial learning strategy. Individuals of all ages who can use written text in English to access knowledge are clearly empowered; they have acquired not only functional literacy, but they also have the potential to acquire *information literacy*, which is defined as 'how to articulate information needs, search for it and retrieve it efficiently, understand and evaluate its authenticity and reliability, communicate it, and then use it to make decisions and solve problems' (ALIES: A Library In Every School!).

The notion of literacy, at any age, goes beyond decoding words in order to understand information: 'literacy in PISA also involves understanding, using, reflecting on and engaging with written texts, in order to achieve goals and to participate actively in society' (OECD 2013: 45). It seems the affective dimension is (at last!) recognized as central to reading. It has been argued that students need compelling comprehensible input – so in the secondary school, for example, a wide *choice* of texts – in order to succeed on the educational path to high levels of literacy and academic language (Krashen and Bland 2014). Young people who are motivated to read and enjoy reading from the outset are empowered – they acquire agency – and the more they use this power, the better they will become. Thus it is vitally important to establish a pleasurable reading culture with young learners (Diehr and Frisch 2012, Bland 2013), in English as well as in the first language(s).

According to Franks' report on drama, and language and literacy learning, drama has been shown to be effective in enhancing reading and writing abilities at all levels, including primary school, due to an increased 'positive affective and attitudinal engagement with learning and schooling' (2010: 248). David Farmer summarizes drama's contribution to literacy in the mother tongue: 'drama develops literacy skills – supporting speaking and listening, extending vocabulary and encouraging pupils to understand and express different points of view. Dramatic activity motivates children to write for a range of purposes' (2011: 1). Therefore it seems likely that using drama can also support children's literacy development in the foreign language.

Young learners do not analyse the language chunks they acquire aurally (through listening) and rehearse orally (through speaking). However, seeing the chunks in writing is likely to speed their ability to unpack them: 'Being able to read may have an impact on how formulaic language is perceived and processed' (S. Kersten 2015: 136). The need to read the scene that will be acted out represents a task-based approach to literacy. For rather than a linguistic goal, the goal is to rehearse a role for a forthcoming performance. This is a powerful incentive to students to reach beyond the functional decoding of words on a page, and enjoy the reading task. With the goal of a performance, children seek to read with understanding – even with vitality and expressive intensity – in order to practise their roles. Thus scripted drama affords *motivated* reading.

Unscripted drama

Unscripted drama is flexible and playful, involves all the dimensions of learning outlined in the introduction to this chapter – cognitive, affective, sociological and physiological – and is extremely valuable, but in a different way to scripted drama. Total Physical Response (TPR) methods can initially be used in warming-up sessions, to activate tired children.

Warming up

Warming-up activities are vital before the drama work begins, 'to prepare the young learners for the physicality of drama as well as to forge the climate of confidence and cooperation essential to the risk taking involved in acting' (Serrurier-Zucker and Gobbé-Mévellec 2014: 24). TPR, a well-known language-teaching method, can fulfil this function flexibly.

Moving Statues

Drama and warming-up activities need, if possible, a large space where the children can move around. A development of TPR particularly for young learners, *Moving Statues,* requires both space and a musical instrument, such as a drum. It is based on a children's party game, Musical Statues, whereby young children dance to music and freeze when the music is stopped suddenly. Any child seen moving is 'out', until there is only one left – who is the winner. In the English lesson variety, the teacher gently beats a drum, and the children move around the space. The teacher can suggest a theme for the children to follow, for example: *Move like a giraffe. Jump like a kangaroo. Fly like an owl.* On a loud rap they freeze – no moving and no sound – so that they can clearly hear the TPR command that follows. This can become an extremely lively game, so the command *everybody freeze,* accompanied by a sharp rap on the drum, must be understood as a rule of the game from the outset, to avoid chaos.

The TPR commands can be so simple that three-year-olds will understand with no scaffolding in the very first English session, such as *Take a partner.* They understand because they are highly motivated to, and it is the kind of command they expect; thus a demonstration from the teacher is necessary only when the word 'partner' is not recognizable to the children, depending on their L1. Over time, complex language can be introduced. If the teacher mimes the action, the children can easily follow. As soon as possible, however, the teacher should stop miming and encourage the children to listen carefully. This is known as the *handover principle*, an important development of scaffolding (see Mourão 2015a: 62). As soon as one child has understood and performs the correct action, the child is praised (in English of course). The others will notice and copy, and thus they learn from each other.

More complex TPR commands train concentration as well as listening comprehension, for example: *Walk backwards! Take a partner and play leapfrog! Your foot hurts – walk very, very slowly to a space and sit down!* Alternatively, the young learners can act out adjectives: *You are tired teachers! You are hungry hamsters. You are angry elephants.* The new language must be introduced gradually and repeated in subsequent lessons. The language is, however, acquired surprisingly fast – aurally and at first receptively. This is due to the fact that it 'requires the involvement of the whole person – the active and integrated engagement of mind and body, involving imagination, intellect, emotion and physical action' (Franks 2010: 242).

TPR in the classroom

TPR as a warming-up activity can also be used in the classroom to consolidate the particular language young learners are currently acquiring – the importance of salience and repetition is a recurrent theme in many chapters of this volume. For example, the teacher can easily smuggle comparisons into commands:

> Take your neighbour as your partner .... Who is taller? Hands up!
> Swap places with your partner .... Which place is tidier? ... Swap back again.
> Jump up high .... Jump higher than your partner.
> Run on the spot .... Run faster than your partner.

TPR can rehearse a certain theme, for example, transport. This is make-believe – the young learners stay at their places and pretend:

> Steer a ship .... The sea is wild .... You feel seasick!
> Now the sea is calm .... You feel better .... Breathe out!
> Ride a bike .... Ride a motorbike .... Slow down!
> Ride on a camel .... Gallop on a horse .... Gallop faster.
> Take a partner .... Get in a car together .... The smaller one drives.
> Your partner drives well .... Enjoy the countryside .... Enjoy the sunshine ....
> Your partner drives badly.... You are scared ....
> The driver stops the car too suddenly .... Get out of the car .... Breathe out!

Finally, TPR can bring fun and relaxation into the classroom at any time:

> Arms up .... Swing to the right .... Swing to the left.
> Shake your hands in the air .... Count the tables.
> Run around your chair .... Write your name in the air .... Draw a circle in the air.
> Sit on your partner's knee .... Give your partner a pat on the back.
> Tickle your partner .... Shake hands with your partner.
> Hands up in the air .... Show your right hand .... Give five.
> Show your left hand .... Give ten.
> Stretch up tall .... Make yourself small.
> Lay your head on the desk .... And have a little rest.

Before turning to improvised drama strategies that are useful for involving higher-order thinking, it will be illustrated how children might fashion their own scripts, through creative writing motivated by well-known tales.

Motivated creative writing: Children write their own dialogue

Young learners who have recently experienced success in learning to write in their mother tongue are usually keen to experiment with writing in the foreign language. When the dialogue to be acted out is based on a well-known story, it is motivating for young learners to be given the opportunity to re-use language they have acquired as chunks by inviting them to fill speech bubbles with their own ideas. Ownership of a task – giving the children authorial power – motivates them to invest effort. The samples of writing below, Figures 12.1 and 12.2, are by seven-year-old young learners, who are only at the very beginning of functional literacy. The data were collected in 2007 during one of my action research projects in a primary school in Essen, Germany, with fourteen children who had only one hour of English weekly. The figures illustrate the motivational power of a familiar fairy tale to encourage responding to stories through writing. The familiarity of the tale, *Three Billy Goats Gruff*, allowed the children to find fitting chunks from their repertoire, which were stored as single units in their mental lexicon. They had acquired the chunks as wholes from oral storytelling, games, from classroom management discourse or through shared picturebooks (Bland 2010: 88–90). Julia gives the troll the lines: *I'm hungry. I like billy goats. Come here!* Ayscha gives Little Billy Goat Gruff the lines: *I'm very little. I'm clever! I want my Mummy. Silly monster! Please behave big monster.* With children of this age, the teacher will often need to act as scribe and provide a model in writing of the chunks the children

FIGURE 12.1 *Terrible troll: sample of colouring and writing (Julia).*

wish to use in the speech bubbles. However, some young learners were also keen to hunt for the relevant picturebooks in the classroom, and used them effectively as a dictionary.

Integrated learning processes and achievements (such as motivated reading, creative writing and drama performance) can be documented and visualized in the *European Language Portfolio*: 'Portfolio work can promote self-determination. It documents personal growth and allows learners to display learning outcomes as evidence for mastery over challenging tasks' (Becker 2015: 264). Both self-efficacy (Bandura 1995) and self-determination

FIGURE 12.2 *Little Billy Goat Gruff: sample of colouring and writing (Ayscha).*

(Deci and Ryan 2000) are considered highly important for intrinsic motivation, social development, critical literacy and personal growth (see Becker 2015: 273–274). Teachers can evaluate the young learners' integration of the skills of writing, reading, listening and speaking through structured observation. The children's attitudes, achievements and their acquisition of effective learning strategies can be celebrated through opportunities for creative writing, drama strategies and drama performance.

Drama strategies

Drama as a creative box of tools offers strategies or processes that can be used with or without play scripts for children. These include activities such as Whoosh, Conscience Alley, Role-On-The-Wall, Collective Role Play, Intrapersonal Role Play, Hot Seating and Teacher-In-Role, with the aim of providing context-embedded, stimulating language-learning opportunities. Read (2008: 8) argues for the use of drama strategies to allow children, following the sharing of a picturebook, to 'think from within the story and explore significant issues'. Using the stories *Billy Goats Gruff* and *The Pied Piper*, some drama strategies are explained in this section that encourage children to think from within the story. None of the processes described are linear, routine or predictable. Characters' thoughts and the plots are explored, with a multiplicity of potential outcomes. It is the open and collaborative nature of drama that makes it so rewarding and satisfying.

Whoosh!

This drama method can be used to familiarize young learners with the plot and characters of a story they are going to hear, a play they are going to act out or a book they are going to read. It can be used with any age group of students. A Whoosh is both very enjoyable and very effective, as young learners can discover even complex stories in a multisensory, memorable way. The children stand in a large circle. The teacher invites children into the circle, to take on roles of characters or objects she describes, with or without improvising dialogue, depending on the repertoire, age and self-confidence of the young learners. Whenever certain characters should leave the scene, the teacher waves her arms and calls out 'Whoosh' to that character. This important stratagem can also send the entire class back to their places, for example, if chaos threatens to take over.

If, for example, the class is to act out *Three Billy Goats Gruff*, a Whoosh can help the children into the story. The teacher tells an outline of the story, for example:

A terrible troll lives in the high mountains. (The teacher chooses a young learner to enter the circle, as the troll.) Look! Here is the troll. He growls, grrrrr, because he is always hungry! (The teacher encourages the child to growl and might also whisper dialogue for the child to repeat: 'I'm always hungry. Grrrrr.') The terrible troll lives under a bridge. (The teacher invites several students into the circle, holding hands in a line, as the bridge.) The bridge wobbles because the troll is so big. (The teacher demonstrates how to wobble.) Little Billy Goat Gruff runs across the bridge. (The teacher chooses a little billy goat.) The bridge goes 'trip-trap, trip-trap, trip-trap' and swings a little. (The children playing the bridge chorus 'trip-trap' and swing.) The terrible troll jumps up and shouts 'Who's that trip-trapping across my bridge?' (The troll jumps up and echoes the teacher in a deep troll voice.) . . .

Before beginning the Whoosh, the teacher can explain that all the children standing in the circle should, on a signal, hold hands and raise their hands high, symbolizing the high mountains, and echo the teacher's lines. In this way key lines can be practised, before or during the Whoosh, as the children playing the mountains echo the teacher in a diminuendo chorus:

Teacher: 'I'm a terrible troll and will gobble you whole!'
Mountains: 'and will gobble you whole! gobble you whole! gobble you whole!'

Conscience Alley

For this drama activity, a moment is chosen when a character has an important decision to make. The children stand, not too closely, opposite each other in two parallel lines. A child representing a character walks slowly between the lines, while the young learners in turn voice ideas that might help the character come to a decision. Using *Three Billy Goats Gruff* as an example, the character Little Billy Goat Gruff might walk through the conscience alley, while the children whisper to him: 'The troll is dangerous. He will gobble you up. The troll is a monster. The grass is greener on the other side! You are clever! You can trick the troll!' . . . When he has passed through, Little Billy Goat Gruff comments on the advice he has received and the decision he will make.

Role-on-the-Wall

This activity is a favourite, as it is creative, interactive as well as reflective. Teams of circa four young learners create a large group poster each of a chosen character. If, for example, the story of *The Pied Piper* is chosen, the different posters could represent the mayor, a mother, a father, a rat, a boy and/or a girl, and the Pied Piper. Each team selects a colour to represent their character. They then draw the character's outline, and fill it with information, such as appearance, qualities, thoughts and actions of their character, using pens of the same colour. When the outlines are full of ideas, the children swap posters in order to annotate the other role posters – using the colour of their own figure and writing from their figure's perspective – on the outside of the other character outlines. Finally the role posters are attached to the wall, for the annotations on the various characters may be further developed as more insights arise.

Role Play

Improvising scenes, such as buying fruit at the market, is an important activity in the language classroom. Everyday scenes, when the children basically play themselves, can be fun and are useful for L2 acquisition. Role play based on a story, on the other hand, is an interpretive strategy, which exercises the imagination. An interesting role-play strategy is the *Storyline* approach – over a series of lessons the young learners 'play the parts of characters in an unfolding narrative, collaborating on tasks' (Ahlquist 2013: 41). This is task-based learning within what can be a compelling narrative framework.

A kind of role play that has some of the creative energy of drama and is highly adaptable is *collective* role play: 'The strategy allows many students to experience role-play at the same time and makes the most of shared knowledge and understanding' (Farmer 2011: 19). An example from *The Pied Piper* is to divide the classroom into groups representing the mayor, villagers, rats, children and the Pied Piper. The teacher asks the groups questions, for example: *Villagers, what do you say when you see your children following the Pied Piper?* Any member from that group can answer in role: *Where are you going? Put on your jacket! Look after your brother! Don't leave the village. Come back soon.* An example from *Three Billy Goats Gruff* is to divide the classroom into groups to represent the troll, the bridge and each Billy Goat Gruff. The teacher asks each group questions, such as: *Bridge, what do you think when Big Billy Goat Gruff gallops over you?* Again, any member of that group can answer in role, for example: *It's noisy. I'm frightened. I'm shaking. Please kill the troll!*

Intrapersonal Role Play

The teacher can invite the children in pairs to represent the conflicting thoughts of a complex character, for instance, the Pied Piper. The young learners improvise the different sides of a personality, while the teacher tours the classroom to offer help. For instance, the 'good' Pied Piper might think aloud: *This is very, very cruel. But the mayor isn't fair! I'm sad, but I need the money.* But the 'bad' Pied Piper could think aloud: *I hate the mayor. I hate the villagers. I'm angry. They can't trick me. They will be sorry!* This is known as intrapersonal role play (Legutke and Thomas 1991: 121). Intrapersonal role play is challenging, but as pair work also collaborative and meaningful. Interpretative drama processes of this kind open up deep thinking about characters. Characters in fairy tales may be analysed through intrapersonal role play. The child abusers – the witch who stole Rapunzel and locked her up, the wicked stepmother in Cinderella – can be analysed and studied playfully when two children improvise their characteristics. Their fearful idiosyncrasies certainly throw light on extremes of human behaviour of which children need to gain some understanding.

Hot Seating and Teacher-in-Role

Hot seating (or questioning-in-role) is rather intimidating for young learners, but there is no reason why the children should not hot seat the teacher. The young learners can give the teacher any role to play – the terrible troll, Little Billy Goat Gruff, the mayor or a rat – and ask the teacher questions. The teacher answers in role. In this way the children can practise asking questions, and the teacher's answers can be a useful language model, recycling language, supporting and extending the children's ideas.

Conclusion

Although drama can jeopardize established routines and preordained outcomes, its rewards in terms of creativity, motivation and flexibility for all participants are considerable. Due to the achieving of a motivating classroom environment, motivated reading and creative writing, as well as richly contextualized communication opportunities, drama can be considered goal-oriented learning: learning that is effective in achieving its goals. A student teacher found the involvement of primary children in a drama project 'totally amazing':

> It reflected how much pupils at this age can understand and also even do and speak in a foreign language they have been learning for only two years. This discovery is actually of very practical use. Knowing that children of that age can manage to understand and act like this encourages me to have a theatre project with my future classes as well. (student teacher, in Bland 2014: 167)

Educationalists in the field of drama, such as Goldberg (1974), Bolton and Heathcote (1998) and Fleming (2004), extol the importance of drama in intercultural education as well as in the recreation of the self. Through the humanistic approach of drama we express content and feelings, we communicate, interpret and create: the new insights gained can help develop intercultural literacy, helping children 'read' their own culture afresh, and build bridges across difference through empathy and understanding.

References

Ahlquist, Sharon (2013), '"Storyline": A task-based approach for the young learner classroom', *ELT Journal*, 67/1: 41–51.

ALIES: A Library in Every School! A Proclamation. Retrieved from http://ensil-online.org/wordpress/wp-content/uploads/2013/11/ALIES-Proclamation.pdf [accessed 16 November 2014].

Bandura, Albert (1995), *Self-efficacy in Changing Societies*, Cambridge: Cambridge University Press.

Becker, Carmen (2015), 'Assessment and portfolios', in Janice Bland (ed.), *Teaching English to Young Learners. Critical Issues in Language Teaching with 3–12 Year Olds*, London: Bloomsbury Academic, pp. 262–278.

Bland, Janice (2009), *Mini-Plays, Role-Rhymes and Other Stepping Stones to English. Book 3: Favourite Festivals* (2nd edn), California: Players Press.

Bland, Janice (2010), 'Bilderbücher als Tor zu Literalität und Lesefreude junger Sprachlernender', in Carola Hecke and Carola Surkamp (eds), *Bildern im Fremdsprachenunterricht*, Tübingen: Narr, pp. 76–93.

Bland, Janice (2013), *Children's Literature and Learner Empowerment. Children and Teenagers in English Language Education*, London: Bloomsbury Academic.

Bland, Janice (2014), 'Interactive Theatre with Student Teachers and Young Learners: Enhancing EFL Learning across Institutional Divisions in Germany', in Sarah Rich (ed.), *International Perspectives on Teaching English to Young Learners*, Basingstoke: Palgrave Macmillan, pp. 156–174.

Bland, Janice (2015a), 'Grammar Templates for the Future with Poetry for Children', in Janice Bland (ed.), *Teaching English to Young Learners. Critical Issues in Language Teaching with 3–12 Year Olds*, London: Bloomsbury Academic, pp. 147–166.

Bolton, Gavin and Heathcote, Dorothy (1998), 'Teaching culture through drama', in Michael Byram and Michael Fleming (eds), *Language Learning in Intercultural Perspective. Approaches through Drama and Ethnography*, Cambridge: Cambridge University Press, pp. 158–177.

Bryant, Peter; Bradley, Lynette; Maclean, Moira and Crossland, John (1990), 'Rhyme and Alliteration, Phoneme Detection, and Learning to Read', *Developmental Psychology*, 26/3: 429–438.

Crystal, David (1998), *Language Play*, London: Penguin Books.

Deci, Edward and Ryan, Richard (2000), 'Self determination Theory and the Facilitation of Intrinsic Motivation, Social Development, and Well-Being', *American Psychologist*, 55/1: 68–78.

Diehr, Bärbel and Frisch, Stephanie (2012), 'Lesemotivation in der Fremdsprache – Erkenntnisse aus der Begleitforschung zum 1. Vorlesewettbewerb Englisch für Schülerinnen und Schüler der Klasse 4', in Heiner Böttger and Norbert Schlüter (eds), *Fortschritte im frühen Fremdsprachenlernen. Ausgewählte Tagungsbeiträge. Eichstätt 2011*, München: Domino Verlag, pp. 10–19.

Długosz, D.W. (2000), 'Rethinking the role of reading in teaching a foreign language to young learners', *ELT Journal*, 54/3: 284–290.

Dörnyei, Zoltán (2007), 'Creating a Motivating Classroom Environment', in Jim Cummins and Chris Davidson (eds), *International Handbook of English Language Teaching*, New York: Springer, pp. 719–731 (Vol. 2).

Farmer, David (2011), *Learning through Drama in the Primary Years*, Norwich: Drama Resource.

Fleming, Michael (2004), 'Drama', in Michael Byram (ed.), *Language Teaching and Learning*, London: Routledge, pp. 185–187.

Franks, Anton (2010), 'Drama in teaching and learning language and literacy', in Dominic Wyse, Richard Andrews and James Hoffman (eds), *The Routledge International Handbook of English, Language and Literacy Teaching*, London: Routledge, pp. 242–253.

Goldberg, Moses (1974): *Children's Theatre. A Philosophy and a Method*. Eaglewood Cliffs: Prentice-Hall.

Garton, Susan; Copland, Fiona and Burns, Ann (2011), *Investigating Global Practices in Teaching English to Young Learners*. <http://www.teachingenglish. org.uk/publications/global-practices-teachingenglish-young-learners> [accessed 4 October 2014].

Johnstone, Richard (2002), *Addressing 'The Age Factor': Some Implications for Languages Policy*, Strasbourg: Council of Europe. <http://www.coe.int/t/dg4/ linguistic/Source/JohnstoneEN.pdf> [accessed 15 November 2014].

Kersten, Saskia (2015), 'Language development in young learners: The role of formulaic language', in Janice Bland (ed.), *Teaching English to Young Learners. Critical Issues in Language Teaching with 3–12 Year Olds*, London: Bloomsbury Academic, pp. 129–145.

Kramsch, Claire (2000), 'Social discursive construction of self in L2 learning', in James Lantolf (ed.), *Sociocultural Theory and Second Language Learning*, Oxford: Oxford University Press, pp. 133–154.

Krashen, Stephen and Bland, Janice (2014), 'Compelling Comprehensible Input, Academic Language and School Libraries', *Children's Literature in English Language Education*, 2/2: 1–12.

Legutke, Michael and Thomas, Howard (1991) *Process and Experience in the Language Classroom*. Harlow: Pearson Education.

Mourão, Sandie (2015a), 'English in pre-primary: The challenges of getting it right', in Janice Bland (ed.), *Teaching English to Young Learners. Critical Issues in Language Teaching with 3–12 Year Olds*, London: Bloomsbury Academic, pp. 51–69.

Pinter, Annamaria (2015), 'Task-based learning with children', in Janice Bland (ed.), *Teaching English to Young Learners. Critical Issues in Language Teaching with 3–12 Year Olds*, London: Bloomsbury Academic, pp. 113–127.

Read, Carol (2008), 'Scaffolding children's learning through story and drama', *Children & Teenagers: Young Learners and Teenagers SIG Publication*, IATEFL, 08/2: 6–9.

OECD (2013), *PISA 2015: Draft Reading Literacy Framework*. <http://www. oecd.org/callsfortenders/Annex%20IB_PISA%202015%20Reading%20 Framework%20.pdf>

Saville-Troike, Muriel (2006), *Introducing Second Language Acquisition*, Cambridge: Cambridge University Press.

Serrurier-Zucker, Carol and Euriell Gobbé-Mévellec (2014), 'The page *is* the stage: From picturebooks to drama with young learners', *Children's Literature in English Language Education*, 2/2: 13–30.

Stevick, Earl (1980), *Teaching Languages: A Way and Ways*, Rowley: Newbury House.

Tomlinson, Brian (2015), 'Developing principled materials for young learners of English as a foreign language', in Janice Bland (ed.), *Teaching English to Young Learners. Critical Issues in Language Teaching with 3–12 Year Olds*, London: Bloomsbury Academic, pp. 279–293.

Wells, Gordon (2009), *The Meaning Makers. Learning to Talk and Talking to Learn* (2nd edn), Bristol: Multilingual Matters.

13

Teaching Young Learners with Technology

Euline Cutrim Schmid
and Shona Whyte

Introduction

Current theories of second language (L2) acquisition emphasize the key role played by interaction and negotiation of meaning in language learning. Interaction is central to language acquisition, as it provides opportunities for learners to produce and understand language, and obtain feedback on their performance (Swain 1995, Long 1996, Blyth 2010). Interactional accounts of language acquisition suggest that language teaching should include the following:

- communication and negotiation of meaning (Long 1996)

- use of language to achieve an objective (Bygate, Skehan and Swain 2001)

- attention to the learner's own personal experiences and needs (Savignon 2007)

- links to language use outside the classroom (Nunan 2006).

The potential of new technological tools to meet these criteria has been extensively discussed (Favaro 2011, Cutrim Schmid and Whyte 2014). For instance, research has investigated how new technologies can be used to (a) create a constructivist learning environment, where learning is an active process of creating knowledge via interaction; (b) enhance student motivation (e.g. Gitsaki and Robby 2014); (c) develop new media literacies (e.g. Warschauer 2006 and 2012); and (d) meet the needs of students with diverse learning styles (e.g. Wall, Higgins and Smith 2005). However, it is important to design didactically meaningful language-learning tasks to fully exploit the potential of technology-rich language-learning environments (Biebighäuser, Zibelius and Schmidt 2012; Cutrim Schmid and van Hazebrouck 2012; Thomas, Reinders and Warschauer 2014; Whyte and Alexander 2014).

Indeed, without attention to its nature and quality, technology-supported interaction may consist in 'gratuitous interactivity' (Plowman 1996: 263) with no clear purpose or learning gain. Aldrich, Rogers and Scaife (1998: 323) define this type of multimedia-based interactivity as a 'reactive model of interactivity' since it is designed to support learning through drill and practice, instead of involving learners actively in the construction of knowledge. Research on the use of interactive whiteboards (IWBs) in language education has also shown a tendency towards *physical* interactivity, where the focus is on students going to the IWB and manipulating elements (e.g. Gray 2010, Cutrim Schmid 2010, 2011), rather than *conceptual* interactivity, 'where the focus is on interacting with, exploring and constructing curriculum concepts and ideas' (Jewitt, Moss and Cardini 2007: 312).

In the EU-funded project, iTILT (interactive Technologies In Language Teaching), forty-four teachers from seven European countries used IWBs to implement communicative language teaching, and their practice was documented through video recordings and interviews. Analysis of IWB-mediated language teaching activities proposed in French and German state schools in the project revealed a general preference for activities involving lower levels of interactivity (Whyte, Cutrim Schmid, van Hazebrouck and Oberhofer 2013, Whyte, Cutrim Schmid and Beauchamp 2014). The findings reveal no clear-cut positive effects on classroom interaction associated with the IWB, and in the primary EFL context there was a preponderance of drill and practice rather than communicative activities. A stronger focus on teacher education in design and implementation of communicative tasks therefore seems important in ongoing work in interactive technologies with young learners.

To this end, the present chapter discusses the advantages and challenges of employing new technologies in the primary EFL classroom with a special focus on the features of task design and implementation which best exploit the excellent opportunities for authentic target language use which technology can provide. The chapter reports on a school-based project on video communication in the primary EFL classroom. The project examines how an IWB can be used to engage language learners in collaborative projects in the target language with students from other countries. The research questions are as follows:

(a) How can an IWB support videoconferencing (VC) exchange between remote partners involving young learners?

(b) How well do task-oriented materials, activities and teaching techniques seem to promote effective learner–learner exchanges?

(c) What light is shed on this communicative situation by commentary from teachers and learners?

Background to the study

The present study adopts a task-based approach to language teaching (TBLT) which fits with much current thinking about L2 instruction (see Pinter 2015, this volume) and also corresponds to the Common European Framework of Reference for Languages (CEFR), which underpins the majority of school programmes in Europe. Some discussion of the use of technology in this context is now necessary. Overviews of technology-mediated language teaching in the fields of Computer-Assisted Language Learning (CALL) and Computer-Mediated Communication (CMC) often distinguish *face-to-face* or traditional classroom environments from *distance* or online learning environments, or *blended* environments, which combine the two. A distinction is also made between *synchronous* or live communication, such as text or video chat, and *asynchronous* communication in the form of blog comments or email, for example. Another opposition involves the use of desktop computers, often in dedicated suites, rather than *mobile* learning. Many educators now consider such classifications to be largely redundant: for Colpaert (2014), for example, it is the *designedness* of the whole learning environment that is important. In other words the learning context must be conceptualized and specified in a methodologically sound manner, and tools should be selected and used on the basis of their pedagogical affordances for each specific context. While recent CALL volumes have emphasized the role of technology in TBLT (Van den Branden, Verhelst and Van Gorp 2007, Thomas and Reinders 2010, Thomas, Reinders and Warschauer 2014), they do not make specific mention of the young-learner context.

Technology offers opportunities for exchanging meaningful information and ideas in authentic tasks. It allows interaction with speakers who do not share a native language and can provide scaffolding to support this interaction. Early work in technology-mediated learning with young beginners suggests that oral, synchronous interaction is best suited to young learners who do not master the written language and cannot sustain motivation over weeks and months (Camilleri, Sollars, Poor, Martinez del Pinal and Leja 2000). Videoconferencing with a distant class thus increases learner motivation and emotional engagement (Favaro 2011) and provides opportunities for authentic communication, which can increase and sustain engagement (Guichon and Nicolaev 2011), as tasks cannot be completed without using the target language, unlike role plays in regular classrooms.

Videoconferencing with young learners is not without challenges, however

> although one of the advantages of videoconferencing is to allow pupils authentic use of the oral language and access to other cultures, it places pupils in a very open context which they do not control and which is also partially beyond the teacher's control. (Gruson 2010: 402)

The complexity of the communicative situation means that teacher support is likely to be important for the successful adoption of effective practices, and recent research-based recommendations for integrating this kind of interactive technology in the language classroom include the following:

- focus on pedagogy rather than tools (Guichon and Hauck 2011)
- expect an implementation dip where pedagogical creativity may be reduced because attention is focused on technological factors (Fullan 2001, Cutrim Schmid and Whyte 2012)
- provide teacher support in context and over time (Hennessy and London, 2013)
- reflect on technology-mediated activities via learner focus-group discussion and video recordings of class interaction (Whyte et al. 2013)
- plan for differential take-up among teachers and encourage collaborative reflection on technology and pedagogy (Whyte 2015).

In the study introduced here we examine how the IWB can provide additional support for live communication among young learners, how teachers' involvement in activities shapes interactional opportunities and how the involvement of participant researchers may support professional development.

Description of the project

The project involved two primary schools in Germany and France with the goals of integrating the IWB into their curricula, preparing learners for authentic foreign language use and enhancing learners' cultural awareness, motivation and autonomy. IWB-based video communication software was used to support whole-class online collaboration by enabling live screen sharing, with a video and audio channel carried by a dedicated server (Whyte and Cutrim Schmid 2014).

Figures 13.1 and 13.2 provide detailed information about the teachers and learners involved in the project.

Over two school years, three teaching units were developed and four 90-minute videoconferencing sessions were conducted as described below.

French teacher	German teacher
Generalist primary school teacher	Generalist primary school teacher
Twenty years of classroom experience	Five years of classroom experience
Technologically fluent (experienced IWB user)	Level of IWB technology expertise relatively low
Previous experience with VC	First experience with VC
Bilingual (French-Spanish) with special motivation for FL teaching	Recent pre-service training in FL teaching (communicative and task-based approaches)

FIGURE 13.1 *Information about participating teachers.*

French learners	German learners
25 pupils – aged 8–9 – **third** of five years of formal primary schooling	25 pupils – aged 7–8 – **second** of four years of formal primary schooling
One single 90-minute session of English per week (**first year of EFL**)	Two 45-minute sessions of English per week (**second year of EFL**)
General pattern of EFL activities: • teacher-led presentation, • carousel activities, individual listening exercises, worksheets, • short closing plenary session.	Varied EFL activities: • lessons taught in English • storytelling, • singing, • role plays, games, • arts and crafts.
Used IWB regularly in all classes	**Beginner users of IWBs**
Previous experience with VC exchange (one Skype session)	**No previous experience** with VC

FIGURE 13.2 *Information about learners.*

1: *Identity Card*

The first VC session was a familiarization session designed as described in Figure 13.3 with interactions in groups of four to five learners.

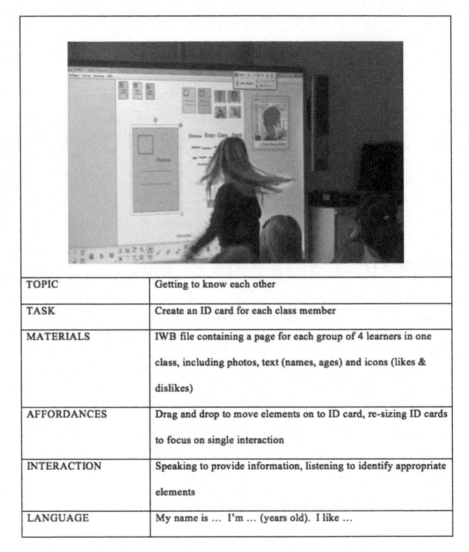

TOPIC	Getting to know each other
TASK	Create an ID card for each class member
MATERIALS	IWB file containing a page for each group of 4 learners in one class, including photos, text (names, ages) and icons (likes & dislikes)
AFFORDANCES	Drag and drop to move elements on to ID card, re-sizing ID cards to focus on single interaction
INTERACTION	Speaking to provide information, listening to identify appropriate elements
LANGUAGE	My name is … I'm … (years old). I like …

FIGURE 13.3 *Session 1 – identity card.*

2: *Funny Animals*

In this session learners described imaginary creatures they had drawn in a previous lesson as outlined in Figure 13.4.

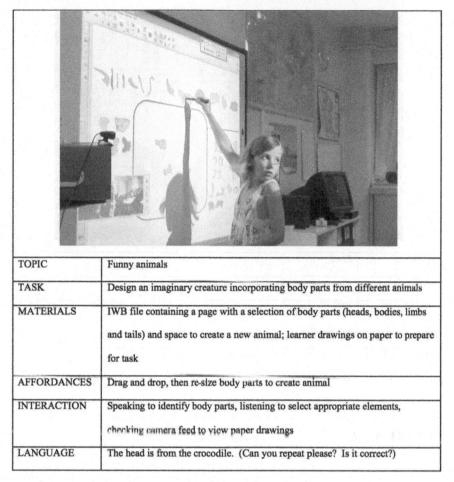

TOPIC	Funny animals
TASK	Design an imaginary creature incorporating body parts from different animals
MATERIALS	IWB file containing a page with a selection of body parts (heads, bodies, limbs and tails) and space to create a new animal; learner drawings on paper to prepare for task
AFFORDANCES	Drag and drop, then re-size body parts to create animal
INTERACTION	Speaking to identify body parts, listening to select appropriate elements, checking camera feed to view paper drawings
LANGUAGE	The head is from the crocodile. (Can you repeat please? Is it correct?)

FIGURE 13.4 *Session 2 – funny animals.*

After describing their animals, each group of learners showed their drawings via the webcam so that the remote class could check if the picture they had created on the whiteboard was correct.

3: Let's Go Shopping

In the third session the young learners practised food vocabulary as shown in Figure 13.5, with one pupil playing the shop assistant and two young learners playing customers to select and pay for different foodstuffs.

TOPIC	Food
TASK	Choose items from shelves to buy in supermarket
MATERIALS	IWB file containing a page for a German supermarket, and another for a French supermarket
AFFORDANCES	Drag and drop food items into shopping trolley
INTERACTION	Shopper: speaking to request food items, listening to understand price
	Shopkeeper: listening to select appropriate elements, speaking to give price

FIGURE 13.5 *Session 3 – let's go shopping.*

4: Breakfast Time

In the fourth session learners prepared a breakfast table for a young learner in the remote class as detailed in Figure 13.6.

During the preparation for the previous session, the teachers discovered differences in eating habits in the two countries: while French pupils usually eat at the canteen, German pupils bring a lunch box and often eat in the classroom. The French teacher thought her pupils would be interested in knowing more about the content of the lunch boxes, so before the Breakfast Time task, it was arranged that some German learners should show their lunch boxes and describe their contents via the webcam.

TOPIC	Food
TASK	Make up a plate for a visitor's breakfast
MATERIALS	IWB file containing a page with a selection of food items
AFFORDANCES	Drag and drop food items; write participants' names
INTERACTION	Speaking to choose breakfast items, listening to identify correct elements
LANGUAGE	I would like milk, bread, yoghurt. Please, thank you.

FIGURE 13.6 *Session 4 – breakfast time.*

Data collection

Data were collected via a variety of qualitative research instruments, including classroom observations and field notes, video recordings of school lessons, in-depth interviews with the teachers and focus group interviews with learners. Data collection and analysis were facilitated by three university students, who worked as teaching assistants to develop and evaluate collaborative mini-projects with the participating teachers and produce academic reports based on their findings. The design encouraged collaboration between in- and pre-service teachers (Cutrim Schmid and Hegelheimer 2014). Another important overall feature of the study is its 'collaborative action research' orientation (Burns 2010), since the in-service and pre-service teachers were supported by university researchers in a process of structured reflection involving data collection and analysis to improve teaching and learning.

Research findings

Interaction was analysed to investigate (a) opportunities for authentic and spontaneous communication among the young learners, (b) the development of teacher and learner competences in managing computer-mediated communication and (c) the perceived impact of the technology-enhanced activities on the young learners' motivation and language-learning achievement.

Analysis of interaction

Analysis of transcriptions of classroom interactions showed high levels of teacher mediation in all videoconferencing sessions, with development towards less teacher intervention and enhanced learner autonomy in later VC sessions. In the following, we analyse episodes from each session to illustrate this development.

In the very first episode from the first VC session, analysis shows that the adults present are all active in framing and facilitating the French pupil Isabelle's introduction to her German partner Anita, directing actions and providing language input on both sides of the exchange. Anita takes the initiative in using the IWB features to complete her listening tasks, but the target language turns are almost all mediated by the teachers. This episode is typical of early VC sessions where young-learner participation was largely structured by the teachers. Pupils were guided throughout the exchanges by gesture and verbally, and teachers tended to repeat pupils' utterances, ratify their actions and supply missing opening and closing routines. Learner–learner interaction was therefore limited, and although pupils performed with some level of confidence and showed understanding of the interactional nature of the activities, they were still very dependent on the teacher. Direct learner–learner interaction was sometimes even prevented by the teachers, when, for example, they created confusion by insisting on the use of complete sentences.

The second episode, from the 'Funny Animals' session, shows participants developing strategies to circumvent problems of sound quality in the exchange. A German young learner called Silvester describes his funny animal to the French learners Charlène and Laura: 'the head is from the crocodile'; 'the legs are from the crocodile'. He repeats each utterance several times, making his speech slower and louder to increase comprehensibility, while the French teacher helps her learners to respond 'repeat, please' and focus on the camera feed when they cannot understand. Unable to hear the next detail, the French teacher prompts her learners to choose any animal body and ask 'is it correct?' After two incorrect guesses to which Silvester responds 'no, elephant' the girls are able to identify the correct element. Laura asks the teacher how to enlarge this body part and she instructs her in French. The German teacher prompts Silvester to show his drawing via the webcam and the French pupils look and smile.

This episode illustrates attempts to minimize teacher mediation and allow learners to negotiate meaning and repair communication breakdowns on their own. They encouraged learners to ask follow-up questions ('how many legs?' 'two or four legs?'). Here Silvester interacted confidently and independently with the remote class, and though the French pupils were less independent, they took initiatives to help each other. There is more learner–learner interaction, since Charlène and Laura were prompted to interact directly with Silvester by using communication strategies such as requests for repetition and confirmation checks ('Is this correct?').

The third episode, from the 'Let's Go Shopping' session, is much shorter than the previous two and illustrates the successful negotiation of a communication problem. Two French children, Marie and Pierre, order food items from Joshua in a German supermarket. Pierre begins with 'I like four orange juice' and Joshua places an orange in the trolley. The French teacher then tells him to say 'no' and repeat what he wants. He says: 'No ... no ... orange juice'. Joshua thinks he means 'oranges' and drags another orange into the trolley. With more prompting, Pierre repeats 'No ... no ... orange juice!' and this time Joshua says 'Ah! Orange juice!' and puts a carton of juice in the trolley. Marie and Pierre smile at each other and Marie then continues: 'I'd like ... I like ... two eggs please'. Seen from the German classroom, Joshua appears to concentrate throughout the exchange, looking directly at the camera feed and reacting promptly without turning to his teacher for help, and showing satisfaction with his success at the end of the episode. The enhanced levels of learner autonomy displayed by Joshua may be due to experience: this learner was participating in his third VC session with a French class. However, data discussed in the next section show that the German teacher's behaviour also played a role.

At the start of the fourth session, fifteen German young learners showed their lunch boxes without preparation, using any linguistic resources at their disposal. The following examples illustrate the increasing accuracy and complexity of young learner productions as the activity progressed:

- Hello, my name is Stefan. I like pretzel of breakfast.

- Hello, my names is Dirk. I like football. This is my breakfast.

- Hello, my name is Josef. I'm eight years old. My breakfast is a pretzel.

All pupils showed great motivation in showing their lunch boxes to the remote class. This is clearly a more open activity than the others, since the learners had not prepared or practised in advance for the activity and therefore had to adapt language in real time during interaction (Cameron 2001). They used various structures to express themselves: 'I like . . ', 'This is . . ', 'My breakfast is . . '. Some pupils also spontaneously provided extra information about themselves 'I'm eight years old' or 'I like football', which shows their strong emotional engagement in the activity.

These findings underline the development shown by all participants in exploiting the potential affordances of the technology to create opportunities for negotiation of meaning, authentic interaction and spontaneous use of language. In the following section, teachers' and young learners' perspectives are explored to shed light on the attitudes and reflections behind the changes recorded.

Teachers' and young learners' perspectives

Both teachers and young learners appeared actively engaged in the critical evaluation of the technology-enhanced tasks throughout the project, and their perceptions reveal both advantages and challenges involved in using interactive technologies in the EFL classroom.

Pedagogical advantages

Real-life scenarios and authenticity of tasks

Both teachers saw the VC project as an opportunity to enhance authenticity and genuine interaction in the EFL classroom, as shown in initial interviews. In the following extract, the French teacher reflects on a common approach to EFL in French schools, based on memorizing vocabulary and grammatical structures.

> The problem with language teaching in France is that we learn lexis and structures and we are engaged in artificial situations and we say, 'Yes, it's fine, they're learning English'. Many people do not know how else to teach and it is reassuring because you tell yourself that they are learning things after all. [. . . With VC] we have realised that it is not true. (French teacher, translated from L1)

For this teacher, designing and implementing VC sessions helped her realize that the language skills acquired through decontextualized exercises do not equip learners for genuine interactions in real-life scenarios.

The German teacher, on the other hand, had already used a task-based approach prior to the VC project and was used to integrating role plays into her teaching to simulate real-life situations. However, she also stressed the essential role of the VC activities in enhancing the level of authenticity of her lessons:

> The pupils' language production during the VC sessions was mostly lower than normal. I think this is because the children experienced this situation as more stressful and real than a normal role play in the English lesson. In normal lessons the children are aware that these are role plays and, if needed, they can always switch into German. During the VC session they don't have this possibility, and of course they have to make themselves understood in the target language, also with gestures and miming. (German teacher)

For this teacher, the fact that the remote class did not share her learners' mother tongue forced them to mobilize all the linguistic and paralinguistic resources at their disposal in order to interact successfully with the French pupils. The French teacher suggested that her pupils also had to 'really listen' to their interlocutors, which is not always the case in the more artificial, practice-oriented interactions which are more common in her regular class sessions. She added: 'Sometimes in class they don't really listen to the others. Here they had to be listening because they had to do something afterwards, and that's important' (French teacher translated from L1). The German teacher saw the shopping role play as particularly realistic, as she explained: 'The French shop was for the children especially motivating, since they could buy the French products in France in a playful way, which is something they would have to do in their holidays. It was similar to a real situation'.

Indeed, even though most VC activities were simulations, the majority of learners seemed to experience them as real: 'I liked that they could go shopping here and we could go shopping there.' The moving of objects on the screen also seemed to contribute to engagement and enjoyment: 'I liked that we could prepare a breakfast table for them and that we could say what we wanted to eat.' Some pupils also emphasized the quality of the digital materials: 'I found it good that the pictures looked so real. It was fun' (young learner quotations translated from L1).

According to the teachers, the authenticity of the task had a positive impact on the young learners' motivation to learn and use the target language, as is shown in the next section.

Enhanced motivation to learn and use the target language

All teachers involved in the project identified increased levels of pupil motivation and engagement during VC sessions. One German assistant teacher was especially impressed by the pupils' enthusiasm and motivation during the project:

> I was really impressed and surprised by the pupils' behaviour. They were always motivated when it comes to the learning of English but I had never seen them as motivated in any of the 'classroom lessons' as they were in the videoconference. They really tried their best to understand the French pupils and also to make themselves understood. (Teaching assistant, Germany)

For the German teacher this enhanced motivation among learners can be traced to a real purpose for learning English: 'They enjoyed it that they were able to interact with the French kids, since they wouldn't be able to speak with them in their mother tongue. They understood why they learn English.' The French teacher agreed that the authenticity of the tasks pushed the young learners to produce comprehensible output and forced them to call up all the linguistic resources they possessed in order to be able to communicate with interlocutors from a different cultural and linguistic background. She noted that her learners 'made a real effort to bring together everything that they had learned [...] to mobilize everything they had learned, and we could really see that' (translated from L1).

The pupils also expressed great enthusiasm during the focus group interviews. The learning experience produced a strong emotional involvement of the children, who especially valued the opportunity to use English to make friends in a different country: 'I found it great that we could talk to the French children in English' (German pupil, translated from L1).

Apart from gains in motivation, teachers' and learners' evaluations also reveal perceived advantages in other areas, such as self-confidence and enhanced communication skills.

Enhanced self-confidence in the ability to comprehend and use the target language

Both teachers mentioned the key role played by the IWB in supporting interaction. According to them, the IWB pages enabled learners to receive visible feedback and confirm their correct understanding of their interlocutors' utterances, since they had to drag elements on the screen in response to their questions or requests. As the French teacher points out: 'Instead of just introducing themselves in a dumb way and the others responding by introducing themselves, the IWB was the element that showed that they had understood. In other words it was an evaluation in a way: "I have understood what you told me"' (translated from L1). The same point was made by the German teacher: 'They gained self-assurance in their own possibilities and skills though the visible feedback on the IWB.'

According to the teachers, the immediate feedback provided by the drag and drop activities on the IWB gave learners a sense of achievement and contributed to their positive self-perceptions of competence in L2. The German teacher noted that the activities also provided opportunities for differentiation, since the weaker students had the chance to work within a basic framework of vocabulary and sentence structures that had been learnt in preparation for VC sessions, while more advanced learners had the opportunity to react more spontaneously during interaction. She stated: 'The children could actively use the previously learned vocabulary or structures, and the activities provided space for openness and differentiation; pupils can either hold on to simpler or use more complex sentence structures and even use language actively by communicating spontaneously'.

Teachers and learners' perceptions have thus revealed various advantages for the language-learning process, including enhanced authenticity, motivation and opportunities for differentiation. In spite of their enthusiasm, however, all teachers involved agreed that the quality of learner output and levels of interaction observed during VC sessions were not optimal. As discussed in the next section, teacher mediation was very frequent and in many activities little was made of opportunities for spontaneous interaction.

Pedagogical challenges

Minimizing teacher mediation

The analysis of the video-recorded data has shown that frequent teacher mediation (e.g. repetitions, ratification of students' actions, prompts, etc.) had an impact on learner–learner exchanges, since the pupils often turned to the teachers during interactions and tended to rely on them for solving communication breakdowns. The teachers were aware of this problem, which was a constant theme in their interviews. The data thus reveal the internal conflicts experienced by the teachers as they tried to balance their roles in managing the smooth unfolding of the VC sessions and in supporting learners' autonomous interactions with the remote class. As the German teacher pointed out, 'My aim was to give as much responsibility to the kids as possible. It depended on how the kid managed the situation'. And in the interview, the French teacher explained:

I almost had to check myself, did you notice? If they didn't understand I didn't want to tell them because I wanted that if they made a mistake, that it would be the others ... When we heard them go 'Oooh' or when they clapped, I wanted them to have that reaction to show whether it was right or wrong. But I had to force myself because it's true you want to [intervene]. (translated from L1)

Throughout the project the teachers felt the need to monitor their own behaviour in this regard to help their learners develop appropriate communication strategies that would allow them to work more independently. The German teacher reflected on this issue: 'In the last two sessions the children were more self-confident and I could step back a bit more. This means that there was seldom the need for repetitions, translations.'

Most German young learners wished they could have interacted more independently during the VC sessions. They talked about anxiety during learner–learner exchanges: 'I found it difficult to talk to the camera because I was so anxious and when I'm anxious I always forget the words' and some pupils wanted more preparation time before the VC sessions: 'we could get more time to practice'. However, most pupils thought their performances were satisfactory. The German learners even compared themselves with the French: 'We are better. We learn a lot of English. They are French, so maybe they don't learn English every day. We've learned English since the first grade' (quotations translated from L1).

Creating more room for spontaneous language production

With respect to the teachers' aim to create more room for language-learning opportunities and spontaneous interaction, data analysis did not reveal many examples of actual learning-related episodes where learners appeared to learn new language or correct non-target-like forms. The teachers believed this was because the VC tasks were designed to practise previously learned language material. As the German teacher pointed out: 'It was a speak-and-respond action. The kids had learned a task before and used what they had learned to communicate. They improved and tested their skills but most did not learn something new, I mean in terms of language learning'. According to the French teacher, 'they didn't learn something in the sense of pure scholastic knowledge' but instead 'made a real effort to bring together everything that they had learned' (translated from L1).

These teachers show a somewhat product-oriented view of language acquisition involving the learning of new language elements, rather than as a process of gaining fluency in deploying language resources in new situations. Yet they showed interest in creating more open-ended tasks, which require thoughtful manipulation of a relatively limited language repertoire. They suggested that such activities would open up opportunities for negotiation of meaning and allow teacher mediation to be directed towards new language elements. As the French teacher stated, 'What I would like to do, but I don't know how to implement it, is this spontaneous thing. In other words for there to be a spontaneous discussion. For example two children who meet and who want to get to know each other, go further' (translated from L1). The German teacher agreed: 'The level was fine for the first session. But the language interaction might be more spontaneous. My kids were proud to say their sentences but they can do much more if they do not have to follow a plan of sentences. Some tried to loosen the plan by changing the order.'

In fact, creating opportunities for spontaneous language production became an important objective for the research team and was also seen as a challenge considering the limited linguistic resources and capabilities of primary-school language learners. In the words of the German teacher, 'I will think about how we could encourage and support more spontaneous/ independent learner-learner interaction'.

The four tasks described above were perceived by the teachers as appropriate for their pupils' proficiency levels and they also agreed that they provided extensive opportunities for language practice in authentic scenarios. However, they also thought that the tight framework provided by the task design and corresponding IWB files also restricted the young learners' language use. As the German teacher pointed out, 'my pupils can do much more if they do not have to follow a plan of sentences'. As previously discussed, the teachers thus expressed an intention to design less-structured VC activities, in which their pupils could select from their own resources to adapt language online in order to communicate meaning, as in the fourth episode described above.

The young learners also expressed a desire to interact more freely with the remote class. For instance, in reference to the Identity Card activity, in which learners had to choose from a set of pictures on the IWB screen when talking about hobbies, one German pupil said, 'It would be cool if we could also say: I like video games, I like cars, I like helicopters'. This indicates pupils' opportunities for self-expression were often limited by the task itself. Indeed, when asked about possible topics for future VC sessions the learners were very ambitious (and perhaps unrealistic) in their prospects: 'we could talk about their grannies or grandpas, or cousins, or where they go on holidays or about pets' (young-learner quotations translated from L1).

Conclusion

This chapter has shown that new technologies can offer opportunities for meaningful language-learning experiences through authentic tasks. The various task-based activities described here illustrate the potential of technology to allow interaction with speakers who do not share a native language and to provide scaffolding to support this interaction. However, the chapter has also demonstrated that simply using new technologies does not guarantee, or even enhance, new meaning making. Our analysis of classroom interaction and teachers' and learners' perspectives has shed some light on a number of important aspects of technology use with young learners.

First, while the project tasks were perceived as more authentic and interactive than traditional activities, teachers and learners also expressed the desire for even greater learner-centredness, allowing opportunities for pupils to use language creatively and experiment with language. The majority of project tasks imposed a tight framework that often prevented this type of language interaction, suggesting that an important challenge with young learners is the balance between adequate linguistic and emotional support and space for learners to create. Second, in early sessions, the unfamiliar environment and technological limitations led to greater teacher mediation; by later stages of the project, the learners developed communication strategies and skills which allowed them to act more autonomously. This pattern corresponds to the implementation dip (Fullan 2001) noted earlier, and may reflect a positive effect of the teacher support in context and over time also reported in previous studies (Hennessy and London 2013, Whyte et al. 2013).

This chapter has discussed various advantages of using new technologies with young learners in the FL classroom, through the description and evaluation of technology-enhanced activities that were perceived as motivating, meaningful and productive. It calls for a stronger focus on task design and task implementation in technology-rich learning environments. Further research needs to be done on the design of technology-enhanced tasks that provide a framework for supporting young learners' language production, while at the same creating room for the development of learner autonomy and self-directed learning.

References

Aldrich, Frances; Rogers, Yvonne and Scaife, Mike (1998), 'Getting to grips with "interactivity": Helping teachers assess the educational value of CD-ROMs', *British Journal of Educational Technology*, 29/4: 321–332.

Biebighäuser, Katrin; Zibelius, Marja and Schmidt, Torben (eds) (2012), *Aufgaben 2.0 – Konzepte, Materialien und Methoden für das Fremdsprachenlehren und -lernen mit digitalen Medien*, Tübingen: Narr.

Blyth, Carl (ed.) (2010), 'Foreign language teaching methods: Speaking'. <http://coerll.utexas.edu/methods/modules/speaking/01/jigsaw.php> [accessed 22 October 2014].

Burns, Anne (2010), *Collaborative Action Research for English Teachers*, Cambridge: Cambridge University Press.

Bygate, Martin; Skehan, Peter and Swain, Merrill (eds) (2001), *Researching Pedagogical Tasks: Second Language Learning, Teaching, and Assessment*, London: Pearson.

Cameron, Lynne (2001), *Teaching Languages to Young Learners*, Cambridge: Cambridge University Press.

Camilleri, Mario; Sollars, Valerie; Poor, Zoltan; Martinez del Pinal, Teresa and Leja, Helena (2000), *Information and Communication Technologies and Young Language Learners*. ECML, Council of Europe. <http://www.ecml.at/tabid/277/PublicationID/38/Default.aspx> [accessed 26 October 2014].

Colpaert, Jozef (2014), 'Interactive whiteboards: Against the odds?', in Euline Cutrim Schmid and Shona Whyte (eds), *Teaching Languages with Technology: Communicative Approaches to Interactive Whiteboard Use: A Resource Book for Teacher Development*, London: Bloomsbury, pp. 1–3.

Cutrim Schmid, Euline (2010), 'Developing competencies for using the interactive whiteboard to implement communicative language teaching in the English as a Foreign Language classroom', *Technology, Pedagogy and Education*, 19/2: 159–172.

Cutrim Schmid, Euline (2011), 'Video-stimulated reflection as a professional development tool in interactive whiteboard research', *ReCALL*, 23/3: 252–270.

Cutrim Schmid, Euline and Hegelheimer, Volker (2014), 'Collaborative research projects in the technology-enhanced language classroom: Pre-service and in-service teachers exchange knowledge about technology', ReCALL, 26: 315–332.

Cutrim Schmid, Euline and Whyte, Shona (eds) (2014), *Teaching Languages with Technology: Communicative Approaches to Interactive Whiteboard Use: A Resource Book for Teacher Development*, London: Bloomsbury.

Cutrim Schmid, Euline and Whyte, Shona (2012), 'Interactive whiteboards in school settings: Teacher responses to socio-constructivist hegemonies', *Language Learning and Technology* 16/2: 65–86.

Cutrim Schmid, Euline and van Hazebrouck, Sanderin (2012), 'Material development and task design for the Interactive whiteboard in the foreign language classroom', in Katrin Biebighäuser; Marja Zibelius and Torben Schmidt (eds), *Aufgaben 2.0 – Konzepte, Materialien und Methoden für das Fremdsprachenlehren und -lernen mit digitalen Medien*, Tübingen: Narr, pp. 119–140.

Favaro, Luciana (2011), 'Videoconferencing as a tool to provide an authentic foreign language environment for primary school children: Are we ready for it?', in Georgeta Rata (ed.), *Academic Days in Timisoara: Language Education Today*, Newcastle upon Tyne: Cambridge Scholars Publishing, pp. 331–339.

Fullan, Michael (2001), *Leading in a Culture of Change*, San Francisco, CA: Jossey Bass.

Gitsaki, Christina and Robby, Mathew (2014), 'Using the iPads for teaching English: Teachers' perspectives', in Marina Dodigovic (ed), *Attitudes to Technology in ESL/EFL Pedagogy*, Dubai, UAE: TESOL Arabia, pp. 277–291.

Gray, Carol (2010), 'Meeting teachers' real needs: New tools in the secondary modern foreign languages classroom', in Michael Thomas and Euline Cutrim

Schmid (eds), *Interactive Whiteboards for Education: Theory, Research and Practice*, Hershey, NY: Information Science Reference, pp. 69–85.

Gruson, Brigitte (2010), 'Analyse comparative d'une situation de communication orale en classe ordinaire et lors d'une séance en visioconférence', *Distances et Savoirs*, 8/3: 395–423.

Guichon, Nicolas and Nicolaev, Viorica (2011), 'Influence de certaines caractéristiques des tâches d'apprentissage sur la production orale en L2', in Elke Nissen, Françoise Poyet and Thierry Soubrié (eds), *Interagir et apprendre en ligne*, Grenoble: Ellug, pp. 61–76.

Guichon, Nicolas and Hauck, Mirjam (2011), 'Editorial: Teacher education research in CALL and CMC: more in demand than ever', *ReCALL*, 23/3: 187–199.

Hennessy, Sarah and London, Laura (2013), 'From international experiences with interactive whiteboards: The role of professional development in integrating the technology', OECD Education Working Papers, 89, OECD Publishing. <http://dx.doi.org/10.1787/5k49chbsnmls-en> [accessed 22 October 2014].

Jewitt, Carey; Moss, Gemma and Cardini, Alejandra (2007), 'Pace, interactivity and multimodality in teachers' design of texts for interactive whiteboards in the secondary school classroom', *Learning, Media and Technology*, 32/3: 303–317.

Long, Michael (1996), 'The role of the linguistic environment in second language acquisition', in William Ritchie and Tej Bhatia (eds), *Handbook of Research on Language Acquisition*, New York: Academic Press, pp. 413–468.

Nunan, David (2006), *Task-Based Language Teaching*. Cambridge: Cambridge University Press.

Pinter, Annamaria (2015), 'Task-based learning with children', in Janice Bland (ed.), *Teaching English to Young Learners. Critical Issues in Language Teaching with 3–12 Year Olds*, London: Bloomsbury Academic, pp. 113–127.

Plowman, Lydia (1996), 'Designing interactive media for schools: A review based on contextual observation', *Information Design Journal* 8/3: 258–266.

Savignon, Sandra (2007), 'Beyond communicative language teaching: What's ahead?', *Journal of Pragmatics*, 39/1: 207–220.

Swain, Merrill (1995), 'Three functions of output in second language learning', in Guy Cook and Barbara Seidlhofer (eds), *Principle and Practice in Applied Linguistics: Studies in Honour of H. G. Widdowson*, Oxford: Oxford University Press, pp. 125–144.

Thomas, Michael; Reinders, Hayo and Warschauer, Mark (eds) (2014), *Contemporary Computer-Assisted Language Learning*. Bloomsbury Contemporary Linguistics Series, New York: Bloomsbury.

Thomas, Michael and Reinders, Hayo (2010), *Task-Based Teaching and Technology*, New York: Continuum.

Van den Branden, Kris; Verhelst, Marchteld and Van Gorp, Koen (eds) (2007), *Tasks in Action: Task-Based Language Education from a Classroom Perspective*. Cambridge: Cambridge Scholars Press.

Wall, Kate; Higgins, Steve and Smith, Heather (2005), 'The visual helps me understand the complicated things: Pupils' views of teaching and learning with interactive whiteboards', *British Journal of Educational Technology*, 36/5: 851–867.

Warschauer, Mark (2006), *Laptops and Literacy: Learning in the Wireless Classroom*, New York: Teachers College Press.

Warschauer, Mark (2012), *Learning in the Cloud: How (and Why) to Transform Schools with Digital Media*, New York: Teachers College Press.

Whyte, Shona (2015), *Implementing and Researching Technological Innovation in Language Teaching: The Case of Interactive Whiteboards for EFL in French Schools*. Basingstoke: Palgrave Macmillan.

Whyte, Shona and Alexander, Julie (2014), 'Implementing tasks with interactive technologies in classroom CALL: Towards a developmental framework', *Canadian Journal of Learning and Technology*, 40/1: 1–26.

Whyte, Shona and Cutrim Schmid, Euline (2014), 'A task-based approach to video communication with the IWB: a French-German primary EFL class exchange', in Euline Cutrim Schmid and Shona Whyte (eds), *Teaching Languages with Technology: Communicative Approaches to Interactive Whiteboard Use: A Resource Book for Teacher Development*. London: Bloomsbury, pp. 50–79.

Whyte, Shona; Cutrim Schmid, Euline and Beauchamp, Gary (2014), 'Second language interaction with interactive technologies: The IWB in state school foreign language classrooms', AILA conference, Brisbane, Australia, Conference paper 11th August 2014.

Whyte, Shona; Cutrim Schmid, Euline; van Hazebrouck, Sanderin and Oberhofer, Margret (2013), 'Open educational resources for CALL teacher education: The iTILT interactive whiteboard project', *Computer Assisted Language Learning*, 27/2: 122–148.

14

Assessment and Portfolios

Carmen Becker

Introduction

Assessment plays a crucial role in the young-learner classroom. It is an important means of identifying the needs of young learners at various levels. Proficiency levels in the target language, plus strengths and weaknesses, can be recognized and further learning supported through assessment. This is valid not only in the case of areas for improvement but also for areas which have improved and need further challenges. Assessment therefore plays a crucial role in identifying optimal support measures for individual learners, and it can have a great influence on the long-term success of young language learners. With the help of assessment teachers can gather valuable information on the effectiveness of their lessons and lesson planning, as well as implementing 'the evaluation and improvement of courses and programs' (Cameron 2002: 220).

Assessment can be informal or formal. Informal assessment is not planned, and is usually 'carried out during the teaching and learning process' (McKay 2006: 21). In contrast, formal assessment follows formal procedures and is planned, such as in tests which have to be completed by all members of a class within a given time and then collected and marked by a teacher (McKay 2006: 21). There are furthermore two common types of assessment, formative and summative assessment. 'Formative assessment is ongoing, usually informal' (McKay: 21) and carried out during the teaching and learning process. It aims to inform teaching and learning by diagnosing the student's proficiency in certain skills as well as by giving feedback and developing individual support measures for each learner (McKay 2006: 22). Summative assessment is a formal type of assessment 'at the end of a teaching unit, term, year, or course, and does not feed back into the next round' (Cameron 2002: 223). It aims at assessing the progress of individual learners and identifying what has been learned during a period of study and how learners compare to others (McKay 2006: 22).

Assessment procedures or tests intended to provide a measure of achievement that interpret the outcomes in terms of the learner's standing within a class or group are referred to as norm-referenced assessment (McKay 2006). According to Cameron (2002: 223), criterion-referenced assessment, on the other hand, is a form of assessment intended to provide a measure of the achievement of individual learners in the target language that can be interpreted in terms of clearly defined criteria such as a response to an item or performance in a classroom task. It can then be used to place learners on a scale of descriptors, using statements such as 'Can answer simple questions using single words' (CILT 2001: 14). Cameron (2002: 224) stresses that criterion-referenced assessment is 'potentially much more helpful' for learners because it supports their understanding of the processes of learning by making the proficiency levels to be reached transparent and by letting them 'see where they are' compared to more accomplished performance.

Experienced language teachers regularly observe learners, interpret their performance and therefore assess them. Consequently, according to Cameron (2002: 220), young learners do not necessarily need to be tested on a regular basis to gain information on their proficiency in the target language. Techniques that go beyond testing, and assess the processes as well as the products of language learning, are defined as alternative assessment. Kohonen (1997: 13) defines alternative assessment as forms of assessment 'that emphasise the communicative meaningfulness and reflect student learning, achievement, motivation and attitudes on instructionally-relevant classroom activities. Its results can be used to improve instruction, based on the knowledge of learner progress'. Such alternative forms of assessment include observation of students, self-assessment and portfolios.

One portfolio model among many is the *European Language Portfolio* (ELP), which was introduced in the European Year of Languages in 2001. After its introduction the ELP spread rapidly. Many European countries developed, implemented and evaluated their own portfolio models and the number of portfolios accredited by the Council of Europe increased drastically. The ELP's success story was supported by a large number of reports on portfolio implementation and use (Schärer 2000, 2004, 2008), as well as empirical studies (Kohonen 2002, Ushioda and Ridley 2002, Perclová 2006, Sisamakis 2006, Bellingrodt 2011) and experience reports from teachers and other ELT specialists (Lippelt, Willgerodt and Windolph 2002, Becker 2003, Windolph and Becker 2003, Rau 2008). Here, it was clearly shown that teachers and learners equally valued the ELP and that the Council of Europe's objectives for portfolio implementation in the areas of learner autonomy development, the support of plurilingualism as well as intercultural awareness and the documentation of learning outcomes could be achieved in different contexts and at different educational levels from primary to higher education. The findings had a large impact on the expectations linked to the ELP and raised high hopes that it could become the significant tool for assessment. It was also hoped that the ELP could become a means for the objective and subjective or personal documentation of the students' language competence, thus aiding transition from primary to secondary level and ensuring the continuity and success of the language-learning process started in primary school (Becker 2013: 58). As a consequence, many educational authorities prescribed the use of ELPs. However, there is evidence that the ELP has not been widely established in practice throughout Europe and has not been accepted by practitioners in English language teaching.

The first part of the chapter will introduce the ELP and its unique structure. Opportunities as well as challenges in portfolio use will be further examined; empirical evidence from a large-scale portfolio implementation study will be evaluated and reasons for the lack of uptake will be explored. Key success factors for portfolio implementation will be identified. In the final section results of the study are employed to construct a model for sustainable ELP implementation.

The European Language Portfolio: Key concepts

The word portfolio was derived from the Italian *portafoglio* and is composed of the verb *portare* (to carry) and the noun *foglio* (leaf). The term refers to a collection of documents or data, which allow the drawing of conclusions about competences or skills of the portfolio's creator (Häcker 2006: 27). Häcker further reports that artists and architects since the Renaissance have used portfolios as application files in order to present their work, individual working styles and personal developments. Today artists, photographers and architects still use portfolios to present their work in order to apply to art schools or be awarded contracts for exhibitions. The adoption of the term *portfolio* by language pedagogy and its analogy to its origin in the arts and architecture were quite intentional. In pedagogy, portfolios are defined as a collection in which learners document their learning products, processes and competences and therefore their individual development and achievements in one or more areas (L. Paulson, P. Paulson and Meyer 1991: 61).

Portfolio work – Theoretical foundations

The use of portfolios in pedagogy has its origins in the US education system. Here a strong dissatisfaction with the established structures and the prevailing teaching, learning and assessment culture arose in the 1970s and the 1980s. With the desire to abolish standardized tests, portfolios were developed as alternative assessment, which could promote meta-communication about education and learning, and would allow the inclusion of process as well as product orientation into the common assessment procedures. The first portfolio movement was initiated in the field of creative writing in language classrooms at universities and schools (Ballweg and Bräuer 2011: 3). It was not until after the grassroots movement had to a great extent established portfolio work that an underlying theoretical foundation was developed.

The theory of *constructivism* serves as the basis for portfolio work. Constructivists view learning 'as a personal process; the learner's developmental level, interests, concerns, personal involvement and current knowledge directly relate to what is learned. Thus not everyone will construct the same knowledge even when provided with what appears to be a very similar learning experience' (Quinn Allen 2004: 233).

The second important theory that serves as a theoretical foundation of portfolio work is the theory of *self-efficacy*. Self-efficacy is the degree of the individual's belief in their own ability to complete tasks and reach goals (Bandura 1995). Portfolios, which document achievements and visualize learning processes, are regarded as an important tool for promoting self-efficacy.

The third theoretical foundation for portfolios in pedagogy is the theory of *self-determination*. It is a theory of motivation put forward by Deci and Ryan (2000) which suggests that people are driven by an active desire to personally grow, experience autonomy and need to feel competent and gain fulfilment. According to Deci and Ryan (2000), new experiences and mastery over challenging tasks are key factors for personality development and motivation. Portfolio work can promote self-determination. It documents personal growth and allows learners to display learning outcomes as evidence for mastery over challenging tasks.

The last theoretical concept underlying portfolio work is the principle of *learner autonomy*. According to Holec (1981: 3), the principle of autonomy is 'the "ability to assume responsibility for one's own affairs". In the context with which we are dealing, i.e. the learning of languages, autonomy is consequently the ability to take charge of one's own learning'. David Little complements Holec's position, adding a psychological dimension:

Essentially, autonomy is a capacity – for detachment, critical reflection, decision-making, and independent action. It presupposes, but also entails, that the learner will develop a particular kind of psychological relation to the process and content of his learning. The capacity for autonomy will be displayed both in the way the learner learns and in the way he or she transfers what has been learned to wider contexts. (Little 1991: 4)

Portfolios promote learner autonomy by supporting critical reflection and independence, by offering choice and room for decision making – for example, learners have to decide which products to display in their portfolios.

The development of the ELP followed on the initiative of the symposium *Transparency and Coherence in Language Learning in Europe* in Rüschlikon, Switzerland, in 1991. The symposium recommended the development of a coherent as well as transparent *Common European Framework of Reference* (CEFR) 'for the description of language proficiency' (Council of Europe 1992: 39). At the same time the Council of Europe proposed the development of a portfolio: 'Once the Common European Framework has been elaborated, there should be devised, at the European level, a common instrument [a language portfolio] allowing individuals who so desire to maintain a record of their language learning achievements and experiences, formal and informal' (Council of Europe 1992: 39).

The CEFR

The main goal of the CEFR as a common basis for the ELP was to provide a common ground for the 'elaboration of language syllabuses, curriculum guidelines, examinations, textbooks, etc. across Europe' (Council of Europe 2001: 1). Furthermore, the objectives behind the CEFR were to facilitate the mutual recognition as well as acceptance of qualifications at the pan-European level to improve the cooperation of educational institutions within Europe as well as to establish a common ground for the evaluation of language competences by developing generally understandable competency scales and descriptors. Accordingly, the aim was to aid European mobility and support plurilingualism and pluriculturalism.

A fundamental component of the CEFR is the description of various language proficiency levels. The CEFR distinguishes between six competence levels from A1 to C2, as outlined in Figure 14.1.

The CEFR includes global scales of language proficiency with descriptors for the skills listening, reading, speaking (spoken interaction and spoken production) and writing and a number of more detailed scales with descriptors

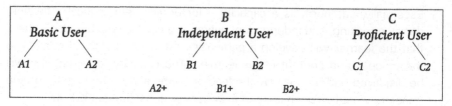

FIGURE 14.1 *CEFR competence levels. (Council of Europe 2001: 32.)*

which, for example, differentiate between situations for language use or text types and are formulated as can-do statements (Becker and Krohn 2006: 212).

The ELP

The ELP was launched at the pan-European level during the *European Year of Languages* as a tool to support the dissemination of the CEFR and 'should be seen as a means of bringing the concerns, perspectives and emphases of the CEFR down to the level of the learner in the language classroom' (Little et al. 2007: 12). The ELP is defined as an 'organised collection of documents, in which individual learners assemble over a period of time, and display in a systematic way, a record of their qualifications, achievements and experiences in language learning, together with samples of work they have themselves produced' (Council of Europe 1997: 3). The ELP is a document in which those who are learning or have learned a language can record their language-learning and cultural experiences. It is targeted at and is the property of the learner. All competence is valued, regardless of whether it is gained inside or outside of formal education.

Comparability of ELPs across Europe is achieved through the use of descriptors taken from the scales of CEFR as well as a set of common principles and a fixed unique structure that has been agreed on for all ELPs. Furthermore, it was agreed that the ELP would be a means of celebrating language-learning experiences, an open-ended record of the learners' achievement in languages, as a document which can be kept by the learner as a valuable source of information and, as well, to aid transfer to the next class or school. The unique common structure with its three parts, the *Language Passport, Language Biography* and *Dossier*, distinguishes the ELP from other pedagogic portfolio concepts in which the learners assemble individual documents or products and outcomes from projects from first draft to final product to form a broad basis for formative assessment (Schneider and North 2000: 167).

The ELP – its three parts

At the primary level the *Language Passport* is a record of the young learners' language-learning experiences in which they record languages acquired at home, including their mother tongue if it is not the majority language, languages learned at school and out of school, as well as contacts with speakers of different languages. The *Language Passport*'s main objective is to document the learners' linguistic as well as cultural identity and intercultural communicative competences (Schneider and North 2000: 173).

The *Language Biography* records the children's specific achievements and proficiency levels reached in the four skills listening, speaking, reading and writing. The pages take the form of a personalized learning diary and are designed to be completed by the learner. They allow children to self-assess their language competence. They can be used in order to celebrate achievements and to encourage children to reflect on their individual progress in different skills as well as the processes and personal targets. The levels of proficiency correspond to the levels established by the Council of Europe in the CEFR.

The *Dossier* is a record of the (young) learners' work in languages and they should add to their Dossiers throughout the year, keeping work in a folder with the portfolio. Examples of things that children could put into the Dossier are pictures, selected written work, documents, photos, souvenirs, texts and examples of work such as audio and video recordings, posters and reading logs. The documents can be reviewed and updated from time to time. The Dossier is a work-file and documents learning processes. It accompanies language learning and illustrates the current level of competence and experience (Schneider and North 2000: 173). The Dossier can serve as a link between process and product orientation. If learners, for example, indicate in the can-do descriptors of the *Language Biography* that they can write an email to a friend, they can include an email they have written to an ePal as a piece of evidence in their Dossier (Ballweg and Bräuer 2011: 6).

When the time comes for transfer to another class or school, examples of learners' work from the Dossier can be selected to accompany them with their portfolio.

The ELP – its functions

From the descriptions above, it becomes clear that the ELP has two main functions. On the one hand, it documents intercultural communicative competence and experiences and therefore has a documentation and informative function. On the other hand, it accompanies children's (and teenagers' and adults') lifelong learning of languages and therefore has a pedagogic and educational function (Langner 2011: 12).

The *documentation function*: The ELP is a personal document that belongs to the learners; it shows their language-learning profile, efforts and achievements and contains certificates as well as personal experiences. It records learners' experience of learning languages during each stage of their education, and passes on with them to the next stage, to provide teachers as well as parents and other caretakers with evidence of the level they have reached and to give some indication of their readiness for further study.

The *pedagogic function*: Keeping a portfolio up-to-date helps young learners participate in a more conscious and active way in their learning process and use all the opportunities available to enhance and diversify it. This approach helps learners take ownership of their own acquisition or learning process and find or strengthen their motivation. It seeks to develop the autonomy of the learner by giving him or her the feeling of satisfying their own and others' needs.

The ELP – Opportunities and challenges

Even though the ELP with its common structure and the direct link to the CEFR differs fundamentally from other more open pedagogic portfolios, research has shown that it can have a positive impact on the primary language classroom and can unfold an innovation potential (Ushioda and Ridley 2002, Kohonen 2003, Legutke 2003, Little 2004, Perclová 2006, Sisamakis 2006, Schärer 2008). As a building block for a new learning and assessment culture (see Figure 14.2) it offers manifold opportunities and comes into effect on

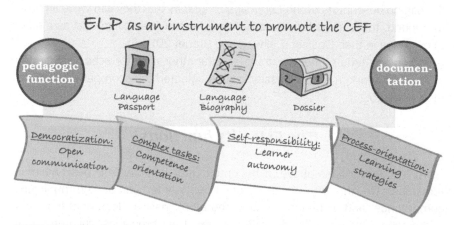

FIGURE 14.2 *The ELP as a building block for a new learning and assessment culture. (Becker 2013: 63.)*[1]

four levels defined by Winter (2011) as *democratization, complex tasks, self-responsibility* and *process orientation*.

Using the ELP in the classroom can improve the communication between teachers and learners and can be used as a body of evidence for an active, truly collaborative reflection of the young learners' progress and language competence. This finally leads to a more democratic open communication (Ushioda and Ridley 2002) and an increased involvement in the learning and assessment procedure. It allows learners to exercise some control over assessment processes by, for example, having a say in choosing what pieces of work they put in their Dossier and focusing on certain competences to be developed further. The open communication concerning proficiency levels and assessment criteria can stimulate learners into being more responsible for their own learning. This includes becoming actively involved in goal setting as well as choosing and applying their assessment criteria by carrying out complex tasks which are directly linked to the descriptors in their ELP (Becker 2013: 63). The learners' active involvement as well as increased ownership of learning and assessment fosters the development of learner autonomy (Ushioda and Ridley 2002, Kohonen 2003, Little 2004, Perclová 2006, Sisamakis 2006, Schärer 2008). Furthermore, the ELP with its checklists in the *Language Biography* provides opportunities for reflecting the learners' individual progress, including attitudes, interests, talents and learning strategies, which include cognitive, affective and social processes and will to a high degree promote process orientation (Ushioda and Ridley 2002, Kohonen 2003, Sisamakis 2006).

In the long run, the shift towards a new learning and assessment culture, with the ELP as building block, can increase the motivation and enthusiasm for learning. The children observe progress as it takes place, and have access to the products of their efforts to show them off to their teachers, friends and families. Teachers do not have to take time away from instruction, nor students from learning for portfolio assessment to take place. The dual focus on products as well as processes serves as a means of information for instruction as it supports teachers and helps them learn from portfolio assessment not only what to teach but also how and when to teach it. Portfolios might therefore in the long run lead to a professionalization of teachers (Sisamakis 2006).

The ELP – Challenges

The research on the use of ELPs shows that its implementation in the language classroom also poses challenges. Those challenges mainly result from the ELP's specific given structure and its direct link to the CEFR. Kolb (2007: 35) argues that the predetermined structure and outer appearance do not leave much room for individual and creative options and may have a negative effect on the intended individualization. She fears that the checklists in the *Language Biography* might lead to a mere processing of model templates by simply ticking off boxes (Kolb 2007: 35). At the same time, the common standards in the form of the CEFR's can-do statements for self-evaluation are not open to personalization and therefore make it very difficult to focus on individual learners. Kolb (2007: 36) also criticizes that the focus on self-evaluation of the developed competences in the four skills may lead to a higher risk of neglecting the reflection of individual processes and learning pathways.

In view of the above, it becomes clear that the ELP can only be implemented successfully when it is used flexibly, and several aspects to support its flexible use and promote process orientation are taken into account. The ELP model to be used needs to be adapted and modified according to the specific classroom context. It also needs to be complemented by the integration of opportunities for documenting processes as well as products. In order to maintain long-term motivation, real tasks must lead to the processes and final products of these processes being integrated into the portfolio. The coursebook employed needs to be closely linked to the portfolio by offering activities for self-assessment. Finally the portfolio needs to be used for individual reflection as well as a basis for communication between teachers and young learners, but also for the development of and reflection on the teaching (Bräuer 2006: 260).

The implementation of the ELP – An empirical study

A large-scale pilot project on ELP implementation was carried out by the Ministry of Education of Lower Saxony, Germany, and was evaluated by Becker (2013). Altogether seventy schools of all school types and 3,200 students and 120 teachers participated (primary and secondary). The project's main objectives were the successful large-scale implementation and long-term establishment of the ELP at primary level, promoting the transition from primary to secondary school as well as the dissemination of the newly developed curriculum of Lower Saxony (Niedersächsisches Kultusministerium 2006) and the paradigm shift towards a competency-based language teaching (see Bland 2015: 1–2). Furthermore, the pilot study intended to promote learner autonomy in the language classroom.

The analysis of small-scale pilot projects with, for example, 360 learners und twenty-two teachers in Finland (Kohonen 2003: 23), 364 learners und fourteen teachers in Ireland (Sisamakis 2006: 81) and 902 learners und fifty-three teachers in the Czech Republic (Perclová 2006) shows that those projects were all mostly positively evaluated; and the ELP in the narrower implementation context showed a high modification and innovation potential.

This gave rise to the question whether a large-scale ELP implementation could be equally successful. The main objectives of the evaluation study by Becker (2013) therefore were the examination of the efficiency of the implementation of the ELP and its modification potential in a large institutional implementation context from the teachers' perspective. Moreover, the study aimed to identify and indicate implementation requirements for teachers and to put forward a basic framework for planning and developing teacher education and training courses for institutional implementations.

The analysis of the quantitative empirical study (n=109), which used standardized questionnaires, identified two levels crucial to portfolio implementation: Level I *Organization and operational support* and Level II *Learning and classroom communication culture*. Level I comprises the elements: (1) regular and planned use, (2) cooperation and operational support, (3) integration of the ELP and its parts in the classroom and connecting coursebooks and the ELP and (4) time. Level II comprises: (1) self-responsibility: learner autonomy, (2) democratization: changes in the communication between teachers and learners, (3) process orientation: learning strategies and (4) complex real-life tasks: orientation towards the CEFR and the competence orientation.

Findings from Level I: Organization and operational support

The analysis of the data shows that the results are contrary to expectations and that uptake in a large-scale implementation context was very low. Sixty-four per cent of the teachers did not want to continue working with the ELP. The motivation to work with portfolios in the language classroom decreased drastically in the course of the project. There is no evidence for regular and systematic use of the ELP. Furthermore, there is hardly any evidence of collaboration by ELP teachers. The data reveals an additive use of the ELP with only a selective integration into the everyday classroom procedures, as the pilot teachers did not put the ELP in the centre of instruction. The data also shows that there is hardly any integration of ELP and coursebooks (Becker 2013). Finally, the evaluation revealed that the time spent on the ELP was very short. Teachers argued that they did not have enough time for portfolio work (Becker 2013: 216).

Findings from Level II: Learning and classroom communication culture

The data analysis shows similar results for Level II. In the large-scale implementation context, the ELP could not unlock its modification and innovation potential at the level of learning and classroom communication culture as described in other pilot studies. Ninety per cent of the teachers report that teaching practice has remained unchanged by the ELP (Becker 2013: 180). The majority of pilot teachers did not openly collaborate and discuss matters of assessment with their students or use portfolios to compare learners' self-assessment with their own evaluation of learners' proficiency levels and therefore did not initiate the democratization of the language classroom (Becker 2013: 178). Especially in the primary classroom, teachers reported not having much confidence in the self-assessment skills of the young learners (Becker 2013: 178). Teachers did not report any effects on the four levels of a new learning and assessment culture as defined by Winter (2011): democratization, complex tasks, self-responsibility and process orientation.

Factors for the lack of uptake

The evaluation of the pilot study clearly reveals several factors for the lack of uptake.

The study confirms that teachers who make changes on Level I, who use the portfolio regularly and systematically in their classrooms, collaborate with colleagues to plan portfolio work and develop a methodology for its integration, as well as link coursebooks with the ELP are significantly more successful in ELP implementation (Becker 2013: 214). Since a majority of teachers did not make the necessary changes, the implementation could not be successful. Several main reasons for non-application could be identified. Firstly, there was a high dominance of coursebooks. Many pilot teachers reported that they do not consider it necessary to use any other tool apart from the coursebook in order to implement competency-based teaching (Becker 2013: 210). There was also no evidence for a paradigm shift towards competency-based teaching: the teachers did not focus on the can-do statements and identify them as competences and proficiency levels to be developed and reached. Finally, the strict focus on the given structure of the ELP did not allow the teachers to flexibly use the portfolio and adapt it according to the individual needs of their working context.

Success factors for extensive portfolio implementation in the young-learner classroom

The ELP pilot study in Lower Saxony showed that large-scale implementation is not a sure-fire success. It cannot be recommended to prescribe ELP use by educational institutions; changes first have to be made on the level of lesson organization. Here regularity and planned use, collaboration and support as well as the integration of the ELP through creating a close connection to the coursebooks used are key success factors. Sufficient time and space for ELP work can only be created by real tasks linked directly to the portfolio arising from concrete lessons (Becker 2013: 216).

For a sustainable portfolio implementation it is necessary to change well-established teaching plans and patterns as well as to initiate a change of the learning and assessment culture (Legutke 2002 and 2003). The ELP needs to be flexibly used by teachers and, finally, the connection between curricula and the ELP has to be made explicit. Other crucial success factors for ELP implementation are accompanying support measures in the form of monthly portfolio meetings, supervision and close support by portfolio trainers (Becker 2013: 219–221). This was also shown by the small-scale pilot studies in Finland where a strong focus within in-service teacher training was put on key issues that relate to the change of the learning and assessment culture as well as concrete links between curricula and the portfolio (Kohonen 2002, 2003) and by studies in Ireland and the Czech Republic where the key success factors of ELP implementation were also identified (Perclová 2006, Sisamakis 2006).

A model for sustainable portfolio implementation

The findings from the pilot study reveal that the ELP is a highly complex tool. The model for a sustainable portfolio implementation as depicted in Figure 14.3 shows that the theories of constructivism, self-determination, self-efficacy and learner autonomy form the ELP's as well as other pedagogic portfolios' foundation. The ELP is a building block for a new learning culture including the levels of *democratization, complex tasks, self-responsibility* and *process orientation*. The structure (*Language Passport*, the *Language Biography* and the *Dossier*) distinguishes the ELP substantially from other pedagogic portfolios. Furthermore, it pursues the goal of documenting and reflecting language acquisition processes based on the proficiency scales of the CEFR, thus also contributing to its dissemination. A successful and sustainable implementation of the ELP is only possible and its innovation and modification potential can only be fully released when all levels of a new learning and assessment culture represented in the model are equally considered. Well-established traditional teaching patterns need to be rethought. Furthermore, it must be ensured that there is an interlink between the ELP and coursebooks through complex tasks and by regularly and meaningfully integrating the ELP into the language classroom. Increased cooperation and collaboration among teachers will help make portfolio work a natural part of the language classroom.

At the same time, the ELP needs to be flexibly used and integrated. Teachers need to independently *reflect* and use the portfolio for evaluation

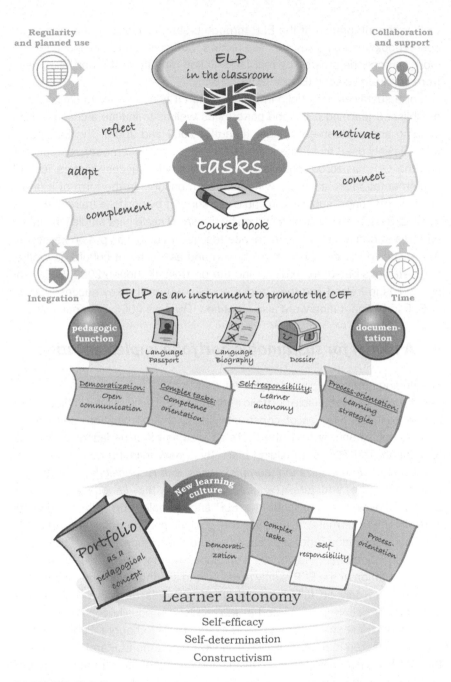

FIGURE 14.3 *A model for sustainable portfolio implementation.*

and assessment. They need to *adapt* the portfolio and modify it for specific situations and contexts, for example, for informing parents about proficiency levels or giving learners concrete individual feedback on target outcomes, progress and acquired competences. Teachers need to *complement* the ELP and create alternative forms for recording processes, for example, by directly linking the *Dossier* and *Language Biography*; and teachers need to *motivate* the children to record their own progress. The portfolio's content has to arise from real working processes, for example, from concrete tasks, in order to promote the young learner's understanding of the CEFR's can-do statements as well as an increased autonomy in self-assessment and motivation to use portfolios. Finally, the content of the ELP needs to be supported and *connect* different areas of language teaching and assessment and needs to be further processed in multifaceted ways, for example, by serving as a basis for giving feedback or for portfolio presentations.

The implementation of the model presented, the inclusion of its underlying theoretical foundations as well as the necessary readjustments at the level of organization and operational support and learning and assessment culture are basic prerequisites for the successful establishment of the ELP in the young learner classroom.

Conclusions

It has been shown that more than a decade after the enthusiastic introduction of the ELP the expectations raised could not be fulfilled. The only successful portfolio implementations were small-scale projects (Kohonen 2003, Perclová 2006, Sisamakis 2006) and there is no evidence for successful large-scale portfolio use in the language classroom. Large-scale ELP use and assessment can only be established if teachers readjust their traditional ways of teaching and make changes at the levels of lesson organization and learning and assessment culture. In order to motivate more teachers for long-term portfolio use, far-reaching support measures of the institutional kind have to be greatly expanded. Portfolio work cannot develop its full potential if it remains a specific measure in an otherwise traditional language classroom, but only if it is used as a building block for a new learning and assessment culture.

Note

1 Figures 14.2 and 14.3 are excerpted with kind permission from Peter Lang from: Carmen Becker (2013), *Portfolio als Baustein einer neuen Lernkultur. Eine empirische Studie zur Implementierung des Europäischen Portfolios der Sprache*, Frankfurt am Main, Berlin, Bern, Bruxelles, New York, Oxford, Warszawa, Wien: Peter Lang (ISBN 978-3-631-62892–8).

References

Ballweg, Sandra and Bräuer, Gerd (2011), 'Portfolioarbeit im Fremdsprachenunterricht – Yes, we can!', *Fremdsprache Deutsch*, 45: 3–6.

Bandura, Albert (1995), *Self-efficacy in Changing Societies*, Cambridge: Cambridge University Press.

Becker, Carmen (2003), 'Lernentwicklung dokumentieren. Das Sprachenportfolio', *Die Grundschulzeitschrift*, 164: 42–44.

Becker, Carmen (2013), *Portfolio als Baustein einer neuen Lernkultur. Eine empirische Studie zur Implementierung des Europäischen Portfolios der Sprache*, Frankfurt: Peter Lang.

Becker, Carmen and Krohn, Dieter (2006), 'Die Arbeit mit dem Europäischen Sprachenportfolio', *SchulVerwaltung Ausgabe Niedersachsen und Schleswig-Holstein*, 16: 211–215.

Bellingrodt, Lena (2011), *ePortfolios im Fremdsprachenunterricht. Empirische Studien zur Förderung autonomen Lernens*, Frankfurt am Main: Peter Lang.

Bland, Janice (2015), 'Introduction', in Janice Bland (ed.), *Teaching English to Young Learners. Critical Issues in Language Teaching with 3–12 Year Olds*, London: Bloomsbury Academic.

Bräuer, Gerd (2006), 'Keine verordneten Hochglanz-Portfolios, bitte! Die Korruption einer schönen Idee?', in Ilse Brunner, Thomas Häcker and Felix Winter (eds), *Das Handbuch Portfolioarbeit*, Seelze: Kallmeyer, pp. 257–261.

Cameron, Lynne (2002), *Teaching Languages to Young Learners*, Cambridge: Cambridge University Press.

CILT (2001), My Languages Portfolio, London: Centre for Information on Language Teaching and Research.

Council of Europe (1992), *Transparency and Coherence in Language Learning in Europe. Objectives, Evaluation, Certification. Report on the Rüschlikon Symposium*, Strasbourg: Council of Europe.

Council of Europe (1997), *European Language Portfolio. Proposals for Development*, Strasbourg: Council of Europe.

Council of Europe (2001), *Common European Framework of Reference for Languages: Learning, Teaching, Assessment*, Cambridge: Cambridge University Press.

Deci, Edward and Ryan, Richard (2000), 'Self-determination theory and the facilitation of intrinsic motivation, social development, and well-being', *American Psychologist*, 55/1: 68–78.

Häcker, Thomas (2006), 'Wurzeln der Portfolioarbeit. Woraus das Konzept erwachsen ist', in Ilse Brunner, Thomas Häcker and Felix Winter (eds), *Das Handbuch Portfolioarbeit*, Seelze: Kallmeyer, pp. 27–33.

Holec, Henri (1981), *Autonomy and Foreign Language Learning*, Oxford: Pergamon Press.

Kohonen, Viljo (1997), 'Authentic assessment as an integration of language learning, teaching, evaluation and the teacher's professional growth', in Ari Huhta, Vilj Kohonen, Liisa Kurki-Suonio and Sari Luoma (eds), *Current Developments and Alternatives in Language Assessment: Proceedings of LTRC 1996*, Jyvaskyla: University of Jyvaskyla, pp. 7–22.

Kohonen, Viljo (2002), 'The European Language Portfolio: From portfolio assessment to portfolio-oriented language learning', in Viljo Kohonen and Pauli Kaikkonenen (eds), *Quo Vadis Foreign Language Education?* Tampere: Publications of the Department of Teacher Education, pp. 77–95.

Kohonen, Viljo (2003), *Student Autonomy and the European Language Portfolio: Evaluating the Finnish Pilot Project (1998–2001)*. <http://31237.vws.magma.ca/pdf/LECTURA%202_Kohonen,%20V.pdf> [accessed 20 July 2014].

Kolb, Annika (2007), *Portfolioarbeit. Wie Grundschulkinder ihr Sprachenlernen reflektieren*, Tübingen: Gunter Narr.

Langner, Michael (2011), 'Das Europäische Sprachenportfolio', *Fremdsprache Deutsch*, 45: 12.

Legutke, Michael (2002), 'Das Juniorportfolio als didaktische Herausforderung: Anmerkungen zur Selbst- und Fremdbewertung im Fremdsprachenunterricht der Grundschule', in Hansa Barkowski and Renate Faistauer (eds), ... *in Sachen Deutsch als Fremdsprache. Festschrift für Hans-Jürgen Krumm zum 60. Geburtstag*, Balltmannsweiler: Schneider Verlag Hohengeheren, pp. 104–120.

Legutke, Michael (2003), 'Sprachenportfolio für Grundschulen – Ergebnisse eines hessischen Pilotprojekts', in Christoph Edelhoff (ed.), Englisch in der Grundschule und darüber hinaus, Frankfurt am Main: Schroedel, pp. 104–109.

Lippelt, Birgit; Willgerodt, Ursula and Windolph, Edeltraud (2002), 'Das Portfolio in der Grundschule in Niedersachsen', *Fremdsprachenunterricht*, 46: 272–277.

Little, David (1991), *Learner Autonomy 1: Definitions, Issues and Problems*, Dublin: Authentik.

Little, David (2004), *European Language Portfolio: Council of Europe Seminar Sponsored by the Ministry of Education, Spain*, Strasbourg: Council of Europe.

Little, David; Hodel, Hans-Peter; Kohonen, Viljo; Meijer, Dick and Perclová, Radka (2007), *Preparing Teachers to Use the European Language Portfolio*, Strasbourg: Council of Europe.

McKay, Penny (2006), *Assessing Young Language Learners*, Cambridge: Cambridge University Press.

Niedersächsisches Kultusministerium (2006), *Kerncurriculum für die Grundschule Schuljahrgänge 3–4. Englisch*, Hannover: Unidruck.

Paulson, Leon; Paulson, Pearl and Meyer, Carol (1991), 'What Makes a Portfolio a Portfolio?', *Educational Leadership*, 48/5: 60–63.

Perclová, Rudmila (2006), *The Implementation of European Language Portfolio Pedagogy in Czech Primary and Lower-Secondary Schools: Beliefs and Attitudes of Pilot Teachers and Learners*, Joensuu: University of Joensuu Publications in Education No. 114.

Quinn Allen, Linda (2004), 'Implementing a culture portfolio project within a constructivist paradigm', *Foreign Language Annals*, 37/2: 232–239.

Rau, Nathalie (2008), 'Working with a treasure-chest', *Die Grundschulzeitschrift*, 22: 42–47.

Schärer, Rolf (2000), *Final Report. A European Language Portfolio Pilot Project. Phase 1998–2000*, Strasbourg: Council of Europe.

Schärer, Rolf (2004), *A European Language Portfolio: From Piloting to Implementation (2001–2004) – Consolidated Report – Final Version*, Strasbourg: Council of Europe.

Schärer, Rolf (2008), *European Language Portfolio: Interim Report 2007*, Strasbourg: Council of Europe.
Schneider, Günther and North, Brian (2000), *Fremdsprachen können – was heißt das? Skalen zur Beschreibung, Beurteilung und Selbsteinschätzung der fremdsprachlichen Kommunikationsfähigkeit*, Zürich: Rüegger.
Sisamakis, Emmanouil (2006), *The European Language Portfolio in Irish Post-Primary Education: A Longitudinal Empirical Evaluation*, Dublin: Trinity College.
Ushioda, Ema and Ridley, Jennifer (2002), *Working with the European Language Portfolio in Irish Post-Primary Schools: Report of an Evaluation Project*, Dublin: Trinity College, Centre for Language and Communication Studies.
Windolph, Edeltraud and Becker, Carmen (2003), 'Das Portfolio in der Grundschule – ein Erfahrungsbericht', *SchulVerwaltung Ausgabe Niedersachsen und Schleswig-Holstein*, 13: 15–17.
Winter, Felix (2011), *Leistungsbewertung. Eine neue Lernkultur braucht einen anderen Umgang mit den Schülerleistungen*, Baltmannsweiler: Schneider Verlag Hohengehren.

15

Developing Principled Materials for Young Learners of English as a Foreign Language

Brian Tomlinson

Introduction

The distinctive fact about the learning of English as a foreign language by young learners is that they have no immediate need to use English and therefore no need to learn it, with the obvious exception of young learners in institutions where English is used as a medium of instruction for other subjects (see Ghosn 2007, 2013a for examples of this situation in Lebanon). The government might want children to learn English, their parents might want them to learn English, their teachers might want them to learn English but we cannot assume that the young learners themselves will want to learn English. As nobody has ever successfully acquired a foreign language without either needing or wanting to, it is very important that materials for young learners persuade them to want to learn the language. This can only be achieved if the experience of learning the language is positive and enjoyable and if it helps increase the learners' confidence and self-esteem (Arnold and Brown, 1999). This can be achieved through an immersion approach (see K. Kersten and Rohde 2015, this volume) or the Content and Language Integrated Learning (CLIL) approach (Bentley 2015, this volume). It can also be achieved through listening to stories (Bland 2015b, this volume) through the use of literary texts such as pictureboooks (Ghosn 2007, 2013b, Bland 2013, Mourão 2015b, this volume), of drama activities (Park 2010b, Bland 2015c), of games (Tomlinson and Masuhara 2010) and of songs (Millington 2011). However, none of these approaches will succeed if they do not make the learning of English an interesting and fun experience and if the materials used have not been driven by and evaluated with criteria based on principles of second language (L2) acquisition in general and young-learner acquisition in particular. It is on such principled criteria that this chapter will focus.

Principled criteria for materials development and evaluation

I have long argued that the criteria for evaluating a set of materials should be developed before beginning to write the materials and that these criteria should be used throughout the development of the materials. I have also argued that both *local* and *universal* criteria should be developed in addition to age-specific, medium-specific and content-specific criteria (Tomlinson 2013: 37–42).

Local criteria are those specific to the actual learning context of the users of the materials and would include criteria related to the gender, age, level, previous learning experience, expectations and interests of the learners as well as to the qualifications, experience and ability of the teachers and the demands of the curriculum and of examinations. Examples of local criteria would be:

- To what extent is the reading of picturebooks likely to be engaging for ten-year-old boys in Saudi Arabia?

- To what extent are the listening activities likely to help the students pass the listening component of the Year Four English Examination in Singapore?

- To what extent are the tasks likely to be cognitively achievable for six-year-old learners in Germany?

Local criteria have to be developed separately for each project and are best driven by profiles of the local context of learning (Tomlinson 2013: 42). They are obviously important but should not take priority over universal criteria if successful acquisition is the goal. In my experience the world is full of materials (and especially of young-learner materials) which are so driven by the requirements of the local curriculum and examinations that it has been very difficult for the writers to ensure the engagement and enjoyment so important for young-learner acquisition of a language. For example, I was involved in a primary textbook project in China in which the materials were constrained by a curriculum that specified which lexical items and which structures should be introduced at which level plus an insistence on testing all the language that was introduced. We thought we had got round this restriction by including stories which also incidentally contained lexis and structure not yet scheduled for teaching. The materials were popular with the pupils but less popular with their parents, who saw their children's test scores go down because of the teachers' insistence on testing all the language in each unit. We then used colour coding to indicate which language items should be taught and tested and which should just be treated as incidental language used to enrich the stories and make them more interesting for the pupils. This did not seem to have much impact on what the teachers actually did though. Similar anecdotes could be told about young-learner materials in many countries where standardization and accountability are of paramount importance.

Universal criteria are those that are applicable to any language learner in any language-learning situation anywhere. They are driven by the beliefs of the developers based on their experience of foreign-language learning as learners, as teachers, as observers and as researchers, as well as their understanding of the literature on L2 acquisition and development. Examples of universal criteria would be:

- To what extent are the reading texts likely to promote connections with the learners' lives?

- To what extent are the tasks likely to give learners opportunities to use the language for communication?

- To what extent are the topics likely to engage the learners affectively?

In projects I have been involved in, I have always developed universal criteria first so as to stress to the developers and evaluators how important these principles are if the learners are eventually going to acquire English and to develop the ability to use it for effective communication.

Key universal criteria for materials development and evaluation

Among the universal criteria for materials development, the following can be considered key: exposure to the language in use, affective engagement, cognitive engagement, meaning-related attention to form and opportunities to use the language for communication.

Exposure to the language in use

Krashen (1985) argued that comprehensible input is both necessary and sufficient for language acquisition. Most applied linguists do not accept that comprehensible input is sufficient (e.g. Sato 1988, Swain 1995, 1998, Ortega 2009: 59–60), but they do accept that it is necessary. Research has demonstrated that learners need to be exposed to language in use which is

- comprehensible – that is sufficiently understandable for the learner to achieve their objective (Krashen 1985)

- rich – substantial in quantity and valuable in variety

- meaningful – of significance and value to the learners' lives

- authentic – that is used for communication rather than for teaching (Mishan 2005, Gilmore 2007, Pinter 2015, this volume)

- recycled – that is experienced a number of times in a variety of ways over a period of time (Nation 2001, 2011).

It seems that input that remains incomprehensible is of no value in helping to achieve L2 acquisition and of little value if eventually worked out through the use of dictionaries, grammar reference books or teacher explanation. An interesting exception occurs in *Chike's School Days* (Achebe 1972), a story about a primary-school teacher in Nigeria who enchanted his pupils by using such long words as 'periwinkle', 'constellation' and 'procrastination'. This makes you wonder about the value of nonsense rhymes which are incomprehensible yet enjoyable. They are unlikely to lead to acquisition of the language items in the rhymes in the short term, but enjoyment of them could lead to positive affect and therefore to acquisition of language items in subsequent input. In fact, it could be argued that the main objective of teaching most young learners English is to help them develop and invest positive attitudes towards English and the learning of it in readiness for a future when they do need English and are in a learning environment with richer input that could facilitate its acquisition.

It is a fact that input is always larger than intake, even in severely input-limited contexts. In other words the amount of language taken in by the brain from exposure for processing is always much smaller than the language available to it. It is also a fact that intake will vary from individual to individual in a class of learners even though they are all receiving the same input. If the input is minimal, as it often is for learners of a foreign language whose coursebooks restrict their input to tiny texts and who have little or no access to the language outside the classroom, then the intake will be miniscule. If the input is also restricted to a few genres and text types, then the intake will not only be too small but also be impoverished. And if the learners only have two or three hours a week of English (as most young learners do, see Ghosn 2013b: 62, Rixon 2015, this volume), then their input will be insufficient for any worthwhile acquisition to take place. Learners of all ages and all levels need rich input. But they should not be expected to learn it all at once: language emergence requires not only rich input but also a lot of time.

Learning basically results from connecting the new to the old and so does language acquisition. It is very important therefore that learners are able to connect their new input to experiences and language which were previously significant to them. This only happens if the new input is salient and meaningful in the sense that it connects significantly with their lives.

Acquisition results from making hypotheses about the use of a linguistic feature from repeated and meaningful exposure to the feature in use. These hypotheses relate to both the form and functions of the feature as well as to when, where and why it is used and not used. Exposure to contrived examples will result in restricted (and maybe even corrupted) L2 acquisition (Bland 2013: 7–9). Effective acquisition requires frequent and varied exposure to the feature in authentic use within a complex context of communication. It seems that acquisition of a linguistic feature can only occur if it is encountered many times, if the encounters are in different contexts and if the encounters occur frequently over a lengthy period of time. Such recycling is essential.

In addition to extensive reading other ways of providing exposure to language in use include:

- extensive listening

- extensive viewing (e.g. of films, videos and live performances)

- extensive performance (e.g. of plays, songs, poems, rituals)

- extended texts in coursebooks

- the teacher talking to the young learners in class

- talks by other proficient users of the language

- frequent use of the internet

- communicating in L2 with other people via email, facebook, twitter, etc.

- using English outside the classroom with fellow learners.

All these ways are possible with young learners and I have experienced successful examples of them being used in China, Indonesia, Japan and Vanuatu.

Examples of specific input criteria for developing and evaluating materials would be:

- To what extent are the reading texts likely to provide a rich exposure to language in use?

- To what extent are the tasks likely to provide recycling of lexical items in use?

- To what extent are the listening texts likely to provide exposure to language in use that connects meaningfully with the learners' lives?

Affective engagement

It is very important that all learners are helped to achieve affective responses to the materials they use, for without affective engagement there is no chance of effective and durable acquisition. This involves the learners

- responding with their emotions – by, for example, laughing, getting excited, feeling happy, feeling sympathy, feeling affection (Arnold and Brown 1999: 1–3, Braten 2006, Bland 2015a: 150–161)

- being positive about the learning experience provided by the materials (Reid 1999: 297–298)

- increasing their confidence and self-esteem (de Andrés 1999, Arnold and Brown 1999: 12).

It could be argued that affective engagement is of even more vital importance for young learners (Hidi and Harackiewicz 2000: 156) and that all components of young learners' materials must achieve affective engagement if they are to be of any value to the learners. Such engagement can be achieved through

- jokes

- cartoons

- songs

- stories

- picturebooks with and without verbal text

- poems

- drama

- games

- tasks which set achievable challenges

- materials which are localized

- materials which are personalized

- materials which encourage and reward creativity rather than insisting on immediate accuracy

- materials which are open.

Language learning for young learners must be a fun, enjoyable experience. It will only lead to language acquisition though if the other key universal criteria listed here are met. For example, songs, games and drama activities which do not provide sufficient exposure to language in use might achieve affective engagement but will not facilitate L2 acquisition.

One way in which we achieved affective engagement and met the other universal criteria on the PKG English Programme in Indonesia (PKG refers to words in Bahasa Indonesia which translate as 'For the teacher by the teacher') was to use TPR (Total Physical Response) Plus activities (Tomlinson 1990, 1994b) using stories, songs, poems, instructions for games, drama activities, painting, problem solving and cooking with eleven-year-old young learners. Rich, comprehensible, authentic, meaningful and recycled input was provided as a stimulus for enjoyable physical activity plus eventual use of language for communication. And, as with all my materials, the learners were often engaged in enjoyably silly or intriguingly bizarre activities (see McDaniel, Dornburg and Guynn 2005 for accounts and explanations of the bizarreness effect).

Cognitive engagement

In addition to feeling while learning, language learners need to think as well (Mishan 2015 forthcoming). Meaningless activities such as drills and other very easy practice activities seem to have very little impact on L2 acquisition (DeKeyser 2007). However, if learners are cognitively engaged by willingly investing thought in a language activity, there is a likelihood not only of facilitating cognitive development but also of facilitating L2 acquisition. The need for thoughtful learning is especially true of young learners. But it is also true of young learners that imposing a too heavy or too analytical cognitive load on them could not only impede their cognitive development but also inhibit affective engagement and prevent L2 acquisition. Forcing young learners to study grammar can have this negative effect as can trying to get them to think about adult topics and issues, which are outside their areas of interest, curiosity and experience or which require high-level cognitive processing beyond the developmental stage they have attained (Ghosn 2013b).

I have found that the best way to achieve cognitive engagement for young learners is to set them achievable tasks, which push them to think but are within their areas of interest, curiosity and experience and are appropriate for their current developmental stage. This can be done through

- jokes, puzzles, riddles (e.g. 'Where do fish keep their money?') and problem-solving tasks (especially those with such silly problems as 'Why did the dog go to a language school?')

- inviting personal responses to listening and reading texts which entertain while raising issues (Mourão 2015b, this volume).

Meaning-related attention to form

Most L2 acquisition researchers agree that noticing how the language is used can facilitate its acquisition (Pienemann 1985, Long 1996, Schmidt 2001, Williams 2005, Fotos and Nassaji 2007, Ellis 2012). Nearly all young-learner researchers also agree that requiring too much attention to language form can kill affective and cognitive engagement and actually prevent intake. What seems to be needed are activities which first of all focus the young learners' attention on global meaning before encouraging discrete attention to a form which has contributed to that meaning (Tomlinson 1994a: 125–126). In my experience it is more useful if the learners (even very young learners) are asked to make discoveries for themselves (e.g. 'What makes the story exciting?'). Or, as I implemented successfully with eleven-year-olds in Indonesia, to maybe even do simple research tasks (e.g. 'Look through the readers on the shelves and find other examples of "but". For each example exchange ideas why "but" is used'). It is arguable that at low levels and for young learners with no metalanguage in English the discussion of discoveries about language use could more usefully be conducted in the first language (L1) rather than in L2 (provided of course that the learners have first of all been exposed to a text in L2 and have responded to its meaning).

Opportunities to use the language for communication

Research shows that it is vital that learners use the target language for communication and do not just practice it (Swain 1995, Ortega 2010, Ellis 2012). This not only provides opportunities for situational feedback on effectiveness but also elicits further meaningful input, especially if the communication is interactive (Swain, Brooks and Tocalli-Beller 2002, Pica

2005). One obvious problem for most young learners of EFL, though, is that there is no need and little opportunity to use English outside the classroom. This means that opportunities must be provided by their materials and their teacher to communicate in English in the classroom and opportunities need to be sought outside the classroom too, for example through the formation of social clubs whose members agree to use English whenever they meet. Inside the classroom the obvious communicants are the teacher and the fellow students. Communication can, for example, take place in unscripted drama activities, as well as in writing activities in which an audience and intentions are specified (e.g. designing advertisements and posters and responding to emails).

Key young-learner criteria for materials development and evaluation

All the universal criteria above are important for the development and evaluation of materials for young learners. In addition I would add the following universal criteria, which I consider are particularly important for young learners, as well as local criteria relevant to the target learners for the materials.

- To what extent do the materials provide a variety of different activities?

- To what extent do the materials provide opportunities for language play (Cook 2000, Tomlinson and Masuhara 2010, Bland 2013: 156–187)?

- To what extent do the materials encourage risk taking (Brown 2001)?

- To what extent do the materials cater for experiential learning preferences (Kolb 1984, Oxford 1990, Kolb and Kolb 2009)?

- To what extent do the materials cater for kinaesthetic learning preferences (Tomlinson 1994b, Asher 1996)?

Examples of principled young-learner materials in action

In this section I would like to offer some exciting examples of principled young-learner materials I have observed in action.

Vanuatu

In Vanuatu, in the South Pacific, I observed a primary-school teacher talking to her class as they lined up outside the classroom. She told them that when they entered the classroom they should sit down in front of their new television. As they had seen pictures of televisions but had never seen a real one, the children were very excited. They rushed into the room and sat on the floor in a semicircle around a cardboard box. The teacher had made the box look like a television by cutting out a screen and painting knobs underneath it. She had also translated a local myth into English and written out the story on a long piece of paper. She had scrolled the paper around a rolling pin and inserted it into the box.

The teacher said, 'Let's watch television', and then slowly turned the rolling pin. The title of the story appeared on the screen and the teacher read it aloud. She then turned the pin again and the story appeared on the screen. She kept turning the pin and the children were totally engaged by the story. After a while the teacher gradually increased the speed of her turning of the pin and the children read faster without any problem. If they encountered a comprehension problem the children discussed it or asked the teacher for help. The teacher froze the screen for a while and then moved on as soon as she could. Each lesson could now begin with watching a story on television, and the children were exposed to rich, comprehensible, meaningful and recycled input while being engaged affectively and cognitively.

In Vanuatu we changed the examination almost overnight from a traditional test of grammatical knowledge to a test of communication by replacing discrete item questions with communication tasks. As the textbook was no longer a useful preparation for the examination, we held weekend workshops on different islands in which teachers wrote a booklet of communication tasks for use in the classroom (Tomlinson 1981). Not long afterwards I had the great pleasure of observing nine- to ten-year-olds having lively discussions in English, acting out scenes they had written and writing poems and stories that they developed from the ones they had enjoyed reading or listening to. Previously in these classrooms I had only heard teachers teaching grammar or children monotonously repeating drills. Now I observed L2 acquisition in action.

Indonesia

As part of the PKG English Programme in Indonesia (Tomlinson 1990), teachers developed materials for eleven-year-old beginners which made exclusive use of TPR Plus activities (Tomlinson 1994b) for the first thirty hours, so as to provide the learners with a fun, non-threatening and engaging introduction to

English which did not require premature production of language and therefore did not result in disheartening errors. The young learners listened to a massive amount of rich, authentic, meaningful English made comprehensible by dramatic performances of the scripts by the teachers, by localization of the texts, by recycling, by trial and error and by observing peers during the physical responses to the stories, menus and instructions for games and other activities. Eventually learners started to speak English when they felt ready and some of them were observed conducting the lesson from the front of the classroom after the teacher had left and even repeating the lesson with still younger children when they went home to their kampong.

After the first thirty hours extensive reading was introduced, through using written and slightly elaborated versions of the TPR Plus scripts written with as many 'good friends' as possible (i.e. lexical items which looked like or sounded like equivalents in Bahasa Indonesia). The learners were encouraged (but not forced) to use English during group discussions and with the teacher. They also took part in activities leading to the writing and performance of stories as well as in scenarios (di Pietro 1987) for which they prepared and then played parts in conflict and problem situations, in which they did not know what their interactants would say or try to achieve. In addition the young learners took part in activities in which they focused on a particular structure in order to make discoveries about its use after first encountering it through an engaging listening or reading text. I will never forget watching an eleven-year-old jump up in excitement in a classroom in Jakarta when he discovered that there were two different types of 'how' words (e.g. quickly and slow) from analysing a text about a birthday party which the class had just had great fun acting out. The teacher had been instructed by the syllabus to focus on regular and irregular adverbs and she had made sure there were lots of them in the story.

The approach used on the PKG English Programme met all the universal criteria outlined above as well as a number of local criteria too. It was conducted on a massive scale (one experimental class in each school throughout the country) and it initially worried many principals, inspectors and parents. Soon, though, it became very apparent that it was popular with the learners. For example, attendance was much better in the experimental classes than in the control classes and often children from the control classes could be seen crowding into the windows of the experimental classes to enjoy what their more fortunate friends enjoyed every day. And, against the expectation of many, in the end-of-the-year traditional grammar-based examinations the learners from the experimental classes outperformed equivalent learners in an examination they had not even been prepared for.

It was in Indonesia too that I observed a teacher stagger dramatically into a classroom carrying an empty box which, as she explained to her bewildered class, was their new class library. She then got each of the forty children for homework to find an interesting text in English and put it in the box the next day. Every week after that for homework she got the children to take a text home to read and to bring it back together with a new one. At the end of term there were more than 400 texts in the box and the children had enjoyed a massive exposure to English both from reading the texts and from finding them (one group had looked for English-sounding names in a telephone directory and had then visited addresses asking the residents if they had anything interesting to read in English).

In another classroom in Indonesia I observed a teacher giving a group of four twelve-year-old language learners the task of finding an interesting text in English to use in the reading lesson. On Fridays they brought a text which they thought would engage their classmates, and on Mondays the teacher used it in the reading class. Each week a different group found a text for the reading lesson. The following term the teacher got the groups to not only bring her a text on the Friday but also bring a lesson plan for using it too. The teacher helped the group to revise their plan and then they used it to 'teach' the Monday reading lesson.

China

In China I observed a class of seven-year-olds faultlessly recite a lesson 'script' they had obviously been coached in so as to impress the visitor from the West. Afterwards I tried to talk to the students. Only three of them could communicate with me. One of the three went each weekend to Foreigners' Corner in the park and talked to speakers of English, one read *World Soccer* every week and one accessed the internet in English every night. All three acquired their communicative competence from finding English outside the classroom which had engaged them.

Conclusion

To sum up I would like to stress yet again that materials for young learners should aim primarily to provide an engaging and enjoyable experience of English. They should not instruct but should entertain. They should not provide lists of contrived examples but should expose the learners to English in use. They should not provide controlled practice but should provide opportunities for use. They should not be closed but should be open. They should be fun.

References

Achebe, Chinua (1972), 'Chike's school days', in *Girls at War and Other Stories*, Oxford: Heinemann.

Arnold, Jane and Brown, Douglas (1999), 'A map of the terrain', in Jane Arnold (ed.) *Affect in Language Learning*, Cambridge: Cambridge University Press, pp. 1–24.

Asher, James (1996), *Learning Another Language through Actions* (5th edn), Los Gatos, CA: Sky Oaks Productions.

Bentley, Kay (2015), 'CLIL Scenarios with Young Learners', in Janice Bland (ed.), *Teaching English to Young Learners. Critical Issues in Language Teaching with 3–12 Year Olds*, London: Bloomsbury Academic, pp. 91–111.

Bland, Janice (2013), *Children's Literature and Learner Empowerment: Children and Teenagers in English Language Education*, London: Bloomsbury Academic.

Bland, Janice (2015a), 'Grammar templates for the future with poetry for children', in Janice Bland (ed.), *Teaching English to Young Learners. Critical Issues in Language Teaching with 3–12 Year Olds*, London: Bloomsbury Academic, pp. 147–166.

Bland, Janice (2015b), 'Oral storytelling in the primary English classroom', in Janice Bland (ed.), *Teaching English to Young Learners. Critical Issues in Language Teaching with 3–12 Year Olds*, London: Bloomsbury Academic, pp. 183–198.

Bland, Janice (2015c), 'Drama with young learners', in Janice Bland (ed.), *Teaching English to Young Learners. Critical Issues in Language Teaching with 3–12 Year Olds*, London: Bloomsbury Academic, pp. 219–238.

Braten, Stein (ed.) (2006), *Intersubjective Communication and Emotion in Early Ontogeny*, Cambridge: Cambridge University Press.

Brown, Douglas (2001), *Teaching by Principles: An Interactive Approach to Language Pedagogy*, New York: Addition Wesley: Longman, Inc.

Cook, Guy (2000), *Language Play, Language Learning*, New York: Oxford University Press.

De Andrés, Verónica (1999), 'Self-esteem in the classroom or the metamorphosis of butterflies', in Jane Arnold (ed), *Affect in Language Learning*, Cambridge: Cambridge University Press, pp. 87–102.

DeKeyser, Robert (ed.) (2007), *Practice in a Second Language*, Cambridge: Cambridge University Press.

Di Pietro, Robert (1987), *Strategic Interaction: Learning Languages through Scenarios*, Cambridge: Cambridge University Press.

Ellis, Rod (2012), *Language Learning Research and Language Learning Pedagogy*, Chichester: Wiley-Blackwell.

Fotos, Sandra and Nassaaji, Hossein (eds) (2007), *Form-Focused Instruction and Teacher Education*, Oxford: Oxford University Press.

Ghosn, Irma (2007), 'Output like input: influence of children's literature on young L2 learners' written expression', in Brian Tomlinson (ed.), *Language Acquisition and Development: Studies of Learners of First and Other Languages*, London: Continuum, pp. 171–186.

Ghosn, Irma (2013a), 'Developing motivating materials for refugee children: From theory to practice', in Brian Tomlinson (ed.), *Developing Materials for Language Teaching* (2nd edn), London: Bloomsbury, pp. 247–267.

Ghosn, Irma (2013b), 'Language learning for young learners', in Brian Tomlinson (ed.), *Applied Linguistics and Materials Development*, London: Bloomsbury, pp. 61–74.

Gilmore, Alex (2007), 'Authentic materials and authenticity in foreign language learning', Language Teaching, 40/2: 97–118.

Hidi, Suzanne and Harackiewicz, Judith (2000), 'Motivating the academically unmotivated: A critical issue for the 21st century', *Review of Educational Research*, 70/2: 151–180.

Kersten, Kristin and Rohde, Andreas (2015), 'Immersion Teaching in English with Young Learners', in Janice Bland (ed.), *Teaching English to Young Learners. Critical Issues in Language Teaching with 3–12 Year Olds*, London: Bloomsbury Academic, pp. 71–89.

Kolb, David (1984), *Experiential Learning: Experience as the Source of Learning and Development*, Englewood Cliffs, NJ: Prentice Hall.

Kolb, Alice and Kolb, David (2009), 'The learning way; meta-cognitive aspects of experiential learning', *Simulation and Gaming: An Interdisciplinary Journal of Theory, Practice and Research*, 40/1: 48–67.

Krashen, Stephen (1985), *The Input Hypothesis*, London: Longman.

Long, Michael (1996), The role of the linguistic environment in second language acquisition', in William Ritchie and Tej Bhatia (eds), *Handbook of Second Language Acquisition*, San Diego: Academic Press, pp. 413–468.

McDaniel, Mark; Dornburg, Courtney and Guynn, Melissa (2005), 'Disentangling encoding versus retrieval explanations of the bizarreness effect: Implications for distinctiveness', *Memory and Cognition*, 33/2: 270–279.

Millington, Neil (2011), Using songs effectively to teach English to young learners, *Language Education in Asia*, 2/1: 134–141.

Mishan, Freda (2005), *Designing Authenticity into Language Learning Materials*, Bristol: Intellect.

Mishan, Freda (2015 forthcoming), 'Comprehensibility and cognitive challenge in language learning materials', in Brian Tomlinson (ed.), *Second Language Acquisition Research and Materials Development for Language Learning*, New York: Routledge.

Mourão, Sandie (2015b), 'The potential of picturebooks with young learners', in Janice Bland (ed.), *Teaching English to Young Learners. Critical Issues in Language Teaching with 3–12 Year Olds*, London: Bloomsbury Academic, pp. 199–217.

Nation, Paul (2001). *Learning Vocabulary in Another Language*, Cambridge: Cambridge University Press

Nation, Paul (2011), 'Research into practice: Vocabulary', *Language Teaching*, 44/4: 526–536.

Ortega, Lourdes (2009) *Understanding Second Language Acquisition*, London: Hodder Arnold.

Ortega, Lourdes (2010), *Second Language Acquisition. Critical Concepts in Linguistics*, London: Routledge.

Oxford, Rebecca (1990), *Language Learning Strategies: What Every Teacher Should Know*, New York: Newbury House.

Park, Haeok (2010), 'Process drama in the Korean EFL secondary classroom: A case study of Korean middle school classrooms', in Brian Tomlinson and Hitomi Masuhara (eds), *Research for Materials Development in Language Learning: Evidence for Best Practice*, London: Continuum, pp. 155–171.

Pica, Teresa (2005), 'Second language acquisition research and applied linguistics', in Eli Hinkel (ed.), *Handbook of Research in Second Language Teaching and Learning*, Mahwah, NJ: Lawrence Erlbaum, pp. 263–280.

Pienemann, Manfred (1985), 'Learnability and syllabus construction', in Kenneth Hyltenstam and Manfred Pienemann (eds), *Modelling and Assessing Second Language Acquisition*, Clevedon: Multilingual Matters, pp. 130–145.

Pinter, Annamaria (2015), 'Task-based learning with children', in Janice Bland (ed.), *Teaching English to Young Learners. Critical Issues in Language Teaching with 3–12 Year Olds*, London: Bloomsbury Academic, pp. 113–127.

Reid, Joy (1999), 'Affect in the classroom: Problems, politics and pragmatics', in Jane Arnold (ed.), *Affect in Language Learning*, Cambridge: Cambridge University Press, pp. 297–306.

Rixon, Shelagh (2015), 'Primary English and critical issues: A worldwide perspective', in Janice Bland (ed.), *Teaching English to Young Learners. Critical Issues in Language Teaching with 3–12 Year Olds*, London: Bloomsbury Academic, pp. 31–50.

Sato, Charlene (1988), 'Origins of complex syntax in interlanguage development', *Studies in Second Language Acquisition*, 10: 371–395.

Schmidt, Richard (2001), 'Attention', in Peter Robinson (ed.), *Cognition and Second Language Instruction*, Cambridge: Cambridge University Press, pp. 3 32.

Swain, Merrill (1995), 'Three functions of output in second language learning', in Guy Cook (ed.), *Principle & Practice in Applied Linguistics: Studies in Honour of H. G. Widdowson*, Oxford: Oxford University Press, pp. 125–144.

Swain, Merrill (1998), 'Focus on form through conscious reflection', in Catherine Doughty and Jessica Williams (eds), *Focus on Form in Second Language Acquisition*, New York: Cambridge University Press.

Swain, Merrill; Brooks, Lindsay and Tocalli-Beller, Agustina (2002), 'Peer-peer dialogue as a means of second language learning', *Annual Review of Applied Linguistics*, 22: 171–185.

Tomlinson, Brian (1981), *Talking to Learn*, Port Vila: Govt of Vanuatu.

Tomlinson, Brian (1990), 'Managing change in Indonesian high schools', *ELT Journal*, 44/1: 25–37.

Tomlinson, Brian (1994a), 'Pragmatic awareness activities', *Language Awareness*, 3/3 & 4: 119–129.

Tomlinson, Brian (1994b), 'Materials for TPR', *Folio* 1/2, 8–10.

Tomlinson, Brian (2013), 'Materials evaluation', in Brian Tomlinson (ed.), *Developing Materials for Language Teaching*, London: Bloomsbury, pp. 21–48.

Tomlinson, Brian and Masuhara, Hitomi (2010), 'Playing to learn: How physical games can contribute to second language acquisition', *Simulation and Gaming: An Interdisciplinary Journal of Theory, Practice and Research*, 40/5: 645–668.

Williams, Jessica (2005), 'Form-focused instruction', in Eli Hinkel (ed.), *Handbook of Research in Second Language Teaching and Learning*, Mawah, NJ: Lawrence Erlbaum, pp. 671–691.

Index

absence 34, 51, 66
additive bilingualism 72, 74, 84
additive language 188
affect 25, 46, 147–8, 154, 169, 269, 282
   affective benefits xi, 5, 35
   affective dimension 1–2, 8, 220,
      222, 227–8
   affective engagement 281, 284–8,
      291, 293
affordances 8, 203, 214, 241, 250
analytical processing 1, 21, 76, 149,
      224, 285
   non-analytical processing mode 220
anxiety 21, 120, 254
aptitude 120
assessment 2, 6, 8, 34, 36–8, 45–7,
      91, 95–9, 106–8, 261–78
   alternative assessment 262, 264
   criterion-referenced assessment
      262
   formative assessment 97, 106, 261,
      266
   norm-referenced assessment 262
   summative assessment 99, 106,
      108, 261–2
at-risk learners 78–9
attitude xi, 24–5, 46, 58, 97, 109, 169,
      171–2, 175, 227, 232, 250, 262,
      269, 282
   negative attitude xi, 14, 21, 78, 120
aural input. *See* listening/aural input
authorities 23, 27, 82, 263
authority 155, 158, 180, 185
autonomy. *See* learner autonomy

Basic Interpersonal Communicative
      Skills (BICS) 33, 94
BC. *See* British Council
BICS. *See* Basic Interpersonal
   Communicative Skills

blended environments 241
body language 83, 152,
      208, 221
   mind and body 222, 229
   whole-body response 162–3, 220
booktalk 205
British Council (BC) 5, 7, 31, 34–6,
      38–40, 45, 47, 92, 104–7, 168

CALL. *See* computer-assisted
      language learning
CALP. *See* Cognitive Academic
      Language Proficiency
caretaker 16, 268. *See also* parents
carousel activities 243
CEFR. *See* Common European
      Framework of Reference for
      Languages
challenging behaviour 59
chant 3, 55, 61–2, 64, 151–2, 163,
      202, 204
   chant-like 150, 191
child-directed speech 190
children's literature 3, 8, 147–66,
      183–217
chorus 151–2, 155, 159, 234
   choral reading 208
   chorus dialogue 225
   echo/diminuendo chorus 152, 157,
      234
cinema circle 186
circle time 57–9, 61, 63–5
classroom management 24, 60, 147,
      154, 230
classroom observation. *See* teaching
      observation
CLIL. *See* Content and Language
      Integrated Learning
CLT. *See* communicative language
      teaching

CMC. *See* computer-mediated communication
code-switching 95, 107
Cognitive Academic Language Proficiency (CALP) 33, 94
cognitive development 2, 42, 52, 55, 77–8, 86, 96, 106, 169, 214, 269, 285
  cognitive abilities/skills 44, 77, 86, 97–8, 102
  cognitive advantage/benefits xi, 5–6, 35, 77–8, 80, 87–8
  cognitive demand/challenge 94, 96, 99, 103, 119–20, 280, 286, 292 (*see also* metacognitive demand/challenge)
  cognitive dimension 8, 21, 219, 228
  cognitive engagement 24, 148, 281, 285–6, 288
  cognitive need for pattern 3, 7, 149, 152
  cognitive niche 189
  cognitive style 120, 136, 220
collocation 131, 133, 144–5
Common European Framework of Reference for Languages (CEFR) 2, 23, 26, 45–7, 99, 171, 241, 263, 265–75
communicative language teaching (CLT) 6, 82, 181, 240, 257–8
CLT approach 114, 170
compelling comprehensible input 227
competences 1–4, 11, 59, 81, 96, 116, 132, 134, 147, 173, 191, 193, 248, 253, 266–7, 275. *See also* intercultural competence; teaching competences
  communicative competence 2, 170, 290
  competence orientation 147, 271
  language/linguistic competence 4, 7, 28, 73, 77, 80, 142, 167, 263, 265–70
  literary competence 156 (*see also* reading skills, literary reading)

competency-based education 6, 96, 270, 272
comprehension fluency 192
computer-assisted language learning (CALL) 241
computer-mediated communication (CMC) 241
consolidating 95, 102, 115, 219, 224, 229
Content and Language Integrated Learning (CLIL) xii, 3, 5–6, 43, 72–3, 84, 91–111, 118, 210, 213, 279
continuity of learning. *See* transition
constructivism 9, 239, 257, 264, 273, 277
contextualize 6, 14, 83, 92, 117, 154, 164, 221, 236
  decontextualize 139, 222, 250
corpora 130, 151
corpus linguistic investigations 130, 161
creative teacher talk 8, 190–2, 195
creative writing 8, 195, 221, 223, 230–32, 236, 264
criteria for materials development 9, 279–293
  local criteria 280, 287, 298
  universal criteria 280–7, 289
cross-curricular learning 99, 105–6, 169, 177–8
cultural awareness 7, 174, 178, 181, 242
  critical cultural awareness 171–72
  intercultural awareness 208, 263
cumulative picturebooks 151, 200. *See also* refrains

digital media/interconnectivity 14, 17, 26, 96, 106, 184–5, 251, 239–259
diversity appreciation 7, 168, 170, 172–5, 178–9, 207
  student diversity 82, 107
double-page spread 204–5, 207
drama xi–xii, 4, 8, 43, 55–6, 94, 152, 155, 193–5, 208, 219–238, 280, 284–5, 287, 289
dubbed/non-dubbed media 33, 40

early French immersion (EFI) 74–6, 85, 89, 149
educational goals of EYL 2, 46, 52, 65, 189–190
effortful attention 6, 78
EFI. *See* early French immersion
ELA. *See* English learning area
ELP. *See* European Language Portfolio
ELT. *See* English language teaching
emergence (of language) 3, 7, 149, 160–2, 283
empathy xi, 8, 69, 158, 160, 174, 177, 189, 195, 202, 236
endpapers 202, 209, 214
English for young learners (EYL) xii, 1–8, 35, 43–4, 47, 94, 223
English language teaching (ELT) xi–xii, 6, 17, 32, 36, 43, 91–2, 95, 99–103, 113, 199–200, 213, 262–3
English learning area (ELA) 58, 61–5
European Language Portfolio (ELP) 9, 231, 261–278
exemplars 138, 148, 160, 162, 193
    exemplar-based acquisition 3, 135, 147–166
Expanding Circle 31–3, 38
explicit teaching/learning 3, 96, 137–8, 140, 142–3, 148, 184
extensive listening 184, 192, 283.
    See also listening/aural input
extensive reading 184–5, 283–4, 289–90
eye contact 191, 193
EYL. *See* English for young learners

facial expression 19, 152, 190, 208, 220–1, 225
feedback xii, 40, 106, 109, 115–16, 119, 122, 124, 126, 239, 252–3, 262, 275, 286
    corrective feedback 83
    negative feedback 115
flashcards 58, 61–2, 64–5, 135
focus on form 3, 75, 82, 117, 293, 286
    delayed focus on form 6, 117
    explicit focus on form 3
formative assessment. *See under* assessment

formats 59–64
formulaic language/sequences xi, 3, 6–7, 61–4, 83, 93, 129–145, 149, 161–2, 187–8, 219, 224, 226–7. *See also* language patterns
formula 62, 131–2, 135, 137–8, 140–1, 160, 187
formulaicity 6, 131, 133, 136, 139
fossilizing 76
4Cs Framework 6, 93–5
frequency 3, 59, 75, 133, 135, 137, 143–4, 161, 164, 192, 224
    usage frequency 3, 137, 161

gap-fills xii, 96, 98, 222
    gap task 115, 121–2 (*see also* telling gap)
generalized success 18, 22, 191
generalist teacher 41, 104
gesture 19, 152, 163, 190, 192, 220, 225, 248, 251
global context xi, 7, 15, 17–19, 32, 48, 67, 69, 76, 167–8, 170, 176, 180–1, 185, 265
    global citizenship 94, 172, 176
    global education 178, 181
    global interconnectivity 25, 17
    globalization 17, 32
    global language 5, 17, 180, 185
    global learning 178, 181
    global mindset 7, 168, 174
    global perspective 22, 85
grammar knowledge 22, 28, 75, 79, 83, 88, 96, 135, 161–2, 282, 288. *See also* focus on form; lexico-grammar
    grammar growth 3, 79–80, 88, 109, 161–2, 224
    grammar performance/processing 75, 114
    grammar sensitivity 7, 148–9, 163, 174
    grammar syllabus 92, 99, 102, 137, 148, 285, 288–9, 222, 250
grammar template. *See under* template
grapheme-phoneme correspondences 151

handover principle 62–3, 65, 229
hands-on activities 82–3, 106
heritage language 7, 13, 173, 177
higher-order thinking 6, 8, 94, 96,
    103, 230
holistic learning xi, 1–2, 55, 82–3, 132,
    169, 220, 222
    holistic structures/activities 83,
        114, 222
    holistic language learning 8,
        219–20
hot seating 195, 233, 236
humanistic learning 222, 236

ICT. *See* information and
    communication technology
identity 20, 169, 178–9, 244, 255
    cultural/intercultural identity 2, 21,
        169–72, 267
    group identity 131, 220
    multilingual identity 2, 21
idiomatic language 130, 132–3, 139,
    144, 162, 224
    idiom principle 130, 132, 144 (*see
        also* open-choice principle)
immersion 3–6, 16–17, 26, 35, 55,
    71–89, 134, 149, 213, 279.
    See also additive bilingualism;
    subtractive bilingual approach
    reciprocal/two-way immersion 73
implicit learning 3–4, 137, 142, 148,
    184, 203
implementation dip 242, 256
information and communication
    technology (ICT) 106–7, 124
Inner Circle 31
input-limited context xii, 3, 6–7, 16, 26,
    148, 161, 176, 184, 282
    unlimited input exposure 71–89,
        184, 282–4
Input Quality Observation Scheme
    (IQOS) 79–80, 89
in-service teacher training 23, 41, 54,
    81, 104, 247, 273. *See also* pre-
    service teacher training
instrumental approach 2, 5, 42, 167
intake 9, 282, 286
intercultural competence 10, 80, 138,
    171–2, 176, 180–1, 220, 236, 267

intercultural/cultural sensitivity 7,
    168, 173, 178
intercultural understanding 173,
    176, 178–9
intonation 19–20, 83, 151, 190, 222,
    224, 225
intrapersonal role play 233, 235
    intrapersonal communication 151
IQOS. *See* Input Quality Observation
    Scheme
IU. *See* intercultural understanding

language awareness 55, 173, 177–9,
    182
language model 33, 55, 148, 151, 171,
    192, 195, 224, 230, 236
language patterns xi, 3, 7, 20, 136,
    139, 141, 147–166, 173, 187–90,
    222, 224, 226
late French immersion (LFI) 75–6
learner autonomy 9, 56, 107, 118, 242,
    248–9, 256, 263–5, 268–71,
    273, 275
learning by doing 96
learning strategies 3, 22, 96–7, 157,
    172–3, 203, 226, 232, 269,
    271
lesson observation. *See* teaching
    observation
lexical items 61, 92, 102, 130, 137,
    141–2, 281, 284, 289. *See also*
    language patterns; vocabulary
    lexical bundles 130, 133, 142
    lexical development 3, 76, 80, 149,
        222
lexico-grammar 6, 129–31, 137, 139,
    161–3
LFI. *See* late French immersion
limited input. *See* input-limited
    context
listening skills 3, 26, 45, 59, 102,
    118, 121, 132, 172, 174, 227,
    229, 232, 265, 267. *See also*
    oracy
    listening tasks 248, 251, 280
listening/aural input 26, 43, 124,
    151–2, 157, 184, 192, 225, 227,
    229, 280, 284, 286, 289. *See
    also* extensive listening

literacy 2–3, 8, 59, 105–6, 136, 172, 187, 213–14, 223–4, 227, 236. *See also* reading skills; writing skills
  critical literacy 213, 232
  functional literacy 76, 149, 151, 227, 230
  information literacy 227
  literacy skills 6, 44–5, 52, 74, 136, 173, 192, 227
  subject literacy 94, 102, 109
  visual literacy 203, 205, 213
literature/literary texts 3, 41, 130, 149, 152, 156, 169, 177–8, 185, 187, 202, 205, 212, 220. *See also* children's literature
  literature-based approach 43, 185, 280
long-term memory 224, 226
lower-order thinking 94, 96, 102

make-believe 20, 58, 154–5, 221, 229
mental flexibility 6, 77, 189
mental lexicon 132, 154, 230
mental model 152, 154
  mental representations 163
metacognitive demand/challenge xi, 6, 119, 292
metalinguistic ability 77–8, 80, 134
methodology xi, 24, 41, 107, 109, 220, 272
Middle French immersion (MFI) 75
mime 61–3, 83, 118, 156, 228
minority language 13
mnemonic 139, 147, 151
mode (of communication) 131, 184, 187, 200, 203, 211, 214, 220, 224
motivated reading 8, 221, 223, 226–7, 231, 236
motivating classroom environment 222–3, 236
motivation 11, 22–5, 46, 58, 64, 76, 80, 91, 118–20, 124, 142, 223, 230, 236, 239, 241–2, 248, 250–3, 262, 264, 268–71, 275
  instrinsic motivation 223, 232
  instrumental motivation 223
  integrative motivation 223

  parents' motivation 58, 76
  resultative motivation 223
  teachers' motivation 64, 110
multilayered opportunities 8, 200, 220
multisensory learning 83, 190, 220–1, 222, 233
multiword expression/unit 7, 131, 133, 135, 139, 142, 224

narrative 8, 76, 94, 141–2, 152, 154, 183–4, 186, 189, 202–3, 209, 211, 213–14, 235
  narrative grammar 186–7
negotiate meaning 8, 22, 114–16, 201, 219, 249
  negotiation of meaning 83, 115, 126, 239, 250, 254
  negotiation of understanding 201
neural activity 3, 17, 152–3, 189
non-analytical processing mode. *See under* analytical processing
non-fiction 94, 102, 106, 209
noticing (active process) 3, 7, 61, 97, 139, 142, 151, 171, 188, 193, 202–3, 229, 230
numeracy 52, 187. *See also* literacy; oracy

open-choice principle 130, 144. *See also* idiom principle
opening (of picturebooks) 204, 207, 209–11, 214
oracy 2–3, 8, 172–3, 187, 191–2, 223–4. *See also* listening skills; speaking skills
oral input. *See* teacher talk
orality 8, 187–8
oral skills. *See* speaking skills
oral stories/tales 8, 184–8
oral storytelling 8, 122, 183–98, 230. *See also* story template; teacher-storyteller
oral tasks 45, 94, 224
otherness 172
out-of-school learning 14, 22, 26, 33, 184, 267
output 75, 94, 96, 114–16, 119, 125, 252–3

Outer Circle 31–3, 38, 45
ownership of task/learning 125, 157, 230, 268–9

paralanguage 190
parentocracy 53
parents 16–17, 23, 33, 39–40, 53, 58, 76, 81–2, 136, 155, 159, 179, 268, 275, 279, 281, 289. *See also* caretaker
pattern. *See* language patterns
peritextual features 202, 209
phonological level 164, 187, 190–1
  phonological awareness 59, 78
  phonological sensitivity 151, 163
physiological dimension 1, 8, 220, 228
picturebooks xi, 3, 4, 8, 20, 43, 58, 62, 118, 138–9, 151, 174, 184–7, 191, 199–217, 226, 230–3, 280, 284
picture dictation 158–9, 194
picture-word dynamic 200–1, 203
plurilingualism 7, 263, 265
postmodernism 208, 211
PPP. *See* presentation/practice/production
prefabricated language 7, 130–1, 136–7
pre-primary/preschool 1, 5, 13, 19, 22–4, 26, 35, 38, 51–69, 74, 76, 79–81, 92, 202, 204
presentation/practice/production (PPP) 113, 117, 124
pre-service teacher training 41, 184, 219, 247. *See also* in-service teacher training
processing load 131
productive skills 3, 7, 75. *See also* receptive skills
pronunciation 20, 26, 150, 156, 224
prop 44, 58, 190, 222
prosodic features 7, 26, 149, 150–1, 160, 190, 222
puppets 55, 60–1, 64, 124
  finger puppet 219, 221
  glove puppet 221

reading skills 3, 26, 43–5, 75–6, 78, 102, 118, 136, 172, 174, 224, 226–7, 232, 265, 267. *See also* extensive reading; literacy; motivated reading

literary reading/literary literacy 152, 176–8, 185, 191, 202, 208–13
reading tasks 102–3, 153, 208, 227, 280–1, 286, 289
rereading 185, 212
realia 83, 135, 190, 221
recasting/reformulating 116, 192
receptive skills 3, 75, 79–80, 149, 192, 229. *See also* productive skills
recto 205
refrains 151, 188, 193–4, 200
repertoire of language 119, 134, 162, 190, 221, 230, 233, 254
rhymes 3, 55, 59, 64, 138–9, 147–66, 193, 204, 224–5, 282
rhythm 4, 147–66, 187, 190, 192, 222, 224–5
risk-taking readiness xii, 6, 20, 116, 118, 120, 224, 228, 287
role play 58, 170, 194, 218, 221, 235, 242, 251. *See also* hot seating; intrapersonal role play; whoosh!
  collective role play 233, 235
  conscience alley 194, 233–4
  role-on-the-wall 233–4
  teacher-in-role 186, 233, 236
routines 23, 58–61, 64, 79, 83, 138, 140, 150–2, 161, 169, 203, 248

salience 3, 7, 139, 149, 151, 161, 190, 229
savoir apprendre/faire 171–2, 175
savoir comprendre 171
savoir être 171–2, 175
savoirs 171–2, 175
savoir s'engager 171
scaffolding 83, 106–7, 109, 115–16, 126, 151, 193, 198, 228–9, 238, 241, 256
  scaffold xii, 56, 62, 83, 162, 192, 203, 213
school libraries 165, 238
script (written/play script) 191, 220–1, 224–6, 230, 233, 289–90
scripted drama 8, 220–1, 223–227. *See also* unscripted drama
  script-like exchange 60–1, 63–4
self-efficacy 9, 231, 264, 273

self-determination 9, 231, 264, 273
semiotics 221–2
settling down 220
social demand 6, 119
sociocultural context 8, 203, 213, 221–2
sociocultural theory 52, 57, 65, 115, 221–2
sociological dimension 1, 8, 219, 228
songs xi, 3, 43, 55–7, 59, 64, 94, 138, 178, 204, 280, 283–5
sound effects 190, 222
speaking/oral skills 3, 6, 14, 45, 74–6, 102, 118, 139, 172, 174, 192, 225, 227, 232, 265, 267. See also oracy
    speaking tasks 114, 120, 241–2
stereotypes 178, 185
stirring up 154
storytelling. See oral storytelling
story template. See under template
storyworld 148, 152, 154–5, 159–60, 162–3
submersion programmes 73
subtractive bilingual approach 73
summative assessment. See under assessment
synchronous interaction 241
    asynchronous interaction 241

target phonology 220, 224–6
task-based language teaching (TBLT) 4, 6, 113–27, 221, 227, 241, 251, 255
    post-task phase 117
    pre-task phase 117, 159
    task cycle 117, 123
teacher-storyteller 8, 183–4, 186–8, 190–2
teacher talk/oral input 1, 22, 138, 151, 283, 288. See also creative teacher talk
teaching competences xi–xii, 4, 22–24, 53–4, 76, 81–3, 110, 151, 171, 190–192, 195, 202, 220, 223–4, 236, 248, 273
teaching/lesson observation 4, 23–4, 62–4, 104, 174, 184, 186, 247. See also Input Quality Observation Scheme (IQOS)

technology 4, 8, 17, 26, 99, 124–5, 167, 177, 239–59
    technology-enhanced tasks 8, 148, 156, 250
'Tell me' approach 212–3, 215
telling gap 200–1, 203, 211
template 136, 147, 160, 162, 164, 270
    grammar template 147–8, 160–2
    story template 8, 186–8, 192
text level 94, 149
thinking processes. See higher-order thinking; lower-order thinking
think, pair, share strategy 195
token frequency 161. See also type frequency
tolerance of ambiguity 19, 149, 224
Total Physical Response (TPR) 55, 118, 228–30, 285, 288–9
TPR. See Total Physical Response
transition/continuity (primary to secondary) 1, 4–6, 22, 24–5, 36–9, 81, 263, 270
    transition/continuity (pre-primary to primary) 38, 81
turn taking 60, 64, 150
type frequency 161. See also token frequency

unscripted drama 8, 220–1, 228–32, 287. See also scripted drama
usage-based approach 2–3, 134–5, 160–1, 222

VC. See videoconferencing
verso 205
very young learners (VYLs) 35, 54, 79–80, 124, 136, 204, 286
videoconferencing (VC) 8, 239–59
visualization 83, 152
vocabulary xii, 7, 44, 80, 83, 92–6, 100, 102–3, 117, 245, 253. See also collocation; formula; formulaic sequences; formulaicity; idiomatic language; lexical bundles; lexical development; lexical items; language patterns; mental lexicon; multiword units; prefabricated language

academic vocabulary 6, 92, 99
vocabulary growth/knowledge 60, 75, 79, 129–45, 154, 159, 192–5, 227
vocabulary lists/atomic perspective 7, 136, 250
VYLs. *See* very young learners

well-formed language 161, 192
whoosh! 184, 233–4
word level 93, 134
writing skills 3, 44, 75–6, 94, 98, 103, 117–18, 121–2, 136, 153, 172, 174, 185, 195, 212, 227, 230–2, 234, 236, 266–7, 287–9. *See also* creative writing; literacy